Gender and Nation
in the Spanish Modernist Novel

Gender and Nation
in the Spanish Modernist Novel

Roberta Johnson

Vanderbilt University Press
NASHVILLE

© 2003 Vanderbilt University Press
All rights reserved
First edition 2003

This book is printed on acid-free paper.

Publication of this volume has been supported by
a generous subsidy from the Program for Cultural
Cooperation between Spain's Ministry of Education,
Culture and Sports, and United States Universities.

Library of Congress Cataloging-in-Publication Data

Johnson, Roberta
Gender and nation in the Spanish modernist novel /
Roberta Johnson.— 1st ed.
p.   cm.
Includes bibliographical references and index.
ISBN 0-8265-1436-7 (cloth : alk. paper)
ISBN 0-8265-1437-5 (pbk. : alk. paper)
   1. Spanish fiction—20th century—History and
criticism.   2. Sex role in literature.   3. National
characteristics, Spanish, in literature.   4. Modernism
(Literature)—Spain.   I. Title.
PI6144.J585 2003
860.9'112—dc22

2003017647

Contents

Preface   vii

Introduction: The Feminist Novel in Spain
at the Crossroads of Modernism   1

1   Women and the Soul of Spain   31

2   Don Quixote as National Icon and Modernist Ideal   69

3   The Domestication of a Modernist Don Juan   111

4   Baroja's, Unamuno's, and Azorín's Failed Feminists   145

5   Biology as Destiny: New National Discourses
    on Gender Inform the Novel of the 1920s and Beyond   185

6   Vanguard Feminists Dream the Nation   224

Conclusion: A Legacy and a Prophecy   275

Notes   281

References   313

Index   337

Preface

When I finished writing *Crossfire: Philosophy and the Novel in Spain 1900–1934*, my sense of accomplishment was somewhat diminished by an acute awareness that the book paid little attention to women writers. The focus of the book—philosophical fiction—precluded a full treatment of the cultural landscape of the period, especially since women did not for the most part write what I defined as philosophical fiction. In contrast with Virginia Woolf's hypothetical Judith Shakespeare of the English Renaissance, published women writers—notably Carmen de Burgos, Concha Espina, Blanca de los Ríos, Sofía Casanova, María Martínez Sierra ("Gregorio Martínez Sierra"), Margarita Nelken, Federica Montseny, Rosa Chacel, and María Zambrano—were present in early twentieth-century Spain. In large part because their literary forms and themes were different from those of the men who played an important role in shaping the criteria of canonical inclusion, however, these women simply did not make it into the literary histories.

This book begins to fill the lacunae left by *Crossfire* and other books on early twentieth-century Spanish literary production that have neglected women writers. I have limited this study to fiction because, although male and female authors approached fiction in significantly different ways, both men and women cultivated the genre extensively between 1900 and 1939 and beyond. Male Spanish authors of the early twentieth century (often referred to as the Generation of '98, the Generation of '14, and the Generation of '27) were more modernist in the traditional understanding of the term, emphasizing technical and verbal innovation in their efforts to represent the contents of an individual consciousness. Women engaged in what I call social modernism, a mode that focuses on interpersonal relations within formal and informal social parameters. Women's fiction, although less aesthetically innovative than male fiction, was known to for its presentation of themes such as women's social roles and unconventional sexual arrangements that were revolutionary by comparison to male novelists' treatment of the subjects. Unlike elitist male fiction, women's fiction was often published in popular venues.

This book opens up the Spanish modernist canon to include the social modernism of women writers, a modernism that focused on domestic issues, gender roles, and relations between the sexes. The lines of division between aesthetic and social modernism are not fixed. Semicanonical male authors such as Felipe Trigo wrote popular novels that argue for free sexual expression. Trigo also tendered certain feminist ideals, such as women's right to work and the need for paid leave for pregnancy and childcare. But because some of Trigo's themes would take my discussions in diffuse directions, I do not include his works in this book.

In part because of the difference in their emphasis, I originally considered devoting this book exclusively to women novelists, but that approach would have simply reversed the lack of balance. Moreover, a single-sex book would not have allowed me to argue, as I do here, that larger sociopolitical discourses (most specifically those on gender) had an important impact on both male and female authors of Spanish fiction in the modernist period. The work of women writers was shaped to a degree by the dominant male culture, and male literary production responded to some extent to the increased visibility that women came to achieve in the public arena at the turn of the century. As I directed attention to aspects of the novels other than philosophical content (as in Miguel de Unamuno's *Niebla,* for example), there emerged a commentary on contemporary gender roles, often of a prescriptive nature.

One of the greatest challenges in composing *Gender and Nation in the Spanish Modernist Novel* was to find significant common threads in the writings of men and women. Although, to some extent, male and female authors operated in different spheres and wrote for different audiences, I sought to highlight diverging approaches to the common interests of both spheres. One salient concern of male and female novelists was the past, present, and future of Spain as a nation, especially its traditions and the role of domestic arrangements within those traditions—that is, the way in which gender informed their view of Spanish society. Novelistic reaction to the proliferating discourse on women and then to the growing feminist movement in Spain is a constant throughout the modernist period (roughly 1900–39). Thus, the intertwining of thought about the way that Spain was or ought to be and the proper place of the genders within a particular model of Spanish society guides the overall design of this work.

As the reader progresses through the book, it will help to keep in mind some working definitions of "gender" and "nation," slippery concepts that have occasioned much theoretical writing since the 1970s. These multilayered terms appear to shift meaning in different contexts. Except when I refer to novelists as being male or female, where the meaning is essentially a biological category or sex, "gender" usually refers to a socially constructed condition in which male- or femaleness is defined by social norms and legal prescriptions. Many of my observations about male and female writers and their novels imply that social conditions influenced the way that men and women wrote and help explain the differences in male and female modernist narrative practices. The term "nation" refers to two basic categories: (1) At the end of the nineteenth century, the idea of the nature of Spain occasioned theorization that led to a variety of national myths, such as (a) the intrahistorical essential nature of the Spanish soul embodied in Castile and Spain's glorious national imperial past and (b) new interpretations of literary figures (especially Don Quixote and Don Juan) that either exalt or vilify the Spanish nation. (2) "Spain" refers to a concrete contemporary political entity analyzed and criticized by writers who sought to influence and change it. Gender formed an important part of both the theories of a Spanish national essence and the efforts to shape the body politic.

This book is organized roughly along chronological lines, beginning with narratives from the pre–World War I era (Miguel de Unamuno's *Paz en la guerra*, María Martínez Sierra's *Tú eres la paz*, Azorín's *El alma castellana* and *Castilla*) that wrestle with the concept of Spain's eternal nature (Chapter 1). Chapters 2 and 3 analyze primarily pre–World War I fiction that incorporates themes from literary classics that allow male and female authors to field topics related to gender within the national tradition. Miguel de Unamuno's *Niebla*, Concha Espina's *La esfinge maragata*,

Gabriel Miró's *Las cerezas del cementerio*, María Martínez Sierra's *El amor catedrático*, and Azorín's more vanguardist *El caballero inactual* exemplify modernist treatments of Don Quixote. Ramón del Valle-Inclán's *Sonatas*, Blanca de los Ríos's *Las hijas de don Juan*, Sofía Casanova's *La princesa del amor hermoso*, Concha Espina's *La niña deLuzmela*, and Carmen de Burgos's *La entrometida* represent modernist revisions of Don Juan.

In the 1920s, the advent of a more organized and aggressive feminism in Spain gave rise to narratives that either denigrated or championed the feminist cause. Chapters 4 and 6, respectively, treat these male- and female-authored novels. Chapter 4 considers novels by the older generation of male modernists—Miguel de Unamuno *(La tía Tula)*, Pío Baroja *(El mundo es ansí)*, and Azorín *(Doña Inés)*—that portray a strong (feminist or protofeminist) female protagonist who is doomed to loneliness and defeat. Chapter 5 examines new medical and philosophical discourses on gender from the 1920s that underpin Ramón Pérez de Ayala's *Tigre Juan y El curandero de su honra;* Carmen de Burgos's *Ellas y ellos y ellos y ellas, El permisionario,* and *Quiero vivir mi vida;* and Rosa Chacel's *Memorias de Leticia Valle*. Chapter 6 concentrates on a series of novels, mostly by declared feminists who used fiction to further some of the goals of the Spanish Republic for which they militated. In addition to a series of novels by Burgos, I also examine Nelken's *La trampa del arenal,* Montseny's *La indomable* and *La victoria,* Espina's *La virgen prudente,* and Zambrano's *Delirio y destino*.

In a way, I have found a new crossfire in the Spanish fiction of the first half of the twentieth century—one in which men and women writers set quite different goals for the nation and its domestic underpinnings. In some cases (as with Miró's and Espina's treatments of the Quixote theme and women authors' reworkings of the Don Juan legend), there is an intertextual crossfire. At other times, the dialogue between male and female novelists is less specific and can be constructed only by juxtaposing the very different kinds of fiction produced by men and women within the same social and political climate. The common thread even here is a reaction to changing gender roles in early twentieth-century Spain. For this reason, I place less emphasis on male writers whose careers were only beginning in the 1920s. I offer examples of some of the rather uniform ways in which male vanguardists such as Ramón Gómez de la Serna,

Benjamín Jarnés, and Pedro Salinas tended to fetishize women. However, because, for the most part, they did not address women's issues in their essays and novels, I have made no more than small mention of José Díaz Fernández, Ramón Sender, and Francisco Ayala, younger canonical male writers who shared political views with the women novelists discussed in Chapter 6.

I owe thanks to many people and organizations for their assistance in preparing this book. I am very grateful to the University of Kansas for granting me a sabbatical leave and to the Guggenheim Foundation for providing me with a fellowship that allowed me to begin my research and writing during the 1996–97 academic year. My colleagues and students at the University of Kansas provided an intellectually stimulating atmosphere in which to develop my ideas. I am especially grateful to Professors Vicky Unruh and Jane Sharistanian for their helpful comments on early drafts of some of the chapters. I thank my husband, Ricardo J. Quinones, for his constant encouragement and his indefatigable willingness to read and critique materials. Emily Gjeltema, my Claremont McKenna College research assistant, provided invaluable assistance in preparing the manuscript for submission. The anonymous readers for Vanderbilt University Press deserve special thanks for their very helpful comments and suggestions. I also thank the editors at Bucknell University Press, *Revista Canadiense de Estudios Hispánicos, Letras Peninsulares,* and *Anales de la literatura española contemporánea* for allowing me to incorporate into this book revised versions of previously published material.

In the interest of maintaining the flow, I have omitted translations where the meaning is clear from the context. Except for those passages where I specifically indicate a published translation as the source, all translations from the Spanish are my own.

Gender and Nation
in the Spanish Modernist Novel

Introduction: The Feminist Novel in Spain at the Crossroads of Modernism

In a 1970s interview, Concepción Vilela, one of Carmen de Burgos's colleagues at a Madrid Normal School in the early twentieth century, described Burgos (1867–1932) as "algo modernista" (qtd. in Starcevic 1976, 129). Burgos, according to Vilela, engaged in activities that other Spanish women of her time would not dare to attempt, such as having coffee alone at a public café. Allying women's modern behavior with social revolution, Vilela considered Burgos rather "bolchevique" for the frank, down-to-earth manner in which she stated her opinions. The designation "modernista" for a socially liberated woman is, however, at odds with other uses of the term "modernist" in twentieth-century Spanish culture. More often, "modernista" refers to Hispanic literary trends associated with writers influenced by Rubén Darío's symbolist/Parnassian language and to Spanish writers who parallel European high modernism, which emphasized individual consciousness and new artistic forms. Although Burgos may epitomize a social modernism and although she lived and wrote in the Spanish modernist period, she is excluded from the literary categories. She, like every other woman writer, is rarely mentioned in studies of the period.[1] Burgos's case, however, is instructive when defining Spanish modernism in general and the role of women writers within it. Vilela's mildly pejorative statement about Burgos's *modernista* attributes reminds us that because literary modernism was a particularly masculine movement, "modernist" women were out of place. Literary modernism emphasized form and philosophy over social phenomena such as women's shifting roles in the modern world. Canonical modernism, cosmopolitan and abstract, subjectivized knowledge and eschewed the realism and domesticity often associated with women. As Ricardo

Quinones notes, "Modernism as an aesthetic is . . . more in search of the virile hard line" (1985, 55).

This introduction outlines some of the themes that weave together the discussions of male and female Spanish modernist fiction herein: (1) modernist novelistic techniques practiced by men and women, (2) the role of domesticity as a metaphor for national concerns, and (3) the rise of a sense of nation in Spain, which was accompanied by discourses on women and gender. The canonically recognized modernist novel in Spain is diverse and heterogeneous, but it coincided with European versions in its emphasis on male consciousness and the masculine subjective experience of the world, a subjective experience that often reflects nostalgia for the past. Even in the teens and twenties, as disaffection with the monarchy increased, twentieth-century male novelists continued to dream of the Spanish past. Male authors included historical novels or novels with an important historical component in their repertoire. An early example is Miguel de Unamuno's *Paz en la guerra* (*Peace in War* [1897]; see Chapter 1), which was followed by Ramón del Valle-Inclán's *Sonatas* (1902–5; see Chapter 3) and *El ruedo ibérico* (1927–28); Azorín's entire novelistic canon (see Johnson 2001); and Pío Baroja's series, *Memorias de un hombre de acción* (1912–13).

Gabriel Miró's and Ramón Pérez de Ayala's major fictions of the teens and twenties also showed a preference for the late nineteenth century over contemporary circumstances. As I note elsewhere, Miró's *El abuelo del rey* (1915) is a saga of the entire Spanish nineteenth century. Pérez de Ayala's *Novelas poemáticas de la vida española* (1916) project a stylized atemporal Spain, and *Belarmino y Apolonio* (1921) resurrects the early Restoration period. Many of the male-authored novels are set in the period of the Carlist wars, when traditional values were pitted against the liberal regime of Isabel II. The implied author's allegiances with regard to these political tensions are ambiguous in these novels. It is not a coincidence that male authors chose to narrate an earlier time in Spanish history, a time before Spanish workers' movements coalesced and gender arrived "as a fully blown historical/cultural/political/epistemic category," in the words of R. Radhakrishnan (1992, 2). Could a certain nostalgia for a time when women and the underclasses played a less public role have anything to do with such historical excursions? It is hard not to be suspicious. While male nationalist theories and many male narrations look to the past, they tacitly urge a social status quo in the present.

Women writers, by contrast, resisted the historical impulse and the obsession with the past, preferring to imagine a Spain struggling to modify traditional constraints. Women chose to depict a contemporary Spain and to imagine a future in which new social configurations would be possible. Significantly, the second chapter of María Zambrano's *Delirio y destino* (1989), a novelized autobiography that concentrates on 1929 and the eve of the Spanish Republic, is titled "Recordando el futuro." Women's configurations of the Spanish nation offer a theory of Spanish history and of women's place in it that is less nostalgic about tradition and more specific about the present. Traditionally private concerns—relations between the sexes, marriage, and domestic situations—are made public. With Zambrano, the women novelists see history as a dream of the future rather than of the past. Zambrano wrote that one must awake every day dreaming the lucid dream, dreaming of what Spain could be. Novels by women incorporate greater class and gender consciousness than the canonical male novels of the modernist period. In fact, the notions of consciousness and self-consciousness are central to the feminist theory and characterizations embedded in virtually every female-authored novel analyzed herein. Many of their narratives concern women's consciousness within private relationships that push conventional social boundaries. They, like Hannah Arendt, understood that "the society of the nation in the modern world is 'that curiously hybrid realm where private interests assume public significance'" (qtd. in Bhabha 1990, 2).

The Spanish male modernism that sought to evade contemporary issues by eternalizing Spain or evoking other historical eras coincided with the European modernist trend described by Lilian Robinson and Lise Vogel: "[Modernism] seeks to intensify isolation. It forces the work of art, artist, the critics, and the audience outside history. Modernism denies us the possibility of understanding ourselves as *agents* in the material world, for all has been removed to an abstract world of ideas, where interactions can be minimized or emptied of meaning and real consequences. Less than ever are we able to interpret the world—much less change it" (1971, 178). There is an almost universal agreement that in artistic modernism the social and the personal drift apart; as Theodor Adorno puts it, "The negation of synthesis becomes such a compositional principle" (qtd. in Eysteinsson 1990, 210).

It is surprising how few of the male novelists' protagonists take an interest in social issues or work for a living: Antonio Azorín in José Martínez Ruiz's *La voluntad* (1902) is a journalist, but we rarely see him ply his trade; Fernando Ossorio in Pío Baroja's *Camino de perfección* (1902) inherits a sum that allows him to travel in search of himself; Andrés Hurtado in Baroja's *El árbol de la ciencia* (1911) is a doctor, but he spends most of his time reading and anguishing; the Marqués de Bradomín in Ramón del Valle-Inclán's *Sonatas* and Augusto Pérez in Miguel de Unamuno's *Niebla* (1914) are independently wealthy. In the male-authored novels, there are few modulations of social class; servants are plot motivators rather than representatives of the working classes. Money, the powerful motivating force in the nineteenth-century realist novel, "at the very least a sign of reality in the novel, that is a sign of the rupture of form by reality" (Vernon 1984, 18), disappears in the male-authored modernist novel and is replaced by ideas. Curiously, the male novelistic format becomes more picaresque (a series of cobbled scenes) as the picaresque monetary motive recedes in importance. Women's novels, like women's lives, continue to center on economic issues in a more integrated plot. If the economically unencumbered modern male protagonist is released from a restrictive plot with a beginning, middle, and end, the protagonists of the women's novels are constrained by more traditional and intricate plotting devices—secrets and their revelation, people moving into and out of the protagonists' lives at strategic moments, arrivals and departures that are less than coincidental—all the strategies that we associate with realist plotting and that male authors consciously avoid. If the male author and his protagonist were free to move from province to city, for the woman author such a move was more fraught with anxiety.

The woman's plot similarly denotes women's dependence on social and legal structures beyond their control. For example, Concha Espina's plot in *La esfinge maragata* carefully arranges social strictures that cage Florinda like a bird. Gothic elements, which occur rarely in the male-authored modernist novel, appear frequently in the woman-authored fictions to underscore not only the sense of entrapment experienced by female protagonists but also their triumph over it: "The Gothic mode typically recreates the story in terms of a double escape/confinement: while this mother is finally subjected to the appropriating vision, she also implicitly defies and eludes it" (Wolstenholme 1993, 156). Thoroughly steeped in the scientific and rationalist traditions, the male novelists avoid supernatural and other elements of mystery and horror associated with the Gothic, even as they mock them in their novels.

Azorín defined the aesthetics of his generation as combining "el grito de pasión de [José] Echegaray," the "sentimentalismo subversivo de Campoamor," and "la visión de realidad de Galdós" (1961, 19). Oddly enough, this wedding of sentiment and realism fits the fiction of female modernists much better than it fits the fiction of male modernists, which consists overwhelmingly of novels of ideas often fashioned according to the innovative narrative techniques that we associate with literary modernism. In women writers' social modernism, form may be more traditional (realist, melodramatic, sentimental), but the message, especially about the social roles of women, is radically new. In 1930, José Díaz Fernández called for a "nuevo romanticismo" that would draw on feminine sensibility (women's "alma espléndida y brillante" [17]) to counter what he considered the sterile intellectualism of the vanguard movements. He failed to recognize that some of his female compatriots—María Martínez Sierra, Carmen de Burgos, Blanca de los Ríos, Sofía Casanova, Margarita Nelken, Federica Montseny, Rosa Chacel, and María Zambrano—had been combining emotion with socially concerned thematics since at least 1905.

Raymond Williams's notion of a "personal realist novel" is helpful in defining women's modernist narrative mode. The personal realist novel combines the individual (perhaps quixotic) vision typical of modernist fiction with the social perspective that we associate with nineteenth-century realism. Williams understands that relationships are a means by which a symbiosis of the personal and the social is accomplished:

> The truly creative effort of our time is the struggle for relationships, of a whole kind, and it is possible to see this as both personal and social: the practical learning of *extending* relationships. In one sense, nineteenth-century realism, scorned by high modernism, has a role in this kind of

work. Realism, as embodied in its great tradition, is a touchstone in this, for it shows, in detail, that vital interpenetration, idea into feeling, person into community, change into settlement, which we need, as growing points, in our own divided time. In the highest realism, society is seen in fundamentally personal terms, and persons, through relationships, in fundamentally social terms. (1959, 211)

The woman-authored novels studied herein manage to meld an (often female) individual consciousness with a seemingly objective critique of social problems through representation of interpersonal and/or family relations. Men and women relate within socially and legally prescribed boundaries that are tested (often rejected or transformed) in such a way that female consciousness has an opportunity to influence social norms. Thus, within realist plot structures, which often add Gothic and/or melodramatic elements and female consciousness of contemporary personal situations, the women's novel gains social purchase. Both Chacel and Zambrano wrote theoretical essays that defended the confessional mode (personal revelation that involves an ethical dimension). The ideas presented in these essays provide insights into not only their own literary practices but also those of other women writers who similarly drew on personal experience in an act of self-consciousness and self-awareness. Relationships and communication, rather than male modernist hermeticism and isolation, lie at the heart of the personal realist mode of the Spanish women writers.

Jürgen Habermas's notion of "communicative reason," which counters modernism's privileging of the individual subject with an alternative discourse, could also be applied to much Spanish modernist women's fiction. According to Habermas, when knowledge is understood as "communicatively mediated," then "rationality is assessed in terms of the capacity of responsible participants in interaction to orient themselves in relation to validity claims geared to intersubjective recognition" (1987, 314). Habermas believes the concept of communicative reason to be superior to "purposive rationality" because it encompasses the moral and practical along with the aesthetic and expressive: "The reason operating in communicative action not only stands under, so to speak, external, situational constraints; its own conditions of possibility necessitate its branching out into the dimensions of historical time, social space, and body-centered experiences" (314). The women modernists examined in the ensuing chapters—Burgos, Casanova, de los Ríos, Espina, Nelken, Montseny, Chacel, and Zambrano—found means to incorporate communicative reason into novelistic structures some years before Habermas formulated his ideas on an alternative to modernist discourse. Thus, the personal realist mode that incorporates communicative reason and action affords what Lynne Tirrell describes as "leaping from the subjective to the objective" (1990, 124) in order to gain moral agency. According to Tirrell, telling stories is necessary for ethical traction, and in storytelling "one develops a sense of self, a sense of self in relation to others, a capacity to justify one's decisions" (125).

Zambrano's revision of Sophocles' *Antigone* (*La tumba de Antígona*, published in Mexico in 1967) emblematizes how literature (storytelling) can create possibilities for women's ethical action within patriarchal law through communicative (and emotional) reason. In Sophocles' play, Antigone's voice is silent after her arrest and entombment for defying Creon's decree prohibiting her brother Polynices from being honored with burial. Zambrano gives voice to this woman who dared transgress political legal authority in order to follow an older and higher moral law dictated by family relationships and her own heart. Zambrano's version begins with a monologue by Antigone in the cave, and in another section Antigone directs her speech to her sister, an absent narratee to whom she exclaims, "Pero yo estoy aquí delirando, tengo voz, tengo voz" (1986, 230). [But here I am talking in a derlirious fashion; I have a voice; I have a voice.] As we see in Chapter 6, *Delirio y destino* was Zambrano's own personal form of storytelling. At the end of Zambrano's *La tumba de Antígona*, the protagonist emerges as if from a dream to enter a world that she herself has helped transform through her heroic act.

What particularly attracted Zambrano to the figure of Antigone was her pure passion; she was, according to Zambrano, a "muchacha que no ha tenido tiempo de pensar en sí misma, cegada por el amor sin mancha; es decir, por la Piedad" (1948, 15) [girl who has not had time to think about herself, blinded by unsoiled love, that is, by compassion]. Zambrano converted Antigone's tomb into social consciousness; we hear her message because ' la tumba de Antígona es nuestra propia conciencia obscurecida. Antígona está enterrada viva en nosotros en cada uno de nosotros" (18) [Antigone's tomb is our own obscured social consciousness. Antigone is buried alive in us, in each one of us]. She represents hope for justice: "Pues sobre la Tierra, la primavera es un delirio de esperanza y en el mundo humano la conciencia, al nacer en su inexorable claridad, es también un delirio de esperanzada justicia" (17). [Well, on Earth spring is a delirium of hope, and in the world of human consciousness, upon issuing forth in its inexorable clarity, it is also a delirium of hopeful justice.] Although her arguments for the use of the rational emotions evoked by literature focus on the realist novel (specifically Charles Dickens), Martha Nussbaum finds in tragedy a similar ability to give the spectator an opportunity to emote rationally: "Indeed, we can say of the mainstream realist novel what Aristotle said of tragic drama: that the very form constructs compassion in readers, positioning them as people who care intensely about the sufferings and bad luck of others, and who identify them in ways that show possibilities for themselves" (1995, 66).

According to Zambrano, Antigone's entombment, her suffering, sponsors the rehearsal of the entire history of a people through the poetic word: "Es una estirpe la que Antígona funda o a lo menos nos da a ver. En el lenguaje de hoy, un arquetipo" (1986, 216). Antigone offers a conscience in a nascent state before it becomes independent of the sacrificed soul, and therefore it does not depend on an independent "I." Her situation mirrors that of all people, not just one individual. Not unlike Williams in defining personal realism, Zambrano has combined the individual's emotions to project something about the communal within the community. In Antigone's particular case, Zambrano has found a truth that is of use to the whole of humanity, what Nussbaum calls the "play back and forth between the general and the concrete" (1995, 8).

In Zambrano's version, Antigone enters into her tomb in a delirious state, lamenting her marriage that did not take place. Zambrano theorizes that only in delirium could Antigone fully understand her ethical situation. Delirium revealed to her that her sacrifice had to be complete in order to emphasize the difference between the state's law and her own moral order. Zambrano's Antigone is an allegory of hope for the future, a phoenix reborn of its own ashes that will stand for a new moral order.

Similarly, the other female novelists studied herein give voice to women who carve out an ethical stand from their personal situations, and much of the ethical work of their fictions is accomplished through an appeal to the emotions that we find in realism and other nonmodernist genres. As in Antigone's case, that stand usually does not conform to reigning social norms and often does not coincide with Spanish (patriarchal) law. Zambrano's version of the Antigone story may well have been directed not only at the original but also at Georg Hegel's interpretation of Sophocles' tragedy. Hegel appropriated Antigone's story to reinforce a dual social duty in which women represent earth, family, and darkness, whereas men signify reason, the state, and citizenship. Zambrano returned to Aristotle's view of Antigone in which there is no such gendered division.

It is difficult to pinpoint the reasons for the differences between male and female modernist fiction. Doubtless, levels of education play a role; men educated to read philosophical works and foreign literature had sources and models not always available to women (women did not have access to Spanish universities until after 1910). As women like Chacel and Zambrano became more educated, they incorporated more modernist practices—philosophical themes, elliptical structures, and reliance on imagery to convey meaning. The meaning of their works, however, retains a social, ethical dimension usually associated with women. But not all of the more highly educated Spanish modernist- or vanguardist-era women writers engage modernist literary forms. The intellectually sophisticated de los Ríos and Nelken, for example, deploy mostly realist techniques in their fiction. In most cases, women writers felt an urgency, born of a variety of personal circumstances, to address social concerns, especially those that related to women's social and legal circumstances.

Spanish male modernism has been understood in part as an exploration of Spain as a nation through radically new art forms. On the surface, gender appears to have been a minor concern. A concept of Spanish modernism that includes women need not forgo national and artistic matters, but it must refocus them to include considerations of gender and domesticity. Nation, family, women, and marriage informed the canonical Spanish modernist novel as well as noncanonical fiction to a larger extent than has heretofore been acknowledged. In fact, the revolutionary fervor that Azorín attributed to his generation was perhaps more domesticating than he wished to admit. Through novelistic characters and situations, writers expressed both their dreams and their disillusionments about the past, present, and future of the Spanish nation. Domestic arrangements within the body politic help define it on both a symbolic and practical level. In the post-1898 debacle—the loss of the last of the Spanish empire—national introspection meant turning inward toward the homeland; in Spanish narrative, family, marriage, and women became a microcosm of the nation and a barometer for measuring its health. As Susan Kirkpatrick observes, "At the turn of the last century, gender became a focus of debates about the possibilities and discontents of modernity" (1999, 117). In this regard, male authors were modernist in their critique of modernity, whereas women novelists often embraced modernity, particularly its liberalization of social roles.

"Domestic" from *domus* (house) conjures the private as well as the public; it can mean "having to do with the home or family" as well as "of one's homeland (native)." "Domesticity" may refer to the "customs of home life" or to the activities of "taming" (animals) and "civilizing" (humans). The dual meanings—family household and national concerns—remind us that the thinking about Spain as a nation that was prevalent at the turn of the century was intertwined with discourse on family matters, especially the role of women in society. As Mary Nash observes, "The public and private divide implied by this discrimination [denial of work identity to women] became a significant feature of gender discourse in modern Spain. The connections and changing boundaries of public and private are a crucial aspect of gender discourse and provide clues to the changing dynamic of gender relations" (1999, 29).

Domesticity in cultural production is often associated with nineteenth-century society and literature, especially the novel, rather than with the more personal and technically innovative modernist narrative. Domesticity and the novel were particularly close allies in the era of industrialization when social roles for bourgeois women required definition and reinforcement. Susan L. Roberson points out that a discourse of domesticity arose in the nineteenth-century United States when the country was "aflurry with competing rhetorics and social, industrial, and political reorientation"; thus, "domesticity provided a stabilizing discourse that prescribed as it described women's roles and space in ways that limited women's competition with the current power hegemony" (1994, 117). With regard to nineteenth-century British fiction, Elizabeth Langland has argued that "middle-class women were produced by these discourses [of domesticity] even as they reproduced them to consolidate middle-class control" (1992, 291). Nash refers specifically to the Spanish case, where the housewife and child caretaker replaced the conventual model of femininity: "The ideology of domesticity provided the foundation of traditional gender discourse in late nineteenth-century Spain. As in Europe and North America, this model of good mothering and housewifery—the product of male thought—generated the notion that women's ambitions had to be exclusively limited to home and family" (1999, 27).

Bridget Aldaraca (1991), Alda Blanco (1993, 2001), Lou Charnon-Deutsch, (1990a, 1990b, 1994), and Catherine Jagoe (1994) have similarly linked domestic ideology to Spanish nineteenth-century fiction, demonstrating that the novel was an important adjunct to conduct books in the process of educating women to a domestic role. Critical accounts of the modernist novel imply (by default) that the novel's role as domestic educator was abandoned at the turn of the century. Most analyses of the aesthetics of not only Spanish modernism but also modernism throughout the rest of Europe would have us believe that domestic agendas were set aside in favor of philosophical and artistic agendas. I suggest that these new concerns in no way replaced the nineteenth-century domestic purpose; rather, they were added to it (with some urgency and often in a more surreptitious manner). Even if (or because) a domestic purpose was buried or embedded in new aesthetic forms and shrouded in philosophical debates about the nature of the Spanish nation, domestic prescriptions became subliminal and all the more pervasive.

For example, marriage is a central domestic issue in novels by both male and female modernists; in fact, marriage and the family became the representational microcosm of the nation. Fictional treatments of this central institution were, however, divided along gender lines. If the men of the Generation of '98 were, or at least considered themselves, radical in their program for the public aspects of the nation and in their approach to artistic forms, they were exceptionally conservative in their deployment of domestic situations in their fiction. Male modernists appear on the surface to eschew observations on domestic arrangements, but most of their novels contain a hidden agenda related to marriage and family matters. Intellectual rebel protagonists Fernando Ossorio in *Camino de perfección,* Andrés Hurtado in *El árbol de la ciencia,* and Antonio Azorín in *La voluntad* all accept traditional marriage in the end. Taken as a body of literature, the male-authored modernist novel has all the earmarks of a conservative social handbook that prescribes the most traditional domestic roles for women. Women novelists, to the contrary, engaged literature to promote a much more liberal program for their sex. In the same year that Unamuno killed off his marriage-snubbing protagonist in *La tía Tula* (1921), Burgos created a woman who rejected marriage, survived quite well on her own, and then passed on her experience to a woman friend.

If modernism in the rest of Europe was nationalist in an international way (James Joyce's deeply Irish modernist fiction blossomed and bore fruit in Paris; Ezra Pound's nationalist sentiments were transferred to fascist Italy), Spanish modernism centered on Spain—its traditions and its contemporary condition. Domestic issues and women's place in forming the nation (especially women's role as domestic educators) emerged in public discourse about the same time as did talk of regenerating Spain in the wake of the 1868 revolution—the period in which the first wave of twentieth-century canonical authors (the Generation of '98) was becoming aware of Spanish public life. The discourse on the nation and the thinking on women, in fact, shared intertwining themes that are not unique to Spain. Political scientist Cynthia Enloe (1989) has observed that nationalism—more so than other ideologies—has space in its vision for women, since no nation can survive without children being born and nurtured. Lora Romero remarks that by "1830 the nature of woman's contribution to society had become a regional obsession amongst intellectuals of the Northeastern United States, and by virtue of the dominance this region exercised over cultural production it necessarily became a national obsession as well" (1991, 115). U.S. educators, she writes, avowed that "in their capacity as mothers, women exercised a tremendous power over the fate of the Republic in the values they taught boys who would grow up to lead the nation. It was therefore necessary, argued these writers, to pay more attention to women's education than had previously been given, lest mothers communicate undemocratic tendencies to their male off-spring" (115).

Although nationalism and the thinking on women were intimately related in most Western nations between 1868 and 1939, curiously this interrelation—which has important implications not only for Spanish history but also for literary production—has not been studied in depth for Spain. Surprisingly histories of feminism in Spain (most notably Geraldine Scanlon's landmark *La polémica feminista en la España contemporánea, 1868–1974* [1975]) and studies of Spanish nationalism (especially Inman Fox's *La invención de España* [1987] and Carolyn Boyd's *Historia Patria: Politics, History, and National Identity in Spain 1875–1975* [1997]) have not considered the discourse on women at the end of the century and the rise of nationalism as parallel and closely interlocking phenomena. While José Álvarez Junco's *Mater dolorosa: La idea de España en el siglo XIX* (2001) foregrounds the grieving Madonna icon as illustrative of Spain's nationalistic view of itself as historical victim, it covers little of the growing discourse on women as citizens of the Spanish state. Nationalism does have a gendered dimension, according to Andrew Parker and colleagues, who note that nationalism is a normative force that adopts an ideal of masculinity "Nationalism favors a distinctly homosocial form of male bonding" (1992, 6). Concomitantly, while male nationalism was defining women's role in the nation-building process, women were motivated to find their own place in the national order through feminist discourse and activity. As highlighted in the chapters that follow, the clash of the discourse on the nation with the discourse on women and later with feminism provided the Spanish novel with ample material for several decades.

The interrelated thinking on gender and nation after 1868, which became incorporated into the Spanish modernist novel, underwent several phases during the period that I call the modernist era. The first phase— from approximately 1895 to 1909, including the Cuban disaster—focused on the essential nature of Spain as a nation and the education of women as an important aspect of the domestic backbone of the nation. The notion of *intrahistoria,* often couched in female iconography, is important to our understanding of significant aspects of the canonical novel of the first decade of the twentieth century. A second phase occupies most of the second decade, which saw a renewed (postdisaster) nationalism emerge with the First World War and the Moroccan campaigns carried out under the reign of Alfonso XIII. Again, nationalist propaganda drew on female imagery. Simultaneously, Spanish writers were awakening to the militant feminist movements in the Anglo-American world, and Spain itself was beginning to see a more vocal if not a more organized feminism. Male authors portrayed feminist activity in their novels, and a number of women began to publish (especially in popular venues) fiction that explored women's status in patriarchal Spain. The 1920s and 1930s form a third phase, in which Miguel Primo de Rivera's dictatorship (1923–30), the Second Republic (1931–39), and the Civil War (1936–39) raised new national issues, including a militant feminism and women's participation in public intellectual and political life. Discourse on women in the 1920s also witnessed a shift from women's education and domestic roles to the biological foundations of gender. The dialogue on the biological nature of gender emerged as a theme in novels by both men and women as a means of addressing the way in which sexual roles reflect the state of the nation. Some novels by men attempted to combat the heightened visibility of women in the public sphere with cautionary tales, whereas women novelists pressed more urgently for alternatives to traditional solutions in women's lives.

From the outset, gender was inextricably linked to a developing nationalism in Spain. The Spanish sense of nation began to coalesce from 1833 forward, when the liberal regime of Isabel II initiated its forty-year campaign to suppress the ancien régime (Bourbon absolutism).[2] Thus, in its beginnings, building the liberal nation-state was associated with a woman (the female monarch), although in its later years her government became allied with conservative Catholic interests. Isabel's gender provided the impetus for the Carlist wars that punctuated Spain's turbulent nineteenth century and provided fodder for male wit (of which Gustavo Adolfo and Valeriano Bécquer's pornographic watercolors are but one famous example). The Spanish-American War of 1898, a crucial turning point in Spanish nationhood, was similarly marked by gender rhetoric and iconology:

The mass call-up was justified in terms of the national interest. The colonies were seen as part of Spain so that the recruits were told they were being sent off to defend the motherland overseas. There was a festive spirit as the troops were seen off in stations and ports, with bands playing and bishops blessing. For the first time in many parts of Spain, national concerns began to vie with local and class identities. Spaniards of all classes and localities were encouraged to internalize images of national identity which were in reality those of the ruling oligarchy. . . . The lion, the ancient symbol of the kingdom of León, was one of the emblems of the Spanish monarchy and appeared on the national shield. Before and during the war, that of a woman also representing Spain often accompanied it in cartoons and illustrations. She was, on different occasions, a matronly mother-figure and a virgin lusted after by a lecherous old Uncle Sam. (Balfour 1996, 109, 110–111)[3]

The ignominious defeat of Spain at the hands of the United States and the loss of Cuba, the Philippines, and Puerto Rico evoked worry about a weak, effeminate nation. Álvarez Junco observes that *afeminamiento* in political language "significaba, y continuó significando hasta bien entrado el siglo XX, la pérdida tanto de fuerza física como de equilibrio o control moral" (2001, 217) [signified and continued to signify until well into the twentieth century the loss of both physical strength and moral control or equilibrium]. He notes that the concept reappeared in 1898, "momento en que tantas tendencias subyacentes de la cultura política del siglo habrían de alcanzar su culminación" (217) [a moment in which so many underlying tendencies of political culture of the century were to culminate].

Although Jagoe, Blanco, and Enríquez Salamanca (1998, 23) provide ample evidence that "woman" as a category became an obsessive topic in Spain around 1840, the intertwining of specific discourses on gender and nation can be located in about 1868 during the so-called revolutionary period between the dethroning of Isabel II and the Restoration (1875). The link resides in Krausist thought, the German philosophy that introduced the Western philosophical tradition into Spain in the 1860s as part of an effort to bring Spain into the modern world. Spanish Krausism viewed education for women, the formative agents of the nation's future citizens, as central to the nation's progress. There were a few lone souls who wrote about the need to improve women's lot in Spain before 1868 (Fray Benito Jerónimo Feijoo's *Defensa de las mujeres* [1726–27], for example), but it was not until the "revolutionary" period of 1868–75 that a real discussion of women's social status, and especially women's education, emerged as part of the broader interests of national rejuvenation.

For example, Krausist educator and rector of the University of Madrid Fernando de Castro sponsored a series of Sunday lectures on women's education in 1869. The topics of the series centered on the range of areas that women's education should cover: religion, hygiene, morals, medicine, domestic economy, the arts, pedagogy, history, literature, physical sciences, and jurisprudence (especially as related to women's issues). Not surprisingly, men, among them prominent political figures Francisco Pi y Margall and Emilio Castelar, gave all the lectures. Castro's inaugural lecture followed the Krausist ideal that each individual had the responsibility to develop his or her potential to the fullest in order for Spain to join ranks with the most advanced nations of the world. He pointed out that other countries had taken important steps to give women equal rights. Although the lectures were primarily concerned with maternity and argued for separate spheres for the two sexes, they were important means of consciousness-raising. The lectures' long-range impact is attested to by the fact that Azorín refers to them in several post-turn-of-the-century articles.

In 1869, Castro founded the Ateneo Artístico y Literario de Señoras. Concepción Arenal, arguably the first Spanish feminist, and Faustina Saez de Melgar, who wrote fairly conventional manuals for young girls, served on its advisory board. As was typical of other associations established between 1868 and the 1920s (when a more modern feminism finally took hold in Spain), many of the activities at the Ateneo Artístico y Literario de Señoras centered on men. Writers such as Juan Eugenio Hartzenbusch, Ramón del Campoamor, Juan Valera, and Gaspar Núñez de Arce gave readings of their work. In 1870, as an outgrowth of the Ateneo, the Escuela de Institutrices and the Asociación para la Enseñanza de la Mujer were created. Prominent men associated with the Institución Libre de Enseñanza—Francisco Giner de los Ríos, Gumersindo Azcárate, Urbano González Serrano, and Martín Ruiz de Quevedo—supported these organizations. By 1880, the Asociación para la Enseñanza de la

Mujer also received some support from the government. The women's education movement continued to gain momentum, and in 1882 the journal *Instrucción para la Mujer* published its first issue.

The Congreso Nacional Pedagógico, held in Madrid in 1882 and attended by 2,182 delegates, one-fifth of whom were women (mostly teachers), devoted much discussion to women's aptitude for teaching young people. There was widespread agreement that women had a natural ability to relate to children. The equation of maternal qualities and teaching evident in conference discussions reappears in some modernist novels (see especially Azorín's *Doña Inés* [1926], analyzed in Chapter 4). Also in 1882, Ministro de Fomento José Luis Albareda rehabilitated the Escuela Normal Central de Maestras; he modernized pedagogical methods and added to the curriculum new subjects such as French, law, sciences, and geography. Shortly thereafter, salaries for male and female teachers were equalized, and in 1888 a pedagogical congress in Barcelona determined that education for boys and girls up to age twelve should be the same.

The years between 1882 and 1892 saw significant advances in women's education, and there was certainly plenty of room for improvement. In 1877, women's illiteracy ranged from 80 to 85 percent (Jagoe 1998, 127). The year 1892 marked an ideological turning point, represented at a well-advertised conference on women held in Madrid. At the conference, unlike at earlier gatherings, the topics were not restricted to women's education, and several women gave major speeches. The conference also admitted debate that more clearly delimited the differing ideological postures on the situation for women. The main positions can be summarized as follows: (1) Women should receive a different education from that of men because of their biological inferiority and their particular responsibilities. (2) Women should receive equal education to that of men but should not have access to all careers, because the social rights of men would be dangerous to women. (3) Women should have absolute equality in education and professions. Emilia Pardo Bazán eloquently defended this last position in her speech, which was published as "La educación del hombre y la mujer Sus relaciones y diferencias" (1892). Jagoe notes that Pardo Bazán "fue la primera en defender una enseñanza dirigida a beneficiar a la mujer y no pensada en la función de la misión de ésta en una sociedad patriarcal" (1998, 131) [was the first to defend education specifically designed to benefit women and not designed with her mission in a patriarchal society in mind]. It would be some years before this idea gained wider acceptance, and even Pardo Bazán could say in 1890 that middle-class men were much more conscious of women's literacy, and they selected wives accordingly: "Hoy un marido burgués se sonrojaría de que su esposa no supiera leer ni escribir" (qtd. in Gómez-Ferrer Morant 1986, 165).[4] Jagoe (1998, 133) points out that the dominant idea that governed women's education in the nineteenth century was that women should be educated for the common, national good, an idea that lasted well into the twentieth century.

If, as Scanlon argues, there was not a full-blown militant women's movement in late nineteenth-century Spain to parallel Anglo-American feminism, there was, as I note, a great deal of discourse about women. In addition to the appearance of public lectures on the subject of women's education, a long list of books was published on "the woman question" between 1869 and the first decade of the twentieth century.[5] These began with Arenal's *La mujer del porvenir* (1869), which had a sustained resonance in the growth of consciousness about women's condition in Spain. Archmodernist Azorín, who owned two copies of *La mujer del porvenir,* wrote articles on Arenal on several occasions. Indicating Azorín's equation of women and nation as essential and eternal coordinates, he characterized Arenal as "España y emoción," calling her also "España, emoción, y también humanidad."[6]

The numerous end-of-the-century books on women evidenced an array of political attitudes from very conservative to quite liberal, but all had the effect of keeping women's concerns in the public eye. Krausist Adolfo Posada attempted to sort through the several kinds of feminism that were influencing Spanish thinking about women in order to negotiate a model that suited the situation in Spain. Between 1896 and 1898, he published a series of articles on feminism in the widely circulated *La España Contemporánea*, which were collected in the book *Feminismo* in 1899. Posada distinguished between a radical feminism that advocated equality for the sexes in education and before the law (the Anglosaxon model) and a feminist radicalism with affinities to socialism and anarchism. He preferred an interclassist nonrevolutionary type of feminism.

His epistolary polemic on feminism with the more conservative Urbano González Serrano was published in 1893.

By the turn of the century, the women's education movement had significantly increased women's public visibility, even in the working classes. In 1906, the Centro Iberoamericano de Cultura Popular Femenina organized a series of courses for women of all social classes designed to make them more economically independent. These measures, although not radical, were beginning to have an effect, and the response was often reactionary as men sought to counter the new female models with traditional depictions of women in their novels. Home and homeland were understood to go hand in hand. George Mosse finds a strong association between nationalism and respectability or traditional domesticity, which allies the nationalist movements with masculinity and rising middle-class values. Mosse points out that national sentiments helped control sexuality and that nationalism adopted the ideal of manliness to further its goals of unification (1985, 10). Some pre–World War I Spanish novels written by both men and women deal either positively or negatively with a more independent life for women. Baroja's *La dama errante* (1908) and *La ciudad de la niebla* (1909) rein in the autonomous woman with conventional marriage. Burgos's *El veneno del arte* (1910; reprinted in *La flor de la playa y otras novelas cortas* [Burgos 1989b]), without concealing the psychological difficulties that the independent woman faces, allows her a margin of satisfaction in the unmarried state.

Interest in defining the Spanish national soul—*intrahistoria* or *la tradición eterna* in Unamuno's terminology, *el alma castellana* in Azorín's—arose concurrently with the developing discourse on women. Like the national discussion of women's education, the search for a Spanish (Castilian) essence, which appeared at the time of the Cuban uprisings in the 1890s and which we often associate with the Generation of '98, had its roots in Krausism. Leading Krausist thinker Francisco Giner de los Ríos divided history into two categories—external history and internal history. For Giner, true Spanish reality resided in internal history, the values and spiritual manifestations of the Spanish people. Sebastian Balfour associates the interest in a tradition of the Spanish people with Spain's identity crisis, which was a more acute form than the more universal ideological and aesthetic upheaval: "Their feelings of pessimism ran deeper than elsewhere because of the seemingly insurmountable contradictions of Spanish society—between traditional and modern, inertia and mobility, rural and urban, peasant and worker, religious and anti-clerical, aristocratic and bourgeois culture, and so on" (1997, 88). Thus, he finds a utopianism in the mythic representations of medieval Castile ("visions of a past society in which social harmony reigned were a compulsive flight from the dilemmas of modernization"), and he directly relates Unamuno's notion of *intrahistoria* to frustration over a sense of impotence in the face of change: "Many petty bourgeois intellectuals sought for a model of identity in an unchanging emotional landscape—a rural arcadia . . . a traditional culture abiding under the turbulent surface of events" (89).

Balfour points out that "social groups who felt threatened by the effects of modernization" (233) favored the imperial myth, which suppresses modern divisions of class and region. It was also very likely a haven from another modern phenomenon—the growing feminist movement. In *tradición eterna* or *intrahistoria,* differences disappear, and women become part of the vast sea of eternal Spain; in fact, they often serve as its symbolic, mythic soul. Eric J. Hobsbawm reminds us of nationalism's need for myths ("Nationalism requires too much belief in what is patently not so" [1990, 14]) and quotes Ernest Renan that "'getting history wrong is part of being a nation'" (qtd. in Hobsbawm 1990, 14).[7] Women as eternal Spanish essence were a significant aspect of the Spanish national myth. As Chapter 1 shows, in male writing of the modernist period, women often became associated with the concept of *pueblo* as an emblem of eternal national tradition. Álvarez Junco points to another kind of traditionalism central to a conservative Catholic nationalism that assumed an increasingly important place in Spain's national identity toward the end of the nineteenth century: "Lo importante de esta mobilization católico-conservadora de finales del XIX es que se defendía en ella la 'tradición española', que a la vez significaba el enfrentamiento del catolicismo con la modernidad, con la revolución, con el materialismo ateo; en el caso de los carlistas, y ahí estaba la disensión, también con el parlamentarismo liberal" (2001, 454). [The important thing about this conservative Catholic mobilization at the end of the nineteenth century is that it defended "Spanish tradition," which at the same time meant a confrontation between Catholicism and modernity, revolution, and atheist materialism; in the case of Carlism, and here lay the division, also with liberal parlamentarianism.]

Tradition, in all these senses, can be a dead weight in the march toward modernity, an inertia that hinders the forward energy of cultures and augurs for the status quo. In *The Protestant Ethic and the Spirit of Capitalism* (1919), Max Weber gave the following example of traditionalism as a precapitalist phenomenon related to agrarian society. Farmworkers were offered a higher wage per hour with the expectation that they would work more hours. In fact, they worked less. They were interested only in maintaining their traditional lifestyle and not in accumulating more wealth in order to live beyond the level to which they were accustomed. Such is traditionalism in premodern societies. Eric Hobsbawm reminds us that invented traditions can serve a similar restraining purpose in modern society: "'Invented tradition' is taken to mean a set of practices, normally governed by overtly or tacitly accepted rules and of a ritual or symbolic nature, which seek to inculcate certain values and norms of behavior . . . which automatically implies continuity with the past" (1983, 1). The invented tradition in literature in many ways helped reconstruct a Weberian traditionalism within canonical modernist fiction, in which women became a national symbol and guardian of the continuity and immutability of the nation. Álvarez Junco notes that between 1868 and 1870, in part because there was no specific monarch as icon of the nation, Spain began to be represented as an anonymous feminine form (2001, 564).

The classics of Spanish Golden Age literature provided a wealth of material for the modernist invention of a national tradition, and for dealing with emerging social groups—the working classes and women—modernist writers needed to reconcile with their vision of Spain's essence or what it ought to be. The great canonical works (such as Fernando de Rojas's *La Celestina, Lazarillo de Tormes,* plays by Tirso de Molina and Pedro Calderón de la Barca, and Miguel de Cervantes's *Don Quixote* and *Novelas ejemplares*) were sources of Spanish national types—*la tradición eterna* of the Spanish people—and domestic arrangements to follow or shun. The classics allowed male authors to shroud a domestic agenda within a nationalist one (the classics reaffirmed Spaniards' preferred view of themselves in the wake of the Cuban disaster as a "pure, warrior race, valiant, chivalresque and Christian" [Balfour 1996, 110]). Male modernist novelists often replaced the failed imperial impulse with a national tradition that they believed lay embedded in the literary classics. As Corpus Barga asserted, "Don Juan y Don Quijote son dos hallazgos, dos descubrimientos más allá de nuestros mares. Son las Américas de la literatura española" (1925b, n.p.). Álvarez Junco interprets the national celebrations of the second centenary of Calderón de la Barca's death in 1881 as a means of reinforcing the conservative idea of Spain as an essentially Catholic country: "Calderón era 'espíritu eminentemente católico' y 'gloria del teatro español'" as well as "'poeta nacional . . . españolísimo . . . espejo fiel de las creencias y sentimientos de la nación española'" (2001, 447). Significantly, many of Calderón's plays center on the rigid Spanish honor code by which women were severely punished (often with death) for any perceived transgression of social (sexual) norms.

As Chapters 1, 2, 3, and 5 show, women writers also looked to the classics for material, although often for different purposes than did male writers. For example, whereas male modernist authors evoked the Don Juan legend with various nationalist (mythic) and/or existentialist intentions, women authors transformed the legend (even subverted it) in order to explore social concerns. To male writers, Don Juan symbolized the eternal essence of Spain as well as Spain's modern dilemma, a tradition-bound country seeking to enter the contemporary world. It is the latter aspect of the Don Juan legend that captured the imagination of women writers who domesticated the Don Juan figure within a contemporary and very specific social milieu. They linked donjuanism to social ills such as prostitution, moral depravity, and social irresponsibility.

In the second decade of the twentieth century, a new constellation of events welded the thinking on the Spanish nation and the thinking on women, or at least marked them as parallel discourses. Spain renewed its extraterritorial influence after the 1898 debacle in a series of agreements with France and Britain between 1904 and 1912 that assigned Spain the role of policing most of northern Morocco. This arrangement also restored the Spanish military's sense of purpose, and its new conscriptive effort provided opportunities for more nationalist propaganda of the kind inspired by the Cuban War. Once again gendered terms projected the nation as a colonial power: "The nation was repeatedly personified as the Mother, abandoned or slapped by an ungrateful son [Catalonia]. . . . The Fatherland . . . was declared intangible because it 'is everything; the air we breathe, our children's cradle, the tomb of our parents. To offend the Fatherland is to offend our own mother. He who allows Spain to be insulted, would allow the woman who carried him in her womb to be insulted'" (Balfour 1997, 187). The socialists also exploited the mother or fiancée image in their campaign against the Moroccan wars (Scanlon 1976, 234). The army in the postcolonial era was depleted, and the campaigns in Africa were mostly disastrous. Burgos debuted as the first female war correspondent during the Moroccan wars, an experience that she incorporated into her novels as well as into her journalism. Somewhat later, Chacel's *Memorias de Leticia Valle* (1945) explored the nationalist pretensions of the Moroccan period alongside gender confusions that arose in the second decade of the twentieth century.

Even though Spain did not participate in World War I, this event gave rise (as it did in the rest of Europe and in the United States) to additional nationalist thinking and changed the nature and importance of the Spanish debate on women. Nationalist sentiment, already revived after the 1898 disaster by the Moroccan military interventions, assumed new meaning for the future of Spain as a nation in the context of the European conflict. As Francisco J. Romero Salvadó indicates, Spaniards were divided in their sympathies; some were Germanophiles, whereas others were Francophiles. Those who sided with Germany "regarded a German victory as the triumph of the concept of nation based on traditional values such as monarchism, discipline, religion, and a hierarchical social order. The Francophiles saw the Allies as representing the "cause of democracy and progress. By demanding that Spain should join that camp they were opting for a future Europeanised, secular and democratic Spain" (1996, 125). The male novelists considered here were also divided; for example, Baroja was a Germanophile, but Azorín was a Francophile.

At the same time that nationalist sentiment rekindled, an increasingly activist Spanish feminist movement emerged after the Great War, largely because price increases occasioned by the conflict forced more women into the workplace. Augmented production demanded by the war effort also created more jobs for women. Once women were out of the home, it was a natural corollary that their feminist consciousness should blossom. The nature of the relationship between public discourse on women and the nation changed. Now women were demanding an equal place at the national table, and the founding of several key institutions ratified a shift in social policy concerning women. In 1915, the Residencia de Señoritas was established as a coordinate of the Residencia de Estudiantes for men. The Residencia Femenina encouraged women's advanced education by providing women with a place to reside while they studied in Madrid. There were very close ties between the Residencia de Estudiantes, so important to the fomenting of the arts and literature in the Spanish Silver Age, and the Residencia de Señoritas. José Ortega y Gasset, Ramón Pérez de Ayala, Eugenio Montés, Ramón Menéndez Pidal, Gregorio Marañón, Juan Ramón Jiménez, Azorín, Pedro Salinas, and Vicente Huidobro all formed part of the intellectual life of the women's residence.

Victoria Kent—who studied law at the University of Madrid from 1817 to 1924, when she received her doctorate—lived at the Residencia, where she was in charge of the library. Kent went on to become the first woman lawyer to appear before the Consejo Supremo de Guerra for the 1930 Republican rebels (Álvaro de Albornoz, Niceto Alcalá Zamora, Miguel Maura Gamazo, Francisco Largo Caballero, Fernando de los Ríos, Santiago Casares Quiroga, Alejandro Lerroux, Marcelino Domingo, Manuel Azaña, Diego Martínez Barrio, Nicolau d'Óliver, and Indalecio Prieto). After she received her doctorate, Kent collaborated with María de Maeztu on a "nuevo plan de estudios" for the coeducational Instituto Escuela, which the Krausist Institución Libre de Enseñanza founded in 1918. By this time, the nationalist idea—that women's education was central to the national goal of bringing Spain into the modern world—had been slowly replaced by a sense that women had a right to be educated and a right to a life of the mind as a good in itself.

Not surprisingly, the second decade of the twentieth century witnessed a significant increase in the publication of novels about women and novels authored by women.[8] The popular venues in which women often published—fiction series such as *Los Contemporáneos* (1909–26), *La Novela Corta* (1916–25), *La Novela Semanal* (1921–25), and *La Novela de Hoy* (1922–32)—were initiated at the end of the first decade and continued to be an important editorial outlet for women throughout the pre–Civil War period. Carmen de Burgos, Sofía Casanova, Blanca de los Ríos, Concha Espina, and María Martínez Sierra all published significant short and long novels during this decade, providing a major body of work that demands consideration in a reevaluation of the Spanish modernist era. Male authors, too, registered women's new social roles in their fiction, with most attempting to circumscribe these roles in one way or another.

Journalism similarly assumed an important female dimension. In 1913, an entirely female editorial staff launched the journal *El Pensamiento Femenino*, which presented feminism as a primarily humanitarian and charitable movement. Although *El Pensamiento Femenino* was short-lived, the need for a vehicle that spoke to women's concerns spawned *La Voz de la Mujer* in 1917, a broadly based effort to unite all women interested in the women's cause. In 1918, the editor of *La Voz de la Mujer*, Celsia Regis, and businesswoman María Espinosa de los Monteros founded the Asociación Nacional de Mujeres Españolas (ANME), which became the most important Spanish feminist organization. Its newspaper, *Mundo Femenino* (1921), took an independent position, attacking the right and the left equally. It criticized the right for advocating women's suffrage and the left for opposing women's suffrage, a hotly contested issue in Spain, because it was widely believed that women under the domination of the clergy would shift Spanish politics to the right. On the whole, however, ANME leaned more toward the right than the left. Its political affiliations were with conservative statesmen such as Antonio Maura, Juan de la Cierva, and Eduardo Dato. Significantly, these were the politicians with whom Azorín was affiliated, and his attempt at liberalism with respect to women's issues often lapsed into an ambivalent attitude toward feminism (see Chapters 1 and 4).

ANME's political posture coincided with a great deal of male writing of the early decades of the century: "1. Oponerse por cuantos medios estén al alcance de la Asociación a todo propósito, acto o manifestación que atente contra la integridad del territorio nacional. 2. Procurar que toda madre española, en perfecto paralelismo con la maestra, inculque en el niño, desde la más tierna infancia, el amor a la madre patria única e indivisible" (qtd. in Scanlon 1976, 204) [1. To oppose by all means within the reach of the Association every proposal, act, or manifestation that goes counter to the integrity of the national territory. 2. To try to insure that every Spanish mother, in perfect parallel to the teacher, inculcate in the child from earliest infancy love of the mother country one and indivisible]. In 1920, ANME opposed the meeting of the International Conference of Suffragists on patriotic grounds (the conference refused to recognize Spain in several important ways). And ANME was ambivalent about the Republic, which was supported by leftist feminists and women writers such as Burgos, Martínez Sierra, Nelken, Montseny, Chacel, and Zambrano.

Thus, feminism in Spain became politically polarized with right- and left-wing factions. Certain sectors of the Catholic hierarchy realized that the church needed to remain abreast of the times and make a show of defending women's rights if it was to keep both educated and working-class women within its fold. In 1912 and 1929, respectively, the Federación de Obreras Católicas and Juventud Católica Femenina were founded. These organizations and many clergy favored women's suffrage, but they supported very limited reform in other aspects of women's social role. For example, Father Graciano Martínez, who wrote *El libro de la mujer española. Hacia un feminismo cuasi dogmático* (1921), opined that a woman should not actively participate in politics because it would shame her husband.

The polarization of feminist discourse in Spain during the second and third decades of the twentieth century ensured lively public debate and a keen public awareness of women's issues. José Luis Aranguren (1963, 232, 234) reminds us that not only the print media but also the new film medium contributed significantly to giving women's new roles a high-profile public image in the 1920s and 1930s. As the discourse on women shifted from the less controversial need to educate women (although to what degree was still in dispute) to a focus on a feminist platform of legal rights, enfranchisement, and divorce, the portrayal of women in fiction also shifted gears. No longer did male novelists ally women with the eternal sea of Spanish history; they now located them in more concrete social situations. The more feminist orientation of public discourse on women (both the liberal and conservative views) is evident in second-decade novels (Pío Baroja's *El mundo es ansí*, discussed in Chapter 4; Concha Espina's *La esfinge maragata,* discussed in Chapters 2 and 3; and Miguel de Unamuno's *Niebla,* discussed in Chapter 2). By the 1920s, when feminism can truly be considered a movement in Spain, some works of fiction, especially by male authors, appear to be works of backlash.[9] During that decade, Unamuno (*Dos madres* [1920] and *La tía Tula* [1921]) and Azorín (*Doña Inés* [1925]) each published novels with unflatteringly portrayed, strong female protagonists who refuse to marry (see Chapter 4).

Debates on gender took a biological turn in the early 1920s, also very likely a response to women's increased public visibility. A number of authors (mostly male) weighed in on the organic nature of gender, and concepts such as the masculinized woman and the feminized man (the latter already a concern in the wake of the 1898 military rout) became part of the national dialogue. This biological discourse received a significant impetus from respected medical authorities, particularly Marañón, whose ideas can be found embedded in novels by Pérez de Ayala, Unamuno, and Burgos published in the 1920s (see Chapter 5). While biological arguments for conventional gender roles attempted to circumscribe women to the home and child rearing, younger feminists such as Nelken and Montseny joined Burgos in employing fiction more insistently to defend women's right to social and legal equality. In the 1920s, Espina, whose solutions to women's need for economic support was usually a practical marriage, wrote the more radically feminist *La virgen prudente* (1929, republished in 1932 as *Aurora de España*). These patently feminist novels are the subjects of Chapter 6.

In 1926, Maeztu, director of the Residencia de Señoritas, in collaboration with Kent, founded an important institution for women's intellectual advancement—the Lyceum Club. Even though she had studied philosophy with Unamuno at the University of Salamanca and with Ortega y Gasset in Madrid and wrote works including *El problema de la ética, la enseñanza de la moral* (1938) and *Historia de la cultura europea. La edad moderna; grandeza y servidumbre; intento de ligar la historia pretérita a las circunstancias del mundo presente para hallar una explicación a los conflictos de la hora actual* (1941), Maeztu is better known for her lectures and her work at the Lyceum Club. Her well-received lectures there eloquently combated the notion that women were inferior to men. The Lyceum Club was an important center of intellectual activity for many women (Federico García Lorca spoke there on occasion, and Miguel de Unamuno read *Raquel encadenada* [1921] to the devotees), but it also became the butt of jokes by men who scorned women's intellectual endeavors. In a somewhat ambivalent gesture, Rafael Alberti dressed as a clown to give a lecture; more pointedly, when Jacinto Benavente was invited to lecture at the Lyceum, he flatly refused, stating, "A mí no me gusta hablar a tontas y a locas" (qtd. in Rodrigo 1979, 135). [I don't like to speak to stupid and crazy women.] Azorín parodied the club in his novel *El caballero inactual* (see Azorín 1965, discussed in Chapter 2). In 1936, Salinas wrote a letter to Margarita Bonmati from his teaching post at Wellesley College, referring to a Miss Oyarzábal, an instructor in the college's Spanish Department, as a "tipo Lyceum, como su hermana [Isabel Palencia]" (Salinas 1995, 31); the reference is clearly not flattering. In his memoirs, Manuel Azaña called the debate between ardent feminist and legislator Clara Campoamor and Lyceum cofounder Victoria Kent on the women's vote "muy divertido" (qtd. in Rodrigo 1979, 72) [very amusing]. Male writers and intellectuals attempted to turn women's efforts to join the ranks of high culture into a national joke, but the cautionary tales embedded in their fiction indicated that they also took it as a serious threat to national stability.

The Lyceum Club, the first women's association not sponsored by the church, also came under attack by the church, which considered it a "lugar en donde facilitaban todo género de lecturas, desde el Corán hasta el Ripalda" (Rodrigo 136). In four consecutive issues (of June and July 1927) signed by a priest who called himself Lorven, *Iris de Paz,* the official organ of the Archicofradía del Inmaculado Corazón de María and the executive committee of the Obra de la Buena Prensa, classified members of the Lyceum Club as women "sin virtud ni piedad," with "las piernas al aire" (qtd. in Rodrigo 1979, 136). The articles suggested that the Lyceum Club was a licentious casino, where women lost their sense of dignity. The club, they continued, was the natural enemy of the family and the husband; it destroyed the home and was a grave danger to society: "La sociedad haría muy bien recluyéndolas como locas o criminales, en lugar de permitirles clamar en el Club contra las leyes humanas y las divinas. El ambiente moral de la calle y de la familia ganaría mucho con la hospitalización o el confinamiento de esas féminas excéntricas y desequilibradas" (136). Carmen Baroja's memoir (see C. Baroja 1998, discussed in Chapter 4) sheds light on what the Lyceum Club meant to intellectually and artistically inclined women who had no other outlet for their talents.

Liberal and conservative male reaction to the activities of the Lyceum Club emblematized men's general concern about women's attempts to achieve social and intellectual parity. In fact, even though there was much public discussion about the rights of women in Spain, very little concrete legislation was achieved before the Second Republic was founded in 1931, when women's militancy was at its zenith (Scanlon 1976, 209). All the women writers included in this study, often socially and politically more radical than their male counterparts, unflinchingly supported a Republican form of government in the 1920s and 1930s, an issue about which many male writers were ambivalent. Ernesto Giménez Caballero scornfully asserted that "la República en España es el triunfo de *la niña*. Un éxito radicalmente femenino . . . avance de la España ginecocrática" (qtd. in Hurtado 1998, 31). This perception may help explain the reservations of some leading intellectuals such as Miguel de Unamuno, José Ortega y Gasset, and Pío Baroja toward the Republican movement. Interestingly, male authors such as Ramón Sender and Francisco Ayala, who were contemporaries of the younger feminist writers and who also supported the Republic and wrote fiction with political content, did not produce novels that pursued gender polemics as did the earlier male writers. Like many leftist intellectuals of the 1930s, these male writers placed the plight of workers and the lower classes above any other social considerations; women's concerns were seen as a distraction to the important business of general social revolution.

One might speculate, as I do herein, that the rash of women's popular fiction produced in the 1920s can claim some responsibility for the shift in public opinion that finally awarded women the right to vote and to divorce and gave them labor legislation and entrées to public office. Burgos may have seemed "algo modernista" when she arrived in Madrid in the first decade of the twentieth century, but by her death in 1932, she had produced a large body of fiction, which, along with that of numerous other women novelists, had radically changed the way that Spanish domesticity was portrayed in fiction and deployed in real life. Working, traveling, and leading independent lives, women's female protagonists recommended and reflected the new options becoming available to their real-life counterparts. Surely the very popular novels published by Burgos, Martínez Sierra, Casanova, de los Ríos, Espina, Nelken, and Montseny helped shaped public opinion that led to these formalizations of women's rights. Borrowing a concept from Jane Tompkins, Michael Ugarte aptly considers Spanish women's writing of the early twentieth century to be engaged in "cultural work" (1994, 264). Divorce legislation, women's vote, and labor legislation were promulgated under the Republic despite the restraining forces of biological and nationalist discourses that argued for circumscribing women within the traditional home. The imaginative powers of fiction projected the new woman beyond these powerful constraints. In *The War of the Words,* Sandra Gilbert and Susan Gubar's book on women and modernity in Anglo-American letters, the authors quote a February 13, 1917 newspaper article in which an anonymous reporter comments, "Some people think that women are the cause of modernism, whatever that is" (1988, viii). If, as I argue here, modernism can be social, then women definitely had a hand in bringing it about.

CHAPTER 1
Women and the Soul of Spain

Theory and reality diverged sharply over women's place in the Spanish national landscape at the beginning of the twentieth century. The male-authored theory of the nature of Spain, which often allied women with the Krausist-inspired transcendental notion of an eternal Spanish tradition or Spanish national soul, clashed with the reality of women's increasingly immanent and concrete role in a rapidly changing national public life. The end-of-the-century identity crisis, brought on by an increasing awareness of Spain's backwardness compared to the rest of Europe and the loss of the remnant of empire in 1898, prompted a search for what José Antonio Maraval (1986) calls "españolidad." Some believed that if only its essential nature were identified, Spain could be set on an authentic and unerring course for the future.[1] This chapter looks at several turn-of-the-century narratives—Miguel de Unamuno's *Paz en la guerra* (1897), María Martínez Sierra's *Tú eres la paz* (1906), José Martínez Ruiz's (Azorín's) *El alma castellana* (1900) and *Castilla* (1912)—that dramatize the search for Spain's eternal soul, *intrahistoria*, or *tradición eterna*.

Intrahistorical time is a complex concept that collapses present and past. In the first chapter of *En torno al casticismo* (published as journal articles in 1895 and as a book in 1902), Unamuno posits an eternal tradition that informs the present; thus, the present always carries the past within it: "Pero si hay un presente *histórico,* es por haber una tradición del presente, porque la tradición es la sustancia de la historia" (1971, 109). Present historical events are but waves on the vast permanent intrahistorical sea:

> Las olas de la Historia, con su rumor y su espuma, que reverbera al sol, ruedan sobre un mar continuo, hondo inmensamente más hondo que la

capa que ondula sobre un mar silencioso y a cuyo último fondo nunca llega el sol. Todo lo que cuentan a diario los periódicos, la historia toda del presente momento histórico, no es sino la superficie del mar, una superficie que se hiela y cristaliza en los libros y registros, y una vez cristalizada así, una capa dura, no mayor con respecto a la vida intra-histórica que esta pobre corteza en que vivimos con relación al inmenso foco ardiente que lleva dentro. (109)

[The waves of history, with their sound and foam that reverberate beneath the sun, roll over a continuous, deep sea, immensely deeper than the layer that undulates on top of a silent sea whose depth the sun never reaches. All that newspapers daily report, all history of the present moment, is nothing more than the surface of the sea, a surface that freezes over and crystallizes in books and registries, and once so crystallized, forms a hard layer, no more important with respect to intrahistoric life than the relation of the poor rind in which we live to the immense burning center it carries within.]

Although theoretically *intrahistoria* is not specifically female, by removing it from the urban newspaper-worthy events that we associate with men and aligning it with rural labors in which women traditionally played a significant role, Unamuno opens it up to a female and domestic dimension. Other adjectives and metaphors in this key passage similarly imbue his concept of *intrahistoria* with a feminine cast: "La oscura y silenciosa labor cotidiana y eterna, esa labor que, como la de las madréporas suboceánicas, echa las bases sobre que se alzan los islotes de la historia" (109) [the dark and silent daily and eternal work, this labor that, like that of the suboceanic madrepores, establishes the bases upon which the islands of history rise]. As we see in a passage quoted later, Unamuno also allies farm labor with women.

Unamuno was a master of insinuating metaphor (here the sea image, which from ancient times has been associated with women and the maternal), and the silence typically associated with women is ubiquitous in the depictions of intrahistorical life:

Sobre el silencio augusto . . . se apoya y vive el sonido; sobre la inmensa Humanidad silenciosa se levantan los que meten bulla en la Historia. Esa vida intra-histórica, silenciosa y continua como el fondo mismo del mar, es la sustancia del progreso, la verdadera tradición, la tradición eterna, no la tradición mentida que se suele ir a buscar al pasado enterrado en libros y papeles y monumentos y piedras. (109)

[Sound lives and sustains itself above the august silence; those that create the bustle of history rise above the immense silent humanity. This silent and continuous intrahistoric life, like the bottom of the sea itself, is the substance of progress, the true tradition, the eternal tradition, not the false tradition that one seeks out in the past buried in books and papers, monuments and stones.]

The reduction of historical substance to the silent, uniform sea-like mass is typical of Unamuno's treatment of his fictional women as well. In theory, Unamuno's intrahistory may be the masses of genderless "folk," but in his early novel *Paz en la guerra,* intrahistory assumes a domestic and female dimension.

In *El alma castellana* and *Castilla,* Azorín also collapsed the present and past in ways that implicate the feminine. Many scholars have interpreted Azorín's obsession with time as a desire to find ways to evade it. Miguel Enguídanos, for example, writes of Azorín's attempt to escape his own time and enter a "tiempo divinal" (1959). Leon Livingstone emphasizes the eternal present in Azorín's narrations, a "momentaneidad," which he describes as instances of "supremo deleite intemporal que constituye un triunfo sobre la realidad temporal" (1970, 327). And Thomas Meehan asserts that "Azorín nos da la impresión que en su mundo de ficción todo sigue existiendo en un eterno presente, que el tiempo no existe" (1969, 661). As Livingstone points out, Azorín thought it an error to make an arbitrary distinction between present and past (1970, 121). Maravall (1968) calls Azorín's treatment of history "microhistoria," a history of the small daily events in the lives of ordinary people in small towns not usually associated with official political history. These interpretations of Azorín's view of time and history are partial, as the Alicantine writer almost invariably constructed a double-sided temporal edifice. One side reveals the eternal view, and the other opens a window onto specific historical situations and institutions (often modern social forms that relate to women and marriage). Women provide the metaphor by which Azorín transposed his message about Spain's circumstances in the early twentieth century onto the eternal essence of Spain.

Male writers tended to associate the heart of the nation—its folk—with the other, someone who is not I; women's identification with "the people," in contrast, is much closer. In Unamuno's *En torno al casticismo,* for example, the notion of *intrahistoria,* the eternal flow of history that can be found only in the country folk and their daily labors, is an idealized view of peasant life. Unamuno's concept of the Spanish "folk" is non-specific; it posits a vague "spirit of the people" that is amorphous, nameless, faceless, and, of course, genderless. In making the past coincidental with the present, both Unamuno and Azorín engaged in what Maravall calls the "comunalización del individuo" (1986, 186) and assumed a conservative position on social roles and domestic arrangements. History (the past) bears much less weight in Martínez Sierra's observations on the nature of Spain, as she concentrated more overtly on contemporary social mores. Moreover, she did not engage in the communalization inherent in the male writers' concept of a Spanish soul, and she did not theorize about the nature of Spain in extrafictional venues until her feminist essays of the second decade and again in her autobiographical *Una mujer por caminos de España* (1952). Her earlier positions are found embedded in her novels and short stories. For example, in the novelette *Aventura* (1907), Martínez Sierra introduced a modern, liberated woman into a rural Spanish setting. The female protagonist completely overrides country traditions, swimming nude in the millpond and dominating her family and suitors with her quick wit and self-possessed demeanor. She does not participate in a silent, long-suffering intrahistorical sea; she is a confident individual who achieves her specific personal goals.

Not only does *intrahistoria* erase temporal distinctions; it telescopes spatial entities as well. The hegemonic Spanish myth at the fin de siècle was that Castile represented the soul of Spain, especially in Miguel de Unamuno's *En torno al casticismo,* Ángel Ganivet's *Idearium español* (1897), and Azorín's *El alma castellana.* The people of Castilian towns and villages were a soul that formed the heart of eternal Spain. By uniting the eternal flow of the life of "the people" with the politically hegemonic Castile in *En torno al casticismo,* Unamuno tacitly asserted the legitimacy of an officially subsumed variety and difference:

Pero si Castilla ha hecho la nación española, ésta ha ido españolizándose cada vez más, fundiendo más cada día la riqueza de su variedad de contenido interior, absorbiendo el espíritu castellano en otro superior a él, más complejo: el español. No tienen otro sentido hondo los pruritos de regionalismo más vivaces cada día, pruritos que siente Castilla misma: son síntomas del proceso de españolización de España, son pródromos de la honda labor de unificación interna y al compás de la sumisión del conjunto todo a una unidad superior a él. (1971, 127)

[But if Castile has made the Spanish nation, it has also become progressively more Spanish, fusing more each day the richness of its internal content, absorbing the Castilian spirit in another—the Spanish one—that is superior and more complex than it. This is the meaning of the lively regionalist urges that daily increase ways that Castile itself feels: They are symptoms of the process of Spain becoming Spanish; they are indicators of the deep labor of internal unification and of the rhythm of the submission of the ensemble to a unity superior to it.]

In a paradoxical way, then, the specific region Castile stands for and encompasses the variety of the Spanish nation, all its distinctive regions—Basque, Catalonian, Galician, Andalusian. Just as past and present become blurred in an eternal present, geography is telescoped, and Castile becomes a synecdoche for all Spain. According to Jo Labanyi, "The instability of history is converted into fixity of place. The emphasis on Castile by Unamuno, Baroja, Azorín and Machado permits the suppression of diversity by creating the illusion of a unified space.... The rejection of history for nature is a rejection of history for myth. As Barthes observes, the goal of myth is to 'immobilize the world'" (1994, 132, 147). Male writers in particular identified personally with Castile's decline and the fading of its glorious past. As Sebastian Balfour notes, "The 'true' Spain was seen to lie in the spirit of the Counter-Reformation and in the Second of May 1808 uprising against the French invaders. The ancestral Castile of the Reconquest also became a model for a renewed Spain. Indeed, Castile exerted a fascination even among those regenerationist writers most critical of the supposed decadence of Spain. Their nostalgic musing over the medieval ruins and the harsh landscape of the *meseta* helped to nourish this conservative myth of national identity (1996, 116). In a similar way, the intrahistorical undercurrent lacks specificity but tends to have a vaguely female identity.

El pueblo (the people) is an abstract concept that facilitates the erasure of geographical divisions, and it has special meanings in the Spanish context not present in other languages. It can mean a "village" or "place"—an assemblage of houses and people with an identifiable sense of community. In this sense, *pueblo* has a rural connotation. It can also convey a broader meaning as "the people of an entire country," often with nationalist overtones. Maravall notes, for example, that in Unamuno's theory, distinctions between tradition, *pueblo*, and nation blur: "El destino fecundo de los pueblos es enlazarse en una patria. . . . En nuestro caso concreto hacer tradición es hacer patria. Y a construir la tradición común española tiene que confluir las tradiciones todos de los pueblos todos que integran la Patria" (1986, 193).[2] In the socialist ideologies that took root in Spain shortly after the arrival of Krausism, *pueblo* refers in a more materialist way to the working classes. Although most meanings of *pueblo* are less idealistic than the German term *volksgeist*, in the Krausist sense that informs *intrahistoria*, *pueblo* acquires a meaning similar to the German transcendent "spirit of the nation."

Instead of being forward-looking, like the workers' ideologies or feminism, *intrahistoria* is nostalgic and yearns for that mythical Golden Age when all was peace, unity, and harmony within the imagined national borders. As Francisco La Rubia Prado points out, *intrahistoria* minimizes external conditions: "Cuando se afirma que en el espíritu colectivo de un pueblo, en el *Volksgeist,* hay algo más que la suma de los caracteres comunes a los espíritus individuales que lo integra, lo que se afirma es que viven en él de un modo o de otro los caracteres *todos* de *todos* sus componentes" (1996, 239).

Both Unamuno and Azorín evoked specific regions via female identifications. When women are associated with a geographical region, their "soul" blends into an eternal landscape. Unamuno observed that the Galician landscape is "femenino;" nature in Galicia is a humanized mansion for men where they can rest and be lulled to sleep "como caricia tibia, un aliento de humedad" (1958 1:544). He notes that "apenas se ve más que mujeres trabajando el campo" [one sees only women working the land], and thus women are "como el paisaje: de carnación muy fraguada, bien tapados los huesos, redundantes, como las que pintó Rubens, con tupida fronda de caballera, con ojos a que asoma la melancolía secular de un pueblo antiguo" (1:544) [like the landscape: of forged carnality, their bones well padded, redundant, like those that Rubens painted, with a thick frond of hair, with the secular melancholy of an ancient people appearing in their eyes]. According to the rector of Salamanca, the low suicide rate in Galicia is a sign of Galicia's strong female character. Azorín also equated women with specific national places (Doña Inés with Segovia or Salvadora with Olbena, for example). In "Oviedo, las bellas amigas," he writes of his beautiful female acquaintances in the Asturian capital: "Y a vosotras . . . Lola, Paquita, Matilde, Rosario, Carmen, a todas vosotras, bellas y espirituales amigas de Asturias, yo os deseo que todos los genios que pueblan estas montañas verdes y estos ríos mansos, os traigan como ofrenda, en vuestras horas tristes el Olvido y la Paz" (1905). [And to you, Lola, Paquita, Matilde, Rosario, Carmen, to all of you, beautiful and spiritual friends of Asturias, I hope that all the geniuses that populate these green mountains and these gentle rivers bring you forgetfulness and peace as a gift.] In "Unas sombrereras," he queries "¿Conocéis a Gerarda? ¿Y a Fenisa? ¿Y a Isabel? ¿Y a Raquel? ¿Y a Guiomar? Todas estas son unas lindas toledanitas" (1906. n.p.).[3]

Women are boundless infinity, spilling out into the atmosphere of entire places. As Azorín writes "Esas mujeres," a section of *Las confesiones de un pequeño filósofo* (1904), women remain in one's soul like a subdued furrow of light and kindness, and one feels an indefinable anguish when they depart. Like Unamuno, he associates the female infinite with the sea :

> ¿Qué afinidad había entre esta mujer y vosotros? ¿Cómo vais a razonar vuestra tristeza? No lo sabemos; pero presentimos vagamente, como si bordeáramos un mundo desconocido, que esta mujer tiene algo que no acertamos a explicar, y que al marcharse se ha llevado algo que nos pertenece y que no volveremos a encontrar jamás. Yo he sentido muchas veces estas tristezas indefinibles; era muchacho, en los veranos iba frecuentemente a la capital de la provincia y me sentaba largas horas en los balnearios, junto al mar. Y yo veía entonces, y he visto luego, alguna de esas mujeres misteriosas, sugestionadoras, que, como el mar azul que se ensanchaba ante mi vista me hacía pensar en lo Infinito. (1990a, 125)

[What affinity is there between you and this woman? How are you going to rationalize your sadness? We do not know; but we vaguely intuit, as though we were bordering on an unknown world, that this woman has something that we do not quite understand, and that upon leaving she has taken something that belongs to us and that we will never find again. I have often felt indefinable sadness; when I was a boy, I often went to the provincial capital, and I sat for long hours at the spas by the sea. And then I saw, and I have seen since, some of these mysterious, suggestive women, who, like the blue sea that widened before my eyes, made me think about Infinity.]

If Martínez Sierra did not share her male counterparts' interest in a communalization of the individual, she did agree with them on the importance of domestic life for the health of the Spanish nation. Her version of domesticity, however, is more modern and does not reduce women to a vast unconscious sea. As we have seen, *intrahistoria* portrays rural and domestic activities as a vast sea of eternity against which specific historical events (war and political actions) play themselves out. The feminine-cast *intrahistoria,* as Gayana Jurkevich (1991) points out, can be compared to the Jungian notion of a collective unconscious. Martínez Sierra, in contrast, emphasizes consciousness, a particular woman's consciousness, her self-consciousness.

For Unamuno, the domestic is closely linked to motherhood, which he considered an almost sacred state. After his father's death before Unamuno had reached his sixth birthday, he formed a special attachment to his mother.[4] It has even been suggested that, during his religious crisis in 1897, he converted his own wife, Concha, into a surrogate mother, a role she continued to play for the remaining forty years of his life (the Unamuno *contemplativo* so ably revealed by Carlos Blanco Aguinaga [1975]). Unamuno also relied on the maternal archetype in his novelistic portrayals of women, even though (or perhaps because) women's roles were changing all around him. Ricardo Quinones observes of a number of European modernist writers that "the mother has become for Modernism the voice of submission to that which is conventionally social, to the larger general processes of life, foremost among which, for her, is the procreative" (1985, 56). Unamuno did not partake of the rejection of the procreative as did non-Spanish modernists, although in his later work he became more ambivalent about motherhood and endowed it with some of the threatening qualities that Quinones finds in Marcel Proust, James Joyce, and D. H. Lawrence.

The peaceful refuge that Unamuno believed women could (and should) offer men from the storms of their own psychological makeup, as well as the slings and arrows of public life, connects firmly to his notion of domestic intrahistory. The third chapter of *En torno al casticismo,* "El espíritu castellano," which focuses on Golden Age literature, spurns adultery and foregrounds the importance of marriage: "No es castiza en España la casuística del adulterio, ni se ha elevado a institución a la *amiga*. Fuera del matrimonio, los amores son de gallo, de Tenorio, no de Werther" (1971, 173). [Expertise in adultery is not a Spanish thing, nor has it become elevated to the institution of the "lady-friend." Outside of marriage, love belongs to the rooster or the Don Juan, not to Werther.] (As we see later, Azorín similarly employed the Golden Age classics to insinuate an ideal of marriage and domesticity into contemporary life.) Castilian women, according to Unamuno, look to men for their fierceness, brutality, and courage. His source for this insight is the proverb "El hombre y el oso; cuanto más feo más hermoso." *Intrahistoria,* the history of common folk, draws upon traditional proverbial wisdom.[5] Unamuno himself called his female characters shadowy figures: "No son, cabalmente, de línea. Pasan por mis obras casi siempre en silencio, a lo más susurrando, rezando, callándose al oído—al oído del corazón—de sus hombres, ungiéndolos con el rocío de su entrañable humanidad" (1966–71, 5:722).

Unamuno's privileging of domesticity in relations between men and women is evident in many of his public statements. When Carmen de Burgos questioned him about his opinions on divorce in 1904, he pleaded innocence by ignorance: "Con el divorcio me pasa lo mismo que con las novelas de adulterio: muy rara vez logran interesarme. Todo lo referente a las relaciones entre uno y otro sexo lo he visto siempre como subordinado a problemas de otra índole (. . .) Mis opiniones a este respecto son de lo más tímidas, de lo más atrasadas, de lo más aburguesadas y de lo menos innovadoras que cabe. Lo reconozco; pero no he conseguido otras" (qtd. in Burgos 1927, 183–84). [The same thing happens to me with divorce as with novels of adultery: rarely do they manage to interest me. I have always seen everything pertaining to relations between the sexes as subordinate to other kinds of problems (. . .) My opinions on these matters are the most timid, the most backward, the most bourgeois and the least innovative imaginable. I recognize it; but I have not achieved any others.] Unamuno's imagination did not stretch beyond traditional domestic arrangements in life or in fiction. His attitude toward relations between the sexes could not be more antithetical to Raymond Williams's (1959) observations on the fundamental importance of relationships—interpersonal connections—to personal realism (the modernist realism that many Spanish women authors deployed in their fictions). Unamuno similarly scorned nineteenth-century realism, perhaps in part because it focuses on material society rather than on abstract philosophical questions.

As does much of the late nineteenth-century discourse on women, Unamuno's works make a clear connection between women, family, domesticity, and the health of the nation. Women are the hope of Spain: "¡Que nos ayudéis, que seáis verdaderas madres de la patria" (1958, 7: 1043). He often equated "la patria" with motherhood: "¿No guardo yo, y bien apretada a mi pecho, en mi vida cotidiana, a mi pobre madre España loca también?" (10:849). Women need to be educated in order to transmit culture to children; this is their biological function, according to Unamuno: "El organismo de la mujer está hecho para concebir, gestar y amamantar al niño. . . . La mujer se queda en casa, y su inteligencia se hace casera, doméstica, estadiza y minuciosa" (1970, 2:705). Thus, women must develop the capacity to reason and should think about the great problems of humanity rather than about trivial matters. In his speech at the Juegos Florales in Pontevedra in 1912, Unamuno invoked women as responsible for the formation of men, who would presumably in turn form the nation: "Os guarda, pues, la tarea de hacer hombres. De hacer hombres, no de parirlos; de formarles viriles, varoniles. . . . Haced, pues, hombres que lo sean; que para mujeres os bastéis vosotras" (1958, 6:342).

In each of the narratives examined in this chapter—Unamuno's *Paz en la guerra*, Martínez Sierra's *Tú eres la paz*, and Azorín's *El alma castellana* and *Castilla*—the notion of a Spanish tradition, a Spanish soul, provides a bedrock identity that resists time and history, an island of salvation from the onslaughts of modernity for the shipwrecked nation. (Modernity frequently means women who do not conform to traditional roles.) Deployment of male and female characters in the fictional elaborations of *intrahistoria* reveal a feminization of the Spanish soul, although the male authors' gendering of that soul differs in significant ways from that of the woman author. Unamuno and Azorín insinuated gender into the *tradición eterna* of their early works by several means. Their architecture of time that elides present and past obscures the progressive changes that favor women's rights and education initiated after the 1868 revolution. Both male authors also privilege collective identity over individual psychology, especially where women are concerned, subordinating variety and difference to universals. The domestic aspects of life and characteristics such as maternal care and peaceful selflessness expected of women emerge as the preeminent qualities of the intrahistoric communal Spanish soul. Unamuno, Azorín, and Martínez Sierra all summon the classics of Golden Age literature to evoke Spanish tradition, although Unamuno and Azorín often employ the classics to construct cautionary tales about changing social roles, while María Martínez Sierra subverts tradition to project new roles.

Unamuno's first novel, *Paz en la guerra* (which was not published until 1897 although he had been working on it since about 1890), constitutes his most sustained dramatization of *intrahistoria* and the eternal tradition, a fictional working out of his ideas about the essential national character set forth in *En torno al casticismo*. Unamuno effects the dramatization by juxtaposing a specific historical event—the third and last Carlist War (1873–75), the final gasp of the most traditionalist of Spanish movements—with the ongoing daily lives of the common folk of a Basque village. Julián Marías points out that *Paz en la guerra* focuses on no one particular character: "Es la novela de un personaje colectivo: se trata en ella de una vida colectiva y comunal, de una existencia no individualizada" (1943, 45). And Martin Nozick observes, "Es durante el bombardeo, sin embargo, que la novela logra un héroe colectivo—el pueblo forzado a comer gatos y ratas, dominado por los rumores, haciéndose ilusiones que pronto se desvanecen, envuelto en interminables discusiones para determinar qué lado tomar en contra de una misteriosa hermandad de masones, librepensadores y anticristianos" (1971, 143). [It is during the bombardment, nevertheless, that the novel achieves a collective hero—the people forced to eat cats and rats, controlled by rumors, forging illusions that soon evaporate, involved in interminable discussions to determine which side to take against a mysterious brotherhood of Masons, freethinkers and anti-Christians.] The people of a small Basque village constitute a mass protagonist, although four individuals—Pachico, Ignacio, and Ignacio's parents, Josefa Ignacia and Pedro Antonio—emerge to represent the whole. Friends from boyhood, Ignacio and Pachico reveal very different temperaments (Ignacio a Carlist ideologue and Pachico an intellectual skeptic). Their life paths diverge when Ignacio joins the Carlist effort; he is a nineteenth-century Quixote who, instead of reading romances of chivalry, reads historical serial novels that fill his head with visions of El Cid and other real and legendary heroes of the past.

Ignacio's quixotism extends to women. Specific women continually dissolve into an ideal at the hands of most of Unamuno's male characters. Apolodoro in *Amor y pedagogía* (1902) and Augusto Pérez in *Niebla* (1914) confuse the individual woman with the ideal of women as a general category. Marina of *Amor y pedagogía,* whose name evokes the sea of eternity, is the archetypal mother. *Niebla*'s Augusto finds that his focus on Eugenia soon becomes diluted by an interest in women as a generic type. His position is theorized within the novel by Antolín S. Paparrigópulos, who posits that men have individual souls, but all women partake of a common soul: "Las mujeres . . . se parecen entre sí mucho más que los hombres, y es porque todas son una sola y misma mujer" (1982, 146). [Women are much more alike than men, and this is because all women are one and the same woman.] Although his portrait of Paparrigópulos is humorous, perhaps satirical, Unamuno expressed similar views himself: "Cuando se conoce bien a una mujer se conoce a todas en cuanto mujeres, se entiende. Y no hace falta acudir a clínica de psiquiatría" (1966–71, 5:723). [When you know one woman well, you know all of them in their being women, one understands. You don't need to go to a psychiatric clinic.] Helena of *Abel Sánchez* (1917) is the eternal archetypal Helen of Troy, the universal fascinator of men. Ángela, the narrator of *San Manuel Bueno, mártir* (1931), acts as the central male figure's passive confessor and confidante. She is left to repeat his story eternally while he achieves historical fame for his works in a contemporary political world of penury and want.

Woman and the earth are especially linked—the great mother archetype—in the intrahistorical subtext of *Paz en la guerra*. Intrahistorical women are amorphous and indistinguishable from the landscape. At one point, Ignacio is attracted to a woman of the people, a blond with cow-like eyes: "Aquellos ojazos de vaca, en que se reflejaba la cima de la montaña" (1966–71, 2:145). [Those huge cow-like eyes, in which were reflected the top of the mountain.] Jurkevich aptly associates the communal nature of Carlism with Carl Jung's great mother through the "maternal qualities of Catholicism, intrahistory, and tradition" (1991, 43). As Peggy W. Watson points out, Unamuno's "women are associated with those unconscious qualities that link them with *intra-historia*. Their role in the novel is highly specific: to dramatize the unambivalent place of home and family within intra-historic life" (1993, 41).

Quixotism like Ignacio's is noble but out of sync with the times. Don Quixote is an ambiguous modernist icon; in postromantic interpretations, which continued to influence some modernist appropriations of him, he is a victimized hero, but he also fails to perceive that the world has changed. He is a romantic idealist doomed in a modern setting. Ignacio is eventually shot rather unheroically when, out of curiosity, he peers over the edge of his trench. His idealistic Catholic monarchism has led to nothing, while life in his home village flows on, if not uninterrupted, much as it was before. Even though Ignacio considered the Carlist king "a man of an earlier time, leading a medieval horde" who "was stirred to his roots by the history he bore at the depth of his soul where the spirit of his forefathers slept" (Unamuno 1983, 138), this kind of tradition does not endure. The contemporary political battle that pertains to men epitomizes the futility of specific historical interventions to influence the continuous present sedimented with layers of the past.

The eternal tradition, the true soul of Spain, resides in the domestic harmony of Ignacio's parents, Josefa Ignacia and Pedro Antonio. They are simple folk; Pedro Antonio is a Carlist-sympathizing chocolate-shop owner who gives his life savings to the failing Carlist effort. Josefa Ignacia asks nothing more of life than to die and join her son Ignacio, which she finally does. This married couple is so completely concordant that they barely need to speak: "Pedro Antonio y José [*sic*] Ignacia por su inconsciencia, por encarnar la tradición y por ser pueblo hasta en sus entrañas, dan la sensación de solidez y seguridad que nos dan las creencias que todavía no han sido puestas en duda" (Elizalde 1983, 216).

Unamuno's conception of women (as represented in his female characters) changed with the rise of the feminist movement in Spain. Josefa Ignacia represents one of two basic types of women that appear in Unamuno's fiction, primarily in the early novels—she is in the category of passive mothers, a category that suggests the intrahistorical idea of women as the peaceful subterranean soul of the nation. Josefa Ignacia is the classically silent, long-suffering Spanish woman, the epitome of perfect domesticity. *Intrahistoria* (domestic, quotidian, and repetitive) is the domain of women, whereas temporal history (war, battles, victories, and defeats) is the domain of men. The *paz*—respite from war and concrete historical events—if not overtly feminine, is definitely domestic. Although all of Unamuno's novels maneuver women into marriage and/or motherhood, the role takes several forms. Carlos Blanco Aguinaga divides Unamuno's female characters into the "furiosas," such as domineering and destructive Raquel and Tula of later novels, and the "mujeres naturales," such as Josefa Ignacia of *Paz en la guerra* and Marina of *Amor y pedagogía*. Marina, "la materia," of *Amor y pedagogía* "pasa como una sombra dolorosa redentora, reparadora, como una madre virginal por entre la locura pedagógica de su marido, que al fin cae desamparado en sus brazos, a la vista del suicidio del hijo, gimiendo "¡madre!" (1956, 72) [moves like a sad redeeming, repairing ghost, like a virginal mother through her husband's pedagogical craziness, who in the end at the sight of their son's suicide falls helpless into her arms, moaning "mother!"]. Lynette Hubbard Seator observes that "[w]oman as function ranges from fecund Earth Mother or castrating witch driving to madness, to a goddess-mother of sanctifying purity" (1980, 51). David W. Foster calls the latter "belles dames sans merci," whose literary provenance he traces to the romantic "Fatal Woman" or "demonically inspired woman" (1966, 322). Ricardo Gullón distinguishes between Unamuno's "madres maternales y no posesivas o maternalmente posesivas" (1961b, 42). He identifies Josefa Ignacia of *Paz en la guerra* and Marina of *Amor y pedagogía* (42) as belonging to the former category.

Carmen Morales adds chronology to her typology of Unamuno's mother figures, noting a significant change in 1920. In the first of three periods that she outlines, the women are real mothers who remain "passive, happy with the possession of a child who gives her fulfillment." In the second, "a new type of woman appears: the possessive one, that is one that governs other people's lives in such a way that she inhabits all their free activity" (93). A hybrid of the first two types of women emerges in the third period; Morales considers Ángela of *San Manuel Bueno, mártir* representative of the "maternally mature [woman], who is neither passive nor possessive but wisely situated in the middle" (1971, 96). She overlooks the fact that Ángela, as a kind of secular nun, has many more characteristics in common with the passive mother figure of the earlier fiction. She has masculine qualities—she is Don Manuel's confessor—but they are more palatable than those of monstrous surrogate mothers like Raquel and Tula. Ultimately, Ángela is denied any life outside her role as Don Manuel's hagiographer. It would seem that after having vented his spleen against the new woman in Eugenia, Raquel, and Tula, Unamuno returned to the positive role model in Ángela.

No married couple in Unamuno's later fiction ever again achieves the domestic harmony of Pedro Antonio and Josefa Ignacia, that domestic peace that Unamuno so valued in his own life. Unamuno's version of married tranquility requires the female partner to submerge herself in maternal roles, nurturing not only her children but her husband as well.[6] As Rosendo Díaz-Peterson (1984, 98) points out, Unamuno believed that the women he drew in *Paz en la guerra* were maternal in the sense of being robust and stalwart; women provide the stuff of national fortitude and continuity. Emphasizing the importance of the traditional family unit for Unamuno, Arantza de Urbieta (1977) formulates a theory of the novel's structure as based on three family units: the Iturriondos, the Aranas, and the Zabalbides. In later novels, Unamuno shows increasing alarm at the disintegration of the traditional family when faced with new female roles that he clearly saw as weakening the harmonious substratum of Spanish society. But in 1897, before feminism had made significant inroads into Spanish public life, Unamuno could portray an intrahistoric Spanish soul in which women and men like Pedro Antonio and Josefa Ignacia form a traditional bedrock on which the peace of the nation can rest.

In 1906, nine years after the publication of *Paz en la guerra*, Martínez

Sierra reexamined the theme of gendered peace in her first long novel *Tú eres la paz*. If *Paz en la guerra* is Unamuno's semiautobiographical consideration of Spanish history as timeless, faceless domesticity (the peace that underlies war and all historical events), *Tú eres la paz* is Martínez Sierra's own biographical reenvisioning of peace as a specific woman with her own individual emotional life. Instead of locating peace as anonymous intrahistorical femininity and domesticity embodied in amorphous everywoman Josefa Ignacia, Martínez Sierra locates peace in a modern woman, who reads, writes, and has a mind of her own. In fact, Martínez Sierra theorized feminist femininity as the drive to create peace (see Blanco 1998, 93).

Martínez Sierra herself was caught in the turn-of-the-century social transition that many intelligent Spanish women experienced. She was born María de la O. Lejárraga in 1874, by dint of which she considered herself in the autobiographical *Gregorio y yo* (1953) a member of Unamuno and Azorín's generation, the so-called Generation of '98. She shared with her cogenerationists a preoccupation with Spain as a nation and for finding new aesthetic forms, but her treatment of female characters in her novels differs radically from that of the male authors. Her publicly acknowledged authorship of an extensive fictional and dramatic corpus was, for many years, obscured by the fact that she signed her works with the name of her husband, Gregorio. It was widely known by their circle of friends, however, that María did the writing, while her husband engaged in entrepreneurial activities. In 1977, Patricia O'Connor revealed the details of the collaboration between the writer María and her husband, who formed a theater company to stage her plays and engaged in various publication enterprises.[7] Martínez Sierra's first long novel, *Tú eres la paz,* is in many ways a feminist answer to male portrayals of women as essential Spanishness. Martínez Sierra may herself have been invisible, an anonymous woman, but this was not a condition that she inflicted on her female characters.

O'Connor has analyzed the complex psychosocial reasons for Martínez Sierra's decision to publish under her husband's name—an unusual arrangement in light of the feminist ideas that she publicly espoused during the years that led up to the Second Republic, when, as María Gloria Núñez Pérez indicates, "fue una personalidad femenina con indudable protagonismo en la vida madrileña" (1993, 128).[8] When Gregorio and María were first married, María supported the couple as a schoolteacher, a profession that frowned on women writers. This obstacle seems to have suited her personal inclination to shun the public limelight. In addition, María's decision to become a ghostwriter may have represented her maternal desire to protect her husband, who was about six years her junior and a less talented writer. Gregorio repaid her selflessness by entering into a life-long affair with the actress Catalina Bárcena, who bore him a daughter. Paradoxically, María's feminism arose from her complex personal and professional circumstances. Through consciousness, self-awareness—a notion at the heart of her feminist theory—she was able to elevate herself above her status as a betrayed woman and "mujer en la sombra," as Antonina Rodrigo (1994) baptized her.[9] Writing—theater, novel, essay, and personal letter—were the mirrors through which she observed, objectified, and even recast her life. Concha Alborg observes that in Martínez Sierra's autobiographical *Una mujer por caminos de España*, "hace análisis de conciencia y llega a comprenderse a través del proceso de escritura" (1996, 490).

Martínez Sierra articulated a theory of the complex existential situation of the female protagonist of *Tú eres la paz* in a 1952 prologue to that novel (see M. Martínez Sierra 1965), which reflects the feminist position that the author had assumed after a period of militancy in the 1920s and 1930s. Martínez Sierra was already formulating this position in 1906. *Tú eres la paz* draws on several strategies to assert its feminist meaning: (1) It is plainly autobiographical, converting a real-life situation into a fictional one that allows the author to assess how a woman in her circumstances can prevail in a patriarchal world. (2) It incorporates at least two major intertexts of contemporaneous male-authored novels—Unamuno's *Paz en la guerra* and Ramón del Valle-Inclán's *Sonatas* (particularly, *Sonata de otoño* [1989]). Martínez Sierra's novel appropriates elements of the male-authored texts with subtle shifts that bear the feminist message. (3) Martínez Sierra's narrative modes—especially, the epistolary and dramatic—facilitate the protagonist's achievement of self-awareness. Martínez Sierra's creation of the complex Ana María foregrounds not only traditional representations of women in fiction by men but also the changing roles that women were assuming at the dawn of the twentieth century. She invokes both the traditional domestic woman who upholds the nation with her eternal labor as mother and homemaker and the modern woman who reads, writes, and moves independently through the world. In this way, as Janet Pérez has noted, "without aggressiveness or polemics, she managed to outline for women a number of alternatives beyond the domestic realm" (1988, 35).

The plot is sentimental and melodramatic, typical of a serial romance, "amerengada," according to one critic Martínez Sierra cites in her 1952 prologue. The author herself described it as a "conflicto de amores juveniles, olvidos, infidelidades masculinas, femeninas esperas desilusionadas, un tono de sentimental intensidad que acaso de persistir hubiera podido caer en sensiblería" (1965, 9). What Martínez Sierra does not say is that the novel also reflects the author's own circumstances. Orphaned at an early age, Ana María is taken in by her grandmother, who inhabits a palace (probably in Galicia) that strongly resembles the Brandeso Palace in Valle-Inclán's *Sonata de otoño*. The novel opens with the return of Ana María's cousin Agustín, to whom she is betrothed. He has been abroad for five years developing his career as a sculptor, and Ana María has written him to return home because their grandmother is terminally ill.

Agustín and Ana María mount an elaborately staged subterfuge to conceal from the grandmother that they have broken their engagement. Agustín has become enamored of a foreign dancer, Carmelina, with whom he has a child, and although Carmelina has since abandoned him and the child for another man, Agustín seems to have lost interest in the provincial Ana María. As the weeks pass, however, Agustín begins to appreciate Ana María's tranquil maternal ways; she is adept at all the domestic arts that create a homey peaceful atmosphere in which Agustín can work on his sculpture. Agustín declares his love for Ana María and asks for her hand, but before the marriage can take place, Carmelina appears at the palace, and the weak-willed Agustín agrees to return to the frivolous, self-centered woman. At this point, the grandmother dies, and Agustín must delay his departure to join Carmelina. Finally, bags packed and faced with the prospect of leaving the peace and tranquility that Ana María offers for the whirlwind life that awaits him with Carmelina, Agustín decides to stay with Ana María.

The rosy ending to a love triangle that Martínez Sierra invented for her 1906 protagonist was not to be her own fate. Although María and Gregorio maintained the appearances of a harmonious marriage, Rodrigo (1994, 110–11) indicates that in 1909 María attempted suicide in Barcelona when she realized that Gregorio had lied to her in order to remain in Madrid with his lover while she traveled to Italy.[10] The coincidences between the characters and the plot of *Tú eres la paz* and the triangle that developed between María, Gregorio, and Catalina Bárcena are too numerous to be merely prophetic, as O'Connor and Rodrigo have suggested. The names of the "other" women (Catalina and Carmelina) are strikingly similar, as are their professions (actress and dancer). The personalities of the two women also coincide; both Catalina and Carmelina are dramatic, egotistical, and erratic. (Ana María calls Carmelina a "mala mujer.") Ana María's nature (selfless and tranquil), in turn, parallels that of the author.

O'Connor gives several dates for the beginning of the relationship between Gregorio and Bárcena. In the biographical section of *Gregorio and María Martínez Sierra*, she writes that Bárcena debuted in the Quintero brothers' play *El genio alegre* in 1906 and that Gregorio met her about the time that he published his poetry collection *La casa de la primavera* (1907). In a later chapter (when she discusses *Tú eres la paz*), she affirms, "If Gregorio was not involved with Catalina Bárcena in 1906, this novel was a coincidence and also proved to be uncannily prophetic" (1977, 85). By beginning the sentence with "If," she now suggests that the relationship was a possibility by that date. I believe that all the evidence points toward Gregorio's having met Bárcena at the time that she debuted in *El genio alegre*.

María and Gregorio went to Paris in October 1905 with a year-long grant that María had sought in order to remove Gregorio from contact with his tubercular family members, as he was beginning to show symptoms of the disease. After two months, Gregorio's health improved, and he returned to Spain. María spent the next three months in Belgium observing teaching methods in a convent school. Thus, Gregorio was alone in Madrid during the winter of 1905–6. As Gregorio was deeply involved with the Madrid theater world, it seems entirely likely that he met Bárcena at a rehearsal or at the opening of *El genio alegre*. During this period of separation from Gregorio, María sustained a very important correspondence with Juan Ramón Jiménez (a great friend to the Martínez Sierras), who could have well indicated to María something of Gregorio's life in Madrid (one of the extant letters from Juan Ramón to María during this period complains that Gregorio was avoiding him). A letter from María to Juan Ramón congratulating him on his receipt of the Nobel Prize for Literature alludes to the secrets they shared: "Juntos, los dos hemos callado tanto" (qtd. in Gullón, 1961a, 108). [Together, the two of us have kept silent on so much.] In the spring of 1906, Gregorio rejoined María in Paris, where she wrote *Tú eres la paz,* completing the work in May of that year. It is particularly significant that María wrote the novel so soon after having lived alone for the first time in her life, so soon after her first long separation from Gregorio since they had made each other's acquaintance in 1897. These circumstances—her solitary state of relative independence in a foreign country and her knowledge or suspicion of Gregorio's infidelity—must have contributed to her desire to gain a certain perspective on her experience by converting it into art.

The self-consciousness in *Tú eres la paz* is not limited to the autobiographical creation of an intelligent, independent woman who is morally superior to a weak man who vacillates between two women on whom he depends in different ways. The novel also reflects the masculinist Spanish literary culture of the turn of the century in which María lived and wrote (perhaps an important reason for her decision to sign her husband's name to her works).[11] The characterizations of Ana María and Agustín bear similarities to some of those created by Martínez Sierra's male contemporaries. Agustín, like so many Generation of '98 protagonists, is associated with art, artifice, and travel and is characterized by the same lack of will that many of the protagonists display.[12] Ana María (like Ignacia of *Paz en la guerra*) has a natural affinity with the earth; Agustín observes, "[Ana María] y esta tierra sois una misma cosa" (G. Martínez Sierra 1954, 211).[13] The earth/woman alliance is an ancient and nationalistic stereotype that connects her to the eternal essence of Spain that Unamuno and Azorín theorized and incorporated into early writings. Martínez Sierra effects a subtle change in the "typical Spanish woman" stereotype by making her mother English. Ana María wants to visit her mother's homeland because "allí una mujer puede ir sola por todas partes sin que nadie se asombre" (193) [there a woman can go about alone everywhere without anyone's being shocked]. In addition, Ana María's "visión terrena" contributes to "la conciencia de su propia insignificancia dentro de la inmensidad del universo que la contiene" (9) [the consciousness of her own insignificance within the immensity of the universe that contains her], the consciousness that is the key to her independence, as we see below.

Ana María is also an art object, a modernist literary cliché especially prevalent in narratives by Valle-Inclán and Azorín. She is framed by the recherché ambience of her grandmother's palace; she is also the subject of Francisco Estrada's poetry and of a sculpture by Agustín. Ana María escapes these artistic imprisonments by imposing her will on both Francisco and Agustín. For example, when she poses for a statue that Agustín is fashioning, she is fully aware of the seductive powers that she holds over him as he gazes upon her hour after hour. The "woman as earth" and "woman as art" stereotypes become a source of strength and individual assertion for Ana María rather than leveling qualities that envelop her in anonymity. They contribute to her ability to perceive herself and her situation and take control of it. Unlike the female characters of Unamuno, Valle-Inclán, Baroja, and Azorín, Ana María is a fully conscious character, and she uses her consciousness to control her own destiny. If the consciousness of male protagonists—Ignacio and Pachico, the Marqués de Bradomín, Fernando Ossorio, or Antonio Azorín—dominates the Generation of '98 novels, in *Tú eres la paz* Agustín's perspective is quite effectively countered by Ana María's more intelligent and morally superior stance. The weak-willed male protagonists of Generation of '98 narratives are solitary beings who live and develop apart from women. In *Tú eres la paz,* in contrast, the female protagonist saves the errant artist with her intelligent companionship and conscious understanding.

Ana María achieves the self-consciousness so important to her ability to exercise her will primarily through theatrical and epistolary means (just as Martínez Sierra herself did). Martínez Sierra wore several masks throughout her adult life. Her principal dramatic role was as her husband's "collaborator," when in fact she was responsible for virtually all the writing that he signed. She also wore the mask of selfless unperturbed wife of an unfaithful husband, while she discretely disclosed her anguish in letters to friends and in her novels and plays. In Tú eres la paz, Ana María also employs a theatrical mask to achieve her goals.[14] When

Agustín breaks off their engagement, she consummately acts the part of complete indifference, a role that she maintains with dignity throughout the entire novel. Within that role, she plays the part of happily betrothed woman and convinces Agustín to assume the guise of committed fiancé whenever they are in their grandmother's company. Thanks to her ability to recreate herself and assume different roles, Ana María finally garners the love and marriage that she desires. By converting her life into a theater, she achieves the distance necessary to gain control over her own destiny and acquire physical and psychological independence. In the event that Agustín carried out his plan to return to Carmelina, Ana Mara was prepared to travel alone to England to widen her horizons.

Martínez Sierra also shared the epistolary mode with her protagonist as a means to understanding and objectifying a complex psychological situation. The author maintained a nearly daily correspondence with Gregorio whenever they were apart and with a number of other artists and writers, especially Juan Ramón Jiménez and Manuel de Falla. Some of these epistolary relations provided an escape valve and a means for reflecting on her situation.[15] For example, Martínez Sierra unburdened herself in a letter to de Falla about the unpleasant scenes that Bárcena mounted to torment her whenever they were working together with Gregorio on a theatrical project (Rodrigo, 1994, 173). She provides her protagonist with the same self-conscious mirror. In two important letters to her friend Juana, Ana María assumes an ironic stance vis-à-vis her paradoxical situation with Agustín. For example, the denouement of the novel is narrated twice. First, the omniscient narrator describes in the sentimental tone of a romance novel the scene in which Agustín, bags packed to depart, changes his mind. Ana María then writes about the same event to her friend Juana. Her ironic, humorous approach to the stock romantic scene annuls the earlier sentimental effect.

In *Tú eres la paz,* which was probably written in the early days of the amorous triangle between María, Gregorio, and Catalina, Martínez Sierra essayed her theory of self-consciousness. Her 1952 prologue to *Tú eres la paz* explains how self-consciousness can achieve female liberation:

> En la conciencia de su propia insignificancia dentro de la inmensidad del Universo que la contiene, sostiene y mantiene, logra la facultad menos ex-

traña de lo que parece, en mentes de mujer de contemplar su 'caso' como si fuese ajeno. Se siente sufrir y se mira sufrir; y de aquel su llorar frente al espejo, saca valor para reírse melancólicamente de su propio drama. Y en novela, comedia, vida o sueño en que los héroes alcanzan el prodigio de sonreír ante sus propias lágrimas, no cabe el amerengamiento, ya que el granito de sal de la ironía disuelve y hace desaparecer hasta el último rastro del caramelo. (M. Martínez Sierra 1965, 9)

[Her consciousness of her own insignificance within the immensity of the universe, which contains, sustains, and maintains her, achieves a condition in a woman's mind that is less strange than it seems, by which she contemplates her case as if it were someone else's. She feels herself suffer and she watches herself suffer; and she gets the courage to laugh melancholically at her own drama from that weeping before a mirror. And there can be no sugariness in novels, comedies, life, or dream in which the heroes achieve the feat of smiling before their own tears, since the little grain of ironic salt dissolves the last trace of caramel and makes it disappear.]

Although Agustín and Ana María marry (the traditional romance ending), they are not portrayed in a typical domestic arrangement. At the conclusion of the novel, the couple is traveling abroad, and Ana María eagerly engages in intellectual gatherings in foreign venues. Martínez Sierra moves her protagonist from intrahistorical, essential Spanish womanhood (identified with a rural regional setting) to a modern cosmopolitan state. Ana María's self-consciousness has carried her from her early identification as the pantheistic soul of Spain to her final stage as an active citizen of the contemporary world.

Unamuno's peace in the whirlwind of political conflict and war resides in eternal domestic harmony and a woman who forgoes individuality to submerge herself in the communal Spanish soul; Martínez Sierra's peace also resonates with domestic harmony, but one that gives the woman an opportunity to grow and engage in intellectual pursuits. Like Unamuno's and Martínez Sierra's, Azorín's early work, such as *El alma castellana* and *Castilla,* pitted Spanish tradition against the contemporary world. As a literary critic and a serious student of Spain's national character, Azorín was especially attracted to the Spanish classics, which he believed enshrined the soul of Spain. In the literary classics, he found unlimited resources to mine and transform.¹⁶ Most scholars have understood his interest in the classics as related to his preoccupation with time and the essence of the Spanish soul. Inman Fox's interpretation of Azorín's use of Spain's literary tradition in his narrative collection *Castilla* is symptomatic. Fox writes that "se medita sobre el paisaje o pueblo como 'pequeña' historia transida por el tiempo—verdadera 'microhistoria' . . . y en que se busca en la literatura una expresión del espíritu nacional" (1991, 11) [it meditates on the landscape or town as a "little" history overcome by time—a true "microhistory" and in which an expression of the national spirit is sought in literature]. Fox did not notice that Azorín's transformations of the classics gave them a modern bourgeois cast, especially in their treatment of domestic issues. The abstract, philosophical projects imbricated in *Castilla*'s appropriation of the classics cannot be overlooked, but they only thinly veil Azorín's commentary on contemporary social mores. The literary classics also provided the opportunity for Azorín to comment on contemporary domestic issues, especially women's role in society, while he sought to define the eternal Spanish tradition. The concern for the conduct of women and their impact on family and ultimately the nation emerged in these early works: Azorín called upon the classics of Golden Age literature to aid him in conveying his message about both national cultural and social traditions.

Azorín's relationships with women and his attitudes toward them are ambivalent. Like Unamuno, Azorín had a special attachment to his mother. His father had a longtime mistress and was rather autocratic.¹⁷ Consequently, Azorín looked to his mother for stability, and she encouraged his reading and literary pursuits. Azorín married but had no children. The details of the nature of his relationship with his wife are not known.

Also like Unamuno, Azorín shifted his views on the changing roles of women over time. Women play a complex role in Azorín's remakes of the classics; they are inscribed in modern life but also form an essential part of Spain's *tradición eterna*. These two roles are not necessarily antithetical to Azorín's notion of an essential Spanish soul, which like Unamuno's *intrahistoria* embodies the eternal flow of time that connects the present with the past. Azorín believed that progress depended on national continuity and that literature was an important vehicle for effecting such continuity. If the past can be found in the present, the classics of literature can be updated to give them a contemporary setting or values without disturbing the spirit of the original work that projects the national essence. A consideration of Azorín's hidden messages about gender in his reworkings of the classics in the pre–World War I era provides an evocative case study of how a modernist procedure (layering of classical reference) can address modern issues such as changing gender roles. Azorín's use of the classics to address gender and nation move from cautionary tales about sexual behavior in the first decade, to models for bourgeois marriage in the second decade, and finally to a recasting of the Don Juan figure in the eponymous novel of 1922, which depicts a national icon who shuns women altogether.

As a journalist, Azorín was well aware of the growing dialogue on women's roles at the turn of the century. Despite the numerous passages in both his early and later work that equated women with the eternal essence of Spain, the bibliography of his journal articles includes a number of essays on women and their social roles.[18] When he began to write in the 1890s, José Martínez Ruiz (as he was known until he adopted the pseudonym Azorín in 1904) assumed a radically progressive stance on such social issues as criminality, the working classes, and marriage. He joined a chorus of male journalists who argued against the institution of marriage; in fact, he was relieved of his post at the newspaper *El País* because of an 1897 article in which he stated that marriage is a profoundly immoral institution, an "indisoluble lazo" (n.p.) that obliges two people to live together against their will. Some of Azorín's arguments against matrimony, however, can hardly be characterized as progressive. He opines, for example, that marriage "es tan absurdo como abonarse a un restaurante a comer todos los días el mismo manjar" (n.p.) [is as absurd as making a commitment to eat the same thing in a restaurant everyday]. He votes for "el amor libre y espontáneo; por la independencia de la mujer, igual al hombre en educación y en derecho; por el placer de las pasiones sinceras; por el goce pleno de la Naturaleza, maestro de la vida" (n.p.) [free and spontaneous love; for the independence of women, equal to men in education and the law; for the pleasure of sincere passions; for the full enjoyment of nature, master of life]. Marriage certainly has a deleterious effect on the character Antonio Azorín in *La voluntad* (see Martínez Ruiz 1902). After wedding the strong-willed Iluminada, he becomes a slovenly provincial who spends his days at the town casino with no vestige of the intellectual life that he had led in his single days.

Azorín's views on such gender issues as marriage, women's education, and social roles were, as I have mentioned, ambivalent and subject to change over time. Azorín waffled rather than join other intellectuals' enthusiasm for Benito Pérez Galdós's 1901 anticlerical play, *Electra,* in which a priest coaxes a young girl into a convent against her parents' wishes. Sometime during the first decade of the century, when Azorín's political stance became less radical, his attitude toward marriage changed.[19] Despite his early reservations about marriage as an institution, he married in 1908, about the time that he declared himself a supporter of the conservative politician Antonio Maura and began to write for the conservative newspaper *ABC.*[20] *El alma castellana* reveals that as early as 1900 Azorín had more ambivalent feelings about women's role in society than he was willing to admit in his journalistic pieces. By 1912, he was covertly arguing in *Castilla* for very traditional social roles for women, a progressively conservative trajectory that contrasts sharply with the increasingly visible feminist public discourse. His fictional practices also fly in the face of those of women writers who, like Burgos, were publishing narratives in which female characters found alternatives to traditional marriage or in which traditional marriage was challenged.

In 1908, Azorín, then a legislative representative, voted in favor of the bill sponsored by Maura to give women the vote in certain local elections. He then discovered that " 'ese intento de feminismo fue lo que suscitó más hostilidad y más escarnio por parte de la oposición liberal" (qtd. in Ouimette 1998, 1:360) [this attempt at feminism was what gave rise to more hostility and more derision from the liberal opposition]. According to Victor Ouimette, Azorín maintained that Spanish women had always exercised immeasurable influence on national politics through the home and family and that it was now a question of simple justice to give them the vote rather than deny it as with the insane and the criminal. In "La mujer moderna," Azorín pronounced, "¡Ah, España, España, como pesan en tu historia las mujeres! Y ¡cuán gran peso no representan en tus hogares! La mujer lo es todo en la vida" (1925, n.p.). [Ah, Spain, Spain, how women do weigh on your history! And, what a great weight they represent in your homes! Woman is everything in life!] In a 1922 article, he stated, "Según sean los hijos, así será la nación. Y es la madre la que debe hacer que los hijos sean buenos" (1922b, n.p.). [The nation will be what her sons are. And it is the mother who must insure that the sons are good.] Azorín countered the liberals' argument that the women's vote would be Catholic and conservative, and he defended women's spiritual independence: "No. A la mujer moderna, en todas partes y cuando ha recabado su derecho en toda actividad humana, es injusto negárselo. En la actualidad, creo que la mujer traerá a la política un poco de la pasión que nos hace falta" (qtd. in Ouimette, 1998, 1:361). [No. When the modern woman everywhere has gained her rights in all human activity, it is unjust to deny it to her. Today, I believe that women will bring to politics a little bit of the passion that we are lacking.]

In his fictional narratives, however, Azorín embeds messages that indicate that women require special protection in order to maintain the health of the nation. Toward the end of *El alma castellana,* Azorín observes, "*Los pequeños hechos* por sí no dicen nada; el arte está en escogerlos, hacerles decir lo que el historiador quiere que digan. Aquí la negromancia" (Azorín 1995, 228). [The small events don't say anything; the art is in choosing them and making them say what the historian wants them to say.] The author is commenting on his own practices in the same book—a social history of Spain's seventeenth and eighteenth centuries in which he draws information from a variety of sources (cited at the end of each chapter). He marshaled these *pequeños hechos* ostensibly to reconstruct the matrix of circumstances that produced the liberal revolution of 1810. The *pequeños hechos* also collectively echo the Spanish sociopolitical climate in 1900, the year that Azorín wrote *El alma castellana* so close upon the heels of the 1898 disaster. Thus, the historical perspective in *El alma castellana* is bifocal. We read the work as though perusing a two-columned page; the first column pertains to the seventeenth and eighteenth centuries and the second to the late nineteenth century. The use of the present tense throughout the narrative helps the reader to collapse the two time frames.

In this light, it is important to note how much of the book is devoted to issues that do not relate to the *alma* (soul), "the immaterial 'I' that possesses conscious experience, controls passion, desire, and action, and maintains a perfect identity from birth (or before) to death (or after)" (Blackburn 1994, 357). If the soul is essence and transcendence, it is counterbalanced by the material and immanent in *El alma castellana*. Material life, particularly as it is associated with women, vies with the spiritual. The little details that Azorín has selected to highlight in the seventeenth and eighteenth centuries are grouped in such categories as estates, the home, domestic life, love (marriage), fashion, picaresque life, the Inquisition, theater, literati, Castilian prose, literary criticism, public opinion, and morality. Note that a number of these topics—the home, domestic life, fashion, and love (marriage)—are normally considered to be within the female realm. Several categories that pertain less obviously to female pursuits—estates and picaresque life—also focus on women. In Azorín's version, the eternal essence of Spain—*el alma castellana*—encompasses both the transcendent and the immanent (which includes gender). In addition, in many chapters of *El alma castellana,* women's social roles—most notably as wife, mother, and prostitute—emerge as important narrative foci.

The ambivalence about women's roles revealed in the contrast between Azorín's public position and the more covert message of *El alma castellana*—what Azorín insinuates in the *pequeños hechos*—is bound up with his view of Spain and its precarious future. The prologue sets the tone. It relates the story of a seventeenth-century gentleman who goes to the theater after dining. One of the characters in the play that he attends recounts a story from Greek history. The story concerns a species of bird—the *calamón* (gallinule)—that was said to commit suicide if the wife of its master was unfaithful to him: "Ahora yo consideraba que todos los pajarillos de las tabernas eran los ahorcados por las traiciones de nuestras mujeres; y que tanto han mudado los tiempos y tan a menos ha venido la fiereza castellana que, si antes matábamos a la infiel, ahora nos comemos tranquilamente las pruebas de la deshonra. ¡Miren vuestras mercedes el símbolo!" (1995, 60). The narration—focusing on women as underminers of personal and national honor—compares two ages, the Greek heroic age and the Spanish seventeenth century, the latter read through late nineteenth-century bourgeois morality. "El símbolo" resonates for a contemporary Spain in which women are stretching the traditional boundaries of domestic morality that many viewed as further eroding a tattered national reputation. *El alma castellana*'s first chapter, "La hacienda" (the dual meaning of *hacienda*—country estate/treasury—links the private and the public spheres), details material ruin with unveiled allusions to female depravity. The description of a sumptuously decorated seventeenth-century house includes a picture of Mary Magdalene and a picture of an old man with his hands tied behind his back, who suckles at a woman's breast. From the balcony of the house is seen an elegant man followed by some women who "hacen maldad de su cuerpo" (74) [use their bodies ill].

Contemporary Spanish women's awakening from a long historical slumber emerges in other ways as well. Facilitating the identification between these seventeenth-century vignettes and the narrative present, Azorín asks: "¿*Cómo* es la mujer española de estos tiempos? ¿Sabemos, acaso, *cómo* es ahora? Seria, silenciosa, humilde y recogida, en las apariencias; levantisca y andariega, en el fondo. Cuando ama, ama con pasión ardorosa; cuando la humillan, se venga" (81). [What is the Spanish woman of that epoch like? Do we know what she is like now? She might seem silent, humble, and modest by all appearances; restless and gadding about underneath. When she loves, she loves with ardent passion; when she is humiliated, she takes revenge.] The referent here is ambiguous; the qualities of "gadding about and vengeful" can apply to either (or both) seventeenth-century or contemporary women. Women's participation in the Spanish consumer riots of the late nineteenth and early twentieth centuries, sparked by an economic crisis that occasioned shortages of basic foodstuffs, enhanced the association of women with civil chaos:

> The traditionalists who controlled the political and cultural establishment for most of the nineteenth and twentieth centuries viewed women's domesticity as part and parcel of the larger vision of Spain that they would defend literally to the death. In contrast, the image of the "modern" public woman was equated not just with social disorder but also with national decadence: the quintessence of anti-Spain. (Enders and Radcliff 1999, 20)

The references to women's lives in *El alma castellana* are prescriptive as well as descriptive. On occasion, Azorín directly alludes to his early twentieth-century female reader: "Quede aquí esta materia: harto delicada para oídos femeniles; demasiado sabida para contada a los varones"

(1995, 99). The author wished to shield his contemporary female reader from references to husbands who prostitute their wives or "los maridos que por precio consintieren que sus mujeres sean malas de su cuerpo" (99), thus recognizing or attempting to postulate a modern morality that no longer tolerates such practices.

Azorín insinuates that his contemporary female reader should devote her time to reading about fashion rather than sexually salacious situations. After a brief allusion to seventeenth-century dress, Azorín asks, "¿Desea alguna curiosa lectora más detalles?" (105). Assuming that she will want more details, the author obligingly continues with a long list of items of apparel. Clothing is a pervasive motif throughout *El alma castellana;* both the seventeenth- and eighteenth-century sections contain chapters on "La moda."[21] Morality and the decline of the Spanish nation are closely allied to styles of dress, particularly those of women; the women in the *hacienda* chapter who "hacen maldad de su cuerpo" wear outlandish garb: "monterillas de plumas, tocas con grandes puntas de Flandes, guardapiés de chamelote con seis pasamanos de oro, jubón de flores, el cabello suelto y lleno de lazos, manillas de aljófar y áureas joyas" (74) [feathered headgear, head-wear with large tips from Flanders, a camlet skirt with six golden laces, a flowered jerkin, the hair loose and full of bows, pearl bracelets, and golden jewels].

In the chapter on seventeenth-century fashion, the narrator observes, "La moda cambia rápidamente. El lujo toma vuelos. Cuanto mayor y más tremenda va siendo la ruina de España, tanto más se explaya la corte en fiestas y aumenta la suntuosidad en el arreo de damas y caballeros. La más simplecilla doméstica se crece de fregatriz a señora, y abandona la modesta basquiña por el guardapiés encarnado, por el franjón de oro y plata, por la ungarina de felpa" (108). [Fashion changes rapidly. Luxury takes flight. As Spain's ruin grows and spreads, the court engages in more celebrations and the sumptuousness of ladies' and gentlemen's dress increases. The simplest domestic servant is transformed from a scullery maid into a lady and abandons the modest skirt for the crimson underskirt, the gold and silver fringe instead of felt.] This passage gathers into the image of the social-climbing servant the late nineteenth-century preoccupations with the working class and social mobility as well as the greater visibility of women in public spaces. Women's clothing also threatened morality in the seventeenth-century. Excessively large skirts hid the fruit of illicit love affairs, so that young women no longer feared the consequences of immoral behavior. The new fashion was not only immoral ("contra la moral, porque ahora se pone 'gran parte de la gala y adorno lascivo en medias, ligas, zapatos y sus rosas'" [109]) but also unhygienic: "contra la higiene porque 'la pompa y anchura de este nuevo traje *(o sea los guardainfantes),* es llano que admite mucho aire y frialdad, que envía al útero donde se fragua el cuerpo humano'" (109). The female body and the nation were ruined simultaneously.

The seventeenth-century section ends presciently with Azorín's description of the feminization of men's garb and manners, foreshadowing the salonized man of the eighteenth century as well as the decadent and dandy of the late nineteenth century. Men went about using fans, and, as if this were not enough, some men also wore "'manguitillos de pieles en las manos'. '¿Qué más hacen las delicadas mujercillas?'" (109) [fur muffs on their hands just like delicate little women]. Military men were becoming alarmingly effeminate:

> '¿Dónde hay hombres en España? Lo que yo veo es mariones [*sic*], que hurtan los usos a las mujeres: de hombres los veo convertidos en mujeres, de esforzados en afeminados, llenos de tufos, melenas y copetes, y no sé si de mudas y badulaque, de los que las mujeres usan. Y siendo así que ayer blasfemavades de los extranjeros que entraban en España con melenas y os olían mal, ¿ahora traéis las mismas y queréis oler bien? A mí me oléis a lo que os olían los extranjeros cuando las traían. ¡Lindos soldados para un aprieto de importancia! Harto mejor os pareciera a algunos una rueca que una espadaña a lo menos hariades más hacienda. Yo espero que habéis de venir a misa de dos en dos dadas las manos, porque sólo eso os falta por hacer.'
>
> La decadencia se acentúa. (110)

[Where are the men in Spain? What I see are queers who purloin women's customs: I see men converted into women, converted from strong to effeminate, full of airs, long hair and pompadours, and perhaps even cosmetics and silliness that women use. And considering the fact that yesterday you cursed the foreigners who entered Spain with long hair and smelling bad, now you do the same and want to smell good? You smell the same to me as the foreigners who used these fashions. Lovely soldiers for an important predicament! It would be better if you chose a woman's distaff rather than a sword because at least you would make more money. I hope you will come to mass by twos holding hands, as that is the only thing you haven't done yet.

Decadence increases.]

The concern with decadence and the feminization of culture detailed here for the seventeenth century echoes similar ideas expressed by Friedrich Nietzsche and Max Nordau at the end of the nineteenth century.[22] The common practice of men and women dressing as members of the opposite sex during carnival became an object of church criticism in the first decade of the twentieth century "because it expressed new and sharper social criticism" (Balfour 1997, 128).[23] And it is not difficult to transpose Azorín's quotations from seventeenth-century texts about ineffectual, feminized soldiers and the pathetic Spanish army to the colonial war of 1898 so fresh in the author's mind when he wrote *El alma castellana*.

The story of a seventeenth-century female cross-dresser provides Azorín with the opportunity to discourage women who assume masculine roles. A widow who inherited her dead husband's estate is accused by her brother-in-law of having an affair with a man of lesser social status than she. A scandal ensues, and she vows to avenge herself, which she does by nailing the tongue, nose, ears, and hands of the perpetrator of her dishonor on her door with a note declaring that she was the author of the horrific revenge. Subsequently, she dresses as a soldier and joins the army. Her female identity goes undetected, except by the narrator of the story, who recognizes her as she plays dice one day. Azorín suggests that such unwomanly behavior seems implausible in the early twentieth century: "Parece hazaña increíble que una mujer, por azares amorosos—como vemos frecuentemente en las *comedias*—corra el mundo en hábito de varón. La cosa tiene visos de certeza; a tal punto llegaban antaño en España los arrestos femeninos" (Azorín 1995, 112). In 1900, Azorín interpreted the morally uncompromised cross-dressing so prevalent in Golden Age texts as excessively bizarre. Cross-gendering and cross-dressing became more prevalent and assumed different meanings in novels that appeared in the second and third decades, for example. In significant contrast to Azorín's nationalistic use of the cross-dressing theme in *El alma castellana* is Burgos's *El permisionario* (1917; reprinted in *La flor de la playa y otras novelas cortas* [Burgos 1989b]), in which Burgos remains more neutral about gender role reversals. She employs them not so much to underline national weaknesses but to explore human emotion and possibly to satirize the national concern with the feminization of a traditional masculine culture. In other novelettes, Burgos fully exploited cross-dressing's potential for social satire, and in *La mujer moderna y sus derechos* (1927), she included an important discussion of the issue.

The image of the masculinized woman that surfaced at the turn of the century in Spain in popular and other cultural venues doubtless reflected concern about women's heightened visibility in the public sphere. Pamela Radcliff notes that press coverage of consumer rebellions in Badajoz in 1898 labeled women protesters "mujeres varoniles" (1999, 319 n. 21) to highlight the perceived social threat in women's assumption of public roles. She also points out that when the women took action to acquire such necessities as food, the implication was that the masculine culture was not adequately caring for its women and children. A 1912 book titled *La educación femenina* worries that if women move into the workplace, men will be forced to assume traditional female duties in the home, "zurciendo la ropa y meciendo la cuna de los pequeñuelos" (Aguado et al. 1994, 370) [making clothes and rocking the little ones' cribs]. This, the text intones, would be tantamount to inverting "los polos de la sociedad doméstica" (370).

The "masculine" woman, who usurps men's role, refusing to marry and settle down to domestic life, emerges as an important figure in male-authored novels during the period when feminism was gaining ground in Spain. The phenomenon occurs as early as 1893, however, in Valle-Inclán's short story "Tula Varona" (see Valle-Inclán, 1992). The protagonist's name reveals the story's gender reversal. Tula is a thoroughly modern woman—a Latin American Creole, separated from her husband and living alone in Paris. She is well educated and flaunts her knowledge before the Marqués, whom she tantalizes and ultimately dismisses. She smokes and engages in the masculine sports of shooting and dueling. Her laugh is strangely "hombruna," and she wears a straw hat without any adornments similar to those that men wear (84). When she cruelly dismisses the Marqués after pretending to seduce him, the narrator describes her as a snake with gleaming eyes, sporting "esa alegría depravada de las malas mujeres cuando cierran la puerta al querido que muere de amor y de celos.... Todo en aquella mujer cantaba el diabólico poder de su hermosura triunfante" (98) [this depraved glee of bad women when they close the door on the lover who is dying of love and jealousy.... All in that woman sang the diabolic power of her triumphant beauty]. In the final scene after the Marqués has left, she undresses before the mirror and strokes her own body, "enamorada de su propia blancura, blancura de diosa, tentadora y esquiva" (99). Interestingly, in an earlier version of the story, Valle-Inclán gave it a more feminist twist. Tula rejects the Marqués's offer to be her slave, saying that his slavery would last only an hour, whereas she would end up being his slave for the rest of her life. That exchange is expunged from the final version, and we are left with only Tula's unreasoned cruelty and narcissism.

Another aspect of modern sexual life that both Azorín and women writers addressed by way of Golden Age references is prostitution. For example, Blanca de los Ríos's 1907 *Las hijas de don Juan* (1907), a modernist version of the Don Juan theme, portrays prostitution as an evil practice spawned by male depravity. Azorín, in contrast, employed a Golden Age backdrop to characterize prostitution as an example of women's depravity. In *El alma castellana*, Azorín refocuses the Golden Age picaresque novel, typically a genre with a male protagonist who engages in a variety of illegal behaviors, to center on female prostitutes. Like his treatment of cross-dressing, Azorín's approach is prescriptive rather than descriptive. He cites sources that claim that prostitution was a revered profession in some seventeenth-century Spanish cities; in Valencia "las mujeres de mal vivir" are more esteemed than anywhere in Europe. The narrator notes with modern astonishment that prostitution was a "nobilísima institución" (Azorín 1995, 121). Prostitution—sex outside of legitimate marriage—gathers metaphorical status as the book progresses; the chapter on love in the eighteenth century is devoted to the custom of the *cortejo* (cortege). Once again, a late nineteenth-century bourgeois morality can be read between the lines; the narrative depicts the *cortejo* as a quaint custom of another era that could not be tolerated in 1900.

After a lengthy description of a day in which the lady and her paramour dress for each other, dine together, and parade about town for all to see their involvement with each other, Azorín prompts the contemporary reader's condemnation of extramarital affairs, in which love is considered a sport:

> '¿Y el marido?' preguntará acaso el lector. ¡Oh, el marido! En *El tocador o el libro a la moda,* catecismo de buen gusto, el autor finge una conversación entre dos damas: cortesana refinada la una, candorosa provinciana la otra. La primera invita a la segunda a ocupar su *vis-a-vis* y dar un paseo. 'Gracias, mi coche me aguarda; voy a pasear con mi marido', contesta la provinciana. Y la madrileña, atónita, asombrada, estupefacta, exclama: '¡Con su marido! Es menester reir a boca llena. ¡Qué gentes! ¡Qué palabras!' (209)

> ['And the husband?' the reader will perhaps ask. Oh, the husband! In *El tocador o el libro a la moda,* catechism of good taste, the author invents a conversation between two ladies, one a refined courtesan, the other a frank provincial woman. The first invites the second to join her in her carriage for a ride. 'Thank you, my carriage awaits me; I am going to take a ride with my husband,' answers the provincial woman. And the woman from Madrid, astonished, surprised, completely taken aback, exclaims: 'With your husband! I have to laugh with an open mouth. What people! What words!]'

Azorín engages his historical source to create an ironic contrast. The eighteenth-century text implies disdain for the provincial view of the *cortejo,* although the disdain contains a veiled irony in presenting the custom imported from France. Azorín capitalizes on this latent irony by inviting the contemporary reader to wonder where the legal spouse fits into the *cortejo* scenario. The contemporary reader's bourgeois moral position naturally casts him or her in the role of siding with the *provinciana* who chooses the company of her husband over that of a paramour.

In the chapter on "La moral" in the eighteenth-century section of *El alma castellana,* Azorín also concentrates on the institution of marriage. Marriage is central to overcoming lax morality: "El matrimonio es uno de los estados que más detenimiento y reflexión requieren en el hombre; principiaremos por el matrimonio" (197). The most important role in the institution of marriage is assigned to the mother: "Deben las madres tener siempre vigilados todos los caminos y sendas de las casas por donde pueden comerciar criados con criadas e hijas con vecinos" (198). The mother should be away from home as little as possible in order to guard against danger. Azorín quotes Palafox, who wrote that "andar fuera de su casa una casada es andar descasada" (198) and also includes a warning about female literacy: "Los libros malos pueden desterrarse y ponerse otros buenos en su lugar; 'pero en que una doncellita sepa escribir, no hallo ni este ni otros bienes, sino muchos riesgos' " (199). Many of these arguments were prevalent in late nineteenth-century discourse about women's work and education, and they contradict messages that Azorín proffered in other venues, such as his famous statements against marriage in *El País* quoted previously.

If *El alma castellana* has recourse to Spanish history to insinuate covert messages about the roles that are inappropriate for women, *Castilla*, which appeared twelve years later, invokes Spanish classical literature to emphasize the proper role for women: wife and caregiver. In the opening paragraph of *Castilla*'s much anthologized vignette "Las nubes," the narrator makes the startling announcement that the star-crossed lovers of Fernando de Rojas's 1499 classic *La Celestina* got married:

> Calisto y Melibea se casaron—como sabrá el lector, si ha leído *La Celestina*—a pocos días de ser descubiertas las rebozadas entrevistas que tenían en el jardín. Se enamoró Calisto de la que después había de ser su mujer un día que entró en la huerta de Melibea persiguiendo un halcón. Hace de esto diez y ocho años. Veintitrés tenía entonces Calisto. Viven ahora marido y mujer en la casa solariega de Melibea; una hija les nació que lleva, como su abuela, el nombre de Alisa. (159)

[As the reader who has read *La Celestina* knows, Calisto and Melibea got married a few days after their clandestine garden meetings were discovered. Calisto fell in love with the woman who was to be his wife one day when he entered Melibea's garden while chasing a falcon. That was eighteen years ago. Calisto was twenty-three at the time. Now the husband and wife live in Melibea's old family home; they have a daughter, named Alisa after her grandmother.]

Of course, the reader knows nothing of the sort; quite the contrary, Calisto's untimely fall from a ladder and Melibea's subsequent suicide are two of the literary events most indelibly inscribed on those who are familiar with Spanish Renaissance literature. Nonetheless, we have accepted Azorín's major recasting of a tragic love affair into a happy domestic arrangement; for the reincarnation of Calisto and Melibea's story in their daughter seems an appropriate means for Azorín to pursue his perennial concern with the nature of time and his desire to discover the eternal essence of Spain in its literary classics.

After the passage in which the narrator announces Calisto and Melibea's marriage, there follows a detailed description of the home of the happily married couple.[24] Azorín transformed the fifteenth-century Melibea, who carried on a sexual relationship with Calisto outside of marriage, into an ideal bourgeois housewife: "Todo lo previene y a todo ocurre la diligente Melibea; en todo pone sus dulces ojos verdes" (160). [The diligent Melibea foresees and takes care of everything; her sweet green eyes observe all.] She is the "ángel del hogar" so often described in women's conduct books of the nineteenth century and reinscribed in the public imagination through female characters such as Juan Valera's Pepita Jiménez and Benito Pérez Galdós's Jacinta de Santa Cruz: "Le cuidan [a Calisto] las manos solícitas de Melibea" (161). Ostensibly, the vignette creates a situation in which Azorín could evoke his favorite subject of the eternal return. At the end of "Las nubes," Calisto and Melibea's daughter meets a young man who is chasing his falcon; thus, history would appear to repeat itself. The wealth of domestic detail at the beginning of the vignette, however, weighs heavily upon its final effect, especially when considered correlatively along with the domestication of other classics in the volume.

In addition to "Las nubes," other well-known vignettes in *Castilla* are domesticating *refundiciones* of Spanish classics, such as the anonymous *Lazarillo de Tormes* and Miguel de Cervantes's exemplary novel *La ilustre fregona*. In "Lo fatal," the hidalgo from the third *tratado* of *Lazarillo de Tormes* is no longer the lazy impoverished nobleman of the sixteenth-century picaresque novel. He is a man of means who encompasses all the virtues that we associate with an enterprising bourgeois gentleman: "En poco tiempo su caudal aumentó considerablemente; era activo perseverante" and he is now domiciled in an "ancho y noble caserón." This comfortable house has a "zaguán con un farolón en el centro; anchas cámaras y un patio" and a pantry "provista de cuantas mantenencias y golosinas pueda apetecer el más delicado lamiznero, y en las paredes del salón, en panoplias, se ven las más finas y bellas espadas que hayan salido de las forjas toledanas" (Azorín 1991, 168). The vignette ends with the hidalgo's visit to his old servant Lázaro, who is similarly commodiously established: "ahora ya casado, holgadamente establecido" (170–71). Of course, we already knew about Lázaro's adoption of a bourgeois lifestyle (if not bourgeois morals) from the original book, but there is no logical reason for the sudden industriousness of Azorín's hidalgo if the main point of the vignette is to identify him as a timeless example of the essential Spanish gentleman who resembles the *caballero desconocido* of El Greco's famous painting.

In "La fragancia del vaso," an adaptation or recasting of Cervantes's "La ilustre fregona," "Constanza ha embarnecido algo con la edad. Es alta, de cara aguileña y morena. Los años han puesto en su rostro una ligera y suave sotabarba" (175). [Constanza has become varnished with age. She is tall, with a dark, aquiline face. The years have added a light, gentle fringe of whiskers to her face.] Not only has Constanza mellowed and aged in appearance; she is now touted as the best of housewives: "Ninguna ama de casa la supera en diligencia y escrupulosidad con el alba" (175). These portrayals of women (and men) from literary classics as positive domestic models are counterbalanced by the cautionary tale "Cerrera, cerrera," which juxtaposes the story of a wild and uncontrollable she-goat from *Don Quixote* with the story of a gentleman who married a woman inferior to him in social class. He ends up a lonely old man after his inappropriately chosen wife has abandoned him.

Azorín continued to draw on the classics throughout his career, often for the same purpose as in these early works—to introduce gender into portraits of the nation. As the ensuing chapters demonstrate, the soul of Spain became identified by both male and female authors with specific classic Spanish literary figures, especially Don Quixote and Don Juan. Just as Unamuno and Azorín differed from Martínez Sierra in their deployment of *intrahistoria* and the *tradición eterna* in early modernist fiction, the treatment of these national literary icons by male and female authors diverged.

CHAPTER 2
Don Quixote as National Icon and Modernist Ideal

After the Spanish army lost eighty ships and one thousand men in the brief 1898 war with the United States, one Spanish newspaper article observed, "We were the only people capable of fighting for honour alone, we were gentlemen, we were Quixotes" (qtd. in Butt 1998, 4). Especially in the first decade after the disaster, many male intellectuals who engaged in the national soul-searching that began before the war and that was intensified by it, such as Miguel de Unamuno, Azorín, and Ramiro de Maeztu, similarly found in Don Quixote an emblem for the national spirit. In early twentieth-century Europe, where technological, political, and social progress were modernity's dominant vision of civilization's future, a Spain that had remained behind in all these areas could point to its idealism as a virtue that placed it in a category all its own (Unamuno famously scoffed "¡Qué inventen ellos!"). Don Quixote's idealism summed up Spain's virtuous opposition to the materialism of modern northern Europe. As Peter Bush writes, "In the late 1890s Unamuno, Ganivet and other members of the *avant-garde* devoted their intellectual energies to working out moral ideas with which to regenerate the Spanish nation. They raised the banner of *quijotismo*. The extreme idealism of Cervantes' literary creation, Don Quixote, was interpreted as the essence of the national spirit. The present state of Spain flowed from the chivalresque madness in its soul" (1984, 472). According to Unamuno, Don Quixote, who "[a] bote de lanza, anárquicamente, enderezaba entuertos" (1971, 169) [lance in hand, anarchically, righted wrongs], pointed toward Spain's path to regeneration. What present-day Spaniards lacked was the rich experience of the Golden Age adventurers, whose activity extended to Flanders, Italy, and the Americas; modern Spain had not found replacements for these energetic exploits.

Cervantes's most famous character inspired meditations on the nation that also directly or indirectly bear upon gender issues, especially women's social roles and marriage. Both male and female writers invoked Don Quixote, although to different purposes. Male authors almost invariably seized on the romantic/postromantic interpretation of Don Quixote as a heroic idealist victimized by a society incapable of understanding him. Women novelists, in contrast, often invoked the foolish, ridiculous Don, which, according to Anthony Close (2000), more clearly represents Cervantes's intention and seventeenth-century Spanish society's understanding of the character. Women novelists who did not completely relinquish admiration for Don Quixote's idealism tempered it with recognition of the demands of the material world.

Don Quixote's perception of women based on his reading in books of chivalry provides a paradigm for analyzing how male and female modernists depicted female characters in their novels. Like many male modernist writers, Don Quixote's feelings about women were ambivalent. The Don's experiences with women ranged from the controlling, manipulative housekeeper and niece to the protofeminist and vocally independent Marcela. His tactic in the face of such baffling female diversity was to transform the women he met in his travels into characters from chivalric or pastoral romances through sheer force of his powerful imagination (the rough peasant Aldonza Lorenzo, for example, becomes the rare beauty Dulcinea del Toboso). Don Quixote's idealism often surfaces in male-authored narratives of the modernist era as a refuge from modern social change. In *La mujer moderna y sus derechos,* after recalling Don Quixote's idealization of women, Carmen de Burgos charges chivalry with having set women back for centuries. It buried them in a false atmosphere of lyrical praise: "Se acostumbraban a no oír más que la canción de sus alabanzas; se entregaron a la molicie, sin idea de ninguna responsabilidad social, como criaturas aptas sólo para el amor" (1927, 67).

Male modernists also adopted Quixote's otherworldly stance as a springboard to philosophical meditations, especially meditations about the nature of the Spanish nation. For example, in *Meditaciones del Quijote* (1914), José Ortega y Gasset considered Don Quixote an essential circumstance of Spain. According to Unamuno, Don Quixote is pure spirit, and Azorín finds eternal truths in the places that Don Quixote visited. Many of the protagonists of male-authored Spanish modernist novels are hopeless idealists of the quixotic type, tilting against the windmills of crass reality. Although their approach to life usually yields unfortunate results, like Quixote, the characters are vindicated in their idealism within a cruel, materialistic world (a materialism often perpetrated by women and marriage).[1]

Unamuno's Avito Carrascal in *Amor y pedagogía* (1902) is an odd modern Quixote whose ideal is a doomed-to-fail outmoded positivism. Pío Baroja's *Camino de perfección* was inspired by several Golden Age classics—Santa Teresa's mystical *Camino de perfección*, as well as the picaresque *Lazarillo de Tormes* and parodic *Don Quixote*. The protagonist Fernando Ossorio undertakes a mystic or quixotic journey through Castile in search of himself, unaccompanied by a practical Sancho Panza. In the end, like Quixote, he accepts the realities of modern life; in fact, Ossorio goes Quixote one better by surrendering to bourgeois marriage. Similarly, the ethereal Antonio Azorín, whose youth is dedicated to reading the likes of the German idealist Arthur Schopenhauer, marries at the end of the novel and becomes mired in material reality—property, children, and household matters.[2] Augusto Pérez, protagonist of *Niebla*, is a declared philosophical Cartesian. Unamuno's Dulcinea, although physically more attractive than Don Quixote's, is, like Aldonza Lorenzo, devoted entirely to earthly matters.

The quixotic male protagonists of these early novels tend to idealize women just as Quixote does, often with similarly disastrous consequences. Consider, for example, Antonio Azorín's idealization of the fragile Justina, who wastes away after taking religious orders; Fernando Ossorio's idyllic view of the maternal and earthy Dolores; Avito Carrascal's quest for the ideal mother in Marina; Andrés Hurtado's desire for the perfect life with Lulú; and Augusto Pérez's tragic misreading of the practical-minded Eugenia. The female characters, who usually have minor supporting roles, often highlight something about the male character's psychology or his masculine ontological project. After the women have fulfilled their supporting role, they die or are otherwise eliminated. (Recall that Unamuno himself recognized—even boasted—that his female characters move silently through his novels like shadows.) Not only did Spanish male modernists—especially, Miguel de Unamuno,

Pío Baroja, Ramón del Valle-Inclán, Azorín, and Gabriel Miró—follow Cervantes in the creation of idealistic protagonists; they also joined the Cervantine tradition of deploying a narrative posture that avoids absolutes.

In *Mimesis,* Eric Auerbach observes that *Don Quixote* does not engage in social criticism: "In the resulting clashes between Don Quijote and reality no situation ever results which puts in question that reality's right to be what it is. It is always right and he wrong. And after a bit of amusing confusion, it flows calmly on, untouched" (1974, 345). In other words, the authorial position in the novel is not absolute: "It is not enough to say that he does not judge and draws no conclusions: the case is not even called, the questions are not even asked. No one and nothing (except bad books and plays) is condemned in the book" (356). In fact, by emphasizing the dichotomy between a personal vision of reality and a reality accepted by the majority of the characters, the possibilities for social criticism that the novel had begun to develop in the picaresque genre diminish concomitantly. This relativism is central to understanding the dichotomy between male- and female-authored novels published in the early twentieth century.

Novels by women who wrote in the first decades of the century—María Martínez Sierra (recall *Tú eres la paz*), Carmen de Burgos, Concha Espina, Blanca de los Ríos, and Sofía Casanova—in contrast, break (sometimes quite self-consciously) with the Cervantine tradition in which masculine idealism or illusion is a central motivating principle. Unlike Cervantes and his modern disciples, these women writers do not maintain the posture of moral relativity that Auerbach notes in the *Quixote,* and they find a variety of narrative means to render biting criticism of such diverse aspects of contemporary society as the legal status of women, marriage, and prostitution. Not only do they avoid "Dulcineafying" the feminine figure; they portray her in her multiple dimensions as a political, legal, working—that is, social—being. Women writers eschewed Don Quixote's futile idealism and often converted his life into a model for contemporary social and political action.[3] Martínez Sierra, for example, invokes Don Quixote as she sets out on her journeys to Spanish towns to proselytize for the Republic: "Y éste era mi temor al empezar mi después intensa carrera de propagandista. Iba en tren por los campos de Castilla la Nueva y entraba en la Mancha. Los tres molinos de viento que aún quedaban sobre la llanura—era en 1932—, suscitaban para mí la evocación del sueño de justicia del Caballero de la Triste Figura" (1989, 82). [And this was my fear when I began what became my intense career as propagandist. I was traveling by train through the countryside of New Castile and entered La Mancha. The three windmills that still remained on the plain—it was 1932—evoked for me the Knight of the Sad Countenance's dream of justice.]⁴ Her mission is practical, but she recognizes in it a quixotic impulse. Her novels similarly meld idealism and materialism in a way that allows the practical to prevail without completely divesting itself of an idealistic dimension.

The tercentenary of *Don Quixote* (Part I in 1905 and Part II in 1916) inspired narratives that rewrite and meditate upon Cervantes's novel. Unamuno's *La vida de don Quijote y Sancho según Miguel de Cervantes Saavedra explicada y comentada* (1928), Azorín's *La ruta de don Quijote*, and Martínez Sierra's *La tristeza del Quijote* were originally published in 1905; Espina's *Las mujeres del Quijote* appeared in 1916.⁵ While quite different in a number of respects, the two books by male authors recreate Don Quixote according to their own philosophical preoccupations, forging a romantic Caballero de la Triste Figura as tragic hero. Martínez Sierra's essay on the *Quixote* examines the role of the emotions in the reading experience, and Espina's book sets Don Quixote aside to concentrate on some of the ancillary female figures in Cervantes's novel. Espina's maneuver is symptomatic of Spanish women writers' tendency to focus on female rather than male subjectivity and their concomitant recourse to certain realist strategies in the process of elucidating the female experience.

Azorín's *La ruta de don Quijote* had journalistic origins. The newspaper *El Imparcial* sent Azorín to La Mancha to visit the same towns through which Don Quixote passed on his travels. Not surprisingly, his experiences in the classic Spanish villages prompted him to continue his meditation on the essence of the Spanish soul and the nature of time and history that he had begun in *El alma castellana*. Here, however, he concentrates more on the national character with fewer hidden messages about gender roles. Both men and women melt into essential Spain. He discovers eternal truths in the Manchegan locales; although each is different, they reveal a common essence. The women are "tan españolas, tan castizas," and the men are "tipos castizos," "viejos hidalgos castellanos," "finos, espirituales caballeros que el Greco ha retratado en su cuadro famoso del *Entierro*" (1992, 100). Spain's greatness, its strength and power, arose from its typical villages: "¿No es éste el medio en que han nacido y se han desarrollado las grandes voluntades, fuertes, poderosas, tremendas, pero solitarias, anárquicas, de aventureros, navegantes, conquistadores? ¿Cabrá aquí, en estos pueblos, el concierto íntimo, tácito, de voluntades y de inteligencias, que hace la prosperidad sólida y duradera de una nación?" (93). [Isn't this the milieu in which the great, strong, powerful, tremendous, but solitary, anarchic wills of the adventurers, navigators, and conquistadors were born? Could one not find here in these villages the intimate, tacit agreement of wills and intelligences that makes the solid and lasting prosperity of a nation?] According to a certain Martín, whom Azorín meets in one of the villages, the journalist is "de los que ponen las cosas en leyenda" (109). Azorín appears to recognize that "true essential Spain" may be only a journalistic interpretation of Spanishness.

Unamuno links Don Quixote's adventures to a drive for personal greatness in an existential sense. According to the rector of Salamanca, Don Quixote's principal motivation is to "cobrar eterno nombre y fama" (1929, 33). The Don's imaginative creation of Dulcinea can be traced to the same drive: "Ansia de inmortalidad nos lleva a amor a la mujer, y así fue como Don Quijote juntó en Dulcinea a la mujer y a la gloria, y ya que no pudiera perpetuarse por ella en hijos de carne, buscó eternizarse por ella en hazañas de espíritu" (73). [Desire for immortality leads us to love a woman, and that was why Don Quixote conjoined woman and glory in Dulcinea, and since he could not perpetuate himself in carnal children with her, he sought to eternalize himself through her in spiritual deeds.] Unamuno also called Don Quixote "pure spirit," since he has undertaken a search for self-perpetuation, a feat possible only in the spiritual realm. Thus, the knight converts all the women into accessories to his immortalizing mission (similarly, the women in Unamuno's own novels are sources of identity and immortality for the male protagonists).

Don Quixote's niece, and women like her who attempt to control men's lives, irritated Unamuno. (On two occasions, the niece is instrumental in having Don Quixote brought home from his knightly adventures, and on his return she attempts to reinscribe him in the domestic order.) The woman who would clip the wings of a man whose imagination and spirit soar is, according to Unamuno, a "rapaza que apenas sabe menear doce palillos de randas" who dares to impose her will on "los hombres de hoy en su patria" (1958, 4:374). She is a weight, an anchor that sinks men (and thus the nation) to the lowest possible level. Unamuno favored Don Quixote's chivalresque idealism over Don Juan Tenorio's superficial Andalusian showiness; he contrasted the pair as representing two different Spains (Don Juan is a *burlador,* whereas Don Quixote is the *burlado*). According to Unamuno, Don Juan Tenorio is an "imbécil, libertino antiliberal;" he is so vacuous that he spends time chasing women in order to fill the spiritual emptiness. He hypothesizes an elderly and domesticated Don Juan married to Don Quixote's niece; the two of them deserve one another "porque si bien lo que busca Don Juan viejo es quien le cepille la ropa, le lleve el caldo a la cama, le ponga bizmas, le dé friegas y le lea los periódicos para distraerle, tampoco descuida la dote" (4:489) [because if old Don Juan is looking for someone to brush his clothes, bring his broth to him in bed, put poultices on him, give him rubdowns, and read the newspapers to entertain him, he is also thinking about the dowry]. It would now appear that the kind of domesticity that Unamuno favored in *Paz en la guerra* is anathema to male ontology and thus to a nation sorely in need of heroes. In the post-1898 national crisis as well as in the aftermath of his own personal religious trauma of 1897, Unamuno increasingly privileged a masculine heroism that paradoxically clashes with female maternity and domesticity. This tension escalates in *Dos madres* (1920) and *La tía Tula,* both of which appeared in the 1920s when women's liberation from traditional roles was acquiring national prominence.

In *La vida de don Quijote y Sancho,* which falls within the first period of Unamuno's novelistic depictions of women as passive and maternal, motherhood is an important metaphor for Don Quixote's being-in-the-world. For example, Unamuno interprets the prostitutes at an inn as mothers (virgin mothers, at that) to the Don Quixote child: "Ved, pues, se las adoncelló con su locura, pues que toda mujer, cuando se siente madre, se adoncella" (1928, 40). [You see then, he turned them into virgins with his insanity, since all women who feel themselves to be mothers become virgins.] Unamuno further notes that Don Quixote would be completely out of place in the contemporary milieu, where sexually suggestive images of provocative women proliferate: "¿Qué diría el casto y continente Don Quijote si, volviendo al mundo, viese el chaparrón de incentivos al deseo carnal con que se trata de desviar el amor? ¿Qué diría de todos esos retratos de mujerzuelas en actitudes provocativas?" (75). For Unamuno, the spiritual Don Quixote converts flesh—woman—into another spiritual entity, something that would perhaps be impossible in the modern world, as the tragic denouements of *Amor y pedagogía* (1902) and *Niebla* (1914) testify.

In *La tristeza del Quijote*, Martínez Sierra also considers the spiritual properties of Cervantes's novel, although she relates them to the response of a real reader who changes over time. As the title of the essay indicates, her analysis of the reader's reaction to the novel focuses on the emotions. She begins the essay with the image of a nine-year-old child opening the novel for the first time, its pages coming to life in the child's imagination. Reading about Don Quixote's adventures inspires the reader's own dream, as his soul fuses with the crazed soul of the kindly knight. He rides with Quixote on Rocinante, viewing life from the Don's perspective. The child's own world becomes that of the hidalgo-cum-chivalric knight. Fired by Don Quixote's golden dream, "la fantasía hecha corazón" (G. Martínez Sierra 1905, 13), he is not dismayed by Quixote's ignominious defeats. When he reaches adulthood, however, the reader's response turns melancholy because he realizes that his hero is crazy.

For Martínez Sierra, Don Quixote manifests pure soul, a feminine soul: "En su alma hay pompa caballeresca y principesca gala femenil y espiritual galantería y amores limpios y músicas y aromas de ambares y orientales esencias" (15). [In his soul there is chivalric pomp and princely feminine charm and spiritual gallantry and chaste loves and music and aromas of amber and oriental essences.] If Don Quixote's nature reveals feminine qualities, it also evokes the feminine emotion of compassion. Those who laugh at Don Quixote, including Cervantes through his narrator, lack compassion: "Los cuerdos no saben compadecer y han olvidado mucho antes que tú entrases por los caminos de la locura, las sendas de la misericordia" (16). Cervantes's cruel attitude toward his protagonist is very unlike the romantic authorial position. In works like *Werther,* the author "siente para su [the protagonist's] dolor compasión femenina, porque todo poeta que lo es de veras tiene en el alma algo de mujer" (18) [feels feminine compassion for his pain because every poet who is really a poet has something feminine in his soul]. At first, the reader experiences anger toward Cervantes and other characters for their heartless treatment of Don Quixote, especially their robbing him of his insanity, his special vision of the world. According to Martínez Sierra, "El primer deber de todo hombre para con las almas de sus hermanas es conservarles la que Ibsen llama *mentira vital*" (22). [The first duty of every man to the souls of his sisters is to preserve for them what Ibsen called the *necessary lie.*] Cervantes (and Martínez Sierra) are in this sense precursors to Rosa Chacel and María Zambrano, who argue from the 1930s forward that the "razón de la sinrazón" (23) is the voice of human truth. Foretelling Zambrano's emphasis on dreaming the future, Martínez Sierra states that mystery, poetry (literature), and dreams are "la madre y la amiga y la arrulladora de todo humano corazón" (25) [the mother and the friend and the lullaby singer of every human heart]. We dream the future, and we allow ourselves to be caressed by what was present and now past "cuando el recuerdo esfuma las crudezas de lo real amable" (25), in the kind of *olvido creador* that Zambrano theorized.

Ultimately, according to Martínez Sierra, the reader's anger at Cervantes subsides because the reader is aware of Cervantes's own sad biography and understands that in many ways Don Quixote is Cervantes. The cruel defeats that the author visits upon his hero are those that he himself sustained in his life full of setbacks and disappointments. Martínez Sierra's reader response interpretation of *Don Quixote,* especially the way in which the reader includes knowledge of the author's biography, has important implications for our understanding of her own novels. As discussed in Chapter 1, *Tú eres la paz* acquires poignancy in light of Martínez Sierra's own romantic triangle, and, as demonstrated subsequently in this chapter, *El amor catedrático* also assumes new dimensions when read against her complicated life.

Espina's *Las mujeres del Quijote* takes fictional biography in a different direction. She sought out the concrete woman in the archetypes created by Cervantes. Her book may well be a reaction to *La vida de don Quijote y Sancho* and *La ruta de don Quijote,* in which Unamuno and Azorín, her male contemporaries, discovered in Cervantes's classic eternal essences and philosophical concepts very similar to those that they themselves expressed in other writings. Espina contributed the following blurb to an edition of *La vida de don Quijote y Sancho* for which the editor had requested comments from other writers: "Unamuno pensador, filósofo y poeta, me parece admirable, interesantísimo, enorme. Su obra literaria en estos géneros adquiere un nivel de cumbre. Desde su altura él ha sembrado ideales y definiciones de *hombredad* en el Arte y en la Vida de España, que muchos se apropian, imitándole sin conseguir la cima de su propósito" (qtd. in Unamuno 1929, 5, emphasis in original). [Unamuno, thinker, philosopher and poet, seems admirable and extremely interesting to me. From his high place, he has sewn ideals and definitions of *manliness* in Spanish art and life that many appropriate, imitating him without achieving the height of his purpose.] Espina's observations, although seeming to offer the praise of a "jacket blurb," subtly remind us of Unamuno's male gender bias as well as of the masculinist prejudice of modernist Spanish letters in general.

Turning away from the hidden domestic and philosophical agendas of Unamuno's and Azorín's books on the *Quixote,* Espina sought to highlight women as strong independent individuals. Espina herself had emerged from traditional female roles to assume a more modern independent life. She married at a young age when her well-off bourgeois family's financial fortunes reversed. Her husband's business took her to Chile, where she took up writing to supplement the family income. Finally tiring of her role as a closet breadwinner, she returned to Spain, separated from her husband, and supported herself and her three children by the pen. Although she has fallen out of the Spanish modernist canon, her novels were hugely popular at the time of their publication. Espina was twice nominated for the Nobel Prize, losing by only one vote in the late 1920s.

In the early pages of *Las mujeres del Quijote,* Espina gently critiques Cervantes for not creating more realistic women: "No llegan todas las del *Quijote,* si ha de decirse la verdad escueta, al punto sazonadísimo de realidad humana y perfección artística en donde resplandecen algunos ejemplares masculinos, aún sin contar los del Hidalgo y su escudero" (1916, 26). She excuses him, however, by observing that he had not had the opportunity to know as many illustrious women as he had outstanding men. Espina highlights a number of female characters (Marcela, Luscinda, Dorotea, Zoraida, Clara, Quiteria, the *duquesa,* Ana Félix, Teresa Panza, the *ama,* and the *sobrina*) by giving each one her own chapter in *Las mujeres del Quijote,* with a role and speaking parts that are much more developed than those in the original text. In some passages, Espina appears to accept the notion of the eternal feminine postulated by the male authors in many of their novels (Josefa in *Paz en la guerra,* Marina in *Amor y pedagogía,* or the eponymous protagonist in *Doña Inés,* for example). The housekeeper and the niece "al cerrar los ojos del sublime hidalgo, entran con él, como imágenes de lo eterno femenino, en la inmortalidad de su gloria" (208) [upon closing the sublime nobleman's eyes, enter with him, like images of the eternal feminine, into immortality of his glory]. There may be a certain irony here in linking the women's "eternal femininity" to the dubious "glory" of a man who lives a crazy illusion and dies when the illusion finally dissolves.

In addition, *Las mujeres del Quijote,* taken as a whole, projects a more concrete and specific vision of women than do the novels and other writings of Espina's masculine compatriots. If the male recastings of Don Quixote remythified an eternal Spain, the Spain of *intrahistoria* and *el alma castellana,* the woman writer's project was to de-Dulcineafy Spain and its women. Some years later, Zambrano interpreted the promoters of the Second Spanish Republic as people who "se disponían a desencantar a Dulcinea" (1989, 166). Zambrano specifically defines the period of agitation for the Republic in the late 1920s as a time in which sexual equality was becoming possible: "Aquella limpia convivencia establecida entre los muchachos de la 'nueva generación', aquella voluntad espontánea de librarse de los infiernos del 'sexo', que permitía la existencia graciosa y alegre de la amistad, de la fraternidad" (166) [that chaste cohabitation established between the youth of the "new generation," that spontaneous will to liberate themselves from the infernos of "sex" that allowed a gracious and happy existence in friendship and fraternity]. In her novel *La virgen prudente*, published on the eve of the establishment of the Second Spanish Republic, Espina joined Zambrano in viewing a Republican form of government as an opportunity for sexual equality.

With this difference between early twentieth-century Spanish male and female Cervantism in mind, I turn to some novels of the early second decade that were inspired by *Don Quixote*—Unamuno's *Niebla* (begun in 1907 and first published in 1914), Miró's *Las cerezas del cementerio* (1910), Espina's *La esfinge maragata* (1914), and Martínez Sierra's *El amor catedrático* (1910). Azorín's *El caballero inactual* (1928) is a vanguardist modification of the earlier modernist versions of the Quixote story within the feminist context of the late 1920s. In each novel, the *Quixote* intertext provides a framework within which the authors inscribed ideas about gender roles and domestic arrangements in early twentieth-century Spain. The many dimensions of the Quixote figure—idealism, imagination, celibacy, encounters with a variety of women, integration into the material world, parody—emerge as important indicators of the author's view of the role of gender in the body politic.

Niebla's Augusto, arguably Unamuno's most quixotic protagonist—like Cervantes's character, pure in body and spirit—instead of traveling about in a geographical sense, moves from story to story. Not coincidentally, this pattern also has Cervantine roots as the many interpolated tales narrated in Quixote's presence considerably broaden the Don's horizons.[6] All the stories told to Augusto center on the subject of marriage, which is ostensibly the focus of Augusto's own story. Augusto has fallen in love with Eugenia after absentmindedly following her in the street one day, and the remainder of the novel narrates his courtship of her. As David W. Foster notes, Eugenia's "influence is felt throughout the tragi-comedy of Augusto Pérez's life" (1966, 322).

Eugenia is a modern, independent woman who works as a piano teacher to pay off the mortgage on her family home, a debt her father incurred before he committed suicide. She is perhaps the first of Unamuno's female characters of the second type sketched in Chapter 1: what Foster calls the "furiosas" or "belles dames sans merci." Eugenia is romantically involved with the feckless and lazy Mauricio, who is unwilling to marry because he does not wish to work to support a wife. The aunt and uncle with whom Eugenia lives consider Mauricio an inappropriate suitor, and when they learn of the well-to-do Augusto's interest in their niece, they declare him their "candidate." Eugenia, however, refuses to be coerced into a relationship with a man she does not love. Eugenia's Uncle Fermín associates her directly with the burgeoning feminist movement by calling her the woman of the future: "¡Ésta es la mujer del porvenir! ¡Mujeres así hay que ganarlas a puño (146).[7] His epithet echoes the title of one of Spain's earliest feminist works, *La mujer del porvenir* by Concepción Arenal, published in 1869.

Eugenia's aunt apologizes to Augusto for Eugenia's behavior, fearing her coldness has dampened his interest. Instead of being repulsed by Eugenia's independence, Augusto is further captivated: "—¡Admirable!, ¡majestuosa!, ¡heroica! ¡Una mujer!, ¡toda una mujer!—decía Augusto" (146). He assures the aunt that Eugenia's strong independent nature is just what he, weak-willed and meek, wants and needs. The uncle, a self-proclaimed mystical anarchist (another version of quixotic idealism), congratulates himself on having fostered Eugenia's independent demeanor. He thus links her to the sociopolitical movements of the day: "¡Ésta es, digo, la mujer del porvenir! ¡Claro, no en balde me ha estado oyendo disertar un día y otro sobre la sociedad futura y la mujer del porvenir; no en balde le he inculcado las emancipadoras doctrinas del anarquismo... sin bombas!" (147). [This is, I say, the woman of the future! Of course, not in vain has she been hearing me lecture day after day about the future society and the woman of the future; not in vain have I inculcated in her the emancipating doctrines of anarchism... without bombs!] By associating enthusiasm for the strong woman with the ridiculous "mystic anarchist" Uncle Fermín and the equally caricaturesque Augusto Pérez, the narrator of *Niebla* begins a campaign against the independent woman that ends with her wicked betrayal of the trusting, decent, loyal Augusto.

When Eugenia's feckless boyfriend Mauricio suggests that she marry Augusto for his money so that they can continue their relationship without his having to work, Eugenia breaks up with him and accepts Augusto's proposal of marriage. Two days before Eugenia's planned wedding to Augusto, after he has paid off the mortgage on her family home and used his connections to obtain a job for Mauricio, Eugenia elopes with her former lover. Such treachery might seem cruel and heartless enough, but Unamuno does not confine his dark portrait of Eugenia to jilting Augusto. Eugenia writes Augusto a farewell letter that ends with a particularly insidious reference to the laundry girl Augusto had briefly considered for a sexual dalliance: "P.D. No viene con nosotros Rosario. Te queda ahí y puedes con ella consolarte" (268). Augusto's distress over Eugenia's cruelty leads him to contemplate suicide, which, after a visit to his author, Unamuno, he carries out.

The ridicule of Eugenia's letter is the final straw: "—Es que no me duele el amor; ¡es la burla, la burla, la burla! Se han burlado de mí, me han escarnecido, me han puesto en ridículo; han querido demostrarme ..., ¿qué sé yo?..., que no existo" (271). [It's not the love that gives me pain. It is the ridicule, the ridicule, the ridicule! They have deceived me; they have scoffed at me; they have made me look ridiculous; they wanted to show me... what?..., that I don't exist.] Unamuno was not content to portray Eugenia as a modern woman capable of supporting herself financially and making her own choice of husband despite incessant pressure from her family to marry someone else. The gratuitous act of writing such a vicious letter casts Eugenia in the role of evil destructor. Foster calls her the "first Fatal Woman in Unamuno's fiction" (1966, 322). She is a species of monster or male devourer (a black widow of sorts) that will be foregrounded more prominently in the novelette *Dos madres* and in the long novel *La tía Tula*. Throughout *Niebla,* Eugenia appears cold and pragmatic; we can condone such an attitude in someone who has not sought a suitor's attentions, but the late hour of the elopement and the cruel letter suggest perversity. It is difficult not to perceive the unnecessary detail of the letter as an attempt to portray the woman who refuses traditional bourgeois marriage (Mauricio is a gigolo) as a threat to honorable men and stable social order. The narrative situation clearly establishes a connection between a strong, independent woman and the death of a decent (if rather innocent and unworldly) quixotic man. Don Quixote was "done in" (according to Unamuno) by the plotting housekeeper and niece (who were, in fact, kindly women who were genuinely concerned about Don Quixote's welfare). Augusto, a modern Quixote, faces even more treacherous circumstances—a woman who, instead of bringing him home to hearth and a comfortable deathbed, cruelly drives him to despair and self-destruction.

Augusto's idealism blinds him to Eugenia's real nature, and he pursues her despite all odds, holding out hope that she will eventually accept his hand in marriage. He even foolishly believes that the modern, independent woman would be his salvation. The stories about marriage interpolated at regular intervals in Augusto's courtship of Eugenia are cautionary tales about the perils of making a poor choice of marriage partner. For example, friends of Don Alburquerque, who is destitute and terminally ill, convince his landlady to marry him, arguing that she will receive a widow's pension in the very near future when he dies. Thus, Don Alburquerque has a place to live out his last few days. Contrary to the doctor's predictions, however, Don Alburquerque recovers, and the landlady is stuck with a husband she does not want.

In other interpolated tales, family and children complicate the married man's life. Don Eloíno has what appears to be a traditional family—a wife and four children—but he reveals to Augusto that the woman with whom he lives, the mother of his children, is the abandoned wife of the man for whom his legal wife left him. Augusto's friend Víctor for his part, was forced to marry his childhood sweetheart at a very early age, when their parents learned that the two had committed an "indiscretion." The indiscretion did not lead to pregnancy, however, and, as it turned out, the couple was later unable to conceive the children they had hoped for. As the years passed, they became accustomed to their childless life and even came to prefer it. Víctor's wife then conceives, and the couple resents the interruption of their peaceful existence. After the child is born, however, Víctor is a happy and devoted father. At the end of the novel, Víctor's family situation—a domestic wife, a child, and a happy home in which he can write his novel—remains the ideal for a contented life. Augusto's quixotic and unfortunate choice of a proto-feminist fiancée thwarts his achievement of domestic felicity.[8] Thus, in 1914, Unamuno's prescription for a stable Spanish social order has not essentially changed from the view projected in the 1897 *Paz en la guerra*, only now the woman has emerged from the intrahistorical sea to become a threat to personal and national peace.

Miró, some fifteen years younger than Unamuno, similarly appropriated Don Quixote as a means to situate relations between the sexes in Spain. Miró did not write a book on the *Quixote* as did Azorín and

Unamuno, but according to Ian Macdonald (1975), aside from the Bible, *Don Quixote* was the major source of inspiration for the Alicantine writer. His 1910 novel *Las cerezas del cementerio* is perhaps the work in which the Cervantine references are most extensively developed. The Cervantine dichotomy, which pits modern material reality against the masculine imagination (especially its idealization of the women), is the central issue in the novel. According to Macdonald, Miró maintained his "romantic inheritance with its notions of the mad genius and the validity of the uniquely personal" (1975, 100). This posture lies completely within the tradition of the modern interpretations of the *Quixote* in which Azorín and Unamuno exalted Don Quixote's idealism and essentialism just five years before the appearance of *Las cerezas del cementerio*.

Miró's modernist treatment of the Quixote theme bears many similarities to, as well as significant differences from, Espina's 1914 *La esfinge maragata*. A commercial success that also won its author the prestigious Fastenrath Prize from the Spanish Royal Academy, the novel presages Espina's project of revising Cervantes's (as well as Azorín's and Unamuno's) literary portrayal of women in her 1916 *Las mujeres del Quijote*. If Espina's *La esfinge maragata* is not a reply to Miró's radically Cervantine novel, it certainly could be. It incorporates the Cervantine intertext in similar ways as and to the same degree as Miró but with very different consequences. Female characters free themselves from the male imagination and seize control of their own destinies. In Judith Kirkpatrick's words, Florinda, the main character, undergoes a passage "into a female community where women define themselves in terms of their own strengths and concerns" (1995, 263).

Both *Las cerezas del cementerio* and *La esfinge maragata* contrast modern, urban Spain with the rural traditional nation. Both novels begin with a young man of romantic-poetic sensibility who is traveling by a modern mode of transportation. Félix of *Las cerezas del cementerio* first appears on board a steamship from Barcelona returning home to his native Alicante to recover from a congenital illness; in the first scene of *La esfinge maragata*, Rogelio keeps an overnight vigil on a passenger train from northern to central Spain. Both of these journeys from the city to the country are framed to contrast modernity and Spanish traditionalism. Each of the two young men encounters a woman on the journey (two women in Félix's case—a mother and daughter, Beatriz and Julia) whose image each immediately begins to construct according to his own criteria, a Dulcineafication of the feminine object.[9] Both Rogelio's and Félix's transformations of real women correspond to female literary archetypes. In *Las cerezas,* Beatriz incorporates elements of Dante's muse, as well as allusions to figures of classical mythology, such as Venus, Psyche, Echo, and Persephone/Proserpine. When Rogelio sees the sleeping Florinda on the overnight train, his imagination transforms her into Sleeping Beauty.

In each novel, the trip takes the principal characters through a provincial city on the way to a remote rural location of a particular region (Alicante and Maragata). In *Las cerezas,* the journey gives free rein to the protagonist's quixotic imagination, whereas in *La esfinge,* the crude realities of rural Spain overwhelm any tendency to romanticize them. The portrayal of Félix follows the Cervantine tradition in which the fantasy-driven male consciousness remains the motivating force throughout the novel.[10] Unlike Cervantes, however, Miró allows his "hero" to die with his romantic illusions of an ideal woman unsullied. Espina, in contrast, breaks radically with the Cervantine tradition: After the early chapters in which we view the world through Rogelio's distorted vision, she removes Rogelio as the novel's principal focalizer. For Rogelio, Florinda/Mariflor is the eternal woman, a perennial enigma, a sphinx:

> En la romántica incertidumbre de sus observaciones veía el poeta surgir a cada instante el vivo enigma de unos ojos claros, de una boca muda, de un talle macizo y un lento ademán; la humilde y robusta silueta de una mujer, de una esfinge tímida, silenciosa y persistente: ¡la esfinge maragata, el recio arquetipo de la madre antigua, la estampa de ese pueblo singular petrificado en la llanura como un islote inconmovible sobre los oleajes de la historia! (1989, 248)

> [In the romantic uncertainty of his observations, the poet saw constantly arise the live enigma of some clear eyes, a mute mouth, a solid figure and a slow gesture; the humble and robust silhouette of a woman, the timid, silent, and persistent sphinx: the Maragatan sphinx, the robust archetype of the ancient mother, the mark of this singular petrified town on the plain like an unmovable island on the waves of history!]

(The reference to Unamuno's notion of *intrahistoria* and woman's important identification with it is unmistakable.) After three chapters in which Rogelio poetically recreates Florinda's beauty, in Chapter 4 he continues his journey on the train, and the readers follow Florinda's trajectory to the impoverished village of Valdecruces (told mostly from her point of view). Both *La esfinge* and *Las cerezas* employ poetic language, tinged with *modernista* overtones in order to project the protagonist's imaginative abilities. In Espina's novel, however, after the initial chapters, it is a female rather than a male character who is endowed with poetic powers.

Because *La esfinge maragata* incorporates the Quixote intertext in two stages, the second filtered through a Mironian-style modern appropriation of the classic, I detail Miró's deployment of Cervantine material first. Born in 1879, Miró wrote little about women outside his fictional works; thus, we can only surmise his attitude toward the growing visibility of women in his milieu. His wife was the daughter of the French consul in Alicante, and therefore we know that he sustained contact with at least one woman of some reading and culture. He also read women writers in order to find, in his words, "la verdad del alma femenina . . . sutilezas y gracias vírgenes" (Miró 1992b, 74) [the truth of the feminine soul . . . virgin subtleties and charm]. In "Literatura feminista: *Yolanda*," one of his few essays that refer directly to contemporary women, he seems to confuse the notions "feminist" and "feminine." Although Miró considers the author *Yolanda* "redentorista," attempting to rescue the members of her sex from masculine enslavement, her "feminismo es exquisito; sus protagonistas no visten de rojo ni logran la perfección dándose de puñadas con los hombres" (76) [feminism is exquisite; her protagonists do not dress in red nor do they achieve perfection by battling it out with men]. He does not like woman-authored books "de hechura masculina, en que los personajes, los fondos de las escenas, el ambiente, el léxico, todo es macizo y varón" (74–75) [of a masculine style, in which the characters, the settings, the ambience, the lexicon are all massive and male]. He avers that women writers may be quite adept at portraying female characters, but they do not "lograr escudriñar el corazón del hombre" (74) [manage to scrutinize the male heart]. Miró himself created almost exclusively masculine subjectivities in his fiction, although he revealed an extraordinary sensitivity to women's need for and right to love and sensuality.

Las cerezas del cementerio is a classic modernist novel in its layering of literary references to reveal a view of the modern Spanish nation. Roberto Ruiz finds in it a modern existential message, a "rebellión metafísica" (1982, 41). If Félix is a Quixote in his idealistic vision (especially of women), he also participates in the modern technological world; he is an engineering student, travels via modern conveyances (at least at the beginning of the novel), and defies the traditionalist view on religion and marriage that his conservative relatives espouse. The novel's chapter titles announce the Cervantine paratext. The first is "Preséntanse algunas figuras de esta fábula," and six of the following twenty-one chapter titles (1, 5, 6, 7, 12, and 20) similarly echo those of Cervantes. Miró manipulates the two interpretations of Don Quixote mentioned at the beginning of this chapter—the preromantic ridiculous knight and the postromantic hero—to garner reader sympathy for Félix. Félix, like Quixote, carries his idealism to risible absurdity. However, by focalizing almost exclusively through Félix's consciousness and endowing his death with a poignant martyrdom, the narrative attenuates his ridiculous side. Félix's self-awareness also endears him to the reader. As Macdonald (1975) points out, Félix himself is conscious of his quixotism, a self-consciousness that asks the reader to overcome any distance created by the character's selfish egotism. This modernist self-consciousness, filtered through a classic literary figure is also a feature of Ramón del Valle-Inclán's modern Don Juan, the Marqués de Bradomín, protagonist of the *Sonatas* published just several years before *La cerezas del cementerio*. As latter-day Don Juans, both Félix and the Marqués reflect complex views of turn-of-the-century Spain that shroud the country's efforts to modernize in ambiguity.

Don Quixote's literaturized version of women is inspired primarily by books of chivalry, whereas the literarily motivated interpretation of relations between men and women in *Las cerezas del cementerio* is deployed in three large systems or codes: the classical (mythological), biblical, and Western literary tradition (mainly Dante and Miguel de Cervantes).[11] These systems converge and collide in such high density that the referents (especially the women) fade behind a screen of allusions. The allusions accumulate and project an eternal feminine essence reminiscent of Unamuno's and Azorín's feminine Spanish soul, one that Miró seemed to be seeking when he read works written by women.[12] The concrete reality of traditional Spain (Félix's family is very Catholic and conservative) that militates against his relationship with a married woman is nearly overwhelmed by modernist literariness.

Beatriz, on what we might call the first level of reality, is a beautiful woman in her thirties whose father married her off to an English businessman to further his own commercial interests. Beatriz and the boorish Englishman have lived separate lives for a number of years. Their daughter, Julia, a younger version of her mother, is on the verge of womanhood. After mother and daughter meet Félix on the ship to Alicante, he becomes a frequent visitor in their home, and there ensues a tacit rivalry between the two women for Félix's affections. Beatriz confides in Félix about her unhappy marriage to the Englishman and her platonic romance with Félix's Uncle Guillermo, who was killed by her husband's associate. Beatriz's sad story is shrouded in layers of literary references, some of which are poetically enhancing, others ironic, and many contradictory. These references construct an interwoven net of textual interplay that completely obscures Beatriz as a living, autonomous woman with a subjectivity of her own. The first time we see her on the boat, she appears in the proximity of the moon and sea: "Se alzaba la roja luna. Y cuando ya estuvo alta, dorada, sola en el azul, y en las aguas temblaba gozosamente limpio, nuevo, el oro de su lumbre, aspiró Félix fragancia de mujer en la inmensidad" (Miró 1991, 94). Since prehistoric times, the moon and the sea have allegorized the female element, especially its fertility functions. The moon also suggests Diana, the goddess of the hunt, protector of women, and the great mother of nature.[13]

These pagan roles contrast with Christian associations in which the mythological woman merges with a suffering Madonna. Beatriz often appears as a nurturing maternal figure to a Christ-like Félix,[14] and she is, of course, a real mother to Julia. The mother/Madonna roles are complicated by inversion and their intersection with other literary references. Beatriz is Julia's mother, but she is also her rival in youthful physical appearance and for Félix's affections. Beatriz's motherhood and links to the earth (she symbolically eats the cherries in the cemetery) associate her with Ceres. Like Ceres's daughter, Persephone, someone carries Julia off and treats her ill. The role is inverted, however, and instead of being Julia's protector, Beatriz is the indirect cause of her daughter's unhappy romantic life.

Félix's filial relationship to Beatriz is similarly paradoxical. Throughout the novel, Félix addresses Beatriz as *madrina,* because he remembers her from his childhood as the friend of his *padrino,* Guillermo. Incest and the eternal feminine converge in the *madrina* epithet (this paradox is reminiscent of Unamuno's interpretation of the prostitutes in *Don Quixote* as mothers to the Don). Beatriz is the great mother, the virginal Dantesque muse, and a destructive Eve (the garden setting in the rural agricultural region of Alicante and the ritual eating of forbidden fruit—the cherries that grow in the cemetery—make the parallel to the Garden of Eden unmistakable). In the opening passage, Félix imagines that he sees women's heads floating in the sea, suggesting the cycle of life and death that the female represents for the victimized male. Félix is ultimately sacrificed for a woman (he dies of his congenital heart disease when he tussles with the husband of a woman he imagines to be unhappily married), just as his uncle and *padrino,* Guillermo, was sacrificed for Beatriz. Not only is womanhood of a whole cloth—the eternally divine and damned virgin and whore—she ensnares the male in a cycle of sacrifice and suffering. Félix is Don Quixote fused with Christ. As an engineering student, he represents an attempt to introduce European modernity into Spain, but his modernity is crushed when he returns full of idyllic illusions to a traditional, rural sector of his country. If women are not directly responsible for his tragic demise, they remain as the eternal earth mothers who take their sustenance from him. In the final scene, the three women who have loved Félix eat cherries from the trees in the cemetery where Félix is buried. Félix's Don Quixote role is, as Unamuno interpreted Cervantes's character, undermined by women's designs and his vulnerability to them. Unlike Unamuno's, however, Miró's depiction of rural, traditional Spain finds little to redeem it.

Espina's *La esfinge maragata* portrays rural Spain in even less positive terms, but the author infuses her novel, which is more class-conscious than Miró's, with great sympathy for women whose lives are tied to the land. She effects this sympathy through a female protagonist whose subjectivity governs much of the narrative. *Las cerezas del cementerio* rarely focalizes through the female characters that serve as Félix's muses. Their subjectivity remains opaque. By contrast, from the beginning of *La esfinge maragata*, Florinda (or Mariflor, as she is known in the village of Valdecruces) displays the same imaginative powers as Rogelio. She becomes the central consciousness that guides the narration after she leaves Rogelio on the train to undertake the journey to Valdecruces by horseback.

Like Félix (and Don Quixote), Florinda harbors romantic pretensions. She tells Rogelio that the man her family has designated as her husband, a cousin who owns a grocery store, is not her ideal. She would prefer a sailor: "Parece que detrás de esa confesión ha volado muy lejos el alma de Florinda a perseguir por remotos mares la silueta romántica de algún velero audaz" (Espina 1989, 65). Throughout her education in the harsh realities of a life of work and privation, Florinda continues to cling to the romantic ideal of the male-female relationships that she has read about in adventure novels and such favorite books as Enrique Gil y Carrasco's *El señor de Bembibre* (in this sense, she could be considered a female Quixote). After the initial chapters of *La esfinge maragata* in which Rogelio's quixotic perspective prevails, the narrative begins a campaign against quixotism. Rogelio's literary perspective disappears when Florinda enters the female world of Maragata, which is a lived rather than a written or writing culture. The fact that Maragatan men do not write letters to women is a recurrent motif, and when Maragatans do write, the effect is deleterious. Marinela is actually frightened by Rogelio's quixotic language ("—¡Salve, oh maragata, augusta *Señora del Páramo*, salve! Con lo cual la aludida [Marinela], escandalizada ante una oración nueva, no escuchada jamás, tuvo al viajero por hereje o por loco" (178). [Hail, oh Maragatan woman, august Lady of the Plain, hail! Upon hearing this new, unusual utterance, Marinela, to whom it alluded, took the traveler for a heretic or a madman.] Don Quixote's greetings to people he encounters on the road echo here as well.

The people of Valdecruces call Florinda "Mariflor," a name more in keeping with her prosaic present. When she lives up to her last name, Salvadores, it is not by acting as a spiritual savior in the tradition of José Zorrilla's Doña Inés in *Don Juan Tenorio* (1844), but by becoming a material provider. Rather than being a pawn of divine intervention, she is a free agent who has made a difficult personal choice. Mariflor follows the romantic model of a woman who waits for the man she loves in spite of numerous obstacles, chief among them pressure from her family to accept the offer of marriage from a wealthy cousin. The marriage would solve the financial difficulties incurred by the poor business practices of Mariflor's grandmother, uncle, and father, which have placed the family farm at risk of falling to a moneylender. Even though she is consumed with romantic notions of love and fidelity to Rogelio, Mariflor is capable of understanding the real social conditions of her relatives and the other townspeople, something that Félix never accomplishes (recall that he dies in the aftermath of a quixotic attempt to "save" a woman from her banal husband). The change in name from Florinda, the lovely "princess" that attracts Rogelio on the train, to the Mariflor of the villagers' coinage signals her release from the literaturized romantic view of her as she enters a world where she is more an agent than an idealized object.

Valdecruces is not the intrahistoric *pueblo* of Unamuno's or Azorín's fictions; it is a particular village sustained by women who till the fields and support their households while their husbands work abroad.[15] Mariflor immerses herself in the poverty-stricken lives of her rural relatives, tending to household chores while her grandmother, aunt, and cousin work in the fields. Félix of *Las cerezas del cementerio* has the same opportunities to engage in rural life (his parents send him to the country to improve his health), but he ignores the invitations to participate in agricultural pursuits in order to devote himself to his affair with Beatriz, flirtations with his cousin, and a search for transcendental experiences on a mountaintop. If *Las cerezas del cementerio* adheres to a high modernist aesthetic in which an individual consciousness governs the depiction of others and their world, *La esfinge maragata* comes closer to embodying Raymond Williams's notion of the "personal-realist novel" in which the social takes precedence over the personal. Relationships with others determine all of Mariflor's choices. Mariflor has an inner life and desires, but they are less single-minded and egotistical than Félix's.

Compared to those elaborated by Miró, the literary references in Espina's novel are greatly simplified. Mariflor calls Rogelio a Quixote, but the association is much more transparent and parodic than in *Las cerezas del cementerio,* and the narrative treatment of Rogelio avoids the devices that achieve sympathy for Félix. Mariflor initiates the association between Rogelio and Don Quixote when she imagines him as the white knight who will save her from the harsh life that she has entered in Valdecruces. She dreams that Rogelio will whisk her away from her dreary impoverished situation: "Era preciso que ella, *Mariflor* Salvadores, la niña mimada y consentida, conocedora de holguras y de halagos, arrostrase, fuerte y audaz, las privaciones y los sacrificios, para que Dios, en premio la nombrara triunfalmente esposa de un artista, musa de un poeta. . . . ¿Por qué lado, por cuál camino milagroso llegaría a libertarla *Don Quijote*?" (Espina 1989, 114). While a downward spiraling web of family circumstances increasingly conspires to make Mariflor's marriage to a wealthy cousin the family's only salvation from economic ruin, her imagination continues to cast Rogelio as Don Quixote, who will rescue the maiden in distress. Rogelio's poetic letters to her fuel the dream: "Otra vez la silueta confusa de un Don Quijote singular, con lentes y aljaba, se adelantó en el campo de la más abundante fantasía para ofrecer liberaciones, paz y ventura a la muchacha en un mensaje que empezaba así:—Mariflor preciosa . . ." (133).

When Rogelio arrives in Valdecruces to court Mariflor, the narrator borrows the Quixote/Rogelio identification from the protagonist but gives it an ironic twist not evident in her perspective. Rogelio arrives on horseback clothed in dandyish fashion, prophesying his unsuitability as a savior of distressed damsels in the forsaken village of Valdecruces: "El andante caballero, visto de cerca, había trocado el yelmo de Mambrino por un jipi, y la célebre lanza por un vástago de roble, llevaba un maletín a la grupa, finos guantes en contacto con las bridas, y aúreos lentes sobre los ojos azules; era joven y parecía feliz" (166). This Quixote has exchanged outmoded armor for stylish modern accoutrements that belie his inability to cope with the serious problems he will encounter in his bid for Dulcinea. Indeed, his first impression of the village is filled with dismay: "Suspiró *Don Quijote* sonriendo; volvió en torno suyo la mirada y quedó atónito, como sobrecogido por la austeridad infinita del paisaje; ni una nube corría por el cielo, ni un átomo de vida palpitaba en el llano. La tierra infecunda se resquebrajaba a trechos, rugosa y amarilla como el cadáver de una madre vieja en cuyo rostro las lágrimas dejaron surcos hondos y fríos" (168).

At this juncture, Rogelio is still able quixotically to transform the misery that he sees into literary fantasy, and he populates the grim landscape with a "tropel de personajes, surgentes de leyendas y becerros, códices y archivos" (168). The "andante poeta," as the narrator calls him, leaves Valdecruces with his illusions intact. Perhaps he cannot change the harsh Maragatan landscape, but he can still hope to liberate the impoverished women trapped there: "Y si aún este propósito [to liberate everyone] fuese desmesurado para acometido por un corazón, un estro y una pluma, le quedaba al artista la certidumbre de poder esgrimir con gloria aquellas nobles armas, para rescatar del mar de tierra, libre y dichosa, a una sola mujer. A cada paso del mulo tomaba más cuerpo esta ilusión en los bizarros sentimientos del joven" (176). Rogelio, however, is a "quijote 'modernista'" (172); his illusions are doomed idle fantasy, because they bear no connection to the real world. Rogelio's interest in his beautiful princess wanes when he finally realizes her impossible economic situation and believes that the wealthy cousin has withdrawn his marriage offer (the desired object loses its appeal when it is no longer coveted by another): "El novio no escribía; mudo en la ausencia, oscurecido como fuyente sombra, perdía su señuelo de Quijote en la llanura de los 'pueblos olvidados'" (305).

Rogelio/Don Quixote disappears from the novel and from Mariflor's imagination. Rather than succumbing to a martyr's death (like those of Don Quixote, Augusto Pérez, and Félix), Mariflor takes charge of her life. She intensifies her work on behalf of her family, pawning her personal possessions and seeking charity to pay household expenses. She also decides to marry her cousin, who in his own rough-hewn way loves her more than does Rogelio. It is not a contemporary feminist solution to a woman's dilemma, but it is a positive and active one. Mariflor has made a generous choice and has become her family's savior, a role that Rogelio, with all his literary imagination, could not accomplish. Practical Mariflor's solution to her family's plight weds the impoverished rural family to modern commercial enterprise. Presumably, the agricultural relatives will have learned a lesson about sound business practices from this recent brush with destitution. Significantly, Mariflor, having left her quixotic illusions behind, will move to the city after her marriage. As Michael Ugarte (1996) and Shirley Mangini (2001) point out, at the turn of the century, the cities of Spain—Madrid and Barcelona—offered women opportunities for greater freedom and autonomy than they were able to achieve in rural locations.[16] Thus, Espina removes her female protagonist from quixotic impulses and rural Spanish backwardness, but Miró leaves his central female characters mired in an eternal cycle of unfulfilled longing at the end of *Las cerezas del cementerio* and transforms Félix-Quixote into a martyr.

In the Valdecruces world inhabited almost entirely by women, Florinda encounters a natural paradigm that contrasts with the idyllic model of the romance; instead of a union with an idealized male who idealizes her in return, she is offered the opportunity to establish genuine ties with her female relatives, especially through her cousin Olalla. The unflamboyant and singularly nonverbal Olalla stands in sharp contrast to Rogelio, the fickle and untrustworthy male with a facility for language. Olalla, who is capable of deep emotional ties and an unflagging constancy, speaks through her physical presence. Unlike the tenuous verbal understanding between Rogelio and Florinda, the pact between Olalla and Florinda is sealed with a physical sign: "Pero el impulso cordial prevalece por debajo del vuelo de las almas, y un pacto de amor se firma con el estallido de un largo beso" (Espina 1989, 98). [But the cordial impulse prevails beneath the flight of souls, and a love pact is signed with the sharp sound of a long kiss.]

As Rogelio disappears from Florinda's perceptual horizon, her strengthening bonds with women emerge in a series of avian images. The dovecote, first introduced to Florinda by Olalla, becomes her haven, an island of peace and solace in her harsh new world. When Marinela's health and illusions fail, she too escapes to the dovecote, situated in the light-filled upper story of an otherwise dark and depressing house. A piece of down from a baby dove adheres to Olalla's feminine form during the first excursion to the dovecote. This image suggests a number of metonymic links between Olalla, the doves, and her role as the titular mother figure within the family: "Y *Mariflor,* al ver un instante ambas cabecitas inocentes refugiadas con regalo en el seno de la moza, recordó al punto aquella dulce caricia en que el pichón recién nacido perdiera un copo de pluma" (122). [And Mariflor, upon seeing for an instant both innocent little heads taking happy refuge in the young woman's breast, immediately remembered that sweet caress in which the newborn pigeon lost a flake of a feather.] The habits of the storks, who mate for life and return year after year to the same nest, are symbolically woven into the narrative at appropriate moments and are evoked most meaningfully during the wedding ceremony of the niece of the priest Don Miguel. When, at the end of the novel, Florinda, now Mariflor, announces that she will marry her wealthy cousin, the doves come to feed from her lap: "Volvióse hacia el carasol para abrir las vidrieras, tomó el centeno en su delantal y todo el bando de palomas acudió a saciarse en el regazo amigo, envolviendo la gentil figura con un manso rumor de vuelos y arrullos" (397). [She turned toward the sun porch to open the windows; she took the grain in her apron and the whole band of doves came to sate themselves in the friendly lap, surrounding the elegant figure within the gentle noise of wings and cooing.] Rogelio's quixotic literary language that is empty of valid human connections has failed, whereas Espina's rendering of a metaphoric relationship between people prevails.

In Cervantes's classic as well as in novels by Unamuno, Valle-Inclán, Azorín, Baroja, and Miró, only men have imaginations that lead them to clash with the real world. Martínez Sierra joined Espina in revealing that women may suffer from the same malady as quixotic men. Both women novelists converted Quixote's singular masculine dream into a two-way reverie in which each sex fantasizes about the other. Espina endows Mariflor with Quixote-like qualities, which she gradually sheds in order to assume a mature womanhood that accepts social responsibility. In Espina's version of the Don Quixote paradigm, Dulcinea awakens from Don Quixote's dream of her and takes on an inner life that becomes much more important than Rogelio's pale imitation of the Knight of the Sad Countenance. Mariflor arrives at a practical idealism that counters Rogelio's useless quixotism. This practical idealism will prove more effective for achieving national progress than the quixotism identified with the Spanish position in the 1898 war.

Martínez Sierra shifted Espina's emphasis on the material world by fusing idealism and materialism in equal proportions in *El amor catedrático*. Instead of engaging in quixotic dreaming, Teresa theorizes about it. She criticizes the visions that women forge for their lives from the earliest age. Right out of the crib, women "puebla[n] sus castillos en el aire con hijos y marido—así por este orden, hijos y marido" (G. Martínez Sierra 1955, 31) [populate their imaginative castles with children and a husband—in that order, children and husband]. Women imagine themselves only within a family realm, "moviéndose ordenadamente en la actividad de la vida doméstica, dentro de la cual caben todos los perfiles de frivolidad, lujo y bienestar que su especial matiz intelectual le sugiera. . . .—Puesta a soñar una mujer tanto placer le saca a las futuras lágrimas como a las risas por venir, que ya es lugar común en poesía lo de que la esperanza y el recuerdo todo lo doran y platean a luz de sol o a ópalo de luna" (31). As the following discussion demonstrates, Teresa gives literature a large role in women's notion of their ideal life.

El amor catedrático attempts to replace the traditional female dream of domestic family life with another model. Like Espina's, much of Martínez Sierra's fiction usually accepts marriage as an uncontested role for women. Martínez Sierra does, however, frame the institution less in terms of a woman's sacrifice and more in terms of equality, companionship, and collaboration. Ana María's union with Agustín in *Tú eres la paz* points toward a marriage of intellectual equals, and *El amor catedrático*'s Teresa enjoys the same educational achievements as her husband, with whom she works professionally. Don Quixote mistakenly transferred the world of medieval chivalry to a materialistic sixteenth-century Spain represented in Manchegan peasants and prostitutes. Instead of using temporal displacement, Martínez Sierra employs spatially diverse markers to distinguish her novel from romance narratives that idealize relationships between men and women, locating her story of love and marriage in the unlikely context of the university.

Martínez Sierra's view of her own marriage to Gregorio as a literary collaboration was doubtless the model for the union that she portrays in the 1910 novel in which a female university student (extremely rare in Spain in the years before the First World War) falls in love with and marries her crystallography professor.[17] Theirs is, if not a marriage of absolute equals (she is eighteen years old, and he is forty-five), a companionable arrangement in which they work together on his (take note) geological projects. This arrangement reflects that of María and Gregorio Martínez Sierra: María wrote novels and plays, and Gregorio reaped the fame that came from his wife's labor.[18] Martínez Sierra presents this unequal equality in a favorable light in this early novel, and when we compare it to the treatment of male-female relations in the fiction of male writers, it represents a significant advance for women, not only in terms of a social-intellectual role but also in deployment of male and female subjectivities through specific narrative strategies.

Valle-Inclán, Unamuno, Azorín, Baroja, and Miró may have relegated their early female characters to stereotypical romantic, maternal, or Eve-like temptress roles in which female subjectivity is never penetrated, but María Martínez Sierra allows Teresa Alcaraz nearly fifty pages of intimate epistolary revelation at the beginning of *El amor catedrático*. Even so, Teresa cannot be considered a true protagonist, as she shares the limelight with two men. The novel, divided into five sections, is narrated by three voices. Teresa's letters to a friend occupy fifty pages. Teófilo, Teresa's husband's protégé, reveals his growing love for Teresa in a thirty-six-page soliloquy. The notes of the professor-husband, Raimundo, some of them philosophical and some pertaining to his relationship with Teresa, cover twenty-six pages. A very brief four-page letter from Teresa to her friend announces her departure for an extended research trip to Australia with her husband. In a final section, Teófilo narrates his liaison with an English woman during a sojourn in Granada four years after Teresa and Raimundo's marriage (thirty-eight pages). This last segment includes observations on the glories of Spain's past that place the novel's personal relationships within a national context. Thus, male and female characters share subjective revelations more or less equally.

In her first letter to her friend Carlota Guillén, Teresa announces her marriage and declares herself to be ecstatically happy. Although this is not exactly the revolutionary material we might expect from a feminist, and it is not comparable to Burgos's more radical stand on marriage and women's roles in her fiction, the novel projects many subtle differences on the marriage theme when compared to the messages of male novelists. As Teresa's letters reflect on her feelings about her university studies and her growing interest in her crystallography professor, they also comment on traditional female reactions to love, engagement, and marriage. These comments form a metanovelistic layer, which constitutes the most important feminist dimension of *El amor catedrático*. Like Cervantes's masterpiece, the commentary on novel writing contained within the main storyline creates an echo against which the reader measures the actions of the novel at hand. Teresa attacks the ideals about male-female relationships and marriage that novels plant in women's minds. Unlike Mariflor of *La esfinge maragata,* Teresa rejects the role of female Quixote from the outset and refuses to be deluded by bookish ideas of love. She is irritated by sentimental novels' depictions of the way a woman feels when she is in love. Novelists portray the initial stages of love as a "cosa bonita," frequently through romantic settings—the countryside in flower, perfumed salons, gentle breezes and poetry, all in ideal solitude that precipitates the emotional bond.

Teresa complains that novels project false images of women, which women then attempt to achieve. Male novelists, she believes, have spread abroad the notion that all women come into the world enamored of a nameless prince. She attributes this mistaken notion to men's impoverished imagination, which "al ponerse a fingir aspiraciones femeniles, no acierta a ir más allá de un pueril cuento de hadas!" (G. Martínez Sierra 1955, 33–34) [upon attempting to imagine female aspirations, does not manage to go beyond a childish fairytale]. She emphatically (and *pace* modernist biases) asserts that life and art are not one and the same. The artificial constructs of novels and plays require logic to achieve verisimilitude. Since life is not artifice, "se prende, germina, florece sobre el más inverosímil e inestable de los terrenos" (55) [it takes hold, germinates, and flowers in the most unlikely and unstable of terrains]. Teresa argues that "la topografía real de almas y situaciones difiere bastante de la imaginada, aun en las novelas más realistas" (25) [the real topography of souls and situations differs quite a bit from the imagined one, even in the most realistic novels]. Her own less than idyllic relationship with Raimundo took a very different course. It coalesced slowly in a solemn academic setting and progressed with a "cierto rumor sordo y molesto como el dolor mal localizado que dicen que se siente cuando dentro del cuerpo se está formando un cáncer" [certain deaf and bothersome tone like a difficult to place body pain when a cancer is forming]. Teresa's physical attributes are likewise antithetical to those deployed in novels that depict ideal women. She has dark, rather smallish eyes; her mouth is red but not at all petite; her chestnut hair is not particularly abundant, and it is not wavy or graced with curls "de esos que en la novelas acostumbran a prender corazones" (57).

Teresa also recognizes men's penchant for fantasizing about relationships; they must dream ("va y viene, habla tal vez, acaso sonríe; pero como si estuviese dentro de una nube" [31]), but the woman never really sees him as he is, and she does not wish to. She concludes that young men dream of beautiful, tall, blond or brunette women of a certain body type, whereas young women dream of an engineer, doctor, soldier, or sailor. Each envisions something that he or she does not have. Men want physical beauty that will give them repose, and women want careers that will provide them with a public presence. Teófilo, in a self-conscious act, acknowledges that men sometimes model their behavior on novels; when Teresa marries Raimundo and embarks for Australia, he decides to give himself "el gustazo de sufrir quince días como en las novelas, a echarnos de cabeza en las aguas amargas" (142). Teresa, for her part, clearly sympathizes more with the female than the male Quixote: "¡Pobres mujeres condenadas por siempre a vivir nuestro ideal en cabeza ajena!" (32). Teófilo, aware that he is playing a literary role, limits his enactment of novelistic behavior to fifteen days.

The male fantasy of the woman as "ángel del hogar" drives the entire central section narrated by the professor, and Teresa seems to accept the angel role in her final letter to her friend. She explains that she learned the role from her mother, who in her advancing age is tiring of playing the part: "No tiene ya el heroísmo de reír sin causa para que en la casa 'no se ponga el sol' " (125). Without the woman's tireless willingness to smile at all costs, the family home now registers a chill. Despite her awareness that the "angel of the house" role grows stale with time, Teresa continues to recommend marriage. She urges her friend to marry and has even selected a husband for her.

Despite her anti-quixotism, Teresa harbored one ideal about a future husband; she dreamt of marrying an "hombre sabio" to join him as a " 'ser complementario' " (33). In the Spain of 1910, this sentiment has a practical dimension. In the early century, an intelligent and educated Spanish woman's best chance of having an academic career was to ally herself with a man engaged in intellectual work.[19] Teresa is also practical in her desire to postpone the wedding until after she has passed all her university exams, but she allows her fiancé to impose an earlier date for the ceremony. Oddly, Teresa overlooks Teófilo, the man whose qualities would make him perhaps the most ideal companion. Teófilo, more than Raimundo, seeks an intellectual companion in a woman, and he espouses certain feminist principles, such as harmonious coeducation for both sexes. He views the institution of marriage as abominable and believes that it will disappear when women realize that it is better to support themselves freely than have a man support them in exchange for a "cadena perpetua" (132).

Raimundo, in contrast, is not at all certain that university education is appropriate for women:

> Siempre he dudado bastante de la capacidad de las mujeres para la investigación científica, y me han atacado un poco a los nervios estas muñecas que se entran por las Universidades a caza de un título que prenderse en el moño, como si no tuviesen bastante para su emperejilamiento con todas las flores que Dios cría y todos los lazos que el diablo inventa. . . . Pero Ciencias . . . , verdad es que a la Facultad de Ciencias pocas vienen, porque ¿qué les importa a ellas la verdad? (100)

> [I have always rather doubted the capacity of women for scientific research, and those little dolls that enter the university hunting for a degree to stick in their hair really rankle me, as though they didn't have enough adornment with all the flowers that God creates and all the laces the Devil invents. . . . But the Sciences . . . , it is true that few come to the Science Division, because what do they care about truth?]

Raimundo opines that women in universities are mere adornment; he views women primarily as mothers. He fears that his wife will go crazy from having read so much: "la invasión de filosofías y místicos que iba ella colocando con toda seriedad entre la austeridad de mis libros de ciencia. . . . Estudia con toda aplicación, porque tiene el vicio poco femenina de aprenderlo todo" (109) [the invasion of philosophy and mystics that she was placing with all seriousness among the austerity of my science books. . . . She studies diligently, because she has the rather unfeminine vice of learning everything].[20]

Hardly insane, Teresa displays strong powers of rational argument. Martínez Sierra follows Cervantes's lead in allowing a female voice to engage in sophisticated discourse about gender (I am thinking particularly of Marcela's speech to the shepherds), but she diverges from her male contemporaries who almost never give women characters the opportunity to make an intellectual argument. Teresa, for example, points out that in philosophical terms "man" refers to humanity in general, including women, whereas "woman" excludes masculine existence entirely: "Hombres somos todos, y mujeres nosotras, exclusivamente; luego no hay en la especie humana más que un ser diferente: la mujer" (12).[21] She argues that, because they are the differentiated category, only women exist. Women are the real and positive within humanity, and men are "mito, una fábula, que podemos versificar a nuestro antojo" (12). Of course, she goes on to point out that women forge their lives according to this myth and thus should not complain if things do not turn out as they wish: "Moraleja: 'La mujer que con *su hombre* entre las manos no acierta a ser feliz, merecida se tiene su desdicha . . . por tonta'" (12). Very likely, Martínez Sierra was reflecting on her own situation in which she had attached her writing career to her husband's name while he was involved with a mistress.

Martínez Sierra ends *El amor catedrático* with the academic married couple in Australia and Teófilo consoling himself with an Englishwoman. The narrative emphasizes that Teresa's marriage does not conform to traditional Spanish bourgeois expectations. Teresa's family is vehemently against the marriage; Raimundo describes the wedding as "abominable" (132), because his in-laws' hostility made the whole experience very unpleasant. Like the situation for Burgos's nontraditional couple in *Los anticuarios,* emigration from Spain is a means to escape an ambience in which an unconventional marriage is difficult to negotiate. Granada, the setting for Teófilo's final meditation, offers an opportunity to place the characters' sentiments within a national context. Teófilo, the more "modern" man, and the one not chosen, ends the novel with a contemplation of Spain's lingering traditions. The national meditation is rooted in Teófilo's views on the nature of Spanish womanhood. His brief affair with the Englishwoman Maud in the quintessential Spanish city Granada invites comparison between Maud and Teresa, whom he believes (perhaps erroneously) to be of "pura cepa española" (112). For her part, Maud refers to the backwardness of Spanish customs with respect to women. By juxtaposing Teófilo's reflections on Raimundo's having spirited Teresa away to Australia ("ese derecho perfecto y detestable, se ha llevado consigo a Teresita, su legítima esposa" [132]) with Maud's recollection, during a visit to the Alhambra, of the sequestration of women in Muslim Spain, the narrator insinuates that, where women are concerned, Spain has not progressed much in the past six centuries.

Teófilo's considerations of Spain's imperial past are intermingled with the reflections on Spanish women's historical enslavement. He melds marriage and nationalism in mutual disapproval, denouncing both matrimony and Carlos V, who reigned over Spain's largest empire. Carlos V was foreign, a "profanación del espíritu patrio" (136). He judges such nationalism ridiculous, "una solemne majadería" (136), an attitude he acquired as Teresa's university companion and as Raimundo's protégé (Raimundo being an "estupendo paradojista" [136]). Teresa, he believes, combines the paradoxical qualities of an absoluta anarchist within her Catholicism; she is charitable and full of common sense. Teresa also rejects nationalism, which conceives the world as carved up into tiny pieces; he quotes her as saying that "no hay más patria que el corazón de los que nos quieren" (136). For Teófilo, Teresa is the ideal woman because she is a religious traditionalist, accepts the female role as angel, and is an original thinker. As Janet Pérez notes (1988, 33), Martínez Sierra tended to portray Spanish women as superior to foreign women (recall the contrast between Ana María and Carmelina of *Tú eres la paz*), this despite her assertion in *Gregorio y yo*, "Me da náuseas todo nacionalismo" (1953, 20).

Teófilo, however, has difficulty overcoming his own nationalistic feelings, especially when certain national monuments move him to a desire for heroism in the cause of his country. For example, when he views the famous patio of the Alhambra, he receives the full impact of Spain's ruined greatness, its unfulfilled promise. He qualifies the feelings that the monument inspires in him as innocent (even puerile) but definitely masculine ("sin duda también masculina" [G. Martínez Sierra 1955, 136]). Teófilo avers that heroic times have waned in the face of a society ruled by law, "un estado de 'ley' que parece la negación absoluta de toda inteligencia" (138). When men legislate, they attempt to make static that which is infinitely mobile, in Teófilo's apt metaphor "aprisionar el agua en una cesta" (137). In Teófilo's view, the law cannot accommodate life's complexities, and his paradoxical ideas about women are true to the idea that life does not conform to absolutes. He defends women's right to sexual relations outside marriage, but he instinctually prefers women who are religious (Maud is a religious skeptic from a protestant background). Significantly, he dreams of the Catholic Teresa while he makes love to Maud. Despite his scorn for nationalism, Maud's stereotypical ideas about Spain irritate Teófilo, and he leaves her in Granada to return to his native Castile when he receives a letter from Teresa, his quixotic ideal of the perfect Spanish woman.

The practical ideal for interpersonal relations that Martínez Sierra forged in her 1910 novel became her basis for a new Spanish nation during her period of Republican and feminist militancy for the Republic in the 1920s. Teresa embodies feminine and intellectual qualities. As Alda Blanco points out, in the feminist essays that Martínez Sierra wrote between 1917 and 1932, she theorized the "wedding [of] femininity to feminism" (1998, 89). Emotions (such as ambition) are not incompatible with marriage, in "a new configuration of the couple, founded on companionship, which presumes economic and legal equality (92). Martínez Sierra argued for social emotions and education that would prepare women to be "dames-errant" whose "individual freedom [would] be intertwined with the desire for solidarity (93). In *Feminismo, feminidad, españolismo,* Martínez Sierra links feminism and nationalism. If mothers voted, she claims, education would improve to create better schools for future citizens (see G. Martínez Sierra 1917, 28). She exhorts women to employ their talents to help save Spain: "Piensen ustedes que si la Patria es como una madre para los hombres, para las mujeres es como un hijo. . . . Y ¿no les da a ustedes un poco de vergüenza que un hijo suyo esté en este momento haciendo tan triste papel en el mundo?" (42). Just as in *El amor catedrático,* in *Una mujer por caminos de España,* she considers Don Quixote's idealistic vision only to reject it for a more pragmatic model. In her journeys across Spain to raise workers' consciousness for the Republic, Martínez Sierra found that Don Quixote's futile idealism was a formidable obstacle to practical materialism:

Quería repetir "in mente" conceptos doctrinales estudiados con encarnizamiento: lucha de clases, plus-valía, organización sindical. . . . ¡Uníos, proletarios de todos los países. . . ! En vano: la magra figura del 'Caballero bien molido y mal andante a quien llevó Rocinante por uno y otro sendero' se obstinaba en alzarse frente a mí, ocultaban las barbas formidables y el fuego de los ojos de Carlos Marx. (M. Martínez Sierra 1989, 83)

[I wanted to invoke doctrinal concepts studied with anger: class struggle, value added, union organization. . . . Unite, workers of all countries. . . ! In vain: the lean figure of the 'battered and poorly errant knight whom Rocinante carried on various roads' insistently rose before me, hiding Karl Marx's formidable beard and fiery eyes.]

Martínez Sierra, like Espina in *La esfinge maragata,* suggests that Spain's solution to its problems must include an idealistic and a material dimension.

Other national types overshadowed the Quixote intertext after the second decade, when new national discourses on gender arose. However, Azorín reconfigured the Quixote model in his 1928 *Félix Vargas*—which he retitled *El caballero inactual,* more closely recalling the Gentleman of la Mancha—in a way that indicates that he was keeping fully abreast of the transformations that were occurring in women's lives in his country. If Don Quixote's attempt to resurrect the Middle Ages in the fifteenth century rendered him "inactual," Félix Vargas removes himself from twentieth-century Spain by immersing himself in the eighteenth century. Don Quixote was a reader of novels set in the chivalric age; Félix is writing a book on eighteenth-century women who were associated with Benjamin Constant—Madame Charrière, Madame de Staël, and Juliette Récamier. Like Don Quixote, Félix joins the contemporary world at the end of the novel, thanks to the intervention of real, modern (as opposed to fictional or historical) women.

Early in the novel, Félix receives a letter from the secretary of the Madrid Fémina-Club that interrupts his deep concentration on the eighteenth-century project. The letter requests that he give a seminar on Santa Teresa to the Club's members. The remainder of the novel focuses on Félix's struggle first to decide whether to write the lectures on Santa Teresa and, once decided, then to actually compose them. He finishes the lectures but only after an encounter with a living modern female—the French woman Andrea. The three types of women—the eighteenth-century French intellectuals, the sixteenth-century nun and founder of convents Santa Teresa, and the modern, independent Andrea—contribute to Félix's *inactualidad,* his lack of contemporaneousness, as well as to his ultimate integration into the contemporary world.

Significantly, four of the women who impinge on his consciousness are French; the only Spanish woman is the temporally remote Santa Teresa. The five women provoke the kind of contrast between the gender mores of Spain and those of other Western European countries that we have seen in *Tú eres la paz* and *El amor catedrático* and that we will see in novelettes by Burgos. The message about contemporary Spanish women (especially women with intellectual pretensions) is not very optimistic, although the ending of the novel indicates that men must take the modern version of womanhood into account if they are to negotiate life successfully in the twentieth century. The letter from the Fémina-Club, doubtless a reference to the Lyceum Club founded in 1926 by María de Maeztu to public criticism from conservative men and the clergy, is the first allusion to contemporary Spanish women. María Granés, the author of the letter, may well represent Maeztu.

Azorín's references to the Lyceum Club (the Fémina-Club) in *El caballero inactual* are ambiguous and do not represent the same degree of irreverent satire rendered by other male writers and intellectuals toward the club outlined in the Introduction to this book. The descriptions of Granés are fairly typical of descriptions of women in Spanish vanguard novels by such writers as Ramón Gómez de la Serna, Benjamín Jarnés, and Pedro Salinas. These authors emphasize women's physical features and exclude female subjectivity. Félix's portrait of Granés focuses on her body rather than on her intellectual qualities. She is "llenita, redonda, todo curvas. Dos curvas de las mejillas, dos curvas los hombros; curva moderada del pecho; dos curvas, sentada, de finas rodillas" (31) [full, round, all curves. The cheeks two curvas, the shoulders two curves; moderate curve of the breast; seated, two curves of fine knees]. Granés's voice is "melosa, dulce, que dice cosas—como algarabía de pájaros—que no se comprenden. Y en eso está el encanto. Sólo al final del enzarzamiento de las frases flébiles y melifluas, la muletilla que Marujita dice saliendo de su melancolía e intentando sonreír: *¿No verdad?*" (31–32) [honeyed, sweet, that says incomprehensible things—like birds' jabber. And that is the charm. Only at the end of the entanglement of the plaintive and mellifluous sentences, emerging from her melancholy and trying to smile, Marujita utters her pet phrase: *Isn't that right?*]. After the observation on her voice, he returns to her curvaceous body, now introducing the voice in a mocking fashion: "Docenas, centenares de curvitas graciosas surgen de pronto en el aire, por todo el ámbito de la casa; curvitas en todas partes. *¿No verdad?* . . . María Granés; su comba pectoral suave; su palabra balbuciente de niña. Y sus abandonos lánguidos, vigorosos. 'Con toda vehemencia'" (32). [Dozens, hundreds of charming little curves arise suddenly in the air, throughout the space of the entire house; little curves everywhere. *Isn't that right?* . . . María Granés; with her soft pectoral curve; her babbling girlish talk. And her languid and vigorous abandonments. "With all vehemence."][22]

Félix's intellectual trajectory, which depends entirely on women, reflects that of Constant with the three French women who are the subject of Félix's book. These women served Constant as important interlocutors while he was elaborating his political theories. During many years, Madame Charrière, although (or perhaps because) she was a monarchist and did not share Constant's Republican ideas, received letters from Constant in which he developed his ideas on the French Revolution and refined his concept of human liberty. In 1785, Constant met Madame de Staël at a critical juncture in the development of his political thought. As she also supported a republic, he was able to continue conceptualizing the ideal Republican state in her company. After the successive failures of the French Republic, Constant began to theorize a monarchical form of government around 1813–14. About that time, he met Récamier, a monarchist, who doubtless encouraged this new direction in Constant's political thought.[23] It is impossible to imagine Constant's life and work without his intellectual and personal relationships with women, just as Felix's life and work depend first on his imaginary relationships with Constant's women and Santa Teresa and finally on his physical relationship with Andrea, whose image becomes intertwined with that of the Saint of Ávila.

Azorín's novel is essentially about the writing process and how it intersects with reality. Félix's immersion in the eighteenth century to the point that he experiences a rapport with the three French women intellectuals ("Félix Vargas vive en la segunda mitad del siglo XVIII francés" [12]) reveals how a writer abandons present reality and acquires a secondary reality based on images that form the written text: "Desaparece la casita colocada en la colina verde. Las imágenes reemplazan a la realidad" (12). In this way, Spain also disappears for Félix, a sensation that gives him great pleasure until the letter from the members of the Fémina-Club jolts him back to reality with their desire to escape their domestic chores in a seminar on Santa Teresa.

Their choice of subject—a sixteenth-century nun—might seem retrograde for a feminist group. Pardo Bazán interpreted Azorín's own interest in the Saint in this way: "'Su impresión de usted tan entusiasta para la gran Santa de Ávila confirma lo que manifesté a usted hace pocos días: La evolución que predije a usted. España no tiene más que pasado; pero un pasado que nos atrae a todos en razón de las deficiencias y las miserias del presente'" (qtd. in Azorín 1962, 286). [The impression you give of enthusiasm for the great saint of Ávila confirms what I indicated to you a few days ago: the evolution I predicted. Spain does not have anything but past, but a past that attracts us all because of the deficiencies and miseries of the present.] Azorín explains that in this context, the word "evolution" has a special meaning; it is not the "explicación del momento presente," but rather "el culto del pasado y el culto a lo presente se entretejen; políticamente, de una escuela ha derivado a otra" (286) [explanation of the present moment but rather the cult of the past and the cult of the present that intertwine; politically one school has derived from the other]. Azorín clearly attributes to Doña Emilia the same concept of time that he himself held—the simultaneity of past and present, which he depicts in the women of three different epochs.

In *El caballero inactual,* Madame Charrière, Madame de Staël, and Julia Récamier are more or less liberated intellectual women; they stand on a middle ground between tradition and modernity, whereas Santa Teresa might occupy a more traditional position as a nun. But Santa Teresa and twentieth-century women share characteristics. Santa Teresa was much more than a religious woman. She was an entrepreneur who founded the Carmelite order and a number of convents. During his long journalistic career, Azorín wrote a series of articles about Santa Teresa in which he admired her energy; he believed that she symbolized an originary national force. In an 1898 article published in *Madrid Cómico*, he characterized her as a national hero because of the difficulty of her undertakings, and although he does not mention Cervantes's character, he portrays her as a kind of Quixote.

When Félix begins to write his lectures for the Fémina-Club, he proposes to transfer the energy that Santa Teresa manifested in the Spanish imperial age to contemporary Spain: "Habría que hacer una Santa Teresa moderna, palpitante, viviendo con nosotros ahora" (Azorín 1965, 24). He attempts to weld the present and the past, imagining Santa Teresa in an automobile with a telegram in her hand. But these devices do not help him bring the Saint to life in a way that allows him to complete his lectures. He needs a contemporary experience, so he travels to Biarritz, leaving behind his books about the past. In Biarritz, he is surrounded with all the trappings of modernity—crowds; automobiles; sounding horns; beautiful, sensual women—and he renews his relationship with Andrea, the catalyst he needs to complete the work on Santa Teresa.

Andrea is married, but she lives an independent life; she represents the modern European woman that Spanish women were only beginning to imitate (for example, the Lyceum Club was modeled on British and U.S. women's clubs). The image of the Spanish woman in locations such as Ávila or Levante evokes for Félix a serene female with melancholy eyes. Andrea, in contrast, is "dependencia e independiente; sujeta a Esteban [her husband] y no sujeta" (82) [dependence and independent; subject to Esteban and not subject to him]. Thanks to the encounter with Andrea, Félix is finally able to capture Santa Teresa's physical being. He especially imagines her feet shod in red and black leather shoes with tight silk stockings instead of the traditional nun's sandals.

Like Maud of *El amor catedrático*, Andrea utters a litany of clichés about Spain as a nation. Andrea and Félix see a Spanish marchioness on the street one day, and Andrea envisions her carrying a little knife like Carmen in the Bizet opera. In her playful summary of what she considers essential Spanish institutions and customs, she also evokes bullfights, *olla podrida,* castles, castanets, autos-da-fé, and the fandango. Andrea's clichés help Félix achieve the necessary perspective on Santa Teresa as a representative of the soul of Spain. The parallels between the saint and modern life are located in her restless nature, *"esa monja andariega"* (101, emphasis in original), and the speed of a telegram. Félix finishes his lectures on Santa Teresa with frenetic acceleration. Finally, the Fémina-Club's request has imposed itself on Félix's career as a writer. He completes the lectures, which will constitute a book, thanks to the presence of the modern French woman Andrea. Thus, the "caballero inactual" turns out to be much more contemporary than he at first appears, especially in his understanding of modern Spain as incorporating the energy and capabilities of independent and talented women. Felix, like Don Quixote, awakens from his romance with the past, but he is not disillusioned, and does not die. He revises his view of reality to incorporate past and present. Significantly, this novel, which alludes to Republicanism via Constant's writings and his association with Madame de Staël, was published on the eve of the Spanish Second Republic so important to women's progress in Spain.

In this novel of the 1920s, Azorín shed much of his interest in an eternal Spanish tradition that propelled his earlier borrowings from the Spanish classics, and he updated his portrayal of women's roles. Like Unamuno and Miró, however, he still found it difficult to accept modern womanhood fully (to wit, the parodic portraits of Maeztu; the Lyceum Club; and Andrea, the frivolous flapper). Espina and Martínez Sierra are much more comfortable with a de-Dulcineafied Spanish woman. Don Quixote as a national icon served as a fulcrum on which male and female Spanish modernists could leverage their ideas about how sexual roles and gender relations inside and outside of marriage should be negotiated in early twentieth-century Spain. As José Álvarez Junco remarks, "Cervantes era el símbolo político perfecto, porque su obra admitía todas las interpretaciones: desde la nacional-católica . . . a la nietzcheana, pasando por la racionalista . . . la antiburguesa o la meramente 'entretenida' " (2001, 590). [Cervantes was the perfect political symbol, because his work allowed all interpretations: from the national-

Catholic . . . to the Nietzschean, passing through the rationalist . . . the antibourgeois or the merely "entertaining."] The figure of the deluded but valiant chivalric knight, whose medieval dreams and exploits were out of sync with seventeenth-century Spain, was an enticing metaphor for the clash of mores between early twentieth-century Spanish social conservatives and liberals. As Chapter 3 shows, Don Quixote shared that role with the equally ambiguous Don Juan Tenorio, who lent himself to a wide variety of modernist interpretations.

CHAPTER 3
The Domestication of a Modernist Don Juan

After José Zorrilla debuted a romantic version of the classic Don Juan legend in 1844, the figure increasingly became associated with national values. José Álvarez Junco notes the role of historical novels and plays in creating a public sense of national tradition in the nineteenth century (both Tirso de Molina's original play and Zorrilla's reworking take place in the Spanish imperial sixteenth century). Álvarez Junco especially emphasizes the importance of masculine virility to the Spanish sense of nation; the Spanish readiness to sword and heroic deeds ("raza de valientes" [2001, 247]) are attributes associated with both Tirso's and Zorrilla's versions of Don Juan. In addition, the Catholic message of Zorrilla's play, which redeems Don Juan, coincided with the Catholic conservatism that increasingly dominated Spain's national image in the later years of the reign of Isabel II. In the nineteenth century (and similarly in the twentieth century), Don Juan was the subject of disperse and often conflicting renditions. For example, David Gies (1994) has noted the many nineteenth-century parodies of Zorrilla's romantic (and redemptive) recasting of Tirso's condemnation of the seducer of women and defier of society's norms.[1]

By the time Don Juan arrives at the modernist turn of the century, he comes laden with a confusing variety of national meanings. Don Juan, like Don Quixote, lent himself to a wide array of political and philosophical ideals; for some he continued to serve as an emblem of national energy, whereas for others he was a decadent degenerate who reflected Spain's contemporary diminished state. Don Juan's overtly sexual nature (as compared to Don Quixote's asceticism) gave rise to even more complex intertwinings of messages about gender and the Spanish nation than did the chaste Knight of La Mancha. In the modernist period, the quintessentially male Don Juan assumes ambiguous sexual connotations, a layer of nuance that was often a metaphor for a troubled nation. Thus, Don Juan became a significant site on which both male and female writers could locate their considerations of gender roles in modern Spain.

This chapter concentrates on a series of modernist reworkings of the Don Juan theme that transform and often eviscerate the unbridled sexual vigor of Tirso's Don Juan, which embodied the energy of imperial power. Very early in the century, the Marqués de Bradomín, protagonist of Ramón del Valle-Inclán's *Sonatas* marshals an elaborate set of literary devices to deflect his moral responsibility and gain sympathy for himself despite his moral transgressions. Valle-Inclán's linguistically competent modernist Don Juan inspired a number of parodies, significantly, many of them by women. Female writers especially reacted to the male modernist's neutralization of Don Juan's socially subversive nature and his elimination of Tirso's and Zorrilla's condemnation of Don Juan's immoral behavior toward women.

Later, other male modernist writers joined Valle-Inclán in adopting the original Don Juan's myriad possibilities to their own nationalist agenda. Valle-Inclán began the process of cleansing Don Juan of his socially irresponsible dimension only to find in him a symbol of eternal, essential Spain and a symbol of Spain's contemporary dilemma as a tradition-bound country seeking to enter the modern world. Miguel de Unamuno and Azorín completed this process in the following decades by respectively transforming Don Juan into an existential hero and a mystic. Valle-Inclán's recasting of Don Juan is less extreme; it retains Don Juan's promiscuous nature but fuses it with ironic self-consciousness and nostalgia for Spanish tradition that imbues it with modern moral neutrality. S. Lázaro Montero notes that the Generation of '98 found both Tirso's condemnation of Don Juan and Zorrilla's salvation of him too extreme: "Ni el Paraíso ni el Infierno. Es mejor el Purgatorio" (qtd. in Martínez Cachero 1960, 124).

Ramiro de Maeztu (María de Maeztu's brother), a contemporary of Valle-Inclán's, Unamuno's, and Azorín's, associated Don Juan's reappearance in modernist iconography with the malaise of his generation.[2] He believed that his own time was, like the seventeenth century when Don Juan first appeared, a troubled era in Spanish history. If the seventeenth-century crisis was a response to the waning Counter-Reformation, the modern turning point was the 1898 war. Like the post–Counter-Reformation period, post-1898 Spain marked a "crisis del nacionalismo" or "crisis de ideales" (1925, 175). The Generation of '98 and the one that followed were marked by "confusión y polémica" (174). According to Maeztu, Don Juan appeared as an irrefutable example of the failure of humanism to reduce good to what is good for man. Don Juan represents what many Spaniards would like to embody—God-given power and energy that require no effort to generate and maintain, "la fuerza por gracia, y no por mérito" (178). Don Juan is an ideal, dream, or myth of immense energy channeled into pleasure, because in moments of crisis, according to Maeztu, we cannot find any other outlets for human endeavor.[3] He equated the modernist crisis with the loss of faith in the possibilities of science; in this uncertain climate, Don Juan reemerges because he marks an alternative to choosing specific ideals. As we shall see, the Marqués de Bradomín redirects his desire for military glory to sexual conquest; even his Carlism is aesthetic rather than ideological.

The Marqués—who, according to Antonio Vilanova, is "la figura donjuanesca y galante . . . cuyo perfil decadentista y romántico le convierte en una versión modernista y actualizada del tipo eterno de Don Juan" (1981, 376) [the donjuanesque and gallant figure . . . whose decadent and romantic profile converts him into a modernist and updated version of the eternal Don Juan type]—appeared almost simultaneously with Spain's loss of empire in 1898: *Sonata de otoño* (1902), *Sonata de estío* (1903), *Sonata de primavera* (1904), and *Sonata de invierno* (1905).[4] In his memoirs, the Marqués nostalgically attempts to resurrect the imperial glories of Spain and the heroism that they afforded conquerors like Hernán Cortés. Valle-Inclán said of his own creation that he was attempting to deal with an eternal theme: "Don Juan es un tema eterno y nacional; pero Don Juan no es esencialmente conquistador de mujeres; se caracteriza también por la impiedad y por el desacato a las leyes y a los hombres" (qtd. in Vilanova 1981, 376, without citation). [Don Juan is an eternal and national theme; but Don Juan is not essentially a conqueror of women; he is also characterized by lack of piety and respect for the law and for men.][5]

For Maeztu, Don Juan represents "cabal españolismo," and Valle-

Inclán counted on Don Juan's national identification in fashioning his Marqués de Bradomín. Maeztu traced the origins of the Don Juan figure and his story to medieval *romances;* he located all the elements that we associate with the Don Juan legend in the Spanish literary tradition and in traditional Spanish customs. The trickster/seducer exists in legend and in works before Tirso's seventeenth-century play (the invitation issued to a dead man occurs in popular ballads, the stone statue has its counterpart in church sarcophagi, the table setting at the funeral banquet is taken from Spanish family practices, and the staging of Zorrilla's play on All Soul's Day is related to the church banquets in honor of the dead). Maeztu associates Don Juan's arrogant, unintellectual nature with the soul of Spain: "Juan es soberbio, no es escéptico, no es intelectual. España no es intelectual ni para dudar, ni para creer" (1925, 146). According to Maeztu, Don Juan is, by definition, a man of appetites without ideals, and Spain has lived without ideals for several centuries; therein lies the "españolismo de Don Juan" (126). Maeztu argues that Don Juan's problem is analogous to the Spanish problem; in understanding his character, we understand Spain: "Lo malo de Don Juan es que no pone su valor al servicio de los ideales superiores que son nuestros deberes, sino al de su albedrío y su sensibilidad" (132). He is incapable of fusing his self ("yo") with the world. Valle-Inclán's modernist rendition of the character incorporates all of these dimensions; he is a harbinger of Spanish traditions in many of his habits and preferences, and his ego prevails over all else. He stands alone against the world: "—Los españoles nos dividimos en dos grandes bandos: Uno, el Marqués de Bradomín, y en el otro, todos los demás" (qtd. in Maeztu 1925, 107). [We Spaniards are divided into two large groups: One, the Marqués de Bradomín and the other, everyone else.]

The two *Sonatas* that narrate a more youthful Marqués are staged in settings reminiscent of the sixteenth-century Spanish empire. The Marqués casts his chronologically first memoir, *Sonata de primavera,* in Italy, where as a captain in the Noble Guard to the Pope, he is the Holy Father's special envoy to the Bishop Gaetani.[6] Both Tirso's and Zorrilla's Don Juans spend time in Carlos V's imperial army in Italy; thus, the Marqués's mission in Italy evokes the imperial ties that Spain once enjoyed with Naples. As Michael Predmore has pointed out, the

Marqués's sojourn in the Episcopal city Ligura is marked by an initial success. Princess Gaetani and her family, whose palace and lifestyle call up the splendor of another age, embrace him and accord him full honors. After his attempt to seduce the princess's daughter, however, he falls out of favor and eventually leaves Ligura in disgrace, defeated both personally and politically.

The second *Sonata* takes place in Mexico, where the Marqués travels to see family holdings acquired during the Spanish conquest of New Spain in earlier centuries. He specifically wishes to recapture the feelings of "un aventurero de otros tiempos" (Valle-Inclán 1963, 84). As Jesús Torrecilla has noted, "El viaje del marqués posee una proyección colectiva y obedece a un impulso de repetir viejas hazañas" (1998, 43). [The Marqués's travels have a collective sense and obey an impulse to repeat old feats.] When the Marqués arrives in Veracruz, his heart swells with enthusiasm; his mind is bursting with glorious visions and historical memories. His noble Christian adventurer's soul feels like losing itself forever in "la vastedad del viejo Imperio Azteca" (98). The Mother Superior of a convent where he and his paramour, the untamed Creole Niña Chole, spend a night articulates his nostalgia for the social structures of another era: "¡Qué destino el de las nobles casas y qué tiempos tan ingratos son los nuestros! En todas partes gobiernan los enemigos de la religión y de las tradiciones, aquí lo mismo que en España" (113). His relationship with Niña Chole is reminiscent of that of the conquerors with Aztec princesses: "Sin duda la Niña Chole era como aquellas princesas que sentían el amor al ser ultrajadas y vencidas" (105).

Carlism affords the Marqués an opportunity to indulge his traditionalism in the last two *Sonatas*. In *Sonata de otoño*, the Marqués refers to his activity in the Carlist wars, but the action that he narrates in that novel is of a more sedentary modern gentleman. The novel takes place almost entirely at the estate of his cousin/lover, Concha, the Palace of Brandeso, which she has fancifully turned into a relic of the Middle Ages, including hiring a page who trains birds to sing. In *Sonata de invierno*, he recalls his participation in the last Carlist War (1873–76), his most active role in his attempt to restore Spain's traditional past. As a Carlist, the Marqués is an adherent of the remaining vestiges of the political faction that struggled against the liberal regime of Isabel II to maintain the political and social structures of the ancien régime. When he yearns for a past that perhaps existed only in books of chivalry, he visits Don Carlos's wife, Doña Margarita: "Comprendí entonces todo el ingenuo sentimiento que hay en los libros de caballerías, y aquel culto por la belleza y las lágrimas femeniles que hacía palpitar bajo la cota el corazón de Tirante el Blanco. . . . Era una lealtad de otros siglos la que inspiraba Doña Margarita" (Valle-Inclán 1989, 195). [Then I understood all the ingenuous sentiment that books of chivalry contain and that worship of female beauty and tears that makes Tirante el Blanco's heart beat beneath his coat of mail. . . . It was a loyalty from other centuries that Doña Margarita inspired.] A reactionary, patriarchal movement countered Spanish liberalism, which was intimately bound up with a female monarch. However, unlike the triumphs of Spain's imperial armies in Italy and the New World in the time of Tirso's Don Juan, the Marqués's Carlists are defeated, and symbolically the Marqués loses an arm for his last valorous effort. Like his country, now a weary shadow of his former self, he is reduced to futile nostalgia about what he once was.

Significantly, the Marqués's remembrances of his adventures, so replete with resonances of Spain's imperial past, focus in each case on a woman. Thus, combined in one character is the sexual promiscuity of the classic Don Juan figure and the conservatism of a nineteenth-century reactionary. His prowess as a soldier fuses with his prowess as a lover, and his fortunes with women parallel his soldierly defeats. His nostalgia is twofold—for a strong, powerful nation and for his ability to attract forbidden women. He has enamored a beautiful aristocratic girl bound for the convent *(Sonata de primavera)*, a hot-blooded cruel Creole in the tropics *(Sonata de estío)*, and his exquisite married cousin *(Sonata de otoño)*. By *Sonata de otoño*, however, the focus of his seductive powers resides in an ill and dying Concha rather than in the healthy woman with whom he began their affair several years before. In *Sonata de invierno*, the last installment, his married lover elects to remain with her husband and breaks off her affair with him. The only seduction that he manages is of his own daughter in a scandalously incestuous affair that results in the girl's suicide. In both his political and his sexual life, the Marqués proves to be, as Joaquín Casalduero has noted, a "paladín de una causa perdida" (1954, 21). Although in *Sonata de invierno* he can still say that he loves the glorious purple of blood and the sacking of villages, he also feels an "acabamiento de todas las ilusiones, un profundo desengaño de todas las cosas. . . . Era el primer frío de la vejez" (Valle-Inclán 1989, 10) [end of all hopes, a profound disillusionment with all things. . . . It was the first chill of old age].

Vilanova has gathered a great deal of evidence that points to Valle-Inclán's reliance on Unamuno's theories of *intrahistoria* (the eternal tradition of Spain) in creating the Marqués. As shown in Chapter 1, although Unamuno believed that Spanish tradition was embedded in its Golden Age classics, he also thought that it was time to put those cultured traditions aside, since they exalted Spain's defects and moribund ideas. Spain now needed to allow the eternal soul of the Spanish people to guide the nation into the modern era of Europeanization. Vilanova argues that this is precisely what Valle-Inclán attempted in Bradomín: "Frente al realism fotográfico de costumbristas y naturalistas vuelve a la creación de tipos eternos, es exactamente el mismo que intenta llevar a cabo el Valle-Inclán de las *Sonatas*, remozando la tradición eterna del Don Juan con una sensibilidad europea, universal y cosmopolita" (1981, 371). [In the face of the photographic realism of naturalists and portrayers of customs, he returns to the creation of eternal types; this is exactly what Valle-Inclán attempts to do in the *Sonatas*, rejuvenating the eternal tradition of Don Juan with a universal, cosmopolitan European sensibility.] José Antonio Maravall, however, argues against a notion of *intrahistoria* in Valle-Inclán:

> Valle-Inclán cultiva, no la intrahistoria—no comprendo como se pueda hablar de ello en este autor—, sino esa antihistoria que es la tradición legendaria. . . . Su estética, su filosofía, su política, se relacionan con la visión estática de una sociedad arcaica. La realidad no está hecha, para él, en forma de cadena, cuyos eslabones se suceden y avanzan, sino de "círculos concéntricos al modo que los engendra la piedra en la laguna." (1966, 122)
>
> [Valle-Inclán does not cultivate intrahistory (I do not understand how one can talk of such in this author) but rather an antihistory that is the legendary tradition. . . . His aesthetics, his philosophy, his politics are related to

the static vision of an archaic society. For him, reality is not made in the form of a chain whose links follow one another and progress but rather in "concentric circles like those formed by a stone in a lake."]

According to Maravall, Valle-Inclán's main objective was to find an alternative to bourgeois constitutionalism, and he was especially hostile to the reign of Isabel II, whom he satirized mercilessly during his entire career. However one chooses to interpret Valle-Inclán's view of history, as I argue below, his *Sonatas* seem undeniably to exhibit nostalgia for the past.

The domestication of Don Juan effected by early twentieth-century women writers had already begun in Valle-Inclán's Marqués. For all his yearning to recover past glory, the Marqués is a quintessentially modernist character, especially in his moral ambiguity. As I have noted, his Carlism is more aesthetic than ideological: "Yo hallé siempre más bella la majestad caída que sentada en el trono y fui defensor de la tradición por estética" (1989, 216–17). Critics have diverged widely on just exactly what he represents—for some, he is either a devilish Don Juan or a benign Casanova; for others, he is allied with the dandy; for others, he matches the epigram to the first edition of the *Sonata de otoño*, which characterizes him as "feo, católico, y sentimental" (185); for still others, he defies these categories.[7]

There is evidence that Valle-Inclán shared the Marqués de Bradomín's nostalgia for a Spain with a stronger sense of purpose. In the more autobiographical *La lámpara maravillosa*, he states:

> Cuando yo era mozo, la gloria literaria y la gloria aventurera me tentaron por igual. Fue un momento lleno de voces oscuras, de un vasto rumor ardiente y místico, para el cual se hacía sonoro todo mi ser como un caracol de los mares. De aquella gran voz atávica y desconocida sentí el aliento como un vaho de horno, y el son como un murmullo de marea que me llenó de inquietud y de perplejidad. . . . De niño, y aun de mozo, la historia de los capitanes aventureros, violenta y fiera, me había dado una emoción más honda que la lunaria tristeza de los poetas: Era el estremecimiento y el fervor con que debe anunciarse la vocación religiosa. Yo no admiraba tanto los hechos hazañosos, como el temple de las almas, y este apasionado sentimiento me sirvió, igual que una hoguera, para purificar mi Disciplina Estética. (1916, 21–23)

[When I was a boy, literary glory and adventursome glory tempted me equally. It was a time full of dark voices, a vast burning and mystical sound, which made my whole being sonorous like a conch shell. I felt the breath of that great unknown atavistic voice like a blast from an oven, and the sound like the murmur of the sea that filled me with disquiet and perplexity. . . . As a child, and even as a youth, the story of violent and fierce adventuresome captains had filled me with a deeper emotion than the lunary sadness of the poets: It was the shiver and the fervor with which one should announce religious vocation. I so admired heroic deeds and courageous souls, and this impassioned feeling served as a bonfire to purify my Aesthetic Discipline.]

Valle-Inclán did not limit his desire for adventure to his imagination and his pen. His family's claim to relations with the old Galician nobility inspired chivalrous sentiments in the author. In the early 1890s, he traveled to Mexico, where he later falsely claimed that he served in the Mexican military. On his return, he assumed the guise of a romantic author in the style of José Zorrilla or Gustavo Adolfo, with long hair and beard and a black cloak. He joined Ricardo Baroja on an expedition to search for treasure in a mine, an adventure that culminated with Valle-Inclán's shooting himself in the leg. He began writing *Sonata de otoño* while he recuperated from the wound. Fusing his own life with that of the Marqués de Bradomín, Valle-Inclán wrote an autobiography for the December 1903 edition of the journal *Alma Española,* in which he incorporated whole passages from his *Sonatas.*

If Valle-Inclán seems to have shared some of the Marqués de Bradomín's nostalgia for a past when men could be heroic adventurers, he also wished to turn back the clock where women were concerned. Valle-Inclán certainly had no use for women in public life. He included feminism among three "tópicos horribles," along with the workers' movements and Americanism. During the 1920s, he was asked what future he would assign to women in Spain. His reply was categorical: "—¡Pero hombre! ¡Qué cosas! ¡Las mujeres! A las pobres se las puede hacer unicamente la justicia de la conocida frase de Schopenhauer. ¡Y ahora ya ni siquiera tienen los cabellos largos! En la presente civilización . . . no tienen que hacer más las mujeres" (qtd. in Arbeloa and Santiago 1981,

318). [But man! What are you saying! Women! One can only do them the justice of Schopenhauer's well-known phrase. And now they don't even have long hair! In the present civilization . . . women have nothing further to do.] His *Sonatas* and other early writings reveal that his idea of women's place in the social spectrum did not change over the more than forty years of his career.

Perhaps the most important modernist element of Valle-Inclán's Don Juan is that he is a writer of fictions, and his most important creation is himself.[8] He distances himself and his past through *modernista* language and the many literary references that he draws on to construct his literary persona. Although no less self-serving than the classic confessions of Saint Augustine and Jean-Jacques Rousseau, the Marqués's "confessions" shift the man-God or man-society relationship to new ground. Bradomín can imagine himself only in relation to a woman, a woman who adores him absolutely and unconditionally. María Rosario of *Sonata de primavera* follows Ophelia into madness over the Marqués's Hamlet-like indifference; la Niña Chole of *Sonata de estío* defies a brutal father/husband for the Marqués's company; the tubercular Concha of *Sonata de otoño* hastens her own death when she complies with the Marqués's sexual demands (he laments Concha's death as the loss of a personal idolater); and the Marqués's own daughter, Maximina *(Sonata de invierno)* commits suicide rather than face her incestuous love for her father.

The Marqués is terrified to realize at the end of *Sonata de invierno* that he no longer appeals to women. He is overcome with the sense of an existential loss of self: "Cuando se tiene un brazo de menos y la cabeza llena de canas, es preciso renunciar al donjuanismo. ¡Ay, yo sabía que los ojos aterciopelados y tristes que se habían abierto para mí como dos florecillas franciscanas en una luz de amanecer, serían los últimos que me mirasen con amor! Ya sólo me estaba bien enfrente de las mujeres la actitud de un ídolo roto, indiferente y frío" (Valle-Inclán 1989, 185). [When one has an arm missing and a head full of gray hair, one has to give up donjuanism. Ay, I knew that those velvety, sad eyes that had opened for me like two little Franciscan flowers in the dawn light would be the last to look at me with love! Now I could only assume the posture of a broken, indifferent, cold idol in front of women.] When María Antonieta, the one woman who still loves him, renounces him to care for her invalid husband, he turns to writing his memoirs. Bradomín thus keeps alive the self that thrives only in the presence of female adoration by recalling and inscribing on paper his past conquests. Significantly, it is a woman, the Marqués's aunt, who formulates what is apparently his favorite description of himself: "Eres el más admirable de los Don Juanes: Feo, católico y sentimental" (185). By emphasizing the Marqués's Catholicism, Valle-Inclán further identifies him as a symbol of the Spanish nation, which, as we have seen, Álvarez Junco considers a dominant characteristic of Spanish nationalism by the end of the nineteenth century.

What distinguishes the female versions of the Don Juan/Bradomín figure from Valle-Inclán's is a notable absence of the kind of parody or irony that Valle-Inclán employed to situate the Marqués in an ambiguous space where neither his ridiculous nor his sentimental side predominates.[9] Irony cuts two ways, as Ross Chambers points out; it can be subversive, "[turn] the tables on the discourse of power," but it can also be enlisted to affirm a conservative position: "Those tables can always be turned again and ironic distance shown to be in complicity with what it opposes" (1991, 101). Although "irony judges," as Linda Hutcheon indicates, it can also reaffirm: "It is as potentially conservative a force as corrective, deriding laughter. Parody, which deploys irony in order to establish the critical distance necessary to its formal definition, also betrays a tendency toward conservatism, despite the fact that it has been hailed as the paradigm of aesthetic revolution and historical change" (1985, 53, 67–68). Women novelists of the early twentieth century employed irony primarily from an objective (realist) narrative standpoint to judge social ills and to secure an ethical position. Valle-Inclán's first-person narrator harnesses the other side of irony—its wry smile, its indulgent wink—to license and legitimize by means of humor and narrator-reader complicity what is in effect deviant or morally unacceptable behavior. For just such reasons as this, Julia Kristeva denigrates parody (which Hutcheon considers the master genre of irony), because parodic literature fosters the principle of *"law anticipating its own transgression"* (1980, 71).

The ironic-parodic cast of the Marqués de Bradomín's narration of his licentious life softens the repulsive nature of his posturing, his egotism and self-aggrandizement. "Boys will be boys" is the interlinear message of the *Sonatas*. It is not surprising that Nietzsche, archenemy of the polarization of morality in terms of good and evil, should have sympathized with a wish to mask one's identity: "I could imagine that a human being who had to guard something precious and vulnerable might roll through life, rude and round as an old green wine cask with heavy hoops; the refinement of his shame would want it that way" (qtd. in Behler 1990, 96). As Ruth House Webber points out (1964, 135), the Marqués's *bagatela* echoes the devaluation of all values in Nietzsche, one of modernism's most pernicious purveyors of invective against women.

Women novelists rejected Valle-Inclán's narratorial positioning of the Don Juan figure as a parodic, self-aware seducer whose sentimentality "saves" him from moral condemnation. They inscribed Don Juan in more real, contemporary settings that undermine his image as a positive national symbol whose masculine energy and links to the Spanish past are qualities that can in some way redeem the nation. The male seducer represented a serious threat to women's precarious position in a bourgeois milieu, at a time when the "angel of the house" archetype was the preferred model for female behavior. The seducer's disruption of peaceful bourgeois life is the subject of the Spanish nineteenth century's two best novels—Benito Pérez Galdós's *Fortunata y Jacinta* (1886–87) and Leopoldo Alas's (Clarín's) *La Regenta* (1884).[10] The woman who did not conform to the hallowed ideals of motherhood and purity had two options: prostitution or the convent. Employment in domestic service was often denied the woman who was viewed as licentious or "fallen,"[11] and since Valle-Inclán ironizes and parodies the male who leads the female into the realm of the forbidden, his invariable representation of women in romantic/*modernista*/decadentist terms haunts the female literary imagination in a particularly ominous way.

A number of novels authored by women during the years following the publication of the *Sonatas* betray anxiety about Valle-Inclán's cavalier portrayal of the male "othering" of the female. Modernist women writers like María Martínez Sierra, Blanca de los Ríos, Sofía Casanova, Concha Espina, and Carmen de Burgos seem to have known, long before studies of the media's impact on society's behavior, that representation can contribute powerfully to prolonging social ills or combatting them. Each found narrative recourses for unmasking and neutralizing Valle-Inclán's sympathetic portrayal of an amoral Don Juan figure, whose fatal attraction to women consistently spelled their gender's doom in the form of insanity, mutilation, or death. The woman-authored novels that reacted to Valle-Inclán's rendition of the Don Juan figure began to appear just a few years after the *Sonatas* and continued to appear into the 1920s, when a more militant feminism marshaled its forces to reduce the Marqués de Bradomín/Don Juan to celibacy and the kitchen.

Martínez Sierra's *Tú eres la paz,* the earliest of the woman-authored novels to address Valle-Inclán's version of the Don Juan myth, converts the moribund Concha into a young, vibrant, independent woman who gains mastery over Don Juan through her keen sense of self-worth. Like *Sonata de invierno,* de los Ríos's *Las hijas de don Juan* (1909) casts the Don Juan figure in a paternal and obliquely incestuous role, only to reverse the *Sonata*'s designation of the Marqués as sentimental martyr. Casanova's *Princesa del amor hermoso* (1910) posits a female version of Don Juan who eventually rejects the role of superficial seducer. As shown in Chapter 2, Espina's *La esfinge maragata* contrasts a literary and imaginative donjuanesque male with the harsh realities of life in the Maragatan region. In her first novel, *La niña de Luzmela* (1909), Espina invented a repentant Marqués de Bradomín–like character. And in *La entrometida* (1924), Burgos converted the aristocratic Marqués de Bradomín into a middle-aged, middle-class aesthete who does not consummate his affairs with women. The women's versions of the Don Juan figure strip him of his illustrious past associated with national glory and transform him into a contemporary national disgrace.

Chapter 1 notes Martínez Sierra's revision of the stereotypical identification of woman and the soul of Spain in her first long novel, *Tú eres la paz.* In that novel, she also addressed Valle-Inclán's literaturized treatment of women in *Sonata de otoño.* Both novels focus on lovers who are cousins, and the two men in the novels share characteristics—the Marqués de Bradomín and Agustín are artistically inclined Don Juans. The principal women in both novels, however, are radically different. The moribund Concha expires in her final encounter with the modernist Don Juan, her subjectivity never having been revealed in the narration. Ana María, in contrast, "joven y un poco poeta," is fully conscious and in command of her situation.

In order to remind the reader that *Tú eres la paz* combats the suppression of female consciousness by such male authors as Valle-Inclán, Martínez Sierra evokes the setting of *Sonata de otoño*. In describing the palace that Ana María's grandmother has decorated, she employs *modernista* language reminiscent of that of the Marqués de Bradomín:

> El palacio escalona tres terrazas sobre el jardín; en la más alta abren grandes puertas-ventanas, y hay más macetas con más flores; las escalinatas de estas terrazas hay que subirlas lentamente, como en reposo de ociosidad elegante; hechas para que las mujeres y los pavos reales desplieguen sobre la piedra blanca de sus escalones la pompa de sedas policromas, sería gran profanación hollarlas con vulgar apresuramiento. (G. Martínez Sierra 1954, 14)

> [The palace sits three terraces above the garden; large windowed doors open onto the highest terrace, and there are more pots with more flowers; one must climb the stairs of these terraces slowly, with the repose of elegant idleness; since they were made so that women and peacocks could unfold the pomp of polichrome silk on the steps' white stone, it would be a profanation to tread upon them hurriedly.]

The fairytale world that grandmother Margarita has created in her palace echoes the fanciful ambience that Concha fashioned at the Palacio de Brandeso. Like Concha's palace, it evokes "vida de antaño" with furniture "de siglos" (15), and the women of both novels are associated with the past through their weaving. If these reminders of Valle-Inclán's *Sonata* escape the reader, Martínez Sierra adds the detail that one hears "los sones de una sonata" (15) emanating from the palace window. Ana María, however, avoids Concha's fate because, as shown in Chapter 1, her author endowed her with an autonomous consciousness that allows her to think beyond the traditional past of her surroundings. She is also educated and an avid reader. In *Feminismo, femininidad, españolismo* (see G. Martínez Sierra 1917), Martínez Sierra argued that women's education was the chief weapon with which to combat donjuanism.

De los Ríos, like Martínez Sierra, was an educated and truly intellectual woman of the fin de siècle, and, like the male modernists, she was well versed in the Spanish classics on which she lectured widely. She was a particular student of Tirso's, the inventor of Don Juan Tenorio.[12] Her biographical/critical study of Tirso received a Gold Medal from the

Royal Spanish Academy, and Alfonso XIII awarded her the Gran Cruz de la Orden Civil on May 23, 1902. Like the members of the so-called Generation of '98, her interest in the Spanish classics was closely linked to her sense of Spain as a nation (for example, she founded the journal *Raza Española*). Her nationalism, however, was not so inward-looking as that of her male counterparts. Like theirs, it revisited imperial Spain, but it also considered Latin America to be part of Spain's national identity. According to M. H. Blanco-Belmonte, "Antes que todos [de los Ríos] soñó con la España peninsular y trasatlántica, con el imperio de Cervantes, con Hispano-América" (1924, 10).

In a lecture that de los Ríos gave at the Ateneo de Madrid on April 23, 1906, she summarized Tirso's dramatic opus as essentially Spanish ("tan español en todo"): "Lo fue, así en su fecundidad generosa, como en sus fatales destinos, porque la historia del teatro de [Gabriel] Téllez es la historia del teatro nacional, la propia historia de España: crear, descubrir, conquistar mundos maravillosos para que otros los posean y los exploten" (1906, 7). She believed that there were "lazos inquebrantables" between "hombres y entre los pueblos" (one hears echoes of Unamuno's and Azorín's notions of the *tradición eterna*). While political regimes and institutions wax and wane, race, history and family remain constant. The present can be changed and the future molded, but the past is unmodifiable. The past, however, is not inert; rather, it is fecund, "es germen vivo y prolífico." It is the root of the present and the seed of the future:

> Lo pasado actúa, vive, persiste y continúa su labor incesante y fecunda en nosotros; lo pasado somos nosotros, que vivimos en la herencia fisiológica y psíquica de las generaciones de que procedemos; que somos el producto, la persistencia, la prolongación de las vidas, de las almas, de los heroísmos, de las culpas, de los dolores y de las glorias de nuestros progenitores. (1911, 6)

> [The past acts, lives, persists, and continues its incesant and fecund labor in us; we, who live the physiological and psychic inheritance of the generations from which we come, are the past; we are the product, the persistence, the prolongation of the lives, the souls, the heroism, the guilt, the pain, and the glories of our progenitors.]

For de los Ríos, Tirso was "un poeta de la gran raza" because "hasta las colectividades (of his plays) tienen alma" (1906, 31). Just as in Unamuno's *intrahistoria,* the past is the permanent underpinning of an ever-changing present. The difference is that in de los Ríos's fiction, the modifiable present and future carry more weight than the traditional past that often overwhelms the present in Unamuno's, Azorín's, and Valle-Inclán's novels. Significantly, on the occasion of the 1924 homage to de los Ríos, not one of the many letters of support sent in was from a member of the so-called Generation of '98. Typically, Jaime Barrena, one man who did write in, credited her success to masculine qualities: "mujer de corazón viril, alma de reina en cuerpo de escritora" who was "señalando el área inconmensurable de los dominios espirituales del idioma" (qtd. in Blanco-Belmonte 1924, 14).

De los Ríos had a particular interest in women in literature, and she developed that interest at length in her lecture *Las mujeres de Tirso* (1910), in which she indicated that Tirso was thoroughly familiar with female psychology through the confessions he had heard as a priest. In *Tirso de Molina,* she argued that Tirso should be a model for other writers in their depiction of female characters, because potential models such as Lope de Vega used female stereotypes—*daifas, celestinas, damas* ("*la dama,* aquella dama-tipo que entusiasmaba a Lista"). She allowed that Lope de Vega had created a few complex and vivid female characters, but they are, she said, only "bocetos psicológicos." They are better than those of Pedro Calderón de la Barca, but they hardly match Tirso de Molino's, whom Lope de Vega might have imitated "realizados no espontáneamente y en la juventud, sino a las vejeces del poeta, cuando éste tenía ya en Tirso tan grandes modelos que imitar." Only Tirso created a complete world that included female psychology: "la mujer de sus tiempos en todas sus individualidades y el alma femenina en todas sus manifestaciones hállanse en el teatro de Téllez; las princesas y damas cortesanas melindrosas, altaneras, apasionadas y resueltas; las doncellitas andantes o mal avenidas con tiránicos encerramientos, como la hechicera beata enamorada *Marta la piadosa*" (1906, 33, 47). She connects the long line of women in Spanish literature—Trotaconventos and Celestina—of whom Tirso's women are granddaughters to the sense of the nation. Because they are drawn in such a human fashion, they are of both historical and universal interest, and they provide female role models for contemporary women: "Vemos en aquellas hembras de temple tan español y tan castizo las líneas genealógicas del árbol opulento de la raza; y los que nos preciamos de descender de madres virtuosas y amantes hasta el heroísmo, vemos en la augusta Reina Doña María de Téllez, el noble tipo étnico de la matrona española, la raíz histórica de aquella egregia estirpe de mujeres de quienes nacieron nuestras madres" (1910, 30–31). Thus, when she theorizes about the "raza española," de los Ríos is thinking less about the eternal soul of Spain than about autochthonous models for modern women.

In addition to scholarly work, de los Ríos wrote several narrations in which she continued her project of exploring the nature of the contemporary Spanish nation: *Sangre española, Melita Palma, La niña de Sanabria* (all published in 1907), *El salvador,* and *La Rondeña* (for which I cannot locate dates). *La niña de Sanabria* takes place in 1898 on the eve of the Spanish disaster. Pepita, "la niña de Sanabria," is an artistic manifestation of the "concepto de raza y la vida psicofísica de la mujer española" (1910, 50) that de los Ríos so appreciated in Tirso. She is exceptionally intelligent and enthusiastic about book learning. As a woman, she can best capture the sense of the nation: "como si aspirase en el aire la ansiedad de la patria." She reflects "la impresión dominante en Madrid en aquellos días de inquietud devoradora;" her feminine nature seems to summarize "el delirante españolismo de su padre, el hondo anhelar del viejo Aurioles, el patriotismo doloroso y torturado del canónigo, la emoción de todos, el ansia nacional disuelta en la atmósfera" [the dominant impression of devouring disquiet in Madrid at that time]. Her very actions embody the nation, picking flowers that bedeck her balconies and affixing them to her breast beneath "la calada sombra flotante de la nacional mantilla" (47). Her father perceives "la propia España encarnada en la gentil figura de Pepita, envuelta en las nacionalidades blondas y ostentando en pecho y cabeza el simbólico auriflama" (56) [Spain itself embodied in the genteel figure of Pepita, wrapped in the light-colored national symbols and displaying the symbolic golden flame on her chest and head].

In the novelette *Las hijas de don Juan* (1909), de los Ríos created a very different and much less idealized view of Spanish women, especially in their association with a Spanish Don Juan. De los Ríos domesticated

Don Juan and converted him into a bourgeois figure who represents the evils of Restoration society. As Kathleen Glenn aptly remarks, "He is the antithesis of the spiritualized Don Juan of Azorín's 1922 novel" (1999, 226), a transformation that I analyze at the end of this chapter. De los Rios's version of the Don Juan story cuts in two directions—it echoes earlier literary versions of the figure while it simultaneously incorporates him into contemporary Spanish life and its social problems. Even though he has taken on many of the trappings of the modern bourgeoisie (marriage, children, financial concerns), traces of romanticism remain beneath the protagonist's middle-class veneer.[13] In an act of rebellion against bourgeois pretensions, he marries a working-class woman named Concha, echoing the Marqués de Bradomín's paramour in *Sonata de otoño*.[14] This Concha, instead of luxuriating at her medieval manor, where she has constructed an imaginary world of princesses and pages, "no conocía, ni aun de nombre, la estética" (de los Ríos 1989, 89). She spends her days searching for bargains and her nights carping at her daughters and husband. The daughters fall into illness and prostitution, having been left unattended by a father who spends most of his time and his income on hedonistic pursuits and a mother who must ply the shops for inexpensive goods to obtain the family's necessities.

For de los Ríos's narrator, the place of donjuanism in contemporary society is self-evident: "Era, pues, don Juan una de las personalidades más típicas del Madrid de la Restauración" (70). In her version, Don Juan's legacy has a social as well as a literary dimension. Don Juan thus achieves the status of a late romantic who fuses a Becquerian essence with the tragic theatricality of José Echegaray and the patriotism of Pérez Galdós's first *Episodios nacionales*. Making the connection between literary and social discourse, the narrator reminds us that the appearance of the *Episodios* coincided with public recitations in high romantic style: "Por entonces, por los días en que los *Episodios* prendían fiebre en las almas entusiastas, y Rafael Calvo electrizaba a los concursos con su declamación candente y con sus fogosas recitaciones de los poemas de Núñez de Arce, amanecía la mocedad de don Juan inflamada en el romanticismo contagioso que era atmósfera del Madrid de aquellos años" (67–68). If de los Ríos's narrator employs a kind of irony in describing the modern bourgeois Don Juan, it is an objective irony that critiques a social situation, whereas the Marqués de Bradomín's ironic stance, deeply informed by romantic notions, positions him above social morality. The romantic literary legacy with its emphasis on male subjectivity and the idealization of women was a powerful ally in modernism's war on realism. Small wonder that women "modernists" found the legacy suspect.

De los Ríos also inscribes the romantic Don Juan figure into the social register: "Don Juan era el histórico seductor *gallardo y calavera* que lo prostituyó todo, menos la estética y la arrogancia, y el prestigio de su romántica persona" (69). [Don Juan was the historical seducer, gallant and liberine, who prostituted everything except aesthetics and arrogance and the prestige of his romantic persona.] This is not Tirso's or Zorrilla's legendary hero or antihero, but a run-of-the-mill representative of Restoration Spain. He is a literary and a social decadent. He prefers art to religion and is a devotee of *flamenquismo* (showy Spanish customs), but his decadence is archaic and does not achieve truly modern amorality: "Quedábase en inmoral, no llegaba a ser *amoral* como los decadentistas actuales" (70).[15] When faced with the choice between their mother's practical vulgarity and their father's tasteful disdain for contemporary reality, Don Juan's daughters, Dora and Lita, prefer the latter. In denying their natural gender connections to their mother, the daughters sow the seeds of their own moral destruction.[16] The process is hastened when Dora and Lita, often left home alone, discover some salacious letters to their father from a paramour. The girls assume more mature and sexually defined identities almost overnight. Dora becomes intensely romantic and takes up religious practices inspired by Saint Teresa of Ávila, and her tubercular condition is said to date from that fateful moment when she read Don Juan's letters. Lita, for her part, becomes more worldly, begins to attend *tertulias*, and engages in flirtations with men.

Significantly, Don Juan, never a focalizer of the novel, disappears from the text after the first ten pages, when the daughters take center stage, and he does not reappear until the novelette's final pages. He remains only as an invisible presence, a pernicious influence to be overcome. The daughters redirect their attention, if not their sympathies, to their mother, who, upon learning of their epistolary discovery, unburdens herself of her years of torture as the wife of the profligate, decadent Don Juan. The sisters form a bond, like the biblical sisters of Lazarus, Martha and Mary: "Dora era, en fin, éter de misticismo; Lita, brasa de pasión; las dos juntas hubieran poseído el cielo y la tierra; ¿qué sería la una sin la otra, si la suerte desataba aquel nudo de contrapuesto gemelismo?" (90). [In the end, Dora was ether of mysticism; Lita, a hot coal of compassion; the two together would have possessed heaven and earth. What would happen to one without the other if providence untied that knot of juxtaposed twinship?]

The daughters' uselessness is highlighted when Don Juan's intemperate ways bring economic ruin to the household: "Dos señoritas inútiles, ¿para qué sirven, vamos a ver? ¡Pues para pedir limosna o... *para otra cosa peor!*" (92, emphasis in original). [Tell me; what are two useless young ladies good for? Well, for begging or... *for something worse!*] Clearly, de los Ríos joined Martínez Sierra and Burgos in employing fiction to argue for women's education, an education that would give women a livelihood. Uneducated girls like Dora and Lita have few options if they must support themselves. Although Concha expresses a modification of the prevailing belief that prostitution was attributable to innate female lasciviousness ("¡No, y como lo lleváis en la sangre, en algo malo acabaréis vosotras! ¡Ésa será la herencia que os deje ese grandísimo canalla!" (92) [No, and since it is in your blood, you two will end badly! That will be your inheritance from that great scoundrel!]),[17] the underlying cause of prostitution is left vacilating between biological and social determinants. Either their father's sexual licentiousness or his fiscal irresponsibility has driven the sisters to stray from traditional morality.

Literature in the form of a novelist—Paco Garba—is the final catalyst in Lita's progress toward prostitution: "Degenerado por herencia, decadentista por oficio ... no era antiguo ni moderno, sino sencillamente detestable" (97–98). [Degenerate by inheritance, decadent by vocation ... he was neither ancient nor modern, but simply detestable.] The narrator understands that fin de siècle literary trends like decadentism, which emphasizes sexual perversion, were extremely damaging to women.[18] Garba is a bad writer, but the upwardly mobile couple who promote his fame are sufficiently uneducated to be incapable of distinguishing good art from bad. So Garba becomes a social success, and Lita, filled with romantic notions of love, succumbs to Garba's posturing: "—Lita, la fuga o mi muerte.... El romanticismo de aquella novelesca fuga, la inminencia de la dicha, el vértigo de la acción asieron de ella" (107, 109). [Lita, either we flee or I shall die. . . . The romanticism of that novelesque flight, the imminence of happiness, the dizzying action took hold of her.] Garba's is the same romantic posture that buries all of the Marqués de Bradomín's women but that ironically "saves" the Marqués himself. In de los Ríos's novelette, the Don Juan figure who perpetrates female ruin is destroyed himself, a move that Reyes Lázaro calls "una versión femenina del calderonismo" (1966, 476). Here the father was the first cause, sowing the seeds of his own dishonor. Evoking Baudelaire, Don Juan, the father, seeks relief for the misery he has wrought on his family by taking morphine and, when forced to witness Lita's degraded life, finally dies of an overdose of drugs and alcohol.

De los Ríos symbolically kills off the Don Juan legacy with Lita's degradation: "En Lita acabó la estirpe de don Juan" (1989, 125). There is no room for Don Juan and his progeny in a Spain that is more hospitable to women. De los Ríos's novelette, written in the melodramatic mode, has many of the marks of that genre's moral allegory in which good is pitted against evil. The daughters are melodramatically typecast, but these stereotypes combine with the Don Juan intertext to represent genuine social problems in the material world—parental neglect, donjuanism, and prostitution. Instead of being presented as yet another self-reflection of the narcissistic Bradomín, this Don Juan is described objectively to prevent him from escaping into the ironic, self-indulgent position. Melodrama's capacity for oversimplifying good and evil delineates a moral attitude, whereas the kind of irony employed by Valle-Inclán in the *Sonatas* leaves the moral message ambiguous. Azorín's ambiguous, layered treatment of prostitution in *El alma castellana* also contrasts with the more direct and condemnatory approach in de los Ríos's novel.

Sofía Casanova, like Blanca de los Ríos (albeit for different reasons), incorporated a nationalist perspective into her fiction. Her relationship to Spain and its cultural tradition were especially complex. She was brought up in Galicia, where she read the Spanish romantics in the family library—Gustavo Adolfo Bécquer, Gertrudis Gómez de Avellaneda, Carolina Coronado, and especially Rosalía de Castro. She married Polish nobleman/philosopher Wincenty Lutoslawski in 1887 and lived abroad in Poland and elsewhere for much of her life, although she traveled frequently to Spain and wrote many articles of international interest for the Spanish periodical press (it is especially important that Casanova spent long periods of time in Spain in the 1920s when feminism was on the rise there). Lutoslawski was a womanizer, probably the model for the Slavic Don Juan that Casanova describes in her book on Russia: "No me era desconocido el tipo del Don Juan eslavo, que justifica su libertinaje para procrear dioses" (qtd. in Alayeto 1992, 39). Like Unamuno's Avito Carrascal of *Amor y pedagogía,* Lutoslawski harbored the quixotic desire to father a son in order raise a genius.

Casanova composed at least two novels centering on the Don Juan myth: *Más que amor* and *Princesa del amor hermoso*. *Más que amor* combines the Don Juan theme with a meditation on Spain by creating a love story in which the man and woman live in different countries. Upon the death of her Polish husband, María, a Spanish woman who resides in Poland, enters into a correspondence with Carlos, who resides in Spain. Carlos and María had met some seventeen years earlier, and Carlos, described as a typical "love them and leave them" Don Juan, has since married. Through the offices of a mutual friend, they initiate an epistolary love affair. This long-distance romance allows Casanova to explore several nationalist issues. The Don Juan figure, Carlos, a Spaniard who resides in Spain, is an emblem for Spanishness, especially in the context of the comparisons that the narrator makes between Spain and Poland throughout the narrative. In developing the love affair between María and Carlos, the novel ultimately queries the nature of race and nation and how nations survive in a healthy fashion.

Like Valle-Inclán's Marqués de Bradomín, Carlos is involved in Spanish political life, which frames him within a contemporary context, but his past is suspiciously close to that of Tirso's and Zorrilla's Don Juan Tenorio. Stories circulate that in his youth he was a "galán profanador de un cementerio" (Casanova 1908, 34) and that he fled abroad to get away from a woman he had seduced. She followed him and committed suicide at his feet. The connection to Valle-Inclán's Marqués is made explicit (as it is in Burgos's *La entrometida*) by involving the woman's sister, who accompanied him in his flight abroad (recalling the Marqués's night of lovemaking with Concha's sister immediately after Concha's death in *Sonata de otoño*).

The novel begins with a nationalist note, a poem invoking "la raza": "Mas antes volver quiero los ojos reverente/a mi sol y a mi tierra, y a mi raza indolente/que no sabe y no puede, cuando siente, pensar" (6), and the notions of *pueblo, raza,* patriotism, and *casticismo* are frequently evoked (see, for example, 5, 10, 13, 16, 17, 61, 134–35, 161). In a letter to a Spanish friend, María ostensibly compares Spain favorably to Poland, which she describes as suffering from a national sadness. However, her observation that "los defectos de una raza acentúanse y se desarrollan implacablemente, si por largo tiempo vive en condiciones contrarias a su naturaleza" (9–10) [the defects of a race become accentuated and develop implacably, if it lives for a long time under conditions that are contrary to its nature] sounds ominously like Unamuno's interpretation of Spain's ills.[19] María foreshadows Maeztu's 1925 observations on Don Juan when she analyzes Carlos's character. Like Maeztu, she believes that Don Juan's insatiable appetite consumed him as well as everything around him: "Dentro de usted un desordenado apetito de vida ha elaborado la negra miel de los amores nefastos. . . . No emana de usted la sombra; no es usted la desgracia. Todas las que sintió y causó son obra *suya*, Carlos. Quién busca el peligro perece en él" (54). [A disorderly appetite for life has elaborated in you a black honey of fatal loves. . . . Shadows do not emanate from you; you are not misfortune. All those that you felt and caused are *your own* work, Carlos. Those who seek danger perish in it.] She accuses him of living in "libros de caballero andante" (56), a posture that would ally him with both Don Quixote and the Marqués de Bradomín. María visits Carlos in Spain after his wife dies, and they decide to marry, but María begins to abhor Carlos when they visit the grave of the woman who committed suicide after he abandoned her. María eventually chooses to leave Carlos and Spain behind and return to Poland. *Más que amor* places the woman in a position of moral superiority over men (for example, Carlos calls María his "colaboradora moral" [160]). Like de los Ríos in *Las hijas de don Juan,* rather than refashion Don Juan to a modern purpose and reinscribe him in the national order as does Valle-Inclán, Casanova prefers to abandon him altogether, eliminating him from the national panorama.

In her short novel *Princesa del amor hermoso,* Casanova refers in a more sustained fashion to the Don Juan theme, unabashedly inverting and subverting many of its traditional qualities (especially Don Juan as hero). Challenging the legendary Don Juan with a contemporary female, "Doña Juana," Casanova incorporates even more direct allusions to Valle-Inclán's Marqués de Bradomín than did de los Ríos (note, for example, the Valleinclanesque "princesa" in the title). Laura, who has been betrayed by her fiancé, the philandering Fernando, decides to imitate his licentious behavior, but in the end she reassumes her initial socially responsible moral posture. Like *Sonata de otoño, Princesa del amor hermoso* begins with a long letter from a woman, Laura, to a Don Juan type, but Casanova reverses some of the details and roles of Valle-Inclán's original. The Marqués of the *Sonata* deliberately includes no more than a phrase of Concha's letter, whereas in Casanova's version Laura's entire communication is quoted. In the first of several defiant gestures toward *Sonata de otoño*, Casanova's narrator quotes only a fragment of Fernando's letter, which is nearly identical in length to Concha's fragment quoted by the Marqués.[20] In her letter, Laura breaks with Fernando, referring to his "fatuidad donjuanesca." She also informs him that she will neither marry nor take up the religious life (the latter being traditionally the only alternative for respectable women).

Laura effectively writes herself out of Bradomín's scenario for the woman as love object, refusing the role of the helpless female dependent on the stronger male's attentions. In the process, she almost writes herself into the role of Bradomín, the superficial seducer: "Voy a divertirme, a *flirtear*, a ver pasar junto a mí las emociones que inspiro y no comparto. . . . Voy a coquetear, sí, a coquetear, que es jugar a los dados y las almas" (Casanova 1989, 160). [I am going to have a good time, to flirt, to watch pass before me emotions that I inspire but do not share. I am going to be coquettish, yes coquettish, which is to play dice with souls.] When her tubercular cousin José Luis (a character feminized not only by his disease but by the intensity of his gaze and the redness of his lips) becomes obsessed with her, her first inclination is to use his infatuation to make Fernando jealous, but she finally rejects such ill use of another's affections.

Like de los Ríos's *Las hijas de don Juan*, Casanova's novelette portrays life and literature as interdependent. Literature can have an important impact on women's lives. According to one of Laura's female acquaintances, modern literature lacks common sense; another prefers love duels in real life to those in literature. Laura herself is attracted to love in both life and literature (165), although she spurns the misogyny in Giacomo Leopardi's love lyrics: "Es desesperante en esa poesía su desprecio a la mujer" (167). Literature's long tradition of casting women in the antithetical roles of evil schemers and idealized objects is perceptible throughout the novelette. Women are either "umbrías virgilianas" (162) or "bienaventurados geórgicos amores" (165), Lady Macbeths or Ophelias (184). Contrary to the gender division in the traditional Don Juan story, José Luis's male view of the world is wholly romantic whereas Laura's is skeptical, even cynical at times. In many ways, Laura prophesies the new Spanish woman—strong, morally courageous, eschewing dependence on men—that will be depicted in a number of novels by women in the 1920s and 1930s. That new woman rejects an independence that assumes typical male attitudes (such as donjuanism) and forges an alternate path that engages in meaningful, morally responsible relationships.

Espina's and Burgos's approach to the Spanish nation is less academic and conceptual than the approaches of de los Ríos and Casanova; in drawing on the nationally associated Don Juan figure, however, they imply a revisionist view of the national tradition that has much in common with the project that underlies the Don Juan narratives of de los Ríos and Casanova. The lives of Espina and Burgos, which followed similar trajectories, provide clues to their view that traditional Spanish masculinity required emendation. Both were married to unsuitable men at a young age. Both had children early, and soon found it necessary to support themselves and their families. Writing became an important source of income.[21]

Espina's roots in northern Spain (Santander) would naturally have called her attention to Valle-Inclán's re-creation of Galicia and other northern provinces in the *Sonatas*. She referred to the Marqués de Bradomín in at least two early novels—*La niña de Luzmela* and *La esfinge maragata*, whose Quixote intertext is analyzed in Chapter 2. Just four years after Valle-Inclán depicted the Marqués de Bradomín lamenting the loss of his daughter/lover, Espina published *La niña de Luzmela*, in which a profligate donjuanesque father of an illegitimate daughter attempts to right the wrongs that he has done to mother and daughter. The novel is not a male memoir like the *Sonatas* (it has a third-person omniscient narrator), but Espina evokes the *Sonatas* in the first section. Here Don Manuel "confesses" to his adopted son, Salvador, his licentious past, especially his having fathered Carmen, the child who lives with him and whom he calls his goddaughter. He identifies himself with the Marqués de Bradomín when he recalls his affair with "una criolla que le adoraba" during an expedition to "las Américas" (Espina 1985, 31). As in *Sonata de otoño,* a symbolic bird presages death (here Don Manuel's rather that of the paramour), and, just as in the *Sonata,* a child asks the chivalresque Don Juan to remove the frightening bird.

Like the Marqués de Bradomín, Don Manuel describes himself as "piadoso y noble," but this Don Juan's sentimental qualities are even more pronounced than those of the Marqués. He explains to his adopted son that he has lived too precipitously and has loved and suffered too much, but he does not believe that he is as bad as his reputation portrays him: "Anduve por el mundo locamente, y pequé y caí veces innumerables; pero otras veces, ¡también muchas!, levanté a los caídos en mis brazos, prodigué a los tristes mi corazón y mi fortuna" (14). [I went about the world like a crazy man; I sinned and fell numerous times; but other times—many times—I raised up the fallen in my arms and offered my heart and wealth to the unfortunate.] This domesticated Don Juan married and dreamed of settling down to family life ("me creí reconciliado con el amo del terruño y con la paz de mi valle; restauré esta casa, soñando vivir siempre en ella idílicos goces; evoqué la visión de unos hijos robustos y de una patriarcal vejez" [19]); however, his wife died almost immediately. Thereafter, he returned to his donjuanesque ways. Because he truly loved Carmen's mother, and in order to atone for the sin of dishonoring her and bringing an illigitimate child into the world, he raises the child on his estate.

On his deathbed, he constructs an elaborate legal plan to ensure that Carmen will continue to be protected and cared for. He divides his large fortune between his adopted son and his impoverished widowed sister, who lives in a neighboring town. The sister may keep the inheritance only on the condition that she raise Carmen as her own child. Salvador, a doctor by profession (his studies paid for by Don Manuel), is charged with monitoring Carmen's happiness under the sister's care. The Don

Juan figure, Don Manuel, then dies, and Carmen's story takes center stage. It is a Cinderella tale that adds three lascivious stepbrothers to a jealous stepsister and a wicked stepmother (aptly named Rebeca for the deceitful biblical Rebecca). Carmen's life at her aunt's has all the elements of a Gothic horror novel. Her stepmother/aunt refuses to believe that she is truly her brother's daughter and torments her continuously. Carmen's beauty fuel's her stepsister's jealousy and her stepbrothers' lechery. Added to these emotions is the congenital mental illness that affects the aunt and one of the stepbrothers. Carmen negotiates these terrors with religious faith and occasionally a sense of humor, especially during visits from Salvador. Fernando, another of Doña Rebeca's sons, also brings a measure of happiness to Carmen's life when he returns from a sailing trip to woo her and ask for her hand in marriage. He turns out to be another Don Juan, who is simultaneously carrying on an affair with a loose woman in the village. Like Don Manuel, he has honorable qualities, however, and finally leaves his mother's home, jilting Carmen, because he realizes he would only cause her misery.

After a crisis in which Rebeca's alcoholic son attempts to rape Carmen, Salvador finally decides to take legal action and remove Carmen from the stepmother's home. This fairytale ending, with the steadfast male rescuing the damsel from Gothic horrors is somewhat mitigated by Carmen's taking control of her destiny by refraining from immediately promising to marry Salvador as he would wish (we have the sense that they will eventually marry, however). Espina has revised Valle-Inclán's approach to the Don Juan figure in which the female characters come to tragic ends, whereas the Marqués carries on with his life finding yet another victim to bolster his aging, sagging ego. Like de los Ríos and Casanova, Espina neutralizes all the Don Juan figures in her novel. She writes Don Manuel and Fernando and his brothers out of the story, leaving only Salvador, the man who is able to appreciate the woman in all her dimensions, especially her kindness and sincerity. Salvador is the Spanish man of the future who will be capable of a lasting, empathetic relationship with a woman.

As indicated in Chapter 2, Espina's Rogelio in *La esfinge maragata* combines the Don Quixote archetype with elements of the Don Juan figure. Rogelio is not unique to the modernist canon in sharing characteristics common to both Don Quixote and Don Juan. Whereas his quixotism shifts to Mariflor, his donjuanism remains to the end as a narratorial critique of his fickle romanticism.[22] Rather than invert the male and female roles as Casanova does, Espina exaggerates the literary gender stereotypes. Rogelio has much in common with the Marqués de Bradomín, whose creator he reveres: "Saluda con reverente pensamiento al peregrino autor de las *Sonatas,* al poeta de *Flor de santidad,* cuya musa galante y campesina trovó en estas silvestres espesuras páginas deleitosas" (Espina 1989, 58). [With a reverent thought, he salutes the singular author of the *Sonatas* and poet of *Flor de santidad,* whose gallant and rural muse fashioned delightful pages in these wild thickets.] As a writer, Rogelio too exploits his relationships with women for their literary value, although Rogelio spins his fantasy a priori, whereas the Marqués de Bradomín narrates his amorous exploits a posteriori. Like the Marqués de Bradomín (and in contrast to the traditional Don Juan), Rogelio genuinely believes that he is in love with the women he pursues. And like the Marqués, he journeys into new geographical space to meet his "princess." Whereas Valle-Inclán situates the Marqués's conquests in papal and princely Italy, exotic Mexico, the highly literaturized Palacio de Brandeso, and the royal camps of the Carlist wars, Espina heightens the discrepancy between literary portrayals of women and women's real lives by setting her novel in the Maragatan region of León, where the agricultural economy can no longer support its inhabitants. Most of the healthy men work abroad, leaving the women to tend the land. Life is a daily struggle to feed and shelter the children fathered by the men on their yearly visits.

Whereas the Marqués de Bradomín engages in a nostalgic retrospective of his excursions into alternative worlds laden with potential for literary escapism, Florinda enters a foreign but all too realistic world of work, suffering, and privation. The Marqués employs the romantic language and tropes associated with late nineteenth-century *modernismo* to seduce women and to vindicate himself and his life; Espina's narrator uses these same linguistic styles to reveal the harm that they can do to women. Valle-Inclán parodies romanticism through the Marqués de Bradomín's clichéd language in order to place the Marqués in an ironic light.[23] Espina, too, evokes romanticism's emotive, idealistic language early in the novel only to have Florinda reject it later by dramatically shredding Rogelio's letters and casting them out among the snowflakes. The Becquerian echoes of Rogelio's letter to the priest announcing his loss of interest in Mariflor are a compelling reminder that men's romantic dreams of women cause pain in the real world. Whereas the Marqués looks back mournfully to a "glorious" past in which he has seduced and directly or indirectly caused the death of more than one woman, Mariflor looks hopefully forward to a future of social responsibility. The implications for Spain's future are clear: Espina proposes pragmatic solutions to social and economic problems rather than nostalgia about outmoded traditions and faded personal and national glory.

In the 1920s, when the Spanish feminist movement had gained some ground, Burgos continued to find inspiration in Valle-Inclán's treatment of the Don Juan figure, now confronting him with a publicly declared feminist in *La entremetida*. Of the five women authors discussed in this chapter, Burgos was the most militant feminist. Her own life could serve as the basis of a feminist novel. She was married to an irresponsible and feckless man at the very young age of sixteen, but she gained valuable experience working in her husband's family's publishing business. After a few years and the birth of a child, she decided to leave her husband and move to the environs of Madrid, where she took a teaching post and began to support herself and her child by teaching classes and writing. Extremely daring, her move for independence from marriage garnered her a great deal of acrimony at the time (to wit, the passage in the Introduction to this book quoting a teaching colleague who referred to her as "algo modernista"). She flaunted her "modern" views of womanhood in even more socially unacceptable ways by entering into an extramarital alliance with the much younger Ramón Gómez de la Serna in 1909 (the relationship lasted for twenty years, and the couple traveled together openly and in other ways made their liaison quite public).[24]

In *La entromerida*, a novelette published in *La Novela Corta* series, Burgos domesticated Valle-Inclán's romantic-*modernista* version of Don Juan by converting him into a bourgeois aesthete whose power over women is more editorial than physical. Recall that the Marqués de

Bradomín, who is invoked on several occasions in the portrayal of Burgos's male focalizer Pérez Blanco, edits the voice of Concha and the other women out of the *Sonatas*. In *La entrometida,* Pérez Blanco's female writer escapes from him and publishes her own story. Pérez Blanco is a middle-aged bachelor, aficionado of good cooking and intimate dinners with a highly select group of young women, most of them married: "No era un galanteador de oficio, ni un seductor, no era más que un *despelusador,* a cuyo contacto las mujeres, sin perder la castidad, perdían la inocencia" (1924, n.p.). [He was not a professional lover, nor a seducer; he was only a hair-musser, in contact with whom women lost their innocence without losing their chastity.][25] Pérez Blanco's ambiguous gender characteristics suggest an effeminate interpretation of Don Juan that Gregorio Marañón and others were proffering in the late teens and early 1920s.

Pérez Blanco enjoys the company of a woman as he does a good book or a fine wine; his donjuanism is limited to the vicarious activities of counselor and confidant, although he claims to have been much loved by women in his youth. The reader becomes wary of these claims, however, when to document his rakish past, Pérez Blanco tells stories that are almost identical to those of the Marqués de Bradomín: "el relato repetido de aquella noche en que la voluptuosidad avivada por la muerte de una mujer respetada, que en su último momento le revelaba su pasión, le hacía abrazar a la hermana de la difunta en el mismo lecho mortuorio" (n.p.) [the repeated story of that night in which voluptuousness enlivened by the death of a respected woman, who in her last moment revealed her passion, made him embrace the sister of the dead woman in the very deathbed]. Pérez Blanco also laments the loss of a fiancée, a widow, who broke off their engagement because her daughters fell in love with him. As Maryellen Bieder points out, "Burgos intertextualizes the self-conscious masculinity of both Valle-Inclán the author, whose outrageous public figure was to some degree as much a fiction as his characters, and his fictional alter ego, the Marqués de Bradomín, Valle-Inclán's decadent recreation of the seducer" (1996, 80). Since the Marqués de Bradomín embroiders his libidinous history with literary tropes, Pérez Blanco's amorous memories are in effect twice borrowed literature.

Pérez Blanco takes a special interest in Clarisa, a declared feminist who has spent time abroad and who plans to mobilize feminist activities in Spain. He undertakes a campaign to redirect Clarisa's life toward more feminine (that is, less public) pursuits and convinces her to dictate her life story to him, including her most intimate feelings and thoughts. When she finds herself in financial difficulty and decides to publish her memoirs for money, Perez Blanco abandons her. In Burgos's rewriting, a "Marqués de Bradomín," who is capable of occupying the space of four novels with his own very public memoirs, cannot abide a woman's similarly revealing her subjectivity. Perhaps he cannot even accept that women have a subjectivity. The end of the novelette finds Clarisa in England, where she has resumed her feminist activities, but she writes to Pérez Blanco that she is wavering between becoming a writer and becoming a prostitute. Clarisa's equation of writing with prostitution, of publishing one's ideas or sentiments with defiling one's body, is significant. By publishing her memoirs, she forfeits her legitimate relationship with Pérez Blanco, the paternalistic male figure; his interpretation of her act renders it illegitimate and prostitutorial. Clarisa's apparent escape from a male editor's influence on her work is left ambiguous. Prostitution, the primarily female profession occasioned by the pressures of male needs and male social forms, becomes a metaphor for the relationship between men and women in the literary as well as the carnal world.[26] The option of leaving Spain in order to pursue a more independent life arises in a number of novels by women—Casanova's *Más que amor*, many of Burgos's novels—and in some male-authored novels as well (for example, Baroja's *La dama errante* [1908] and *La ciudad de la niebla* [1909] and Azorín's *Doña Inés* [1925]). Throughout the modernist period, Spain remained a troubled nationality for those who sought new gender identities.

Like Burgos, Azorín and Unamuno adapted the Don Juan theme within the context of 1920s feminism in *Don Juan* (1922a) and *El hermano Juan o El mundo es teatro. Vieja comedia nueva* (1929), respectively.[27] Their interpretations of Don Juan in a feminist context, however, differ radically from hers. In their versions, Don Juan escapes gender difficulties not through emigration but through interior exile, casting their gaze beyond the immediate material world. Unlike the women authors, who created feminist remakes of the Marqués de Bradomín, Azorín and Unamuno eliminated all vestiges of the moral engagement that we find in Valle-Inclán's and in women authors' renditions. They converted Don Juan into a timeless essence, an existential hero that is quietist and passive rather than active and aggressive. Azorín's *Don Juan* not only eschews the moral subject matter of the original versions of the Don Juan story; his title character is little more than a reminder of the Spanish literary tradition, an excuse to excavate the Spanish *tradición eterna* through detailed portraits of Spain's villages and people. He has even abandoned the overtly cautionary and prescriptive use of Golden Age classics of his earlier narratives, finding other ways to insinuate his views on gender relations. *Don Juan* opens with a genuflection toward the Don Juan legend: "Don Juan del Prado y Ramos era un gran pecador; un día adoleció gravemente" (1922a, 9). Azorín then recalls the Spanish literary tradition, evoking Berceo's *Milagros,* which recounts numerous occasions in which the Virgen has saved lost souls, transforming worldly appetites into spiritual ones. Such will be this Don Juan's story.

Don Juan has already set aside his philandering past and has initiated a humble existence in a Spanish village. This scenario provides Azorín with the opportunity to devote chapters to various characters that populate this unnamed "pequeña ciudad," a metaphor for every small Spanish town. "El espíritu de la pequeña ciudad," is the title of an early chapter, followed by brief chapters that portray important religious figures—the bishop, various nuns—and civil types, such as a colonel in the Civil Guards, the schoolteacher, the doctor, the president of the Audiencia, and several women and children. In the last chapter, Don Juan is one of a company of people who go to the train station to say good-bye to a family that is leaving the town. One member of the family shouts from the train, "Adiós, España, tierra del amor y de la Caballería" (177). [Goodbye, Spain, land of love and chivalry.] The spiritual Spain in which the church dominated village life may be a thing of the past, but Don Juan refuses to succumb to modern pressures, and in the epilogue he is now a monk, "el hermano Juan." Azorín's Don Juan has forsaken worldly riches and women for spirituality: "—Hermano Juan: no me atrevo a decirlo; pero he oído contar que usted ha amado mucho y que todas las mujeres se le rendían.—El amor que conoczo ahora es el amor más alto. Es la piedad por todo" (179). ["Brother Juan: I don't dare to say it; but I have heard tell that you have loved a great deal and that all the women surrendered to you." "The love that I know now is the highest love. It is compassion for everything."].[28] The message of *Don Juan* is clear. Women must be excised from a man's life in order for him to achieve a "higher" spiritual plane.[29]

The novelistic treatment of masculine national figure Don Juan in the first half of the twentieth century constitutes a sustained gauge for registering male and female authors' attitudes toward a range of domestic issues. Valle-Inclán's ugly, sentimental, Catholic Marqués de Bradomín, modern in his nostalgic posturing, represents many qualities, especially extreme male egotism and a disregard for a morality that takes women's needs into account. Women writers strove to neutralize Valle-Inclán's morally slippery Don Juan through modified realist strategies that reveal a feminine and feminist consciousness. As the feminist movement solidified in the 1920s, Don Juan metamorphosed into an asexual being in narratives by Burgos (the sybarite), Unamuno, and Azorín (a monk). Don Juan's encounter with feminism in Burgos's *La entrometida* produced inconclusive results. Domesticated Don Juan Pérez Blanco forced feminist Clarisa into exile when he failed to bring her completely under his control and coerce her into speaking only through him. Her plans for the future are ambiguous, even frivolous perhaps.

As Chapters 4 and 5 demonstrate, novels by Miguel de Unamuno, Azorín, Ramón Pérez de Ayala, and Benjamín Jarnés that incoprorate the Don Juan figure in the 1920s are equally ambiguous. Pérez de Ayala's *Tigre Juan y El curandero de su honra* (1925) complicates the Don Juan intertext with Calderonian overtones and an intensely ironic style that catches the reader up in its densely layered artfulness. Jarnés's *El convidado de papel* (1928) gives Tirso's stone statue a vanguardist fillip by converting it into salacious photographs of women that circulate clandestinely in a seminary. Confronted by militant feminism, Unamuno, Azorín, and Pérez de Ayala portrayed female characters as threatening, whereas Don Juan became the beleaguered symbol of a nation at risk—not from foreign powers like the United States, as it was in the 1890s, but from within, from the gender that they had earlier attempted to convert into the timeless symbol of the nation's essence. In each novel, women's actions transgress social norms, and in the case of Unamuno's *La tía Tula*, they assume monstrous proportions. Unamuno's and Azorín's versions of the Don Juan theme, which lack Valle-Inclán's irony, are earnest attempts to convert Don Juan into a timeless, blameless emblem of Spanish tradition. The rise of women's social and political power was seen as draining away national energy, symbolized, according to Ramiro de Maeztu, in Don Juan.

CHAPTER 4
Baroja's, Unamuno's, and Azorín's Failed Feminists

Carmen de Burgos's *La entrometida* (1924) reflects the schizophrenic situation in which Spanish women found themselves in the 1920s. They were caught between increasing expectations for equality and independence and the old social norms that were still firmly in place. As in both the rest of post–World War I Western Europe and the United States, the Spanish 1920s was a period of social and political change. Women assumed striking visibility, shortening their hair and their skirts, going out alone, and smoking in the street and in other public places. Spanish feminism finally found official organization in groups such as ANME, although they often had a conservative orientation. If Spain was slow to embrace feminism, it was ahead of the curve in testing fascist dictatorship. The increasingly ineffective monarchy of Alfonso XIII finally ceded to a military dictatorship in 1923. As a sign of the times, the dictator Miguel Primo de Rivera declared himself a feminist and during his regime even instituted a few fairly benign measures that favored women—work legislation, posts in municipal government, and university education—although these hardly satisfied large numbers of women or solved domestic problems. During Primo's dictatorship, Republicanism swelled, and in it feminism found an ally. Many feminist leaders were strong advocates of a Spanish Republic. In contrast, most of the male writers discussed herein, including those whose novels had female protagonists, did not unconditionally endorse the Republican cause.

As noted, the lives of Pío Baroja, Miguel de Unamuno, Azorín, and Ramón del Valle-Inclán almost exactly paralleled the rise of the feminist movement in Spain. Born just before or just after the September 1868 revolution, when the discourse on women was entering national consciousness, these authors wrote narratives that registered and reacted to an increasingly prominent feminism and changing roles for women in the first two decades of the twentieth century. In the second and third decades, Baroja, Unamuno, and Azorín each produced a novel with a strong female protagonist who ultimately fails in her personal relationships and comes to a rather unpleasant end. Baroja's *El mundo es ansí* is from 1912; however, Unamuno's *La tía Tula*, his only long novel with a female protagonist, and Azorín's *Doña Inés* (1925) were penned after 1920, when Spanish feminism was asserting itself as an identifiable movement. Both Tula and Inés defy the bourgeois ethos for women to marry and establish themselves as domestic housewives. The Don Juan theme prevalent in literature throughout the modernist period and present in these anomalous male-authored novels with strong female protagonists takes on new dimensions in the male-perceived feminist context.

Although each of the authors approached feminist discourse from a different perspective, such issues as historical versus eternal woman and women's relationship to domesticity are found in all three. I cannot address the psychology of these authors in relation to women, but it is interesting to note that each had a special relationship to his mother. Baroja lived with his mother until her death in 1912. As noted in Chapter 1, after Unamuno lost his father at age six, he formed a special attachment to his mother, as did Azorín, whose autocratic, philandering father caused him to look to his mother for stability. The reactions of these writers to female authors, which was ambiguous at best, demonstrated their aversion to high-profile women. Unamuno and Azorín both revered Santa Teresa and were deeply indebted to her simple, direct, straightforward style and presentation of the human condition. Both respected (and were influenced by) the older Emilia Pardo Bazán, but there is no evidence that they considered any contemporaneous female author worthy of notice. For example, very shortly after Concha Espina sent a dedicated copy of *La niña de Luzmela* to Azorín, she found it in a secondhand bookstore. He did, however, write a favorable article about her in the 1950s, when they both ostensibly supported Francisco Franco's regime. In "A una aspirante a escritora," Unamuno declared that "la lengua literaria es 'pantalónica,'" and in "A la señora Mab" he declared that women should find "su propio tono, el tono genuinamente femenino" (Unamuno 1970, 696, 708). Women, he said, excel at the private letter (697).

Baroja was the first of the three male authors to include a feminist character in a novel: Miss Pich of *Paradox, rey* (1906), who is a rather flat caricature, significantly of English nationality. English feminism was the earliest and most strident feminist movement in Europe and by the late nineteenth century had infiltrated the Spanish male consciousness as a particular threat that might spread to Spain. Baroja was also the first of the major Spanish male modernist writers to create female protagonists. Although he wrote vehemently against the institution of marriage in the first decade and proclaimed himself a "partidario acérrimo" of divorce when queried in Burgos's survey (qtd. in Castañeda 1994, 116), his novelistic plots favor traditional domesticity. In *Camino de perfección*, Fernando Ossorio ends his philosophical quest with marriage and child rearing. His wife, Dolores, is the quintessential angel of the house. In 1908 and 1909, Baroja produced a pair of novels (*La dama errante* and *La ciudad de la niebla*) with a female protagonist, María Aracil, who attempts to live independently in England, where there existed greater freedom for women. She survives most of the events narrated in the two novels—orphanhood, anarchistic turmoil, and exile—as an independent woman, but finally succumbs to social pressures for marriage and domestic duties at the end of the second novel. The Spanish María must surrender her autonomy and appear content and fulfilled within housewifery. By the pre-Republican era, Baroja had become overtly more reactionary, stating that divorce was an institution for rich countries and that if women were granted the vote, they would support communists and priests: "¡Ni hablar!" (qtd. in Arbeloa and Santiago 1981, 58).

As early as *El mundo es así* (1912)—although feminism at that time was still very much a foreign phenomenon in Spain, something associated with other countries—Baroja endorsed traditional female roles within a milieu much more consciously aware of feminism. Thus, the protagonist of *El mundo es así*, Sacha, is Russian. Having grown up in a male-dominated Russian family, Sacha defies her father's wishes and decides to study medicine in progressive, open Geneva.[1] Baroja's position in this novel might seem feminist for the sympathetic portrayal of the intelligent female protagonist. Like Blanca de los Ríos and Sofía Casanova, he disparages the Don Juan figure that other male novelists convert into an icon of national tradition and spirituality. The narrative situation is, however, complex and leads to other conclusions.

The Basque author's precociousness in creating female protagonists and addressing feminism can perhaps be attributed to his sister, Carmen Baroja. Much of what little we learn about Sacha's psychology suggests that Baroja at least subconsciously had his sister in mind. In her memoir (written in the 1940s but not published until 1998—a classic case of a female-authored manuscript that languished in a trunk), Carmen declared herself a feminist: "Era la época del feminismo. Yo era francamente feminista, veía la poca diferencia que había entre los dos sexos. Encontraba [a] muchos hombres estúpidos, tan estúpidos o más que las mujeres, y que, sin embargo, gozaban de un sinfín de prerrogativos en todas partes, desde las mismas ideas ancestrales, pasando por la literatura, hasta la Iglesia, etcétera. Esto me sublevaba" (1998, 68). Carmen's memoir profiles her brother Pío and sheds light on his treatment of feminism in his fiction.

Carmen tellingly titled her memoir *Recuerdos de una mujer del noventa y ocho;* thus, like María Martínez Sierra, she identified herself with the male generation. She was the youngest of a family that already had three sons, two of whom became well-known artists and writers. Carmen also had artistic inclinations, displaying a special flair for metal and enamel work in the years before she married in 1913. She struggled her entire life with the social strictures placed on women who wished to develop artistic and intellectual talents. Her frustration and bitterness over her own situation vis-à-vis those of her brothers are everywhere evident in her autobiography. Her upbringing was "muy *a la española*" (45); as she put it, "Era por demás rígida para mí en cosas pueriles y sin importancia, y muy laxa para his hermanos en cosas que yo, ya entonces, consideraba importantes" (45). [Besides it was rigid for me in silly and unimportant things and very lax for my brothers in things that I, already then, considered important.] After her marriage to Rafael Caro Raggio, she felt the constraints of traditional womanhood even more acutely: "Ya no tuve derecho más que a hacer mis labores domésticas y llevar la carga de muchísimas cosas" (45). She writes that if she had had the means, she would have taken her children and left home, but she had no way to make a living. Her declarations make Burgos, Espina, and Casanova, who did leave husbands and support themselves with their writing, seem all the more courageous.

During the Civil War (1936–39), Carmen's most famous brother, Pío, took flight to France. Carmen's husband was trapped in Madrid, so she grew produce at their summer home in the Basque village Vera del Bidasoa to feed herself and her children. She comforted her children by writing a story about a protective elf *(duende)*, which she read to them each night. How many other Judith Shakespeares were unable to shake the bonds of traditional Spanish womanhood to break into print?[2] Carmen's literary talents emerge in her autobiography, when she conveys how she felt as a traditional wife and mother by likening herself to a coach horse in Dickens's *The Pickwick Papers*. The Pickwickian coachman explains that his horse would fall down if released from the coach, but, while the horse is in harness, the wheels keep him going: "Las famosas ruedas de familia, casa, etcétera, me han llevado por el camino vulgar y seguro" (46). Carmen's brothers were extraordinarily egotistical: "El egoísmo de Pío siempre ha sido terrible; ahora ya da[ría] risa si no diera pena. A Ricardo le pasa igual [con] el egoísmo y la roñosería" (54). They learned from their mother to take for granted that she and their sister would provide every convenience. The brothers were free to pursue their art, but Carmen was tied to household and family. The situation was particularly painful for Carmen because she was aware that she was their intellectual equal: "Yo creía que si las mujeres, empezando por mí, a quienes veía en mi propia casa, en mi propia familia, a muchas con magníficas cualidades, no éramos más inteligentes era por nuestra falta de preparación, por nuestra falta de conocimientos" (68). [I believed that if the many women with magnificent qualities whom I saw in my own house, in my own family, beginning with myself, were not more intelligent, it was because we lacked preparation, because we lacked knowledge.] Because her mother favored handwork over reading, Carmen (who eventually wrote a book on embroidery) was forced to read furtively. Life for the bourgeois woman—sewing, fashion—bored her "to death," and she read as much as possible: "A pesar de mis trabajos, estudios costuras, lecturas, etcétera, yo me aburría de muerte" (57).

Despite Pío's protestations about his lack of Spanishness (in other words, his self-perceived progressiveness), Carmen considered her brother extremely conservative in family matters. Even though he never married and he wrote publicly against the institution of marriage, his novels reveal a hide-bound Spanish traditionalism in domestic affairs. Carmen confirms the interlinear message of the novels: "Él ha sido y ha vivido con ideas absolutamente españolas; llamo españolas a éstas relativas a las mujeres y a los asuntos amorosos y, sobre todo, a la moral de la familia" (68). [He has been and has lived with completely Spanish ideas; I term "Spanish" those ideas that relate to women and to matters of love, and, above all, to family morality.] The first years of her marriage (1913–25) occupy only a paragraph in her memoir. She was doubtless depressed by the confinement of marriage. Although her years as a single woman had not been unconstrained, she had traveled to Paris with her brother Pío in 1906 and had initiated a vocation in metal and enamel work.

Carmen's mood changed radically when she became a founding member of the Lyceum Club in 1926. She was also involved in the theatrical group El Mirlo Blanco, organized in 1925, which began in the home of Ricardo Baroja and his wife, Carmen Monné. For many years, the Barojas maintained three separate apartments in the same building: One floor was occupied by Carmen Baroja, her husband, and their children; another floor was occupied by Ricardo Baroja and Carmen Monné; and the third floor was occupied by Pío and his mother. Carmen Baroja headed the art section of the Lyceum Club, where Joaquín Sorolla y Bastida's daughters, among many others, exhibited. Carmen mentions that although the lecture program was very popular, she personally was unable to take advantage of it. She was often involved in the setup and arrangements for the lectures, but because her husband was inflexible about the dinner hour, she had to leave for home before the lectures began: "Rafael, si no estaba para la hora de cenar, que solía ser muy temprano, se ponía hecho una furia. Así que casi nunca me enteraba de lo que habían dicho" (91).

Toward the end of her memoir, Carmen dedicates a few pages to ruminations about her brother Pío's novelistic art. She gently criticizes him for not taking an interest in his immediate surroundings and suggests that his limited optic produced a deep flaw in his writing: "Así, en sus *Memorias,* si dicen mucho respecto a juicios literarios, anécdotas de escritores, etcétera, no pueden interesar a quien busque en ellas la manera, el proceso de formación de los sentimientos" (199). [So, if his memoirs say a great deal about literary judgments and anecdotes about writers, etc., they would not interest anyone looking in them for the manner, the process in which sentiments are formed.] Carmen had quite sophisticated ideas about how to describe one's own psychology or that of another person. First, she suggests, one must uncover the person's true being and feelings, something that she believed Pío had never bothered to do. Equally unaware of what motivated himself or others, he had formulated an abstract scheme about human psychology at some point and never bothered to change it.

Carmen believed that Pío's method produced a serious defect in his novels. She described his characters as "formados, cortados psicológicamente por los distintos patrones que tenía en su mente, patrones hechos de retazos de aquí y de allá, el chaleco de uno, los pantalones de otro, una bota de cada color y la americana del de más allá. Gentes que van y vienen en la vida de un lado a otro viendo cosas, tirando tiros, hablando, viajando . . . todo verdadero, todo tomado de la realidad, pero no verdaderas personas" (200) [formed, cut psychologically from different patterns that he had in his head, patterns made from pieces taken from here and there, a vest from one, the pants from another, a boot of each color, and the jacket from the one over there. People who come and go in life from one place to another, taking shots, talking, traveling . . . all true, all taken from reality, but not real people]. Carmen's observations may apply to both the male and female characters in Pío's novels. Most of the male protagonists hold certain traits in common—introspection, search for self, philosophical musings—but the reader is allowed an intimate and privileged knowledge of the character's inner life. Sacha, in *El mundo es ansí,* perhaps Pío's best-known female protagonist, offers an interesting case study in his approach to female psychology, which he handled in a decidedly different fashion. Although Sacha is ostensibly the focalizer of a narrative that includes her letters and diary, her interiority is often no more than a vehicle for observations about places or other people. This technique contrasts sharply with Martínez Sierra's narratives that privilege female consciousness through the epistolary mode.

Pío chose an unusual narrative plan for his "feminist" novel, which has been studied in depth by Carlos Longhurst (although without reference to its implications for Spanish feminism).[3] Longhurst asserts, for example, that with the diary technique, the reader not only feels closer to Sacha but also unconsciously identifies with her viewpoint. A diary, he says, can promote the false sense that we are witnessing the "genuine inner life of the character" when in fact the character is "fabricating a self rather than revealing it" (1977, 77). I argue that Sacha is not really allowed either to reveal herself *or* to fabricate a self, because the narrative is continually deflected onto other matters—the locale of her actions or the psychology of a male character, such as José Ignacio Arcelu.

Gilbert Smith is the only critic to seriously engage with the novel's depiction of feminism, but he ultimately judges the subject of feminism to be dominated by a more universal philosophical message. My view differs from that of Smith in that, as I see it, although the title and some of the plot—especially the relationship between Arcelu and Sacha, which comes very late in the book—point toward universal issues such as the arbitrary cruelty of life, women's position in society, rather than humanity in general, is a dominant theme of the novel. The management of feminism in *El mundo es ansí* is intimately bound up with the novel's narrative strategies. Sacha's story—her youth in Russia, her years as a medical student in Geneva, her first marriage to the Belgian Jew Ernesto Klein, her divorce, and her equally disastrous second marriage to the donjuanesque Spaniard Juan Velasco—is told by a variety of narrators filtered through a central editorial voice, presumably male. As Smith points out "A male voice . . . controls and edits the entire text" (1989, 361).

This narrator/editor, a friend of Velasco's, attends Velasco's wedding to the Russian divorcée Sacha. After the wedding, the narrator locates several sources that complete Sacha's story, including her life before her marriage to Velasco—her Russian childhood, medical school in Belgium, and the first marriage to Ernesto Klein—and her life in Spain with Velasco.[4] The most significant source of information about Sacha is Madame Frossard, a Swiss feminist who knew Sacha well and who conveniently provides the narrator with letters and a diary. Smith notes that "the transference of narrative authority primarily to Sacha, and in a secondary way to Madame Frossard, establishes an authenticity in this narrative that, the prologue seems to suggest, will be constructed in such a way as to prove some point in favor of the feminist ideology" (364). Smith rightly concludes that this strategy is deceptive and that the novel's message is not feminist.

Madame Frossard's interpretation of Sacha's story is a feminist interrogation of women's subjugation to patriarchal men; thus, Sacha's fate as a failed independent woman becomes a male commentary on the feminist movement in Europe. The male editor/narrator is ultimately judging Madame Frossard's feminist approach to Sacha's story. Having ascribed a feminist orientation to a salient source of information, Baroja colors much of what we learn about Sacha's important years in the feminist milieu of Geneva. The complex embedding of the narrative could have been sustained without an ideologically oriented source. Why not a vacuous landlady of the kind that Baroja portrayed in many of his other novels? Over and above Madame Frossard's feminism is her desire to relay Sacha's story to the narrator in order to convince him of "lo protervo de la conducta de los hombres en general y de los españoles en particular" (P. Baroja 1990, 69) [the perverse conduct of men in general and of Spaniards in particular]. The narrator, for his part, carefully undermines Madame Frossard's credibility as a feminist by adding coquetry to her list of qualities: "Era una mujer ingeniosa, alta, con los ojos pequeños y la nariz de loro, muy emperifollada y coqueta, a pesar de su edad" (68). [She was an ingenious woman, tall with small eyes and a parrot nose, very gaudily dressed and coquettish, despite her age.]

When we place the ambiguous portrait of Madame Frossard in the context of the patently negative descriptions of masculinized female medical students in Geneva, a pattern of questioning the motives and the mission of the feminist movement emerges. The seed is planted in the prologue when, in a diatribe against "sufragistas y feministas," Velasco avers, "No se puede vivir con una mujer sin religión" (67). The male editor/narrator, presumably informed by Madame Frossard, who received her notion of the student culture from Sacha, provides the following information about the female medical students: "Sacha, con su tez blanca y sonrosada, sus ojos azules y su cabello rubio, parecía una muñeca de porcelana entre aquellas mujeres de facciones duras, de color cetrino, como enfermas de ictericia. . . . Todas estas muchachas habían perdido el aire femenino. . . . Otra muchacha . . . daba la impresión de una inteligencia de hombre en cuerpo femenino" (84–85). [Sacha, with her white, blushed complexion, her blue eyes, and her blond hair, looked like a porcelain doll among the women with sallow-colored hard features, as though they were ill with jaundice. . . . All these girls had lost their feminine air. . . . Another girl . . . gave the impression of a man's intellect in a woman's body.] They are, in short, "estudiantonas" (88). Semeneski's wife is "mandona" (117), and Madame de Staël was a "sargentona" (129). The number of voices and points of view that intervene in these observations is complex and often confusing.

The second part of the novel, which Sacha narrates in the epistolary mode to her medical school friend Vera, recounts Sacha's travels to Italy after her divorce from her first husband, Ernesto Klein. The circumstance offers an opportunity to disclose Sacha's psychological condition after a failed marriage, but only a few references to her "alma vacía de emociones y de pensamientos" (149) hint at her state of mind before the remainder of the section becomes an objective travelogue.[5] Pío's travels in Italy provided details for the "impresiones retinianas" that fill numerous pages. In Italy, Sacha meets Velasco, who will become her second husband. A classic Don Juan, Velasco is a stereotype, as Carmen observed many of her brother's characters to be. Pío once commented, "El éxito de Don Juan entre las mujeres estriba en su falta de chispa y de gracia y humor" (1934, n.p.). [The success of Don Juan with women was based on his lack of spark and of charm and wit.] He also indicated that women prefer serious, sensual men, because "las mujeres son como los judíos: serias, ceremoniosas y sensuales" (n.p.) [women are like Jews: serious, ceremonious, and sensual].[6] Sacha, who displayed considerable spunk in her earlier years, even shooting a gun at Klein when she became completely disgusted with his egotistical behavior, loses her independent spirit in the company of the Spanish Don Juan: "Era un caso de sugestión, de captación de la voluntad. Velasco disponía, mandaba, y Sacha dejaba hacer" (P. Baroja 1990, 180).

Sacha's diary constitutes the third part of the novel. She turns to the diary form because her correspondent, Vera, who has married Leskoff, one of their former medical school companions, is preoccupied with her new domestic life. One would expect a diary, unburdened of narratee, to offer even greater impetus for intimate revelations than the letters, but again these opportunities are deflected in favor of extensive observations on Spain, especially observations on the role of women. Sacha takes a dismal view of the education that Spanish women receive in her adopted country. Aristocratic women learn only to pray and do handwork, which leads to "un carácter de coquetería, de ñoñería y de infantilismo verdaderamente desagradable" (201) [a coquettish character, a truly disagreeable silliness and infantilism].[7] They are spoiled, interested only in fashion and boyfriends. Women spend their time thinking about the parties that they attended during the last season and that they will attend in the next. Spanish women have a rather distorted view of women in other countries, assuming that they are "un poco hombrunas y muy decididas" (201) [rather masculine and very strong-willed]. Sacha is particularly distressed at the way that Spanish men talk about women as though they were chattel: "Se habla de ellas como de caballos. No es raro oír decir a uno:—¿Qué tal es esa mujer? Y al otro que contesta:—Es una buena jaca" (203).

The appearance of Arcelu, her husband's cousin (whose monocle and extravagant dress betray Azorín as the model), interrupts Sacha's observations on Spanish society. Arcelu becomes Sacha's constant companion, while Velasco, who has tired of family life and taken a mistress, spends most of his time elsewhere. Sacha and Arcelu, both intelligent and somewhat disillusioned, find solace in each other's company. Oddly, Arcelu's potential as a means for the narrator to further explore Sacha's psychology is not realized; in fact, the reverse occurs. Nearly half of the important section (toward the end of the novel) after Arcelu appears is devoted to exposition of his worldview; meanwhile, Sacha is relegated to the role of interlocutor. The narrator appears to be more comfortable with male than with female subjectivity (a situation repeated in both Unamuno's *La tía Tula* and Azorín's *Doña Inés*). We learn of Arcelu's views on many subjects—literature, science, painting, and life in general—and we learn that, like so many of Baroja's male protagonists, he lacks will. As Longhurst notes, Arcelu's ideas are "a mixture of perceptive comments, ingenious extemporizing, outrageous explanations and eccentric suppositions. Arcelu's disquisitions bring out his personality very well" (1977, 53).

Arcelu's personality accrues a subtlety and complexity lacking in the female protagonist. He is a sympathetic figure because he befriends the unhappily married Sacha ("es un hombre muy amable y muy atento conmigo," she says [P. Baroja 1990, 214]), but his tendency to introspection and associability irritates Velasco. Arcelu describes himself as having "un instinto de destrucción grande; ahora, que como no tengo voluntad ni perseverancia no lo he podido realizar nunca" (220) [a great instinct for destruction; but since I lack will and perseverance, I have not been able to carry it out]. Complicating the sympathetic portrayal of Arcelu is the narrative irony with which his extreme biologism is presented. His racial and national theories sound absurd (for example, he divides all of humanity into what he calls "gorillas," the idealists, and "chimpanzees," the realists). Sacha's view is more reasonable and balanced, but the contrast places Arcelu in the unusual position of likable eccentric.

Sacha's marital situation finally reaches a crisis, and she decides to separate from Velasco. Inertia on the part of both Arcelu and Sacha prevents them from then forming the romantic relationship that the reader has been led to expect. Sacha, bitterly disappointed in her marriage to Velasco, leaves Spain to return to Russia. Upon learning of her abrupt departure without a farewell, Arcelu requests that his newspaper assign him to cover the political turmoil in China. Sacha blames the breakdown of her marriage on her husband's refusal to provide a true home for her and her child. His donjuanesque nature dictates that he prefer to live in hotels and move from city to city. Sacha, in fact, blames all of Spain's ills on a national inability to make the home a central feature of daily life:

> Mi vida es una vida de movimiento continuo; ir al teatro, al museo, subir a la Giralda, hacer visitas, corretear por las calles.
> Una vida así me parece demasiado exterior, demasiado superficial para que me guste. No sé, la verdad, si podré acostumbrarme.
> No comprendo bien la manera de ser española. . . .
> Éste es un pueblo con dogma, pero sin moralidad, con gestos, pero sin entusiasmo, con franqueza y sin efusión. No lo comprendo bien.
> Gran parte de su manera de ser creo que procede de la falta de hogar. La calle les parece a estos meridionales el pasillo de su casa; hablan a las novias en la calle, discuten en la calle; para la casa no guardan más que las funciones vegetivas y la severidad. (200)

[My life is one of continuous movement; going to the theater, to the museum, climbing the Giralda, visiting people, hanging around the streets.

A life like that seems too exterior for me, too superficial for my taste. I really don't know if I could get used to it.

I don't understand the Spanish way of life very well. . . .

This is a country with dogma, but without morality, with gestures but without enthusiasm, with frankness and without effusion. I don't understand it well.

I think a large part of the way they are comes from the lack of home life. For these southerners, the street is like the hallway of their house; they talk to their girlfriends in the street; they discuss in the street; they save only the vegetative functions and severity for the house.]

Thus, Sacha, who began as the dedicated intellectual woman with a clear sense of her medical vocation, gradually becomes more domestically inclined, but a donjuanesque Spaniard thwarts her domestic urges. She is not even able to form a long-lasting relationship with a kind and intellectual man like Arcelu. She is now trapped in an impossible limbo—she has lost her intellectual and professional footing, but she is not suited for the traditional domestic realm either.

Sacha's friend Vera, a woman with no intellectual pretensions, is the female character who prevails. The coquettish and feminine Vera stands out in the masculinized female student culture of Geneva. (Sacha, similarly, is more feminine than the other Geneva students, but she lacks the female coquettishness.) Pairing the feminine, intellectual Sacha with the equally feminine but unintellectual Vera, Baroja, who often used opposing characters to make a point, sets the stage for his final message about which kind of woman will succeed in the modern world. Vera is more devoted to fashion and socializing than to her studies. She would have preferred dressmaking or hat design to medicine: "Le hubiera encantado ir al teatro, estrenar trajes bonitos, llamar la atención. . . . Le gusta hablar de amores, de trajes, de joyas. . . . Cree tener más condiciones para cocinera que para médica" (86, 87, 89). The epilogue of the book narrates Sacha's visit to Vera and her husband in Geneva. The couple's life seems idyllic; they have a lovely house in the country and a beautiful little boy. Vera is completely and happily devoted to her domestic duties: "Sacha la encontró muy hacendosa, muy burguesa" (257), whereas Sacha ends up lonely and miserable in Moscow. The final message of the novel is that the intellectually endowed woman, even if she attempts the domestic life, will fail, whereas the woman who is naturally domestic will find happiness. Even though Vera and Sacha are foreigners, Sacha's sojourn in Spain suggests that Baroja was trying out models of appropriate sexual roles and domestic arrangements for the Spanish nation. He offers no positive role models. The donjuanesque Velasco is thwarting national stability by eschewing domesticity. The country seems to need intelligent women like Sacha, but she fails to find an appropriate domestic partner.

Smith notes that toward the end *El mundo es ansí* abdicates the theme of power relations between men and women and the intelligent woman's inability to find an appropriate place for herself. Instead, he highlights "the solipsistic insensitivity inherent in all people, men and women alike" (1989, 367). Smith concludes that "the question of feminism is posed [only] because it is an example of an active engagement with firmly entrenched societal patterns" (367–68). Even though through his male narrative filters, Baroja constructs a web of antifeminist rhetoric and sentiment into which Sacha's story is placed, *El mundo es ansí* is not an antifeminist diatribe. There is a great deal of narrative sympathy for Sacha's intelligence. Sacha can hold her own with male interlocutors on any subject, and she forcefully counters Leskoff's anti-Semitism. The ultrafeminine Vera, in contrast, is portrayed as frivolous (at least until she marries and becomes a mother, whereupon she assumes greater maturity and dignity). Nonetheless, the message of the ending that favors traditional marriage and domesticity cannot be ignored. A woman of independent spirit ends badly, whereas her stereotypically feminine friend who embraces marriage and home ends well.

Baroja was fully aware that he was preaching to a female readership in Spain. The chapter "El amor y la literatura," which appears toward the middle of the novel, reflects on the role of literature in women's lives and on the perceived need to address a "female psychology." When Sacha becomes disenchanted with her marriage to Velasco, the wry narrator blames the literature that women read: "La literatura ha hecho creer a los hombres y a las mujeres que en determinadas circunstancias se desarrollan en ellos fuerzas espirituales que les llevan a las alturas de una felicidad inefable" (P. Baroja 1990, 136). [Literature has made men and women believe that under certain circumstances spiritual forces develop in them that carry them to the heights of ineffable happiness.] The narrator asserts that the concept of "female psychology" was invented. Female psychology is projected as "buena y mala, sensual y casta, amable e impertinente, seca y sentimental' (138) [good and bad, sensual and chaste, pleasant and impertinent, dry and sentimental], and the woman attempts to conform to the stereotype. Despite these rather astute observations (remember that it is 1912), the narrator concludes quite unhelpfully, "En el fondo ni en el hombre existe algo más que lo humano, ni en la mujer algo más que lo femenino" (138). [In the end in men there exists only the human and in women only the feminine.]

If *El mundo es ansí* engages with feminism in a relatively overt manner, Unamuno's novels that have strong female characters (although they do not mention feminism directly) acquire, as we observed in *Niebla,* significant shades of meaning when read in the context of contemporaneous feminist discourse. Unamuno abhorred feminism, which he mentioned often in his extranovelistic writing. He saw it as the masculinization of women, a "masculinismo femenino" (1958, 7:362). Unlike Martínez Sierra, who argued in *Feminismo, feminidad, españolismo* against a "marimacho" feminism and for a feminine feminism (G. Martínez Sierra 1917, 127, 129), Unamuno declared that not only is feminine feminism impossible but it is also invariably oppressive: "Bajo el dominio, no ya de la mujer, sino de lo femenino . . . viene a parar a un estado de que hace falta una recia sacudida para poderse libertar. Cae bajo un feminismo de una cierta vanidad, vanidad voluble, quejillona a veces, a veces zumbona" (1958, 7:822). He believed that national stagnation could be attributed to such "vain" and "complaining" feminism. Woman's role was to assert a domestic heroism, to be a companion to her husband and a strong and intelligent educator of (especially) her male children: "Esa entrañable convivencia en el hogar debería ser, además, la mejor cura de la pereza, y con ella de la soberbia y la envidia . . . y el mejor abono de las artes de la paz, únicas que llevan a los pueblos a la dicha y la gloria duraderas" (7:588). The true spirit of women "se nota en el hogar, el propio ser femenino se revela en la manera de gobernar su casa y hacer sus labores" (qtd. in Doyaga 1969, 15) [is evident in the home, the very feminine being is revealed in the way she governs her house and does her chores]. As noted in Chapter 2, Juan Rof Carballo calls this aspect of Unamuno's thinking "epidemiología familiar" (1964, 84).

Tres novelas ejemplares y un prólogo and *La tía Tula,* both from 1920, incorporate the masculinized woman Unamuno railed against in his extranovelistic writing. As noted in Chapter 1, some studies of Unamuno's literary treatment of women exist, but little critical literature has attempted to understand Unamuno's depiction of women as reflecting the wider historical-social moment of the second and third decades of the twentieth century in Spain.[8] Unamuno himself mentioned several of his novels in the context of feminism. He believed that *Abel Sánchez* and especially *La tía Tula* sold exceptionally well because of the "propaganda de lectoras, de mujeres . . . que saben qué es eso de feminismo" (1958, 10:699) [propaganda of female readers, of women . . . who know what feminism is]. He conversed with Emilia Pardo Bazán about the plot of *La tía Tula* in feminist terms: "Se engarzó con ella en una discusión sobre 'etnología feminista' o 'feminismo etnológico'" (qtd. in Doyaga 1969, 24).

As shown in Chapter 2, by the completion of *Niebla* in 1914, the new, more modern woman makes her appearance in Unamuno's cast of characters, albeit not as the lead figure. *Niebla* was seven years in the making, but *La tía Tula* took some eighteen years to complete.[9] Circumstantial evidence suggests that Unamuno regained interest in his novel about an independent woman when women's public visibility increased in Spain in the post–World War I era. By the 1920 publication of *Tres novelas ejemplares y un prólogo,* he was keenly aware that women made up a large share of the readership of novels: "En España, hoy, el consumo de novelas lo hacen principalmente mujeres" (1958, 9:423). (He quickly corrects the term "mujeres," which does not designate marital status: "¡Es decir, mujeres, no!, sino señoras y señoritas" [9:423]) His tone in the prologue is decidedly paternalistic, if not scornful. He considers the novelettes "exemplary" because they are cautionary tales for women. Women, he avers, normally read novels recommended (or prohibited) by their confessors or "sensiblerías que destilan mangla o pornografías que chorrean pus" (9:423). And, although they do not necessarily avoid novels that make them think, they flee from those that could move them unless the emotion ends in "¡Bueno, más vale callarlo!" (9:423). Clearly, Unamuno was not thinking of novels by Martínez Sierra, de los Ríos, Casanova, or Burgos.

Even more assertively than *Niebla,* the "novelas ejemplares," while they ostensibly field Unamuno's perennial themes of identity and self-perpetuation, depict stories about women's appropriate social comportment. All three of the *Novelas ejemplares* center on problems of marriage and family, and two of the novels, *Dos madres* and *El marqués de Lumbría,* feature the strong black widow type of woman who destroys the men with whom she becomes involved. The third, *Nada menos que todo un hombre,* centers on a more feminine woman who ultimately garners her obdurate, egotistical husband's love and devotion. However iconoclastic Unamuno may have been on many issues, as noted in Chapter 1, he was a strict traditionalist in family arrangements.

In many respects, *Dos madres* and *La tía Tula* are companion novels in which the female protagonists, Raquel and Tula, desire motherhood without marriage. Raquel, in *Dos madres,* is apparently barren, and Tula never engages in sexual activity. Both women choose surrogate mothers and are strong-willed and manipulative enough to force marriage between the surrogate mother and a weak-willed man. Like Eugenia in *Niebla,* both Raquel's and Tula's behavior assumes a monstrous quality unnecessary to the plot or to the psychological-cum-philosophical drama that motivated the work. Both novels engage the Don Juan legend to characterize the weak-willed male character destroyed by the monstrous female. Thus, Unamuno links the failure of the man to the larger issue of Spanish national decline. Don Juan, emblem of the once-strong Spanish nation, is now reduced to simpering dependence on a strong-willed, even vicious and destructive woman. The man wants and argues for a traditional family unit, but the woman denies him the fulfillment of that wish in favor of a solitary, monomaniacal motherhood as the lone all-powerful woman. The interlinear message is that feminism threatens the health of the nation, which in turn depends on a traditional family unit.

In *Dos Madres,* Raquel, whose name and story echo those of biblical women, is a childless widow engaged in a long-standing affair with Don Juan. This Don Juan, however, has abandoned his sexually promiscuous life and is now monogamous. When their union fails to produce offspring, Raquel encourages Juan to marry his childhood sweetheart, Berta. Although Juan would rather marry Raquel, at Raquel's insistence, he marries Berta, whose parents are happy to finally place their daughter in the matrimonial estate. Raquel's voraciousness knows no bounds; she absorbs and destroys everything around her. The novel begins ominously: "¡Cómo le pesaba Raquel al pobre don Juan! La viuda aquélla, con la tormenta de no tener hijos en el corazón del alma, se le había agarrado y le retenía en la vida que queda, no en la que pasa. Y en don Juan había muerto, con el deseo, la voluntad" (Unamuno 1958, 9:424). [How Raquel weighed on poor Don Juan! That widow, with the torment of not having children in her soul's heart, had grabbed hold of him and retained him in what remains of life, not in that which passes on. And Don Juan's will had died with his desire.] When Berta and Juan's first child is born, Raquel takes possession of her; in the meantime, Raquel has also managed to gain control over Berta's parents' fortune. Juan has already signed over his own assets to Raquel. Finally, Juan commits suicide, and Berta, pregnant with their second child and bereft of financial means, is forced to accept Raquel's offer to support her in exchange for custody of her firstborn.

In the first paragraph of the novelette, Unamuno establishes the centrality of formal family arrangements to the denouement. The narrator refers to the liaison between Raquel and Juan as "aquel hogar solitario, constituído *fuera de la ley*" (9:424, my emphasis). This illegal union—a family that is not a traditionally sanctioned unit—is a menace. Rapacious language characterizes Raquel. Juan is "absorto por ella. . . . Y don Juan se sentía arrastrado por ella a más dentro de la tierra. '¡Esta mujer me matará!'" (9:424) [absorbed by her. . . . And Don Juan felt himself being dragged down into the earth by her. "This woman will kill me!"]. Berta, the woman who accepts legal marriage, is described as "angelical" (9:428), whereas Raquel is "demoníaca" (9:428).[10] Berta's parents cast Juan in the role of a "pobre náufrago de amores," although they do not know that Raquel's home is a "puerto de tormentas" (9:429). Raquel has "ojos negros y tenebrosos" [dark, gloomy eyes]; she is like "una noche sin fondo y sin estrellas" [a bottomless night without stars] pushing him toward an abyss. She is his inferno, death itself. After the baby arrives and Raquel assumes the role of surrogate mother, she sings to the child in a strange and unintelligible language. It is as though she arrived from a far-off land, "un mundo lejano, muy lejano, perdido en la bruma de los ensueños" (9:450). When Juan hears her, he experiences the dream of death, and an insane terror fills his hollow heart.

If, as David W. Foster (1966) suggests, the depiction of Raquel as a "Fatal Woman" has its roots in romanticism; a weakling Don Juan is decidedly antiromantic. Unamuno's will-less Don Juan is the antithesis of his prototypes in Golden Age and romantic models. As Isabel Criado Miguel points out, the "desmitificación del tipo de Don Juan, del donjuanismo, de lo que atañe a su carácter, procedimientos de seducción física, etc., no comienza hasta el positivismo del XIX como pura reacción antirromántica" (1986, 115) [demythification of the Don Juan type, of donjuanism, of what concerns his character, procedures of physical seduction, etc., does not begin until the positivism of the nineteenth century as a pure antiromantic reaction]. Criado Miguel claims for the protagonist of *Dos madres* the position of first modernist demythified Don Juan (a Don Juan who lacks physical vigor and masculine decisiveness). She overlooks Valle-Inclán's wry modernist portraits of the Don Juan figure in the Marqués de Bradomín, perhaps because Unamuno's Don Juan appears more decisively demythified than the Marqués de Bradomin. Unamuno's Don Juan is demythified by a woman rather than by his own hand. In fact, the roles of male seducer and female victim are completely reversed in *Dos madres*. Raquel absorbs Don Juan's very essence, his manhood: "Yo voy a hacerte hombre; voy a hacerte padre" (Unamuno 1958, 9:437). She converts him into a mere instrument of her desire to become a mother.

As noted, other male characters in Spanish modernist novels are indecisive and will-less (Antonio Azorín in the early novels by José Martínez Ruiz and Pío Baroja's Fernando Ossorio in *Camino de perfección,* Andrés Hurtado in *El árbol de la ciencia,* and Arcelu in *El mundo es ansí*), but these qualities are inherent to their natures rather than directly attributable to a woman's diabolical machinations.[11] The narrator of Unamuno's *Dos madres* asserts that Don Juan "perdía aquella voluntad que no era suya, sino de Raquel" (Unamuno 1958, 9:429) [lost his will, which did not belong to him but to Raquel]. As Criado Miguel indicates, Raquel's role is "privar al mito de cualidades que le son inherentes y dotarlo de sus contrarios, deterioro que se advierte porque se conoce el modelo al que responde este personaje, que en la novela atiende por Don Juan, tratamiento que lo indentifica y lo segrega de los otros personajes" (1986, 116) [to take from the myth those qualities that are inherent to it and endow it with its opposites, a deterioration that one notices because one knows the model to which the character corresponds, which in the novel answers to the name Don Juan, a treatment that identifies it and separates it from other characters]. He loses his distinctive character and becomes any Juan: "[El] pobre Juan, ya sin don, temblaba entre las dos mujeres" (1958, 9:432). In his portrayal of the struggle between the "terrible mother" Raquel and the victimized Juan, Unamuno joins other European male modernists, such as Marcel Proust and James Joyce, in whose novels, according to Ricardo Quinones, "the maternal relationship . . . inspired the most poisonous behavior" (1985, 55). Quinones finds that canonical modernist writers, instead of seeking to liberate themselves from their fathers, sought "to achieve freedom from the[ir] mother[s]" (55). D. H. Lawrence, he notes, "discovered his great and true theme: the terrible pathos of men defeated by the superior will of independent women" (60). Quinones does not link this phenomenon to the rise of the feminist movement in Europe but to a "rejection of the values of historical continuity" (60). In Spain, where the mother figure (as José Álvarez Junco [2001] amply demonstrates) is so closely linked to nationalist thinking, canonical modernist writers are struggling against the attempts of that traditional national figure to redefine her role.

Unamuno's *El marqués de Lumbría,* the second *novela ejemplar,* similarly incorporates a diabolical woman who psychologically castrates a male figure. The Marqués of Lumbría has two daughters, both of marriageable age. Luisa, the younger daughter, finds a suitor before the older daughter, Carolina, who enters into an affair with her sister's fiancé, Tristán, before the wedding. Carolina then goes to a distant village to have their child; meanwhile, the marriage between Luisa and Tristán takes place. The married couple has a son, the presumed heir to the Marqués's estate. When Luisa dies shortly after giving birth, Carolina brings her own (illegitimate) son to live at the estate; she and the widower marry, and she maneuvers her own son into the position of heir. Tristán becomes a will-less puppet in her designs. Again, the issue of legitimate versus illegitimate male-female relations is central to the story, and the illegitimate relationship (read: woman) and child are portrayed as monstrous and destructive.

Unamuno's *Nada menos que todo un hombre,* the third *novela ejemplar* (probably written first, as it was published separately in 1916), creates a different domestic situation. Here the male is dominant and reduces the female to desperation. Alejandro Gómez, a wealthy *indiano,* marries the extraordinarily beautiful Julia, who accepts his hand because her father is destitute. Alejandro is incapable of showing Julia any real love and uses her as one more object to display his wealth and power. Julia's exasperation at Alejandro's seeming indifference drives her to declare that she is having an affair with a nobleman who frequents the house. Alejandro's egotism knows no bounds, and he has Julia committed to an insane asylum for pronouncing herself an adulterer. In order to secure her release, Julia confesses to having lied about the affair. After reducing Julia to near madness with his psychological mistreatment, Alejandro finally reveals a deep love for her: " '¡Pues no he de quererte, hija mía, pues no he de quererte! ¡Con toda el alma, y con toda la sangre, y con todas las entrañas; más que a mí mismo! Al principio, cuando nos casamos, no. ¿Pero ahora? ¡Ahora sí! Ciegamente, locamente. Soy tuyo más que tú mía.' ¡Julia! ¡Julia! ¡Mi diosa! ¡Mi todo!' " (1958, 9:508–9). [Well, of course I love you, my child, well, why shouldn't I! With all my heart, and with all my blood, and with all my entrails; more than myself! A t first, when we got married, no. But now? Now, yes! Blindly, insanely. I am yours more than you mine. Julia! Julia! My goddess! My everything!] The "example" or message here is that the submissive wife will eventually win the devotion of even the most obdurate husband. Shortly after Alejandro's declaration of love, Julia falls ill and dies; the inconsolable Alejandro then commits suicide. Interestingly, the portrayal of Alejandro, whose initial heartlessness and egotism could be compared to that of Eugenia, Raquel, or Carolina, ends on a sympathetic note. The monstrous qualities of the dominant women intensify as their story progresses, whereas the male's domineering character is submerged in an existential angst with which the reader is encouraged to empathize. On her deathbed, Julia asks Alejandro who he is, and he responds, "¡Nada más que tu hombre . . . , el que tú me has hecho!" (517). [Nothing more than your man . . . , the man you have made me!]

Tula, protagonist of *La tía Tula*, apparently exhibits the same existential anxieties as her male counterparts.[12] She resists situations in which she will lose her identity and seeks immortality through her surrogate children. Geoffrey Ribbans especially points to her nature as a "supreme individualist" (1987, 411) who "imposes her will, consciously and consistently on herself and on her acquired family" (413) in order to "determine and follow her authentic self, although she is racked by doubts that she is simply adopting a false *persona*" (413). As is invariably the case in Unamuno's fictions, *La tía Tula*'s narrative situation is designed to illustrate the ontological problems that Ribbans has identified. Tula's sister, Rosa, attracts the attention of Ramiro, who courts her somewhat indecisively until Tula forces his hand. A growing fondness for Tula occasioned Ramiro's indecisiveness about Rosa, but Tula rejects his advances and insists on his honoring his pursuit of Rosa. Once the marriage takes place, Tula intervenes in several ways to ensure that the couple will have children immediately.

Tula assumes the care of Rosa's three children. Rosa dies shortly after the birth of the third child, exhausted from the rapid succession of births manipulated by Tula. At this point, Tula joins Ramiro's household to become a surrogate mother to her dead sister's children. Ramiro seeks Tula's hand in marriage, but she refuses. In desperation, Ramiro has an affair with the serving girl Manuela, who becomes pregnant by him. Tula then insists that they marry and adds their two progeny to the brood that she considers her own. Manuela dies giving birth to her second child, and Ramiro's death follows shortly thereafter.

Ostensibly, Tula's desire for children and her aversion to sex and marriage are tied to her existential need to maintain her individual identity and perpetuate herself through her adopted children.[13] Tula refuses Ramiro's proposal of marriage after her sister dies, because she does not wish to be a stepmother to Rosa's children. She is averse to being "la otra," which would cast her as an existential shadow. The parallels between Tula and Augusto Pérez (*Niebla*) are many; Tula has also been characterized as a female version of Joaquín Monegro (of *Abel Sánchez*). Rof Carballo calls *La tía Tula* "la novela de la envidia femenina," (1964,

74). Like Augusto, Tula eschews carnality to engage in a vicarious relationship with the real world. Also like Augusto, she overemphasizes the mental to the denigration of the carnal (embracing the Cartesian split between mind and body). Although both Tula and Augusto modify their attitude toward carnality in their final days, they meet unhappy (even tragic) ends. Both characters struggle valiantly to assert their existential independence, to be themselves rather than just a mirror of someone else, "el otro" or "la otra." Although similar in philosophical or existential terms, they diverge in character. Tula combines Augusto's existential plight with Eugenia's strong, manipulative character (Augusto, like Don Juan in *Dos madres,* Tristán in *El marqués de Lumbría,* or Ramiro in *La tía Tula,* is weak-willed in the face of a strong, domineering woman).[14]

If Augusto's existential problem—his fictional nature—is completely independent of his sexuality or his relationship to Eugenia (which merely precipitates his crisis), Tula's dilemma is inextricably bound up with her biological and social situation as a woman. Her existential failure derives from her refusal to engage in a traditional marital relationship with any of the men that seek her hand—Ramiro, Ricardo, and Don Juan. Tula believes that her existence (her individual identity) depends on maintaining her independence from both Rosa and Ramiro and on possessing her adopted children. Gullón calls Tula's drive to maternity a "disfraz de la voluntad posesiva" (1964, 206) [disguise of a possessive will]. She promises Rosa on her deathbed that she will not allow Rosa's three children to have a stepmother. Rosa insinuates that the best way for Tula to prevent this is to marry Ramiro. She thus implies an absolute identity between herself and Tula. In terms of their role as mother to Rosa and Ramiro's children, they are, in fact, identical. If Tula were to marry Ramiro, she would become "the other," a prospect that she abhors. She imagines that if she were Ramiro's wife, he might think of Rosa as, she, Tula, lay next to him in bed: "No sería sino el recuerdo . . . , algo peor que el recuerdo de la otra!" (Unamuno 1990, 122–23). Augusto experiences the same dilemma in his "relationship" with Eugenia, but his existential crisis is more developed: After Unamuno reveals his fictional status to him, Augusto exhorts, "Yo quiero ser yo, yo, yo."

Unlike Augusto's existential discourse, however, Tula's is combined with the social discourse of feminism. Much of what Tula says about her situation echoes what Spanish feminists (especially after the First World War) were saying about women's general social condition—their subordination to a patriarchal legal system, their lack of options outside marriage. Carlos Feal calls Tula "un formidable reto a la sociedad (masculina) en que vive, en cuyo seno se resiste profundamente a entrar," (1988, 70) [a formidable challenge to the (masculine) society in which she lives, into whose bosom she profoundly resists entering]. He adds that she proposes "nada menos que una reforma social" (70).[15] María Elena Bravo likens her to Antigone for her defiance of male law, pointing out that both women fail in their attempts to transgress patriarchy: "Las mismas leyes [as in Antigone's case] son denunciadas por Tula que al ponerlas a prueba paga un alto precio, el de su fracaso como ser humano integral" (1989, 415). Tula argues consistently for women's independence from traditional roles, and she contests conventional images of women. When Ramiro comments that she could have married if she had wished, Tula replies that women cannot seek suitors; only men can do that. Women must wait to be chosen: "Y yo, la verdad me gusta elegir, pero no ser elegida" (Unamuno 1990, 98).

Although in one of his essays Unamuno equated motherhood with eternal life ("la madre se descubre madre, o sea inmortal y eterna" [1958, 11:800]), Tula links her existential situation to her sociosexual role, something none of the male "agonistas" in Unamuno's novels do. Ramiro asks Tula why she did not become a nun, which evokes the reply that she does not like others to order her about. When the doctor Don Juan remarks, "Cada hombre es un mundo" (1990, 145), she retorts, "Y cada mujer, una luna, ¿no es eso, don Juan?" (145). [And each woman a moon. Isn't that the case, Don Juan?] Don Juan reaffirms the traditional female role as angel of the house: "—Cada mujer puede ser un cielo" (145). When Don Juan suggests that he and Tula marry and raise her adopted children together, she accuses him of seeking a sexual "remedio" and/or a domestic servant. She reflects on women's traditional role: "¡Cuando una no es remedio es animal doméstico y la mayor parte de las veces ambas cosas a la vez! Estos hombres . . . ¡O porquería o poltronería! ¡Y aún dicen que el cristianismo redimió nuestra suerte, la de las mujeres!" (155). [When one is not a remedy, she is a domestic animal and most of the time both things at once! These men . . . Either filth or idleness!

And they still say that Christianity redeemed our fate, that of women!] Moreover, she considers that Christianity "es religión de hombres . . . masculinos el Padre, el Hijo y el Espíritu Santo." (155). Indignantly, she observes that the Lord called his mother "servant" rather than mother.

A number of critics have pointed out Tula's dual nature; she combines masculine and feminine qualities in the kind of sexual ambiguity (masculinized women and feminized men) that was common to 1920s gender discourse. Paciencia Ontañón de Lope calls her "la característica mujer fálica, es decir revestida de los atributos masculinos, que envidia y desea—y logra poseer—, circunstancia que la convierte en hembra castradora" (1986, 386–87) [the typical phallic woman, that is to say, dressed in masculine characteristics; she envies and desires—and manages to possess—a circumstance that converts her into a castrating female]. Carballo sees her as having become a "varona por despecho amoroso, por haber sido su hermana y no ella la elegida" (1964, 75) [male-female out of love spite for her sister's having been chosen rather than her]. Gonzalo Navajas deploys the Lacanian terms Symbolic and Imaginary, the former to refer to the masculine realm of Law or the "order of values imposed on the individual from outside" (1975, 118) and the latter to refer to "inner, intuitive life" (118) often associated with the female. Navajas interprets Tula's problem as an inability to reconcile the two realms: "I shall propose that in Tula this balance does not exist since her life has been overpowered by the Symbolic" (118). Carballo calls her "anti-erótica" (1964, 87), and Feal (1988) locates her failure in trying to be both a father and mother simultaneously. Harriet Turner (1989) points to her dual masculine/feminine nature through a study of the sun/moon polarity of images. She convincingly argues that Tula, a manly-thinking woman forgoes a negatively viewed carnality. I do not, however, agree with Turner that Tula eventually escapes Unamuno. She is held firmly in his antifeminist grasp and is eliminated as a danger to traditional Spanish society.

As Gullón (1961b) and Turner (1989) observe (for different reasons), Tula is a monster. She is a hybrid; she is a strange combination of both male and female whose dual characteristics make her an aberration, something to neutralize. Tula's sin is not so much that she is not domestic but that she has refused to marry and legitimize her domestic situation. Tula equates marriage with servitude; thus, she limits her domestic commitment to childcare and avoids the constraints of male-dominated marriage. Tula's existential situation, grounded as it is in her sexuality (her virgin motherhood), can never achieve the abstract intensity of Augusto's or Joaquín Monegro's. She is anchored in her physical body, although she paradoxically refuses carnal engagement in the sexual world, which the narrative suggests is her natural place and obligation. Augusto's existence is primarily mental (he never engages in sex), but ultimately he genuinely desires matrimony with Eugenia and abandons his ascetic ways for a suicide of corporal excess (overeating). Augusto's avoidance of the body is a philosophical error; Tula's is socially unacceptable. She unnaturally eschews marriage out of repugnance for its physical aspects. Her confessor describes her appropriate social role as man's savior, instead of her chosen path as a strong, independent woman: "—Es que esa fortaleza, hija mía, puede alguna vez ser dureza, ser crueldad. Y es dura con él, muy dura. ¿Que no le quiere como marido? ¡Y qué importa! Ni hace falta eso para casarse con un hombre. Muchas veces tiene que casarse una mujer con un hombre por compasión, por no dejarle solo, por salvarle, por salvar su alma" (Unamuno 1990, 133).

The confessor is, in fact, rehearsing the "ángel del hogar" role assigned to women in many nineteenth-century tracts and novels, although the role is presented in a less straightforward manner. Tula is not simply an example of an undomestic woman who wreaks havoc on the home in which she inserts herself. She dies regretting the life that she has lived, a life in which she has forced others into marriage and childbearing so that she could raise children without having to engage in sex or a relationship with a husband—in other words, the whole domestic package. The children she has raised—her sister's and those of her brother-in-law and his second wife—scornfully reduce her memory to the generic name "la tía," a sad end to a woman who attempted to establish her existential being through her devotion to a surrogate family. Unamuno relegates Tula, a new breed of Spanish woman who lives according to her own ideals outside of Spanish tradition, to the ash can of oblivion.

Doña Inés, Azorín's undomestic woman, also ends with adopted children. If the early Azorín diverted the classics of Castilian literature to construct a positive exemplum for female conduct, by 1926, in *Doña*

Inés, he joined Pío Baroja and Miguel de Unamuno in creating a female protagonist who embodies a negative example of modern Spanish womanhood. *Doña Inés* is arguably Azorín's most ambitious conversion of a Spanish classic. Like his *Don Juan*, discussed in Chapter 3, its major intertext is José Zorrilla's quintessentially romantic play *Don Juan Tenorio*. *Doña Inés* employs the romantic intertext to an even greater extent than the earlier novel as a springboard to consider contemporary sexual mores. The meditation is facilitated by comparing a modern woman to Zorrilla's Doña Inés, a convent-raised potential novitiate who was to be the archseducer's supreme conquest. Thus, Zorrilla added an "angel of the house" model to Tirso de Molina's *El burlador de Sevilla o el convidado de piedra* (1621). The play was first staged in 1844; Azorín's novel is set in 1840. In the romantic play, Don Juan, like his seventeenth-century counterpart, is a seducer and a braggart. Three quarters of *Don Juan Tenorio* centers on Don Juan's amorous seductions of women and his valorous conquests of men in battle and in duels. Instead of being consigned to hell for his sins as he is in Tirso's work and in Mozart's opera on the theme, in Zorrilla's version, Don Juan is saved by falling in love with the pure and innocent Doña Inés.

He kidnaps Inés from her convent after sending her a love letter designed to seduce her, and he kills her father when he discovers them together at Don Juan's palace in Seville. After many years of living abroad to escape justice, Don Juan returns to Seville to find both his father and Inés dead, the latter of a broken heart. The father has disinherited his son and devoted his fortune to constructing an imposing pantheon to honor all those who perished at Don Juan's hand. Inés's most important role comes in the scenes in which, as a messenger from God, she confronts Don Juan in the pantheon. Inés is the voice from the other world, the angel from God asking the sinner to repent and be saved. This role coincides with the nineteenth-century view of women as harbingers of morality and the agents of salvation for men who stray from domestic virtue. In a 1924 article, Corpus Barga writes that Zorrilla added "la feminidad, todo lo virgen y contrario a Don Juan, su pareja Doña Inés" (n.p.) to Juan's masculinity. Corpus Barga first suggests that Inés was absorbed by Don Juan but then corrects himself and gives Inés a freestanding part: "El drama de Zorrilla, en vez de *Don Juan Tenorio* no se deba llamar *Doña Inés de Ulloa,* el verdadero drama de Doña Inés, más que el de Inés de Castro" (n.p.).

As though Azorín were answering his colleague's suggestion in his 1926 novel, he borrowed Zorrilla's romantic angelic female who rescues the most wicked of men from condemnation, and he converts her into a modern, cosmopolitan liberated woman. The manipulation of time in the novel is crucial, and (as I have developed at length in Johnson 1993c) central to the novel's contemporary message. The year 1840 was a critical moment in Spanish history. The despot Fernando VII had died just seven years earlier, and his daughter Isabel II was finally consolidating her reign. Her ascension to the throne in 1833 had occasioned a bitter civil war (the first of the Carlist wars) between, on one hand, reactionary factions that preferred a male heir who could continue Bourbon absolutism and hierarchical privileges and, on the other hand, more moderate elements that championed Isabel as a socially reforming constitutional monarch. As Elena Catena notes, "En los años de 1840 a 1848, España vive la desazonante situación de un mundo en trance de cambios fundamentales; agoniza una sociedad tradicional y avanza inconteniblemente otra nueva y de signo muy contrario" (1973, 54). [From 1840 to 1848, Spain lived the discomforting situation of a world in the throes of fundamental changes; a traditional society was dying and a new one of a very opposite character was advancing uncontrollably.] Toward the end of the novel, the narrator reminds us that the story that we have just read is emblematic of wider social movements: "Europa entera marchaba hacia algo desconocido e inquietador. España estaba revuelta. En Madrid había estallado, en septiembre, una revolución. Asonadas y motines habían perturbado a España en este año 1840. . . . Un arte abigarrado—el romántico—refleja una sensibilidad anárquica" (Azorín 1973, 213). [All of Europe was moving toward something unknown and disquieting. Spain was in tumult. In September, a revolution had broken out in Madrid. Mobs and riots had disturbed Spain in this year of 1840. . . . A motley art—romanticism—reflected an anarchic sensibility.] Similarly, vanguardism and feminism were provoking dismay in the traditional sectors of Spanish society in the 1920s. The narrator of *Doña Inés* pertinently mentions Flora Tristán, a nineteenth-century socialist active in the French revolution of 1848. He describes her as an "apóstol de las reivindicaciones obreras y ha lanzado, en 1843, la fórmula de la unión de todos los trabajadores" (214) [apostle of workers' revenge, and in 1843 she launched the formula for the uniting of all workers]. Her book *L'Union ouvrière*, he says, was a manifesto that subverted and brought down all traditional beliefs. Civilization based on Roman law was exhausted: "La imagen material de la vieja y lejana España se va rompiendo a pedazos; una nueva y poderosa forma trabaja por nacer" (220). [The material image of the old and distant Spain was breaking into pieces; a new and powerful form was laboring to be born.]

A number of narrative devices remind the reader that the nineteenth-century revolutionary period is being viewed through a modern, twentieth-century lens. If the nineteenth-century revolutions focused on workers and class society, the twentieth-century revolution centered on women. Doña Inés is dressed in 1840s fashions, but her attitude is that of a sexually liberated woman of post–World War I Europe. She is independently wealthy and has never married. At the beginning of the novel, the protagonist is walking alone through the city (presumably Madrid) on her way to an assignation with Don Juan in a room that they have rented for their love trysts. The narrator's eye scrutinizes her physical appearance: "Una observación atenta podría hacernos ver en el cuerpo de la dama que las líneas tienen ya un imperceptible principio de flacidez. Se inicia en toda la figura una ligerísima declinación. En la cara fresca todavía, la piel no tiene la tersura de la juventud primera" (73–74). [An attentive observation would make us see that the lines of the lady's body now have the imperceptible beginnings of flaccidity. Her whole figure has begun a slight decline. The skin of the still fresh face does not have the taughtness of early youth.] The narrator does not specify Inés's age, but clearly she is not in the first bloom of youth. She is perhaps in her mid- to late thirties (Salvadora de Olbena, protagonist of Azorín's eponymous novel of 1944, is thirty-two years old, and although no longer very young, she does not yet show the same signs of age as Inés).[16]

Doña Inés's face also bears the marks of melancholy. She is a woman whose life experiences have left their traces on her body and spirit. After a long wait in the room where she trysts with Don Juan, Inés receives a letter from him; although the text is not given, the letter clearly breaks off the relationship. In a stunning reversal of the key scene in *Don Juan Tenorio* in which Inés receives a poetically seductive letter from Don Juan in her convent, Doña Inés tears up the missive and casts it out the window of the house of assignations. Instead of carrying out a seduction, the modern letter ends an illicit affair. Don Juan then disappears from the novel without having made a personal appearance.

If the male protagonist Don Juan looms large in Tirso's and Zorrilla's versions, not to mention in the many other nineteenth- and twentieth-century remakings of the myth, in Azorín's novel, he is reduced to an invisible correspondent. One would expect the concomitant reassignment of narrative interest to Doña Inés. She appears, however, in only approximately half of the fifty-two chapters of the novel. Inés is the focus of the early scenes in Madrid in which she is waiting for her lover, but when she moves to her property in Segovia, attention shifts away from her to the lovingly described Castilian countryside, the provincial houses of the city, and colorful minor characters reminiscent of those in *El alma castellana* and *Castilla*. The sexually liberated, independent Inés, however, is not the soul of Spain that she would have represented in those works, and she must eventually be exiled from her "fatherland."

The exceptionally simple plot centers on a brief romantic interlude in which Inés and the local poet are attracted to one another. When the poet kisses Inés in the cathedral, a scandal ensues, and the reactionary townsfolk make Inés's life in Segovia unbearable. She finally decides to distribute her property to relatives and friends and depart for Argentina, where she founds a school for children of impoverished émigré Spaniards and lives out her life as a lonely, unfulfilled old maid. The novel could be interpreted as a feminist critique of a Spain that has no place for a woman like Inés, who wishes to live independently and enjoy love relationships outside of traditional marriage.[17] As a young girl, she felt alienated from the society in which she lived: "[La] sensación de cercanidad y distanciamiento del mundo, a un tiempo mismo, debía repercutir a lo largo de toda la vida de la niña y constituir el núcleo de su personalidad. La esquividad, el apartamiento, la enconada aversión hacia una sociedad estúpida y gazmoña habían de impulsarla poderosamente por un lado" (Azorín 1973, 97). [The feeling of simultaneous nearness and distancing from the world must have had repercussions throughout the girl's life and constructed the nucleus of her personality. The evasion, the withdrawal, the aggravated aversion to a stupid and priggish society had pushed her powerfully to one side.] The feminism of the novel (if one can call it that) is more aesthetic than social. Although Inés experiences a number of emotionally distressing events (including the end of her affair with Don Juan), we are never allowed access to her subjective states on these occasions. The narrator maintains an objective, camera-like view of her at all times. For example, she is described from an exterior nonsubjective position when she receives the letter from Don Juan: "El sobre ha sido roto. La mirada de la dama va pasando por los renglones. ¿Habéis visto la lividez de un cuerpo muerto? Así está ahora el rostro de la señora; mortal ha quedado Doña Inés. Y con movimiento lento, lentísimo, como lo haría una consumada actriz, ha dejado otra vez Doña Inés la carta en el velador" (80–81). [The envelope has been torn. The lady's gaze moves over the lines. Have you seen the lividness of a dead body? That is the way the lady's face is now; Doña Inés looks dead. And with a slow, a very slow movement, the way a consummate actress would do it, Doña Inés has left the letter on the table.]

Doña Inés's perception seemingly governs the scenes during her stay at her Segovia properties, but the narrative viewpoint is objective rather than subjective:

> Doña Inés recorre la ciudad y pasea por los contornos. . . . El río se desliza manso en el fondo de la cañada. La verdura, a un lado, cubre la margen y asciende hasta la población. Las huertas forman cuadros de hortalizas en que las altas matas de guisantes están rodrigadas con cañas. Los frutales se entremezclan entre los tablaros verdes. Y el follaje va reptando por el repecho y se cuela por los portillos y entraderos de la ciudad. Ya en estos días de junio los árboles han acabado de pulular. La sombra, encerrada durante el invierno en el subsuelo, ha ido ascendiendo por los troncos; ha henchido las yemas de las ramas, se ha asomado poco a poco en los renuevos verdes, y ha acabado—extendidas las hojas—por cubrir, invadir, llenar los árboles y el paisaje. El río, el Eresma, se desliza apacible en el fondo. Sobre sus cristales tersos, las frondas de las orillas se inclinan y besan las aguas, como si los árboles, sedientos, estuvieran bebiendo de bruces. (155)

[Doña Inés traverses the city and walks in the outskirts.... The river slides gently in the bottom of the ravine. Green covers the bank on one side and ascends toward the town. The fields form squares of vegetables in which the high pea plants are staked with bamboo. The fruit trees are scattered among the green patches. And the foliage snakes around the short, steep incline and slips through the openings and entrances of the city. Now in these June days the trees have finished budding. The shade, enclosed during the winter in the subsoil, has ascended through the trunks; it has swollen the buds of the branches, has appeared little by little in the renewed greens, and has ended up—with the extended leaves—covering, invading, filling the trees and the landscape. The river, the Eresma, glides peacefully at the bottom. Above its terse glass, the fronds on the banks bend and kiss the water, as if the trees, thirsty, were facing downward to drink.]

In fact, the perspective lapses into the universal "nosotros":

En el silencio profundo, gozamos de la armonía maravillosa del verde sobre la piedra dorada. En ninguna ciudad española se da como en Segovia tan perfecto el concierto entre las viejas piedras y la hoja verde lozana. Los momentos van deslizándose y las sombras de los troncos se van alargando. Si nos llegáramos hasta el cercano monasterio del Parral, en ruinas, con los techos desfondados, con las estancias llenas de escombros, con las vides labruscas enroscadas a los maderos carcomidos, escucharíamos en un apartado aposento caer en un pilón el chorro de una fuente y al mismo tiempo, como réplica a este murmurio, en lo hondo, en un subterráneo, el son pausado, intercadente, del agua que se entrederrama, que se derrama despacio, con lentitud. (136)[18]

[In the profound silence we enjoy the marvelous harmony of green on the golden stone. In no Spanish city does one find such perfect agreement between the old stones and the luxuriant green leaves as in Segovia. The moments go slipping by and the shadows of the trunks are lengthening. If we were to go to the nearby ruins of the monastery of Parral with its caved-in roofs, with the rooms full of debris, with the wild grapevines curled around the worm-eaten wood, in a remote room we would hear the flow of water from a fountain fall into a trough and at the same time, like a replica of this sound, in the depths, in a subterranean place, a deliberate, irregular sound of water that spreads out, overflows slowly, sluggishly.]

A similar process occurs whenever an opportunity arises for Inés to demonstrate that she can engage in abstract thought. After she has seen the sculpture that depicts her ancestor Beatriz, whose story parallels her own, she wonders if time exists, but before she can develop the thought, the narrator introduces Inés's Uncle Pablo, who is also preoccupied with the nature of time (175).[19] On another occasion when Inés begins to think about time, the narrator eludes her consciousness, converting the subject into one of general concern introduced by a universal "we" (176). Once again, as in Baroja's *El mundo es ansí,* the male author avoids formulating a true female subjectivity and shifts her personal vision to the universal (recall Sacha's letters about her stay in Florence). Such treatment is very different when Baroja or Azorín narrates from the perspective of a male protagonist; then the landscapes form an intimate part of the protagonist's individual consciousness.

Uncle Pablo is the character in *Doña Inés* whose inner preoccupations and view of the world are most carefully developed. The reclusive Don Pablo lives on the top floor of a large house; his wife, Pompilia, occupies the first floor. The two rarely see each other (I return to their unusual marital arrangement later). Uncle Pablo's psychology is complex and genuinely interesting. As a historian who lives entirely in the past, he has completely disengaged himself from the contemporary world and is pathologically preoccupied with time. Sometimes he is aware of the monotony of life, and he attempts to engage with the world around him, but he soon realizes that when in the throes of activity, he cannot think. His innermost self is then blank, and he retreats once again to his hermetic existence.

Uncle Pablo's subconscious retains authentic involuntary primitive states, which cannot be evoked at will: "De pronto, inesperadamente, una voz, un ruido, un incidente, cualquiera, le hacían experimentar al caballero con prodigiosa exactitud, con exactitud angustiadora, la misma sensación que quince, veinte o treinta años antes había experimentado" (116). [Suddenly, unexpectedly, a voice, a noise, some incident made the gentleman experience exactly, with anguishing exactness, the same sensation he had experienced fifteen, twenty, or thirty years before.] He can see the future in the present with all its potential for disaster and death. He has named this phenomenon "el mal de Hoffmann," after the

German writer, who suffered from a similar psychological aberration. Paradoxically, many of the insights that we gain into Uncle Pablo's character come from his conversations with the female "protagonist," whose psychology remains sketchy. For example, he reveals to Inés his dream of an anthropomorphic image of Eternity and he talks extensively of his visit to the area where the Barbizon school painted. Significantly, while Pablo holds forth on the Barbizon school, Inés sits passively having her portrait painted.[20]

Pablo is writing the history (which mirrors Inés's story) of an ancestor of Inés's, Beatriz, who lived from 1425 to 1466. Beatriz, married to a crude and insensitive man, fell in love with a troubadour. When her husband discovered the affair, he had the poet killed and placed his long blond locks in Beatriz's jewelry box. Upon seeing the shorn hair, Beatriz went mad; she lived only a few years longer, secluded in a country house. Leon Livingstone (1970), Thomas Meehan (1969), and Gonzalo Sobejano (1972) have interpreted this repetition of a woman's story in two different historical periods as reflecting the Nietzschean notion of the eternal return. María Doménica Pieropán (1989), however, argues that the parallels between Inés's and Beatriz's lives are deceptive and that the differences are more important than the similarities: Pieropán finds a feminist intention in the novel.[21] She notes that Inés is free to travel and takes control of her own situation, choosing not to marry and to leave Spain for a new life in South America, whereas the medieval woman was essentially imprisoned, bereft of decision-making power. Pieropán gives only two examples of Azorín's feminism from extratextual sources—the *El País* articles on marriage from 1897 and an article from 1929 in which he stated that the great problem of all civilizations, even in modern times, is the way that society views women ethically, juridically, and aesthetically and the concept that they have of themselves. He asserted that all ideological and political movement will center on women: "No habrá, para la marcha de la Humanidad, un problema más hondo y más trascendental que éste. Todos los tradicionales valores morales y jurídicos han de ser revisados" (qtd. in Pieropán 1989, 234). [For the advancement of humanity, there cannot be a deeper and more transcendental problem than this. All the traditional moral and judicial values must be revised.]

Azorín's public stands on many subjects are often at odds with the more covert messages that he reveals in his fictional works (he was a political chameleon, changing his ideological alliances several times over his long career). He was a master of presenting various sides of an issue and committing himself to none of them. An article titled "La mujer moderna," which Azorín wrote in 1925 at the same time that he was composing *Doña Inés,* reveals this ambivalent posture One hand, he argues that women should be liberated from church-dominated ideology that denies them a thorough education, but on the other hand he urges for woman's circumscription within a happy home that she creates for her family. The article begins with a reference to the Residencia de Señoritas directed by María de Maeztu, who, according to Azorín, has worked tirelessly to make the Residencia "un centro notabilísimo, verdaderamente europeo" (1925, n.p.). He describes the Residencia as a place where girls from all social classes and nationalities study, read, meditate, and learn to be good citizens and housewives. He uses adjectives such as "casa limpia, ordendada, sana" to categorize this "mansión" where "[se] vive bien" (n.p.). From this description, he moves to a consideration of what is required for a woman who will eventually establish a family, an undertaking that he considers very difficult. To aid him in his depiction of women's role, he refers to Fray Luis de León's *La perfecta casada* written in the sixteenth century to recommend women's submission to an external ideal. Fray Luis instructed that tradition should mold women in the bosom of the family. There should be no psychological independence: "Le basta a la casada, para ser perfecta, con ser buena. Y ser buena es principalmente cumplir con sus deberes tradicionales. Todo el círculo de acción de la mujer está reducido al ámbito del hogar. Fuera del hogar, no existe nada para la mujer. Las preocupaciones de la mujer deben ser: los hijos si los tiene—, el esposo y las normas espirituales señaladas por la tradición" (n.p.). [In order to be perfect, it is enough for the married woman to be good. And being good is principally fulfilling the traditional duties. The woman's entire circle of action is reduced to the space of the home. Nothing exists for the woman outside the home. The woman's preoccupations ought to be: the children, if she has them, the husband, and the spiritual norms indicated by tradition.]

Later in the same article, Azorín evokes nineteenth-century Bishop Félix-Antoine-Philibert Dupanloup, who also commented on women's proper education. Bishop Dupanloup opined that not only should women read; they should read critically and studiously with pen in hand. However, the bishop imposed certain limitations on the kinds of materials that women should read. Thus, Azorín believes that because the bishop also places limitations on women's thoughts and actions, any advances in thinking about women that he might seem to offer over Fray Luis are false. Through a rather abrupt transition, Azorín brings us back to the Residencia, the kind of education that women receive there, and their future social roles, which he defines as "el gran problema que oscila entre la tradición y la innovación" (n.p.) [the great problem that vacillates between tradition and innovation].

Azorín wonders what attitude a stay at the Residencia will impart to young women. Will they carry with them a sixteenth-century ideal or one more consonant with the twentieth century? He enjoins the (male) reader to consider what kind of woman he wants for his lifelong companion: "la que obedezca a una presión externa o la que se ajuste, en sus actos, en sus pensamientos, a una estricta y dulce neutralidad?" (n.p.) [the woman who obeys external pressures or the one who adheres in her acts and her thoughts to strict and sweet neutrality?]. Equally calamitous are an obsession with the home and an antidomestic inclination:

> No puede haber paz, serenidad, ecuanimidad, donde hay preocupación en cualquiera de los sentidos: en contra o en favor. La vida dulce y grata de familia, la da, únicamente, la autonomía espiritual. Una presión externa es la pesadilla de todos los días, la divergencia en la opinión, la rencilla, la desavenencia, la obediencia a algo forastero y ajeno a nosotros y que en nuestra vida se ingiere y manda. (n.p.)

> [There can be no peace, serenity, equanimity where there is worry in any of the senses: for or against. Only spiritual autonomy gives sweet and pleasant family life. External pressure is the nightmare of every day, the divergence of opinion, the quarrel, the disagreement, the obedience to something outside and alien to us and that inserts itself into our life and dominates.]

He concludes that the ideal family life should not be subject to external pressures.

Echoing Martínez Sierra's *Tú eres la paz,* Azorín assures that only in neutrality can the domestic state achieve the peace necessary for fruitful work. Azorín goes a step further in relating the peace thus achieved with national progress. Ultimately, Azorín's arguments against the recommendations of Fray Luis and Bishop Dupanloup are designed to promote a happier home, where the only pressures come from the husband. Thus, his argument is strangely circular. The whole point of women's education should be toward the establishment of a peaceful haven in the home, since "el progreso social, político, de las naciones depende de las mujeres" (n.p) [the social, political progress of nations depends on women]. Women do not need to intervene directly in political life in the same proportion as men because they have ample influence through the home: "Influyen, en el hogar, sobre el ciudadano, sobre el gobernante. ¿Queréis daros cuenta de la marcha de España en el orden social, en el orden político? Examinad a las mujeres de los políticos; ved a qué influencias exteriores obedecen; y ved cómo ellas traducen, trasladan esa presión al cerebro del hombre ligado a ellas de por vida"(n.p.). [In the home, they influence the citizen, the politician. Do you want to know how Spain is doing in the social or political order? Take a look at the wives of the politicians; see what external influences they obey; and see how they translate, convey that pressure to the brain of the man tied to them for life.] As long as external concerns impinge on home life, the country cannot advance, and there is nothing that the most advanced, liberal politicians can do if they are chained to a traditional norm. Thus, the women of the Residencia should ponder these indisputable social facts: "La casa limpia, clara, sana, bien, perfectamente bien. Nada tan grato. Pero, y en la casa clara, sana y limpia, ¿qué vamos a poner? ¿Cuáles van a ser las horas que la mujer proporcione al marido: horas de desabrimiento, de lucha sorda y obstinada u horas de dulce paz, de maravillosa y bienhechora neutralidad?" (n.p.). [The house, clean, clear, healthy, fine, perfectly fine. Nothing so pleasing. But, what are we going to put in the clear, healthy, clean house? What hours is the woman going to give her husband: hours of bitterness, deaf and obstinate struggle or hours of sweet peace, of marvelous and beneficent neutrality?] Women determine the course of Spanish history: "Como Dalila al gran Sansón, sus tijeras van cortando poco a poco la idealidad, el entusiasmo, la fe, la creencia en un porvenir de justicia y de humanidad. No son así, claro es, todas las mujeres. Millares y millares las hay ya de tendencia distinta. Pero si quedan algunas con sus tijeras cortadoras de innovaciones en las manos, dulcemente, muy dulcemente quitémosles las tijeras terribles para que ellas no puedan dañar" (n.p.). [As Dalila did to the great Samson, her scissors are little by little cutting ideality, enthusiasm, faith, belief in a future of justice and humanity. Of course, not all women are like that. Thousands and thousands are of a different tendency. But if there are any left with innovation-cutting scissors in their hands, let's gently, gently take away those terrible scissors so that they can do no harm.]

The message of the article registers the same ambiguity as *Doña Inés*. In the novel, Azorín appears to present a forward-looking view of women's roles through a female protagonist who is unmarried and has freedom to travel and take charge of her own life. But Inés does not establish an "hogar." Therefore, she is a disruptive element who must be exiled to another continent and neutralized by being installed in an alternative form of childcare, as headmistress of a school for poor children. The long passages that emphasize the well-ordered house in the novel are indicative of the subterranean pull toward a less mobile and volatile life than the one that Doña Inés led before her self-imposed exile. In the Madrid house of assignations where Inés met Don Juan clandestinely, the "losetas han perdido el barniz y se deshacen en un polvillo tenue" (1973, 75) [flagstones have lost their varnish and they are disintegrating into a fine, soft dust]. In Don Juan's Madrid house, "los salones están oscuros. Todas las luces de la casa han sido apagadas. . . . En el patio, angosto y negruzco, se ven de día por el suelo papeles rotos, vidrios, pedazos de tabla" (83) [the rooms are dark. All the lights of the house have been turned off. . . . In the daylight one sees torn papers, glass, pieces of wood in the narrow and blackish patio]. In Doña Inés's Madrid house, everything is closed off: "Cerrado el balcón, cerrada la puerta, el aire de la cámara, en esta noche de primavera, es cálido y denso" (85). [The balcony is closed, the door is closed, the air of the bedchamber is hot and dense on this spring night.] In Segovia, however, where Inés grew up in a traditional family, the house is orderly, clean, and open: "A la derecha y a la izquierda se abren las puertas de espaciosas salas. El zaguán está amueblado con sillones y un canapé provisto de mullidas colchonetas. Extenso y frondoso huerto respalda la casa; anchuroso patio linda con el huerto" (94). [To the right and to the left, doors of spacious rooms open. The entry is furnished with overstuffed chairs and a sofa with soft cushions. An extense and shady orchard backs the house; a wide patio borders the orchard.] Chapter 10 of the novel is devoted entirely to describing the interior and exterior of the house and all the domestic objects associated with it.

In Chapter 11, we are introduced to Uncle Pablo and Aunt Pompilia's house, a house divided, in which the husband lives apart from his wife on separate floors. The state of affairs is awry here; Pompilia is constantly moving all the furniture about: "Desaparecen consolas, sillones, canapés, cuadros. Sólo quedan insustituibles las cornucopias con un azogue apagado. Tía Pompilia no puede permanecer quieta. . . . Los muebles sufren un zarandeo continuo de sala a sala; marchan por los corredores; se ladea violentamente para entrar por las puertas angostas; se les desconchan los chapeados y se les tuercen las patas" (104). [The consoles, chairs, sofas, and pictures disappear. Only the sconces with cloudy mirrors remain irreplaceable. Aunt Pompilia cannot keep still. . . . The furniture undergoes a continuous shifting from room to room; it gets moved through the hallways; it is tipped violently to get through narrow doors; its veneers get chipped and its legs get twisted.] Chapter 17 details an orderly and domestic morning at Doña Inés's family home. Her companion/housekeeper, Plácida, motivates the servants to set the household in motion and gathers flowers for the house. Plácida's room is especially important, as Plácida will eventually enter into marriage with the poet Diego. Her room is indicative of the kind of life the narrator condones: "En el armario está colocada con cuidado la ropa. Blanquean las primorosas texturas segovianas de lino; cada tabla del armario está cubierta de un paño blanco; sobre el paño se levantan los montones de ropa" (126). [The bedclothes are carefully placed in the armoire. The finely woven Segovian linen shines white; each board in the armoire is covered with a white cloth; the piles of linens rise from the cloth.] If Chapter 17 describes the productive morning in Inés's Segovian home, Chapter 29 centers on the afternoon, which witnesses a second cleaning and peaceful sedentary domestic activities after the midday meal. After Inés and Diego's scandalous embrace in the cathedral, her home is much less attractive: "Puertas y ventanas están cerradas. . . . Compresos en la casa cerrada, cerrado el paso hacia fuera por la densidad del ambiente" (201). [The doors and windows are closed. . . . Compressed in the closed house, the dense atmosphere closes off access to the exterior.] The bishop visits Uncle Pablo to suggest that Inés should marry in the wake of the cathedral kiss scandal. Uncle Pablo, who seems unworldly but who understands Inés fairly well, thinks to himself, "¡Cualquiera le hace a mi sobrina que se case, y a estas alturas!" (194). [Who could possibly make my niece marry at this point!] At times Inés represents the "eternal woman" of *El alma castellana* and *Castilla* (especially her household in Segovia that follows the traditions of centuries), but she is also a new woman, and, as such, she cannot be accommodated in Spain.

Inés is a "modern" woman caught in the web of Spanish tradition, but in denying her a voice and subjectivity, the tradition-bound Segovia and environs overwhelm and trap her in the eternal cycle of female exile for carnal transgressions. We might compare her end to that of Clarisa in Burgos's *La entrometida* (published just the year before in 1924). Clarisa also chooses to live abroad, but rather than adopt a pseudomaternal role, she once again engages in the feminist activities that had occupied her before she returned to Spain from the New World. Spain is a hiatus, a place where Clarisa's feminist program stalls and where her independence is derailed. Similarly, Spain effectively quashes Doña Inés's sexually independent life when she refuses to marry and settle down there, but Azorín chooses to enshrine her in an alternative form of domesticity in Argentina. Thus, Inés joins Sacha, Raquel, and Tula as a failed feminist (or independent woman). Her end is less pathetic than Sacha's and her characterization less negative than Raquel's and Tula's but no more forward looking. The assumption of a masculine-style independence in all four women is not viewed as unambiguously positive (and in Unamuno's case is patently negative). As Chapter 5 shows, during the 1920s, the blurring of masculine and feminine qualities evident in these four female protagonists was theorized as a national disease.

CHAPTER 5
Biology as Destiny: New National Discourses on Gender Inform the Novel of the 1920s and Beyond

If at the turn of the century and in the first decade of the twentieth century, woman-centered discourse marshaled social arguments in favor of women's education to further national progress, by the 1920s and 1930s, scientific, biologically centered discourse dominated public conversations about gender. Biological considerations on the nature of the sexes fueled new polemics over gender, some concerned with gender roles as naturally determined and others with cross-gendering. Mary Nash points out that doctors were influential in disseminating a "modernized gender discourse based on a reconceptualization of motherhood as women's social duty" (1999, 33),[1] and María del Pilar Oñate associates the biological discourse on gender with the rise of feminism: "Médicos y biólogos, al ocuparse de estos problemas [the biological nature of gender], rozan más o menos directamente los temas feministas" (1938, 239). In the late second decade, Gregorio Marañón, physician, politician, and essayist, began publishing a series of influential articles and books that promoted biological arguments for gender definition. And beginning in 1923, José Ortega y Gasset's new journal, *Revista de Occidente,* published a number of articles on gender by scientists and philosophers that had a wide-ranging influence in intellectual circles. Much of this material ultimately deals with male effeminacy and/or female masculinization, often metaphors for exploring men's and women's roles in marriage and women's fitness for public life. These issues are salient subjects of the novels analyzed in this chapter.

This chapter begins by considering a series of works by Ramón Pérez de Ayala, Miguel de Unamuno, and Carmen de Burgos that respond in one way or another to Marañón's ideas on gender, and it ends with Rosa Chacel's *Memorias de Leticia Valle,* read within the context of the gender polemics that appeared in the pages of *Revista de Occidente.* These novels reveal a wide range of reactions to sexual theories proposed by Gregorio Marañón, José Ortega y Gasset, and Georg Simmel, among others, in settings that clearly reflect concerns about a Spain that was moving toward social modernity. Perhaps predictably, Unamuno was patently opposed to women's assumption of what he considered male traits and men's assumption of traditionally female roles; Pérez de Ayala attempted to be more modern in creating an acceptable feminized male; Burgos fielded a variety of sexual hybrids with ambiguous results for any gender's place in Spanish society; and Chacel created an entirely new woman who conjoins male and female qualities equally in an effort to undo the traditional Spanish past.

Marañón, whose ideas on sexuality raised public consciousness of gender ideology to new levels in the 1920s and 1930s, was a versatile man. He was fully engaged in Spanish politics while he maintained his medical practice and kept up his essay writing. In 1914, for example, he joined Ortega y Gasset and Pérez de Ayala in founding the Liga de Educación Política, whose express purpose was to educate the Spanish public for more general and enlightened participation in Spanish political affairs. He wrote works of a historical nature in which he applied his interest in biology to national periods: *Raíz y decoro de España* (1933), *Ensayo biológico sobre Enrique IV de Castilla y su tiempo* (1934), and *El conde-duque de Olivares (La pasión de mandar)* (1936). If his essays on sexuality marshal arguments to exclude women from political life, in *Biología y feminismo,* he states that women are not inferior, only different from men (1920, 7). In "Sexo y trabajo" (1924b), Marañón established two basic instincts—social action in men and maternity in women. As Nash points out, for Marañón "full-time dedication to children was a woman's duty and in line with the legacy of traditional domesticity, her cultural identity was still constructed through motherhood" (1999, 34). Marañón noted that women naturally included masculine traits as did men feminine qualities (1926; see Marañón 1969), but he was troubled by men he considered to be overly effeminate. This concern became a major theme in his many essays on Don Juan, which Isabel Paraíso considers "afán vivísimo de mejora de España, tradicionalidad y europeísmo" (1998, 317). Don Juan, earlier judged by some male writers a symbol of masculine national energy, now assumes feminine characteristics.

Marañón was not alone in this new interpretation of Don Juan; toward the end of the First World War, just when women's presence was emerging as a significant fact of Spanish public life, Pérez de Ayala also theorized an effeminate Don Juan.[2] Which of the two friends initiated the theory is difficult to determine. Pérez de Ayala published articles on Don Juan in 1916 and 1917 (later collected in *Las máscaras* [1963d]). These articles put forth ideas on sexuality and Don Juan that Marañón developed in 1920 and later: (1) Men and women both encompass characteristics associated with the opposite sex, but women remain in the realm of the sexual, whereas men rise above the physical. (2) Don Juan's tendency to deceit and his childlessness place his masculinity in doubt. Pérez de Ayala leaned heavily on Arthur Schopenhauer and Otto Weininger for his ideas on gender, and it is possible that Marañón's notions on Don Juan derive from the same sources or from discussions of them with Pérez de Ayala.[3] For example, in a later (1919) version of his essay "El satanismo" (Pérez de Ayala 1963f), he adds a quotation from Marañón's recently published *La edad crítica*, in which he claimed that the attraction that Don Juan holds for women is a feminine trait, since biologically the male is normally attracted to the female. In *La edad crítica*, Marañón states that he read Pérez de Ayala's articles on Don Juan only after completing his own book (see García Mercadal 1963: 375–76, n. 1).

Importantly, Pérez de Ayala ties his interpretation of Don Juan to Spain's national character, which he considers a combination of Western (Greco-Roman) and Eastern (Semitic) tendencies. Don Juan's attitude toward women reverses the Western medieval tradition of chivalric love, which placed women on a pedestal. In developing and expanding these ideas, Marañón moves Pérez de Ayala's more philosophically abstract argument fully into the realm of the biological, replete with biological classifications and Darwinian overtones. In his essay "Notas para la biología de Don Juan " (1924a), Marañón devised a taxonomy of lover types for each gender—"el tipo intelectual, el tipo emotivo y el tipo instintivo"—which enabled him to use Don Juan as an emblem for arguing against public roles for women. For Marañón, Don Quixote epitomizes the intellectual lover, while he belongs in the male instinctual masculine group, although Don Juan hovers near the feminine border (24–25). Othello is purely instinctual/masculine, but "Don Juan es, punto por punto, lo contrario; de hermosura correcta y afeminada, incapaz para la lucha social, corre tan sólo en las apariencias detrás de *las mujeres*. . . . El amor de Otelo es espontáneo e irreflexivo. El de Don Juan es un amor meditado, frío y sin riesgos, pudiéramos decir que industrializado" (25). [Don Juan is the opposite on every point; of a correct and effeminate beauty, incapable of social struggle, he only appears to run after *women*. . . . Othello's love is spontaneous and unreflective. Don Juan's is a meditated love, cold and without risks, industrialized we could say.]

According to Marañón, it only seems that Don Juan chases women; it is really women who follow him and surrender themselves (one wonders at Marañón's ability to interpret literary texts!). Don Juan lives only for women, before whom he places himself in a passive attitude "de centro de atracción" (26). For Marañón, the center of gravity in the Don Juan–woman relationship resides in the woman. Don Juan lives to love, avoids sociopolitical life, and cultivates lying, traits that ally him with femininity. Even though Don Juan is ingenious, he lacks creative genius, "que es, desde sus grados más modestos hasta los más potentes, la característica de la mente viril" (31). Men, according to Marañón, can be ascetic and forget their sexual nature, something women cannot do, because they are made for love and maternity. Men, freed of the preoccupation with sex, can devote themselves to "la actuación social en sus múltiples modalidades" (32). Don Juan, like women, invests all his sexual energy in "[el] amor propiamente dicho, a expensas de una precaria actividad social, tal como hemos visto que ocurre en la mujer" (33) [love per se, at the expense of precarious social activity, as we have seen happen with women].

Lying, an act that Don Juan shares with women, is, according to Marañón, a biologically based defense mechanism of the weak, "análoga a la tinta de los calamares o a tantos otros subterfugios defensivos que la historia natural nos ofrece" (42) [analogous to squid's ink or so many other defensive subterfuges that natural history offers]. Children and women lie out of self-defense, and, like them, Don Juan, whose energy is intermittent, is able to carry out his amorous exploits only indirectly, through "tratos y comadreos femeninos" (42). Pérez de Ayala doubtless discussed these ideas with his wife, Mabel Ricks, a native of Allentown, Pennsylvania. Ricks, a founding and very active member of Madrid's Lyceum Club from 1926 forward, was clearly familiar with the U.S. feminist movement, which was much more militant than the movement in Spain at that time. Pérez de Ayala's overt response to Marañón's extreme biologism is ambiguous (in his preface to Marañón's *Ensayos sobre la vida sexual,* he called Marañón's ideas "emoción dramática, emoción novelesca, emoción lírica" [1969, 21]).[4] In his novels, Pérez de Ayala was able to hide behind character and plot to satirize his friend's outlandish proposals, although the message of *Tigre Juan y El curandero de su honra* is essentially the same as Marañón's—that women are not fit for public roles.[5]

In 1916, about the time that he was incorporating Schopenhauer's and Weininger's ideas on gender into his essays on Don Juan, Pérez de Ayala published three short novels—*Prometeo, Luz de domingo,* and *La caída de los Limones,* under the title *Novelas poemáticas de la vida española*—in which he enlisted gender to make certain points about Spanish national life. For example, in *La caída de los Limones,* the local political boss (in the corrupt Restoration system of government) is a woman; the political power of her family comes to a bad end when her brother (a singularly ineffectual man who is incapable of fulfilling the political role expected of him) rapes and murders a beautiful young woman. In *Tigre Juan y El curandero de su honra,* Pérez de Ayala not only explores national political problems through gender but also creates characters that are complex parodies of many domestic and national issues.[6] As J. J. Macklin observes, "The reference to La Gloriosa . . . as part of Juan's youth helps date the novel in the 1880s, as does Colas's departure for Cuba" (1980a, 27). These references mark significant moments in the national consciousness. Alicia Andreu explores the many ways in which the paired novel draws on the Don Juan legend to contemplate various facets of Spain as a nation. She concludes that by rewriting "el mito de don Juan en sus múltiples vertientes, con el cual ha construido España el andamiaje de gran parte de su cultura . . . [Pérez de Ayala] cuestiona aquellos valores que han dado lugar . . . a la formulación inicial del mito y . . . a su perpetuación a través de la constante repetición" (1992, 391) [the Don Juan myth in its many facets, with which Spain has constructed the scaffolding of a great part of its culture . . . Pérez de Ayala questions those values that have led to the initial formulation of the myth and . . . to its perpetuation through constant repetition]. I would add to Andreu's perceptive analysis that, in large part, Pérez de Ayala achieves his subversion of Don Juan as a national myth through his treatment of gender.

Don Juan actually bifurcates into two characters—(1) the title character, Tigre Juan, and (2) Vespasiano, Tigre Juan's best friend, whom he loves "como su otra mitad ideal" (1990, 199). Like Burgos's Pérez Blanco of *La entrometida* and Azorín's Don Juan of the eponymous novel, Vespasiano is a man of dubious sexuality, a symbol of a nation that suffers from troubled virility (lack of strength). The title character, Tigre Juan, also blends genders and national types. He is a tiger in appearance only, for the would-be restorer of his sullied honor (in the style of Calderón de la Barca's *El médico de su honra* [1637]) turns out to be a domesticated house cat (although this gender modification is not ultimately as negative as Vespasiano's).

Tigre Juan is a misanthropic, misogynist merchant, owner of a medicinal herb stand in the public square of Pilares (Oviedo). Thus, he is a *curandero* in several senses—in the literal as well as the figurative, Calderonian sense. He is identified with Spanish tradition in both folklore (folk medicine) and high culture (the Golden Age honor play). His family names—Guerra (war) and Madrigal (poetry)—ally him with Spain's two past glories. Tigre Juan espouses extremely misogynistic views. He has avoided the company of women for many years, and his shadowy past may include the murder of a wife. Paradoxically, Tigre Juan is fond of children and has adopted the orphan boy Colás, on whom he dotes.[7] In young adulthood, Colás, spurned by the object of his love, Herminia, abandons Tigre Juan's home and leaves Pilares. Tigre Juan, unaware of the identity of Colas's love object, becomes smitten with Herminia. Herminia's grandmother and guardian urges her into an engagement with the well-off, heretofore-misogynistic Tigre Juan. Tigre Juan, fully cognizant that he lacks courtship skills, enlists the aid of his friend Vespasiano, an infamous Don Juan. Once the couple is married, Vespasiano lures Herminia away with him in typical donjuanesque fashion. Vespasiano subsequently abandons Herminia, who is pregnant with Juan's child. Despite his sullied honor, Tigre Juan allows Herminia to return home, and he assumes the unlikely role of mother figure to the child.

The narrative's position vis-à-vis gender roles encompasses a variety of possibilities that both reflect and confound many of the ideas elaborated by Marañón. At one extreme is Tigre Juan's ludicrous misogyny represented in the classic Spanish literary tradition's portrayal of masculinity and honor (including the murder of a wife for the slightest suspicion of infidelity). Taking some of his material from Marañón, he reveals his misogyny primarily in conversations with Colás. For example, Tigre Juan asserts that society would be untenable if it consisted of only women ("de mujeres solas no podría haber sociedad, ni civilización, ni progreso" [Pérez de Ayala 1990, 77]), a conclusion that can also be inferred from Marañón's assertions that only men reserve their libidinal energies for social activity. Like Marañón, Tigre Juan posits women as liars, "de condición flaca y engañosa" (73). And like Marañón, he associates the feminine and the diabolical (although not via the Don Juan metaphor): "El género humano acércase hasta Dios por el hombre; abájase hasta la serpiente, que es el diablo, por la mujer" (73). Alluding surely to contemporary discussions of feminism's pernicious influence on domestic life, Tigre Juan says, "Las cosas de tejas abajo andan por extremo confusas, a causa de los enredos de las mujeres" (80). [Things under the roof are getting extremely confused because of women's mischief.]

However, in other aspects, Tigre Juan's interpretation of Don Juan diverges from Marañón's. For Tigre Juan, Don Juan is a Christ figure or saint who redeems men by taking revenge on women and vindicating all men. He mounts a highly specious argument to sustain this questionable view. He avers that Don Juan turns the tables on women (embodied in Eve) for committing the original sin. Don Juan saves men from the terrible sin of ridicule and turns ridicule back on women: "El ridículo y la irrisión revuelven sobre la mujer, de donde proceden" (79). Taking a more moderate position, the narrator follows Marañón in declaring that the sexes inhabit completely separate spheres: "Hombre y mujer encierran dos universos esencialmente herméticos, incomunicables e ininteligibles entre sí, al modo de dos pedernales, que por muy en tangencia que se hallen no dejan de permanecer aislados" (68).

Colás occupies a more liberal position on women's roles than does Tigre Juan, the narrator, or Marañón, espousing ideas that echo feminist ideals.[8] He handily deflects Tigre Juan's antiquated notions about women. Nonetheless, Colás interprets Don Juan as an "afeminado," almost exactly in Marañón's terms. For example, he points out (just as does Marañón) that Don Juan has never had a child; he has never impregnated a woman. However, he turns Marañón's interpretation of Don Juan to a feminist purpose. Don Juan, he notes, falsely serves as the image of "el hombre más hombre" (78) conjured by many men. Echoing some of the messages in novelettes about donjuanism by Blanca de los Ríos, Sofía Casanova, and Carmen de Burgos (see Chapter 3), Colas asserts that if women deceive men, it is because there are Don Juans. If there were no Don Juans, women could not deceive men. In fact, he says, women don't deceive men; other men deceive men. As Colás observes, "Don Juan y las mujeres andan trocados los papeles. No es que engañe a las mujeres; ésa es una modificación que él mismo urde y propala. Ellas solas se engañan, habiéndole tomado por muy hombre" (81). [Don Juan and women have changed roles. It isn't that he deceives women; this is a modification that he himself plots and promotes. Women deceive themselves, having taken him for a very masculine man.] For Colás, Vespasiano embodies his ideas of a feminized Don Juan; his "ojos lánguidos," "labios colorados y húmedos," "pantalones ceñidos," "muslos gordos," and "trasero saledizo" all contribute to his being "algo amaricado" (85).

Tigre Juan also exhibits feminine (maternal) traits, despite his misogyny and self-proclaimed radical masculinity, and these qualities evoke reader sympathy for him. Tigre Juan manifests his femininity in his kind heart, his affection for children, his attempts to perform works of charity, and finally in the maternal role that he assumes with his own child. Thus, Tigre Juan is a healthy amalgam of the masculine and the feminine. His masculinity, nuanced by positive feminine qualities, contrasts with Vespasiano's very effeminate donjuanism (an incarnation of Marañón's definition of the figure). In turn, Vespasiano, the effeminate male, has his counterpart in the masculinized woman Doña Iluminada, a middle-aged widow who has long harbored an unrequited love for Tigre Juan. Both are sterile, but the energy from her sterility is directed toward life-promoting activities such as sponsoring a union between her ward

Carmina and Colás. Vespasiano, in contrast, "era la esterilidad insumisa, que se engaña a sí propia y pretende engañar a los demás, desviviéndose en hacer pasar el libertinaje como exceso genesíaco, derroche de potencia y voluntaria renuncia a la fecundidad" (198) [was unsubmissive sterility, which deceives itself and attempts to deceive others, anxious to make libertinism seem like a genesic excess, a wasting of potency and a voluntary renouncing of fecundity]. Vespasiano awakens an unhealthy attraction in women, partly because of his ambiguous anatomy, some of which is decidedly feminine ("como la sobarba, el abultado pecho y el trasero, no menos rotundo, sino también por sus actitudes sugestivas, de corrompida molicie, y su experimentada madurez, a semejanza de la perdiz para el gastrónomo, que la halla más sabrosa en un punto de incipiente descomposición" (201) [like the noseband, the bulky chest and no less rotund rear, but also because of his suggestive postures, the corrupt flabbiness, and his experienced maturity, like the partridge for a gastronome, who finds it tastier at the point of incipient decomposition]. His tactile gaze that reaches out like elastic tentacles to caress their object also contributes to his appeal to women. His gaze makes women feel as though he were undressing them with translucent, viscous arms that emerge from his eyes.

Although women on the whole are more sympathetically portrayed in *Tigre Juan* than they are in Unamuno's novels, they are not allowed much more freedom of intellectual expression. Ultimately, the message for women is very similar to that in *Dos madres* and *La tía Tula*: Marriage and care giving are the only appropriate roles for even a modern woman of the 1920s. Sara Suárez Solís (1986) and Thomas Feeny (1985) label this message, which they find in all of Pérez de Ayala's novels, "antifeminist." Paralleling the development of male figures as openly sexually ambiguous are the women who hover in the shadows both sexually and socially. Doña Iluminada always appears in interiors: "Se escondía allí un manantial de tiniebla" (Pérez de Ayala 1990, 66). Tigre Juan considers her a virgin martyr, insinuating that her husband, much older than she, did not perform his masculine duties.[9] She has a nearly magical ability to understand Tigre Juan; meanwhile, she remains a complete mystery to him. Iluminada fulfills her need to nurture by adopting a child whose impoverished mother has died.

Herminia, following Orestes's wife, whose name she bears, remains in the shadow of male interaction, which she motivates but in which she does not participate. Like many male-authored novels of the Spanish modernist period, *Tigre Juan y El curandero de su honra* is replete with dialogues on philosophical subjects. Herminia occupies narrative space during these dialogues in order to demonstrate her marginal relationship to them. Herminia's grandmother (suggestively named Doña Marica) holds a regular *tertulia* attended by Tigre Juan and several other men in their home. When the men enter, Herminia utters a greeting, from a "rincón de sombra" (147). Her grandmother bids that she come out of her lair, but "Herminia llegó, lenta y temblorosa, desde la zona negra e impenetrable, como desde el más allá, hasta la penumbra fluida y verdemar que la lámpara efundía" (151) [Herminia emerged slowly and trembling from the black and impenetrable zone, as from the great beyond, into the fluid sea-green half-light that the lamp emitted]. Tigre Juan faints at the sight, as he believes he has seen the image of his dead wife, Engracia, and Herminia sinks back into her hiding place, "a sumergirse de huida dentro de la oscuridad" (151). After the reconciliation between Juan and Herminia, men carry on several philosophical dialogues while the women sleep.

The priest, Doña Iluminada, and Doña Marica understand Tigre Juan's desire to marry Herminia as the natural order of things. Herminia, however relegated to the shadows she may be, has other ideas. First of all, she is in love with Vespasiano. She accepts marriage to Tigre Juan, but the narrator ironically (and perhaps misogynistically) observes that "como hija de Eva, por imperativo de su feminidad," she rebelled against the established order ("leyes dictadas por el hombre, a las cuales la mujer está sujeta"), attempting to destroy it. Cast in this light, Herminia, is a feminist, but her weapon is sin "mediante el consentimiento en el pecado, puesto que, desde el Edén, el pecado femenino trastornó el humano destino, y a cada instante desvía de su curso la vida de los hombres" (195). It is likely that Pérez de Ayala's acerbic wit was attacking the words he had heard on the lips of his feminist American wife and her associates at the Lyceum Club.

Although Herminia marries Tigre Juan, she longs for freedom from the bonds of traditional marriage (Tigre Juan is, not surprisingly, a very paternalistic husband), and Vespasiano has no difficulty in luring her away. When Vespasiano installs her in a house of prostitution in another town, Herminia observes the illicit lives of the women who inhabit the brothel and repents having fled her conventional home. She knows, however, that she has engaged in unforgivable behavior, even though she has not actually committed adultery with Vespasiano. She assumes that Tigre Juan would murder her in Calderonian fashion, if she were to return. Colás and Carmina, Doña Iluminada's ward, who have undertaken an itinerant life together, rescue Herminia from the brothel and urge Tigre Juan to accept his wife back into his home. They easily convince Herminia, who has affirmed that Tigre Juan is a true man (as compared to the effeminate Vespasiano) and that she has been misguided. The narrative format for the section in which Herminia and Tigre Juan are separated is divided into two columns, each containing the thoughts and actions of one of the married characters. In the column that focuses on Juan, he is referred to as "virile" and "immortal" for having fathered a child. Herminia finally settles on the man who represents the traditional aspects of manhood that society expects, the man who is willing to put his love at the service of marriage and childbearing. Vespasiano argues that the essence of love is freedom, but ultimately Herminia understands that such freedom is an illusion.[10]

During his rescue of Herminia, Colás advises a young man to flee Spain with Carmen, a prostitute he loves; thus, he links gender roles, especially prostitution, to the ills of Spain.[11] Modern feminism revitalizes Tigre Juan, the emblem of classic (imperial) Spanish masculinity, and Colás's tolerance prevails. The future of Spain resides in the fully masculine male who adopts feminine characteristics rather than in strong independent women. In a 1927 article, Pérez de Ayala invokes national epics like the *Iliad* to argue for the importance of "hombredad" to all aspects of human endeavor: "La mengua de hombredad estorba la plenitud, cuando no estraga por su raíz la eficacia, de todo linaje de conducta; social, religiosa, artística, literaria o científica" (n.p.). [The decline of manliness is an obstacle to plenitude, when it does not spoil the efficacy of all types of activity—social, religious, artistic, literary, or scientific at its roots.] Tigre Juan's extreme masculinity might appear diluted when he assumes the maternal duties of childcare; in fact, however, he is usurping Herminia's dominion over the child. Tigre Juan gets into bed with Herminia during the birthing process; he participates in the birth with her to convey his role as the sole progenitor. This action is presented as an ancient custom of Juan's region, an "ingenuo y humano simbolismo, aunque al parecer *contra natura,*" which "encerraba alto sentido y social trascendencia: afirmar la línea de varón y transmitir al descendiente el apellido paterno, con que la contada prole legítima se diferenciaba de la innumerable cría anónima, pues la mayor parte de los habitantes en aquella serranía eran hijos de madre soltera y padre desconocido" (Pérez de Ayala 1990, 293) [ingenuous and human symbolism, although apparently *contra natura,* which contained lofty meaning and social transcendence: to affirm the male line and transmit the paternal surname to the descendent, with which the limited number of legitimate offspring were differentiated from the numerous anonymous children, since the majority of the inhabitants of that mountainous country were children of a single mother and unknown father]. If this practice has a patriarchal aim, Tigre Juan's assumption of other maternal roles cannot be similarly interpreted. First of all, the male child is named for Iluminada and Herminia, simply converting these feminine names into Iluminado and Herminio, Mini for short. Tigre Juan insists that Herminia alternate bottle feeding with breast feeding early on so that he can feed the baby. In the final image of the married couple, Herminia sleeps while Juan cuddles the baby in his arms as they depart for an extended train trip.

Colás had initially argued against institutionalized unions between men and women, because sanctified unions often result in discord, "infierno permanente" (313). For Colás, a contract is valid only when it upholds the free will of both parties that have entered into it. (This reasoning sounds very much like some of Burgos's feminist arguments against marriage.) It is significant that Colás, who argues so fervently against marriage, is also disillusioned with the nation and nationalism. When he left Pilares a disappointed lover, he joined the Spanish military in the Philippines, where he lost a leg. He returned "un desilusionado, un huérfano de emoción patriótica" for "esa incorpórea madre de todos, que se suele llamar la madre patria" (217) [disillusioned, orphan of patriotic emotion for that bodiless mother of all, which we call the mother country]. Tigre Juan's disastrous first marriage, in which he believed his wife had committed adultery, occurred in the Spanish colony of the Philippines, where Juan was an occupying soldier. The theme of emigration that we have seen allied to nation and sexuality in a number of narratives throughout this study is central to the concept of what Spain was and what it ought to be during the modernist period.

In Colás, an orphan who was raised by the complexly gendered Tigre Juan and who challenges his adoptive father with progressive ideas about women, resides the mutilated but perhaps only hope for a twentieth-century Spain. Ultimately, Pérez de Ayala's seemingly more liberal stance toward gender roles—his parody of donjuanism and his attribution of feminine characteristics to the sympathetic Tigre Juan—is undermined by the reaffirmation of traditional marriage and the silent, unexceptional wife dominated by the strong, albeit domesticated, male.[12] Ten pages after his reasoned arguments against marriage, Colás announces that he and Carmina have married in civil as well as religious ceremonies. Delighted, Tigre Juan congratulates him on taking the reasonable course of action. Ever contentious, Colás proclaims that if marriage were reasonable, he would not have gotten married, but the fact remains that he has married and entered into a civil state regulated by laws and tradition. As Miguel Ángel Lozano Marco astutely observes, "El tema fundamental de esta novela doble es . . . la unión matrimonial concebida como generosa entrega del uno a otro, y la fusión de ambas vidas en el hijo" (1990, 27). [The fundamental theme of this double novel is . . . the matrimonial union conceived as a generous surrender of one to the other, a fusion of both lives in the child.] Lozano Marco also notes that paternity (not maternity) "se muestra como un todo indisoluble" (27) [shows itself to be an undisolvable whole].

The final discussion on Vespasiano between Tigre Juan and Colás that once again recalls Marañón's ideas on gender ties up the several threads that have woven together national and gender concerns. Tigre Juan now accepts Colás's interpretation of Don Juan as emasculated. All that he does is false, and falsity does not endure. Especially pernicious, he observes, is that Don Juan does not leave children in the world, nothing permanent (a more existential and Unamunian version of Marañón's biological observation on Don Juan and procreation). Despite Vespasiano's challenge to Tigre Juan's traditional Spanish honor code ("fanático del deber y del honor" [Pérez de Ayala 1990, 64]), he has survived, thanks to a more flexible attitude and his new paternal/maternal role. Tigre Juan, who once equated a woman's adultery with a soldier's desertion of the battleground, embraces Vespasiano rather than killing him as the traditional Spanish honor code would require. He tells Vespasiano that he is an integral part of himself—the ultra macho Tigre Juan needs the feminine Vespasiano: "Eres una parte de mí mismo que me falta; como yo debiera ser una parte de ti" (338). He also calls him deficient and castrated, which leaves the final message ambiguous. What is not ambiguous is that Tigre Juan knows that he possesses Herminia absolutely after her attempted escape and return. She has prostrated herself before Tigre Juan and asked him to murder her. Thanks to Vespasiano's having lured her away, Tigre Juan now possesses her much more completely than he did before.[13] In *Tigre Juan,* Pérez de Ayala considers Spanish patriarchalism from several different angles, including Marañón's theses on gender, and he ultimately concludes, with Marañón, that, even though men are more domestic than they once were, Spanish public life belongs in the hands of men.

Echoes of Marañón also surface in Unamuno's *El hermano Juan o El mundo es teatro. Vieja comedia nueva* (1929), which, like *Tigre Juan y El curandero de su honra,* evokes Golden Age theater ("vieja comedia") and new gender arrangements (the "nueva" of the title).[14] The message of *El hermano Juan* is, however, much more sinister than that of Pérez de Ayala's novel, which resolves gender conflict by conflating male and female attributes in the title character. The play, like *Dos madres,* is an existential work that converts the Don Juan figure into the "hero of tragic proportions" that Anthony Cascardi attributes to the treatment of Don Juan by what he calls "several members of the Generation of 1898" (1988, 156).[15] The Don Juans in both *El hermano Juan* and *Dos madres* are engaged in the same struggle for identity as most of Unamuno's other characters (the second part of the title, "o El mundo es teatro" signals the theme). Marañón's ideas on Don Juan's gender afforded Unamuno the opportunity to consider gender and existence in a more explicit way than he had in *La tía Tula* or *Dos Madres*.[16] The female characters in these works are not Don Juan's sexual pawns; rather, they are threatening figures that rob Don Juan of his selfhood, posing the kind of existential problem noted by Cascardi (without direct reference to Unamuno, but surely with Unamuno in mind):

> The fear which thus is generated and which in many ways transcends the problems of self-division, is precisely that to which we are exposed in Tirso's play. This is the fear, characteristic of modernism that the performing self, the inessential self, the self of mobile desires and prattle ultimately may eclipse the central self. Stated in slightly different terms, this is the fear or the absorption of the self by its roles. (1988, 157)

Unamuno effects this modernist division through women characters who absorb Don Juan's role as a masculine figure.

Published in 1929, on the eve of the Second Spanish Republic that gave women many of the legal advantages for which Spanish feminists militated throughout the 1920s, *El hermano Juan*'s references to women's new public profile are hardly subtle. Antonio, the doctor, claims that women, instead of cutting their Sampsons' hair, cut their own hair and traipse off to football games or boxing matches to shout themselves hoarse "como una verdulera"; they even run for public office "para hombrearse" (Unamuno 1959, 935). The lead female character, Elvira, notes that women have every right to assume masculine traits, since men have given themselves over to "mujerearse" with a feminism "que se disfraza de masculinidad" (935). The predominant message in the play adheres to the most radical antifeminist discourse of the period. Roberto Novoa Santos's views are typical of the times:

> Mas cuando aparece esporádicamente en la sociedad una mujer preeminentísima, hemos de ver en ella el sostén vivo de una aberración sexual, o bien hemos de considerar su aristocracia mental como expresión de un estado de inversión de uno de los más importantes caracteres secundarios del sexo. Así como es conocida la inversión de ciertos caracteres somáticos y fisiológicos, definica como *masculinismo y virilismo,* conocemos también un tipo de inversión psíquica, que corresponde a la *masculinización* de la mente femenina. (1929, 49)

> [But when a very preeminent woman appears sporadically in society, we should see her as the living incarnation of a sexual aberration, or rather we

should consider her mental aristocracy as an expression of a state of inversion of one of the most important secondary sex characteristics. Just as we recognize the inversion of certain somatic and physiological characteristics, defined as *masculinism* and *virilismo*, we also recognize a kind of psychic inversion that corresponds to the *masculinization* of the feminine mind.]

Like Azorín's Don Juan, Unamuno's character eschews carnality for a spirituality that radiates tradition, history, and universal humanity, but Unamuno includes questionable masculinity in Don Juan's characterization. At the beginning of *El hermano Juan,* Don Juan has already abandoned his profligate past and has initiated a more introspective phase. Unlike most of the reworkings of the Don Juan theme, however, Unamuno's provides his character with more psychological background (for example, he was raised among girls). His relationship to women is not that of the traditional seducer. In fact, Elvira sequesters Don Juan in order to make him a man and, thus, herself a woman. When she observes that he is not like other men, Juan replies, "Hay quien sospecha que no lo soy" (Unamuno 1959, 916; the "quien sospecha" is doubtless Marañón). Juan does not conform to the traditional strong male gender stereotype, and therefore he does not exist in an ontological sense. Thus, Unamuno seamlessly collapses gender and philosophical categories while he questions the biologism to which Marañón reduced the Don Juan figure.

Ultimately, Juan is reduced to a shadow existence. Rather than portray a diabolical Don Juan, Unamuno creates diabolical women. Antonio comments, "Es algo demoníaco que os habéis hecho las mujeres. Este... ¿hombre? Hombre... ¡no! (936). Juan's existential problem is that women have appropriated his masculinity. He is condemned to be alone: "¡Condenado a ser siempre él mismo..., a no poder ser otro..., a no darse a otro... Don Juan... ¡Un solitario!..., ¡un soltero!... ¡y en el peor sentido!" (951). Don Juan, who was the national problem, the "imbécil, libertino antiliberal" in Unamuno's early essays is now an existential outcast, a lonely anguished existential hero emasculated by strong women. It is, however, a fitting end, because the original Don Juan violated "la costumbre, la santa costumbre, el cauce de la vida más íntima y entrañada, el amor humano, el que funda y basa la tradición, la historia, la humanidad" (868) [the custom, the saintly custom, the bedrock of the most intimate and deeply buried life, human love, that which founds and forms a base for tradition, history, and humanity]. His sin was not that he defiled women but that he breached traditional male and female roles.

Unamuno openly joined the biological debates about Don Juan's sexuality in his prologue for the 1934 edition of *El hermano Juan*. The reference to Marañón is unmistakable: "¿Es Don Juan acaso la pura masculinidad—no precisamente virilidad o varonilidad—, el puro catabolismo que diría un pedante de biología, sin lo común a los hombres todos, varones o mujeres, sin hombría y sin verdadero sentido de paternidad?" (870). [Is Don Juan by chance pure masculinity—not exactly virility or maleness—pure catabolism, as a pedant of biology would say, without what is common to all people, male and female, without manliness and without a true sense of paternity?] By 1934, the Republic had been in place for three years, and it had promulgated significant legislation that favored women's rights. The early years of the Republic saw the legalization of divorce and civil marriage, as well as enfranchisement for women. As Martínez Sierra pointed out in her lectures published as *La mujer ante la República* (1931), under the Republic a woman had become director of prisons, women sat on the High Court, and they now held positions as notaries and registrars and were eligible to run for legislative office; by the end of that year, three women (Clara Campoamor, Victoria Kent, and Margarita Nelken) had been elected as representatives to the Cortes. Unamuno's attempt to fold women into masculine psychology in the 1934 prologue to *El hermano Juan* appears especially out of tune with the times. Since he had tried to convert Don Juan into an existential case study in his play, he is at particular pains to deny the biological in Don Juan: "Queriéndose a sí mismo y no a sus queridas. Lo material, lo biológico, desaparece junto a esto. La biología desaparece junto a la biografía, la materia junto al espíritu" (Unamuno 1959, 858). [Loving himself and not his mistresses. The material, the biological, disappears along with this. Biology disappears along with biography, matter along with spirit.] Don Juan is a representer; he knows he is an actor on stage, always dreaming and making women dream of him. The libido is nothing more than a "término latino [que] han puesto en moda los especialistas biológicos" (862). Biology has no place in the interpretation of Don Juan; he is a spiritual rather than a material phenomenon, "no de física, sino de metafísica" (862). Don Juan is a solitary pleasure seeker, who, like a frog spreads his seed without real contact with the female of the species. He takes special exception to the biologists who "se enredan ... en teorías sobre homosexualidad, y como el goce, que es el medio, borra el fin, que es la reproducción" [get entangled in theories of homosexuality, and like pleasure, which is the medium, erases the goal, which is reproduction] (862). According to Unamuno, perhaps homosexuality has its origins in a dark Malthusian instinct: "Gozar el goce del momento, gozar inmediatamente lo mediato, sin sentido de la finalidad, que es la reproducción, la continuidad y continuación de la especie" (860–61).[Enjoy the pleasure of the moment, enjoy immediately what is mediate, without a sense of the end, which is reproduction, continuity and continuation of the species.]

He finds in Don Juan the same impulse that he attributed to Don Quixote, the search for eternal fame, which he now asserts can be achieved only through a complete blending with the female of the species:

> En latín *homo* (en acusativo *hominem,* nuestro "hombre") es el nombre de la especie que incluye a los dos sexos: *vir,* varón, y *mulier,* mujer—por no decir "macho" y "hembra"—, y que podríamos traducir por persona. Tan "hombre", tan persona es la mujer como el varón cuando dejan de ser macho y hembra. Y en alemán, *Mensch* abarca a los dos, al *Man,* o Varón, y a la *Weibe,* o Mujer. Es la categoría común de humanidad. Y cabe decir que el verdadero hombre, el hombre acabado, cabalmente humano, es la pareja, compuesta de padre y madre. Y a ese hombre acabado le hace el nombre. Pero no ciertamente el que parecía buscar ese pobre Don Juan soltero, esto es, solitario. . . . Con el hombre acabado, con la pareja humana, aparecen la paternidad y la maternidad conscientes. (862)

[In Latin *homo* (accusative *hominem,* our "man") is the name of the species that includes the two sexes: *vir,* man, and *mulier,* woman—in order not to say "male" and "female"—and that we could translate as person. The woman is as much "man," as person, as is the man when they stop being male and female. And in German, *Mensch* covers the two, the *Man,* or

Male, and *Weibe,* or Woman. It is a category common to humanity. And one can also say that the true man, the complete man, fully human, is the couple, composed of father and mother. And the name makes this complete man. But certainly not the one sought by that poor Don Juan, the bachelor, that is, the solitary man.... With the complete man, with the human couple, conscious paternity and maternity appear.]

Having rehearsed all the biological and philosophical arguments that the Don Juan figure suggests, Unamuno returns to the notion that there is a natural order of things (is this not biology?): "el sentido de maternidad—y con ello de paternidad—que es arranque de la historia, de la tradición, del nombre, para la religiosidad" (862) [the sense of maternity—and with it paternity—which is the beginning of history, tradition, the name, for religiosity]. Unamuno patently rejected Marañón's thesis about Don Juan's femininity, which would make his victims lesbians ("¿Es que, como sostienen ciertos autores, sienten la supuesta feminidad de él? ¿Acaso por una suerte de homosexualidad femenina? ¡Quía! Es que le compadecen" [866]).

Not surprisingly, Unamuno once again cast women in the role of mothers. If the prostitutes in *Don Quixote* were mothers to the Manchegan knight, Don Juan's victims play the same role for him. They are grateful that he takes notice of them and recognizes them as corporal and psychological beings—in other words, that they exist. Continuing the metaphysical (or more correctly, ontological) argument, Don Juan wishes to make women mothers (even though he does not achieve it), for "reproducirse es conservar la identidad espiritual del linaje, la personalidad histórica.... Es anonadarse como individual separado y distinto. Y Don Juan sin saberlo, se buscaba en sus víctimas. No quería morirse sin más" (866) [to reproduce oneself is to conserve the spiritual identity of the race, the historical personality.... It is to annihilate oneself as a separate and distinct individual. And Don Juan, without knowing it, sought himself in his victims. He did not want to just die with nothing more]. Feal argues that by converting Don Juan into the seduced rather than the seducer, Unamuno casts him in the role of child (1984, 55).

Unamuno interprets his *hermano* Juan as collapsing the paternal and maternal function (we are reminded of Pérez de Ayala's Tigre Juan): "Los hombres verdaderamente padres se sienten madres; sienten la comezón y hasta el escozor de sus tetillas atrofiadas" (870). Also like Tigre Juan, the telescoping of male and female means that the male possesses maternal qualities. Perhaps, Unamuno muses, Don Juan is a drone bee—"para cada reina . . . hay varios zánganos, lo más de los Don Juanes, supernumerarios o sustitutos" (Unamuno 1966–71, 5:723). The civil state, he continues depends on the real mothers and fathers "que crían la familia y conservan el enjambre" (5:723). It is another variation on the theme of traditional sexual union and child rearing that we saw in *Niebla, Dos madres,* and *La tía Tula.*

Man should subsume woman. Unamuno could not imagine any other arrangement than completely separate spheres, which paradoxically collapse into the male sphere in some ethereal spiritual plane: "el amor . . . que hace a la mujer y a su hombre hombre. Los dos un hombre solo, una persona, dos espíritus en una carne. Que es lo mismo que dos carnes en un espíritu" (Unamuno 1966–71, 5:722). The fusion of maternity and paternity equals humanity. Paternity is masculinity, and therefore also maternity. Don Juan, he continues, is more like the drone bee, whose sole function is to impregnate the queen. He is a "celestino" (go-between). Unamuno quotes Don Quixote, who claims that the profession of go-between is " 'oficio de discretos y necesarísimo en la república'—no dijo en el reino—'bien ordenada, y que no le debía ejercer sino gente muy bien nacida' " (871) [vocation of the discrete and very necessary to the well-ordered republic—he did not say kingdom—which should not be carried out by anyone but the wellborn]. The fact that Unamuno particularly notes a republic reminds us that he is linking gender and politics. The shrill tone of the prologue suggests Unamuno's exceptional alarm at the roles that women were assuming in Spanish public life under the Republic.

Contrasting significantly with Pérez de Ayala's and Unamuno's incorporation of hybrid sexualities into their works of the 1920s to highlight what they perceived as threats to traditional family stability are several novelettes by Burgos—*Ellas y ellos o ellos y ellas* and *El permisionario*—both published in 1917, shortly before Marañón's famous essay on Don Juan's ambiguous gender. Burgos preceded Pérez de Ayala in deploying transgendered novelistic characters to query social roles within the body politic. In *Ellas y ellos*, she, like Pérez de Ayala, incorporated the Calderonian honor theme, but in doing so, she did not camouflage her message about contemporary gender arrangements with philosophical ruminations on the meaning of great figures of Spain's glorious literary past. Rather, she employed gender amalgams and cross-dressing to question traditional marriage. *Ellas y ellos o ellos y ellas* daringly deploys homosexuality, lesbianism and transvestism to probe Spain's reaction to the moral confusion of the modern world.

Set in Madrid, probably toward the end of the First World War, *Ellas y ellos* portrays a society in sexual chaos. Unlike *El permisionario*, which places a heterosexual couple within a range of other sexualities, *Ellas y ellos* does not include a single traditional heterosexual couple, married or otherwise. Sexual freedom is an emblem of the general social liberation that the First World War ushered into Europe, including Spain, even though Spain did not actively participate in the war.[17] At the Hotel Majestic (aptly named to capture the new international ambience that Spain acquired in the World War I era), aristocrats and pretentious bourgeois mix "sin escándalo" (Burgos 1989b, 5) and, in turn, associate with decadent artists and women of easy virtue. The few foreigners who come to Spain also congregate at the Majestic, "un soplo de extranjerismo, de modernidad" (6). The Majestic is a little island of freedom and modernity within traditional Spain, "algo como la soltura que se adquiere al pasar la frontera y hallarse en un mundo más tolerante" (6). The streets of Spain, harbingers of traditional Spanish ways, are, however, never far away. There one finds the old caste system undiluted and the facades of the houses proclaim social inequality: "Fuera había un ambiente rígido, hambriento, desesperado, ineducado, hostil, que acosaba al gran hotel y que parecía espesarse a su alrededor" (6).

Mass protagonism, somewhat in the vein of Vicente Blasco Ibáñez, whose naturalism influenced Burgos in her early novelistic career, overshadows any single character. (The mass protagonist of *Ellas y ellos* is, however, aristocratic and bourgeois in contrast to the working-class mobs of Blasco Ibáñez's novels.) Within the kaleidoscopic movement of people, Manuel, an effeminate man married to Mercedes, manages to rise above the general din. Manuel's story is a modern version of the classic Calderonian honor play. A homosexual, he marries Mercedes with the idea of having an idyllic, platonic marriage, but Mercedes finally leaves him to join the free "high society" described in the first part of the novelette. Manuel is the object of pity and the butt of jokes in the sexually "liberated" social classes that attend fêtes at the Hotel Majestic.

Manuel appears to have accepted his wife's new life, although he is always watching her from a distance to see if she is romantically involved with anyone else. Mercedes has, in fact, become attracted to her constant companion, the seductive lesbian Luisa. One day, while Luisa and Mercedes are engrossed in an intimate tête-à-tête at the theater, Manuel murders Luisa in a fit of jealousy, rage, and impotence. He had tried and failed to adopt an open attitude toward a sexual liaison between his wife and another woman: "Hombre o mujer, ¿qué más daba? Buscó su puñalito en el bolsillo y lo clavó de un golpe en el seno blanco de aquella mujer que le robaba su felicidad" (87–88). He killed "como un héroe de la España antigua, y sin embargo no tenía en favor suyo la simpatía que hay siempre para el hombre que venga su honor" (88) [like a hero of old Spain, and nonetheless he was not favored with the sympathy there always is for the man who avenges his honor]. Ultimately, the old solutions to marital infidelity, just like traditional sexual arrangements, are inadequate for a modern setting. Modernity seems to demand new approaches to perennial human emotions: "Aquel hecho de una pasión extraña y brutal, representaba un dolor nuevo, incomprendido que arrojaba como prueba fehaciente de su existencia un cuerpo ensangrentado en medio de la concurrencia atónita ante el hecho incomprensible, pero decisivo" (89). [That fact of a strange and brutal passion represented a new incomprehensible pain, which, as a confirming truth of its existence, threw a bloody body into the middle of an astonished crowd in the face of the incomprehensible but decisive event.] Such a radical shift may, however, be impossible.

Burgos never relinquishes a belief in fundamental human characteristics that cross historical barriers. (As we see later, she also endorses a certain biological determinism.) Manuel finally understands that genuine emotions are involved in any kind of human sexual relations ("había algo que tocaba al corazón" [89]), and when people do not take emotions seriously, tragedy always lurks in the wings. The message of *Ellas y ellos* (and of Burgos's other novels that portray alternatives to bipolar gender roles) with respect to the new gender identities in post–World War I Spain is inconclusive, perhaps reflecting an ambivalence about nonheterosexual identities and her own mixed experiences as a nontraditional woman. As discussed later, in *El permisionario* (1917), *Quiero vivir mi vida* (1931), and *El veneno del arte* (1910), Burgos was a master of maintaining an ambiguous perspective on shifting gender roles. In *Ellas y ellos,* the Calderonian solution to a wife's infidelity (even with another woman) is clearly antiquated, but the reader is encouraged to sympathize with Manuel, whose sexually liberated wife, Mercedes, is hardly portrayed as the model woman of the future.

El permisionario, set during World War I, similarly compares traditional marriage to alternative sexual arrangements. Fernanda (a female name formed from a more common masculine name) married Luis shortly before he went off to the French front, and now, after several months of separation, he has been granted a leave to meet her in Nice. Their conventional heterosexual relationship is first threatened by Luis's jealousy of Fernanda's friendship with another man, until Fernanda reveals that the man is a woman. Then Luis's attention toward a beautiful young widow at the casino piques Fernanda's jealousy. Later we learn that the woman is a lesbian. These two incidents of mistaken sexual identity that disrupt the serenity of the heterosexual pair are a sign of the larger sexual revolution taking place in Europe during the Great War. Finally, Fernanda and Luis remain locked in their hotel room focused on one another: "Hubieran tomado por la vida real una representación de teatro, y ahora vieran por entre los desgarrones del telón cómo se disfrazaban los actores y se pintaban con corcho y con albayalde" (1989b, 403). The story ends with the couple refusing to go out into a society so fraught with dangers to their traditional marriage.

By the late 1920s, Burgos had entered into the national discussion on gender with overt and covert references to Marañón's ideas. Her brief mention of Marañón's notions of bisexuality in her essay *La mujer moderna y sus derechos* seems to agree with his biological interpretation of gender, a position somewhat at odds with other arguments in the book that emphasize the importance of society and the legal system in shaping gender roles. A careful examination of the passage in which she cites Marañón reveals that Burgos ingeniously dilutes Marañón's extreme biologism. Citing Greek myths in which men engendered by the sun and women engendered by the earth produce androgynous beings, she first points out that man is the only animal to consider his female companion inferior. Today, she says, these notions of "la primitiva bisexualidad de los seres" (26) have been converted into scientific theory (she specifically cites Marañón). Tip-toeing around Marañón, whom she respected for his positive role in the Spanish feminist movement, Burgos attacks his (and Pérez de Ayala's) sources, Weininger and Schopenhauer, taking pains to indicate that Marañón softens the misogyny of the German thinkers.[18] She especially distinguishes Marañón from Sigmund Freud, whose all-encompassing sexual interpretation of human life she qualifies as "monstruoso" (34).

Burgos further scrutinized Marañón's theses on gender in her last long novel, *Quiero vivir mi vida* (1931).[19] The protagonist, the beautiful Isabel, is never satisfied, even though her husband, Luis, is excessively attentive to her every whim. Her dissatisfaction is attributed to "la lucha de los instintos femeninos y viriloides unidos en su naturaleza" (25). The narrator's interpretation of Isabel's malady coincides with that of Luis's friend Alfredo, a doctor and thinly disguised representation of Marañón. In a long discussion with Isabel's husband, Luis, who is concerned about his wife's wild mood swings, Alfredo refers to the ancient myths of androgyny cited by Burgos as fallacious in *La mujer moderna* and pronounces Isabel "un caso de intersexualidad." According to Alfredo, the problem is purely endocrinological and can be treated surgically. Burgos seems to feel that she can more safely examine Marañón's ideas by dialogizing them within a novelistic context than by examining them in an essay format. She thus places her critique in the voices of the novel's characters at a comfortable remove from her own voice.[20] In a dialogue between Isabel and Alfredo regarding the nature of the sexes (86–90), Isabel accuses Alfredo (Marañón) of a "cierto espíritu de contradicción" (89), to which he replies, "No lo niego" (89).

The true causes of Isabel's frustration may just as likely be the marriage state itself, which spawns jealousy and malaise that were not present before the couple became legally united. In his prologue to the novel titled "Breve ensayo sobre el sentido de los celos," Marañón writes that the work "desarrolla un conflicto de la psicología y del instinto de la mayor modernidad, de un interés actual apasionante" (1931, 7) [develops a very modern psychological and instinctual conflict, which is of passionate current interest]. Isabel attempts (and to an extent succeeds) in living a fairly independent life, spending a great deal of time with female friends and even taking a lover. The title, *Quiero vivir mi vida*, is a refrain that is repeated at key intervals throughout the novel. Isabel's "masculinism" is, in fact, a strong independent character, which does not fit the traditional female stereotype. Contradicting the biological explanations for Isabel's behavior put forth by Alfredo are other passages in which education is tendered as a cause for women's condition: "La mujer de nuestra raza suele ser honesta por temperamento. Se la educa diciéndole que su misión en la tierra es sólo la de casarse y tener hijos" (Burgos 1931, 99). [A woman of our race is usually honest by temperament. She is educated in the idea that her mission on earth is only to marry and have children.] Isabel's father educated her in masculine pursuits, and Isabel herself "jamás concedía . . . que sus desigualdades de carácter tuvieran un origen puramente fisiológico" [never conceded that the ups and downs of her character had a purely physiological origin] (205).

Isabel's independence and coldness toward her husband provoke him into an affair with a young woman in his office. They have a child together, and Luis sets his mistress up in an apartment. When Isabel's lover commits suicide because she has tired of him, Isabel's volatile psychology takes yet another turn. She becomes excessively religious, further alienating her husband. Finally, a malicious friend reveals to Isabel her husband's secret life with his mistress and their son. Isabel's jealousy overwhelms her, and she murders Luis with a pair of scissors. Thus, her story reverses the classic Calderonian honor play in which a jealous husband murders his wife. If Pérez de Ayala modified the Calderonian wife-murder plot to create the more modern Tigre Juan who accepts an errant wife back into his home, Burgos removed the husband entirely from hegemony over his wife's fate and endowed the wife with power over her husband. Burgos appropriates the sexual jealousy that was traditionally the province of men for women and portrays Isabel with the capacity to act on strong emotions.

After killing her husband, Isabel, who has often expressed the wish to be a man, inhales her husband's fleeing soul. In the context, we understand this attempt to assume a male identity as not so much a biological but a social desire. Men's affairs outside marriage are socially (and legally) condoned (Isabel's behavior in her extramarital affair mirrors that of a husband): "Volvía al lado de su marido con esa tranquilidad con que vuelven los hombres al lado de sus esposas después de una infidelidad a la que no conceden importancia" (169). [She returned to her husband's side with that tranquility with which men return to their wives after an infidelity to which they give no importance.] In addition, men are allowed to express jealousy and to avenge themselves of wives who stray. Isabel gives herself the rights that the social and legal systems have denied her. (Burgos may well have been playing out a fantasy for women who, like Burgos and Martínez Sierra, have longtime male partners who betray them with younger women.) Burgos's treatment of the breakdown in fixed boundaries between male and female identities differs from that of Pérez de Ayala. In her novels with characters that cross gender lines, there is no falling back on male dominance in the heterosexual couple or on strictly maternal roles for women. In Burgos's fictions, Spain has entered a new era with respect to social roles for men and women, and even without the satisfactory establishment of a new order, there is no return to traditional models. When there is a more traditional couple, as in the case of Fernanda and Luis of *El permisionario,* they must lock themselves away in a decidedly unsatisfactory social isolation.

Born in 1898, some thirty years after Burgos, Rosa Chacel—whose early adulthood coincided with the rise of feminism and Republicanism—moved Burgos's ambiguous deployment of mixed gender identities to new levels in her novel *Memorias de Leticia Valle.* A portion of the novel appeared in the journal *Sur* in January 1939, and the novel was published in its entirety in Buenos Aires in 1945. In many ways, *Memorias de Leticia Valle* continues the gender polemics raised by Marañón and propagated in Ortega y Gasset's journal *Revista de Occidente.* As both Magdalena Mora (1987) and Juli Highfill (1999) point out, *Revista de Occidente* assisted the emergence of the "woman question" from the margins of the Spanish public imagination, helping to catapult it to a prominent position on the national stage. *Revista de Occidente,* a bellwether for Spanish intellectual life from 1923 until the early 1930s, regularly included articles about and by women.

Mora categorizes the material about women presented in *Revista de Occidente* in the following way: (1) commentary on women as different from men, (2) biased information about the contemporary social, public role of women, (3) images of women presented in biographical essays and fiction by men, and (4) analysis (usually fairly negative) of the artistic and literary work of women from various countries. She also divides the material on women in *Revista de Occidente* into two overlapping periods: from about 1923 to 1930 and from the late 1920s on. Between about 1923 and 1930, articles by José Ortega y Gasset, Georg Simmel, Gregorio Marañón, and Carl Jung judged women's biology and psychology to be innately opposite to men's; they especially highlighted what they believed to be women's limitations. By the end of the 1920s, articles on women were less general and abstract, focusing on concrete moral (and other) issues that related to women in contemporary situations in precise locations. Issues of *Revista de Occidente* in the late 1920s also saw more articles by women, which combated some of the negative views toward women that were contained in the male-authored articles.

In articles from the first period, oppositional dichotomies such as nature/culture, immanence/transcendence, and subjectivity/objectivity emerge as central organizing principles. Simmel, for example, centers his article "Lo masculino y lo femenino" (1923) on objective masculine principles, which he defines as the social, intellectual, and artistic. The feminine, he claims, is less easily detected and exists to serve and complete the masculine. Woman's essence is consonant with sexuality and the erotic; woman is immanent. For women, maternity is the absolute, whereas men participate in a transcendent duality. In "Para una caracterología," Ortega y Gasset (1926) argues that in women the soul—the emotions—predominates over spirit. (It is possible that María Zambrano's 1924 article "Hacia un saber sobre el alma" inspired Ortega y Gasset's meditations on this subject.) Predating Luce Irigaray's sexual interpretation of Plato's cave metaphor by a number of decades, Ortega y Gasset employs the cave allegory "el útero cavernoso y arcano" (1923, 241) for women in "Oknos el soguero." The phallus, in contrast, "inicia la ascención hacia . . . una cultura solar y fulgural" (241). Chacel not only participated in the *Revista de Occidente* dialogues on gender in the 1930s with a well-reasoned response to Simmel's ideas published there; she also incorporated notions from those debates into her narrative masterpiece *Memorias de Leticia Valle.*

An only child whose enlightened parents lavished on her not only education but also encouragement for her artistic talents, Chacel was fortunate that her natural brilliance (she had a prodigious memory that lasted to the end of her very long life) and strong character did not suffer the constraints that did the talents of other intelligent women of the early century. Chacel married the painter Timoteo Rubio in 1923 and spent five years with him in Rome. During those years, Chacel avidly read *Revista de Occidente,* and through an autodidactic process became an existential philosopher/novelist who continued the philosophical legacy of Unamuno and produced philosophical writings that coincided chronologically with those of Jean-Paul Sartre and Albert Camus.[21] Her philosophical position is akin to that of Simone de Beauvoir, whose understanding of existence is less metaphysical and more corporeal than that of male existentialists.[22] Also diverging from male existential writers, Chacel placed gender at the center of her novels of self-creation. In *Memorias de Leticia Valle,* existence, rather than "preceding essence," is a coming into being in a gendered society. Gender precedes existence and shapes it, and the process of acquiring existence, coming into being, impacts on gender. In addition to engaging in the public dialogue about the nature of gender in the 1920s and 1930s, *Memorias de Leticia Valle* gives a feminist response to much of what constituted the male-authored novel of the early twentieth century—modernist aesthetics; approaches to gender roles; and the transformation of the Don Juan theme, especially Ramón del Valle-Inclán's *Sonatas* (Leticia's last name is a clue, and Valle-Inclán was Chacel's teacher at the Escuela de Bellas Artes).[23] Inspired by a Fyodor Dostoyevsky novel in which an older man seduces a very young girl (as well as by a similar story that she read in a Spanish newspaper), Chacel wrote a narrative in which the seduction of an eleven-year-old girl and a middle-aged man (her tutor) is mutual. Rather than face public shame when the affair is discovered, the man commits suicide.

Chacel identified with Ortega y Gasset's intellectual leadership in a number of ways; on at least one occasion, she even avowed adherence to his aesthetics in which form and technique overshadow personal and political concerns (see Chacel 1956). In practice, however, her aesthetics were patently personalist (a vanguard personalism, rather than the realist personalism of Martínez Sierra, Burgos, and other older women writers). Her novels are "self"-conscious in a way that recalls Martínez Sierra's deployment of the self in *Tú eres la paz*. Chacel, in opposition to Ortega y Gasset and like Unamuno and Martínez Sierra, envisioned a self that could and should in some way be related to an art created by it.[24]

Chacel's relationship to Ortega y Gasset and Unamuno, the two living models for her as thinkers/writers in the Spanish 1920s and 1930s, is complex and has yet to be fully sorted out. We must read between the lines of her essays and fiction and sift through the sparse correspondence for clues. Moreover, Ortega y Gasset's patronizing patriarchalism was temporally, if not always geographically, very close at hand, whereas Unamuno was a distant, grandfatherly figure in age as well as proximity. Susan Kirkpatrick and Teresa Bordons point out Chacel's opposition to Ortega y Gasset's ideas on gender in their analysis of Chacel's novel *Teresa:* "Throughout her life, Chacel declared her adherence to many aspects of Ortega's thought, but her engagement with the story of a woman who lived, as she herself did, in an era of revolution, led her to think through and clarify her disagreement with Ortega on the matter of women's nature" (1992, 289).[25] As correspondence between Chacel and Zambrano indicates, Chacel also disagreed with Ortega y Gasset on the Republican initiative, especially in the early stages of the movement. Both women were very disappointed when he returned to Francoist Spain after the war. They both clung to their Republican ideals and returned to live in Spain only when the dictator was near death (in Chacel's case) or had died (in Zambrano's case).[26]

Memorias de Leticia Valle incorporates the theories about sexual identity that Chacel outlined in her *Revista de Occidente* article "Esquema de los problemas prácticos y actuales del amor" (1931) and developed further in her book *Saturnal* (1972). Additionally, the novel embodies her ideas about the confessional genre, which also has gender implications. In "Esquema de los problemas prácticos," Chacel countered Ortega y Gasset's strong tendency to a bipolar division between the sexes and his idealization of the female body. Love, for Ortega y Gasset, is unidirectional (always male toward female): "The normal man 'likes' almost every woman he encounters. This fact permits the nature of profound choice, which love possesses, to stand out all the more. . . . The indifferent man will find beauty in the broad lines of her face and figure—what, in fact, is usually called beauty" (1967, 87). Without mentioning Ortega y Gasset, in whose *Revista de Occidente* she published her article on the problematics of love in contemporary life, Chacel confronts Simmel, one of his German sources who wrote on women in the love relationship. She particularly challenges Simmel's idea that " 'la mujer descansa en su belleza, sumida en la bienaventuranza de sí misma' " (Chacel 1931, 141) [woman rests in her beauty, submerged in her own bliss].

As a number of male writers concerned themselves with the masculinization of women and the feminization of men, Chacel criticized the "feminización de la mujer." Ortega y Gasset's construction of the "opposite" sex and Simmel's tendency to understand gender in terms of binary opposites contribute to this feminization that she finds so abhorrent: "La tesis de los absolutos contrarios, es de tal modo insostenible que el mismo Yung, apenas expuesta, reconoce como fuera de toda duda el hecho de que la mujer actual pasa por la misma fase que el hombre, y acto seguido establece un parangón entre la situación crítica que atraviesa" (Chacel 1931, 147). [The thesis of absolute opposites is so untenable that when it was first posited, Jung himself recognized that beyond all doubt women today are going through the same phase as men, and he immediately established a comparison with the critical situation that men are undergoing.] According to Chacel, the effect of a theory centered on binary opposites is to exclude women from the realm of cultural creation:

> No existe, pues una oposición efectiva entre la esencia general de la mujer y la forma general de nuestra cultura como Simmel cree. . . . Todo esto parece, a primera vista, que atañe a los destinos de la cultura y, por tanto, queda aquí fuera de lugar. Pero no es así; en la teoría de Simmel, no es un plan cultural concebido racionalmente lo que se ventila, es el fundamento íntimo de una mitad del género humano que se encuentra en el trance singularísimo de empezar a cobrar realidad en su ser consciente, que debe ingresar fatalmente en la ola de superactividad espiritual que anima a nuestro siglo y a la que se ofrece por solución antener con gran consecuencia un dualismo radical: reconocer que la existencia femenina tiene otras bases,

fluye por cauces radicalmente distintos de la masculina, construir dos tipos vitales, cada uno con su fórmula autónoma. (136, 137, 138)

[There does not exist a real opposition between the general essence of the woman and the general form of our culture as Simmel believes.... At first glance, all this seems to concern the destiny of culture and thus remains out of place. But that is not the case; in Simmel's theory, it is not a rationally conceived cultural plan that is aired; it is the intimate basis of half of the human species that finds itself in a very singular critical moment of beginning to gain reality in its conscious being, which should necessarily enter into the wave of spiritual superactivity that animates our century and is offered as a solution to rely consequentially on a radical dualism: to recognize that feminine existence has other bases, flows through radically different channels from those of men, to construct two vital types, each one with its own autonomous formula.]

For Chacel, women enter culture by means of their rebellion against it. If Ortega y Gasset stresses Don Juan as a symbol of rebellion, Chacel turns the tables and points up the rebellious acts of women, once Don Juan's victims: "Una de las cosas que con mayor evidencia pueden demostrarnos la adhesión de la mujer al mundo espiritual, a la cultura, es precisamente su primera manifestación de rebeldía a ella" (14). [One of the things that can demonstrate to us with greatest evidence women's adherence to the spiritual world, to culture, is precisely her first sign of rebellion against it.] Chacel was concerned about *how* a woman gains an existential presence: "Pero es demasiado obvio que sin *ser* no hay *querer*, y vice versa. Lo que no es imaginable es que semejante cosa—no *querer*, no *ser*—me pasase a mí" (1981a, 69). [But it is too obvious that without *being* there is no *love*, and vice versa. What is unimaginable is that such a thing—not *loving*, not *being*—would happen to me.]

Leticia is a precociously intelligent, androgynous figure who constantly moves between the masculine world of ideas and intellectual conversation associated with her tutor Don Daniel and his wife Luisa's feminine world of kitchen, children, and music. She is the embodiment of woman's entrance into culture via her rebellion against it; she eschews the polarized existences of Daniel and Luisa that allegorize the Cartesian tension between mind and body. Don Daniel's approach to knowledge is entirely book oriented; he is the Simancan archivist, and his study is so lined with books that there is no room for artwork. Don Daniel cruelly ostracizes Leticia whenever she abandons her books for a few days to engage in other more female-identified activities associated with Luisa. Through Don Daniel, *Memorias de Leticia Valle* also revisits central issues of the debates on Spanish education for women, especially separate spheres for men and women, to suggest a neutral zone in which household endeavors and intellectual pursuits unite in a single person. Don Daniel's role as custodian to one of the most important Spanish archives of materials related to the Spanish empire places him in an especially significant position as the keeper of the Spanish past and tradition. The location of the story in Valladolid and Simancas, in the heart of Castile, reminds us of the difference between Chacel's approach to gender and nation and that of Unamuno and Azorín, who situated the eternal feminine Spanish soul in these old Castilian towns. Leticia's father, a soldier in the Spanish army, which fought a losing battle in Morocco in a vain attempt to recover some of the imperial legacy, also symbolizes Spain's moribund glory.

Leticia defies her two father figures—her biological father and Don Daniel, who symbolize the Spanish masculinist tradition—by approaching the world through her body (her senses) and by revealing her position through the confessional genre. In an essay that Chacel wrote on the confession (or the personal in literature)—the genre that Rita Felski calls "a type of autobiographical writing which signals its intention to foreground the most personal and intimate details of the author's life" (1989, 87)[27]—Ortega y Gasset's presence is everywhere marked by his absence. We can similarly speculate on Chacel's crusade to reintegrate the personal into the literary as a reaction to the Ortega y Gasset–informed aesthetics of contemporary male novelists such as Benjamín Jarnés and Ramón Gómez de la Serna, whose vanguard approach to fiction created women not only as objects (the traditional position of the female in art) but as obsession.[28] In a reversal of women's radical objectification as visual spectacle, women authors of the vanguard era cultivated more subjective forms of writing in order to reassert their position as subjects. Note the number of autobiographies by women associated with the vanguard era: María Martínez Sierra's *Una mujer por caminos de España* (1952),

Zenobia Camprubí's *Diario, I* (written in English between 1937 and 1956; published in Spanish in 1991), and María Teresa León's *Memoria de la melancolía* (1970) in addition to Chacel's *Desde el amanecer* (1972), *Alcancía. Ida* (1982), and *Alcancía. Vuelta* (1982) and María Zambrano's *Delirio y destino* (1989).

Chacel finds a positive value in novels with a confessional dimension. Her theoretical scheme for confession includes a sense of guilt, which, along with solitude, is a fundamental requirement of the genre. For Chacel, confession is "última voluntad": "La que no es esto, no es confesión; es lo que generalmente se llama *memorias*" (1970, 10). [Anything that is not a last will and testament is not confession; it is what is generally called *memoirs*.] These qualities, she believes, are preeminent in Cervantes (especially *Don Quixote*) and Unamuno but are lacking in Galdós: "Galdós escribe mal en cuanto *no quiere confesar*" [Galdós writes badly in as much as *he does not wish to confess*] (75, emphasis in original). She does not mention the *memorias* of the Marqués de Bradomín (he is, of course, a fictional memorialist), but she certainly would not have defined his narrative as a confession.[29] As he tells it, his story is highly contrived and anything but a testament. Also lacking in all the male-authored novels discussed herein (including those by Unamuno) is a sense of guilt, which Chacel associates with confession.

John Paul Eakin notes that Roland Barthes changed course in 1978, wanting "to escape from the prison house of critical metalanguage and through simpler, more compassionate language to close the gap between private experience and public discourse" (1992, 18). Eakin argues, I believe convincingly, that what triggers reader recognition of the autobiographical mode or self-revelation is Philippe Lejeune's notion of an autobiographical pact between author and reader, which is related to Normand Holland's idea of "reality testing" (20). Readers have a different experience with texts that bring them closer to the writer's life. Chacel instinctively sought to form the kind of pact between author and reader that Eakin, borrowing from Lejeune, theorizes.

Kathleen Glenn (1991) has commented on the fluidity between the boundaries of fiction and autobiography in *Memorias de Leticia Valle,* which is, in Chacel's own estimation, a prelude to her avowed autobiography *Desde el amanecer*: "El breve recuerdo de este colegio lo esbocé, cuarenta años más tarde, en las 'Memorias de Leticia Valle,' apócrifas, de hecho, y tal vez por esto mismo omití una cosa que perteneció a mi verdadera historia" (Chacel 1981a, 71). [Forty years later, I sketched a brief remembrance of that school in *Memorias de Leticia Valle,* which was, in fact, apocryphal, and perhaps for that reason I omitted something that pertained to my true story.] Through Leticia's experiences with Don Daniel and Luisa, Chacel fictionalizes her own awareness, as a young girl, of the chasm that separated the worlds of her mother and father. Gender and genre boundaries are confounded in both books.[30] The fictional as well as the autobiographical girl negotiates a precarious position between finely chiseled masculine and feminine stereotypes. Being is not the universal Sartrean polarization between *l'être et le néant;* instead, it entails locating a new space between masculine and feminine identities. In the process, Chacel forged an erotoaesthetics ("La conjunción eroticoestética era indisoluble" [186]) that shifts the female-obsessed unidirectional male vanguard gaze to a diffused female gaze or sphere of attention.[31]

In Chacel's vanguard personalism, the self is hard-won and fragile and should not be subjected to linguistic frivolities, the playful, "pneumatic" vanguard aesthetics that Ortega y Gasset described in *La deshumanización del arte.*[32] Instead of embodying an airy tendency to ephemerality, parody, and play, her art "bodies" forth. Male vanguard narrative is game-like, self-conscious in a metafictional sense (for example, in Jarnés's *El convidado de papel*—a vanguardist permutation of the Don Juan theme—the numerous autobiographical elements are overwhelmed by literary self-consciousness). Chacel's self-consciousness, in contrast, is substantive and physical, eschewing the male verbal pyrotechnics that parody past literary tropes and obfuscate the self. In her autobiography, *Desde el amanecer,* Chacel indicates that she abhorred parody (1981a, 44); as Smith puts it, for Chacel, "language is thus taken to be a wholly transparent medium, the vehicle of authenticating personal testimony" (P. Smith 1992, 21).

Both male and female novelists of the vanguard period converge in their interest in language as an artistic medium; however, male language focuses on objects, often evoking a playful relationship in the consciousness of things (Gómez de la Serna's *greguerías,* for example), whereas Chacel shifts attention to a self-discovery from within a corporeal position in the world. Validated by their participation in the hegemonic intellectual elite and thus having less need for self-affirmation, male vanguardists could draw away from life and move toward the realm of the purely aesthetic, focusing on their craft and its medium in language—what Shari Benstock calls the "mystical emphasis on the Word" (1986, 28). *Estación. Ida y vuelta* (1930), Chacel's novel that is most frequently associated with the vanguard, occasionally engages in the vanguardist *greguería* but only very rarely. And unlike the countless ephemeral women of the male vanguard novel evoked by male protagonists' linguistic voyeurism, her protagonist (although male) eventually returns to his responsibilities as a husband and father.[33]

For Chacel, writing was literally a lifeline that called for self-revelation, self-expression. Leticia Valle, like Chacel in *Desde el amancer,* is a self that acts, that effects changes in social values and resituates itself vis-à-vis society. Chacel's interest in confession as a philosophical subject and as the centerpiece of literary creation affirms with Donald Guss that selfhood "is at the base of freedom, as it is of language, society, and daily practice" (1994, 487). She joined Maurice Merleau-Ponty *(avant la lettre)* in assigning the body a central place in selfhood. The perceiving body is a source of knowledge that facilitates the freedom necessary to have an effect on the world. In contrast to Sartre's dreadful freedom, Chacel's existential self-consciousness illuminates life and affirms its possibilities for growth and self-knowledge.

Life, as Chacel understood it, begins with the body, "el alma carnal" (1981a, 119), the biological woman rather than woman as metaphor (as Susan Suleiman paraphrases Alice Jardine, "woman as discursive entity or metaphor, and *women* as biologically and culturally gendered human beings" [1990, 13]). Unlike Unamuno's and Azorín's versions of the Don Juan story, which separate Don Juan from his body and convert him into an ascetic, Chacel's version in *Memorias de Leticia Valle* returns him to his corporeal self. His body eventually overwhelms Don Daniel, the intellectual man and seducer. In fact, Chacel's own literary self is firmly connected to a body, a position that directly challenges the lingering rationalism of Ortega y Gasset's philosophy. Physical illness was central to Chacel's intellectual formation. In *Desde el amanecer,* Chacel describes being confined to her room during her many colds and fevers: "Todo lo que pasaba allí en mi alcoba, tenía la dimensión de un esquema cultural, de un proyecto o, más bien, de un semillero de vida literaria. . . . Todo ello era entrañablemente irracional, diré, si con esto logró dar a entender que era como un amor abismal, corporal, hacia el espíritu" (1981a, 39). [Everything that went on there in my bedroom had the dimension of a cultural scheme, of a project, or rather, of a seed bed of literary life. . . . It was all intrinsically irrational, I will say, if with that expression I can indicate that it was like an abysmal, corporal, almost spiritual love.]

Physical sensations are closely related to verbal phenomena ("Crear es físico" [149]); when a fellow student repeats the words "¡el gusanillo de la conciencia!" [the little worm of consciousness] (71) in a school recitation, Chacel suddenly feels a pain in her armpit: "Hasta los treinta o cuarenta años, ante toda convulsion de mi conciencia he seguido sintiendo una aguda punzada en la axila izquierda" (71). [Until I was thirty or forty years old, I continued to feel a sharp pain in my left armpit whenever I experienced a convulsion in my consciousness.] In *Los títulos,* Chacel wrote of Zambrano's metaphor of the heart as central to her understanding of human perception. For Zambrano, the body and the mind are inseparable, and the heart symbolizes the union. Chacel quotes Zambrano: "En su ser carnal el corazón tiene huecos, habitaciones abiertas, está dividido para permitir algo que a la humana conciencia no se le aparece como propio de ser centro" (qtd. in 1981c, 74). [In its carnal being, the heart has hollow places, open rooms; it is divided in order to allow something that cannot appear as central to the human consciousness.]

Leticia's senses (her physical body) tell the hidden story that she refuses to narrate overtly (her identification with Luisa's maternal and feminine qualities, which does not exclude an intellectual and sexual attraction to Daniel).[34] Coming into knowledge of oneself and the world is at the center of *Memorias de Leticia Valle.* Carnal knowledge forges its way through the labyrinth of boundaries and obstacles of male rationality. Leticia's way of knowing is not limited to words on pages; she absorbs information primarily through her senses. Early in *Memorias de Leticia Valle,* the protagonist explores the limits of vision in darkness; her memories of her now absent (inexplicably disappeared) mother are tactile: "Sentía que la piel de mi cara estaba enteramente pegada a su brazo y la palma de mi mano pegada a su pecho. . . . El amor era aquello!" (1981b, 10, 12). [I felt that the skin of my face was completely stuck to her arm and the palm of my hand stuck to her breast. . . . That was love!] When Leticia feels confused about how to react to a situation, "se ensordece." The senses, not the intellect (although it is one of her best assets), are her window on the world; she frequently evokes the *cinco sentidos* (five senses) all together or individually (100, 102, 147); to embrace, to touch, is to know (102). She is fascinated by her cousin Adriana's dancing because it transforms her cousin's body alternately into male and female personages.

Light is literally the medium of illumination. Although the masculine world of the intellect appears to intrigue Leticia more than female confines and activities, strategic use of light reveals another scenario. Luisa is often associated with the positive values of light perception: "Ni siquiera la costumbre que adquirí de entrar en él a diario pudo borrarme la impresión que me causaba su luz al llegar a la puerta. . . . La obra estaba rematada y las dos nos quedamos a la puerta un rato mirando cómo la luz atravesaba los visillos, brillaba en el agua de la damajuana y se extendía por el encerado del suelo, por los respaldos de las sillas y por las cornucopias" (33–34, 41). [The impression that the light from the doorway made on me as I approached was never erased, not even by the habit of walking though it every day, as I eventually did. . . . The work was finished and the two of us stood in the front doorway awhile watching how the light passed through the curtains, sparkled on the water in the demijohn, and spread over the waxed surface of the floor, along the backs of the chairs and the sconces.][35] Daniel, the agent of intellectual development, "se puso de espaldas a la luz" (46) [stood with his back to the light]; light works on Daniel (as in a scene in which Leticia observes the shape of his body through his shirt), but neither his presence nor his actions light up existence. Leticia feels cold after her first lesson with the archivist (significantly, her body also experiences cold when, horrified, she witnesses the drowning of some unwanted puppies [78]). History at the hand of imperial archivist Don Daniel is aggressive and violent: "Según hablaba [Daniel], el lápiz aquel tomaba actitudes de lanza, de cruz, de pendón" (49). [Depending on what he was talking about, the pencil resembled a spear, a cross, or a banner.] The masculine symbols are not veiled. Leticia experiences bodily pleasure when she encounters history on her own terms rather than on Don Daniel's. For example, when she views the statue of the Rey de la Cerveza, she imagines the king eating (15).

Seeing is paramount in Leticia's growth into self-consciousness. In Abigail Lee Six's article on Chacel's autobiography, she theorizes two types of gaze: (1) the voyeuristic, in which one sees without being seen (I would associate this type with Suleiman's obsessive male viewing of the female in surrealism), and (2) a mutual gaze, as when mother and child look at each other (1992, 80). Chacel had already made use of these gestures in *Memorias de Leticia Valle* to delineate masculine and feminine spheres. Leticia's only memory of her mother focuses on the sense of touch and a mutual gaze: "Recuerdo cómo me quedaba un poco en el aire al incorporarme, y seguramente entonces la miraba y ella me miraría" (1981b, 10). [I remember how I hovered in the air a bit as I sat up, and I must have looked at her then, and she probably looked at me.] Her first meeting with Luisa is signaled by a mutually frank and open gaze: "Entonces me pareció que nos decía adiós con una mirada tan franca, tan abierta" (33). [Her gaze seemed so frank, so open, as she said goodbye to us.] Looks that involve Daniel are radically different; Leticia and Daniel look at each other (observe one another), but never at the same time and never with mutual confidence. One of the last times that he looks at her, it is a "mirada inquisitorial" (159); significantly, Don Daniel is once again allied with archaic Spanish institutions. Leticia takes her revenge for these inquisitorial looks when she focuses her eyes on Don Daniel during her public recital of José Zorrilla's poem about an Arab warrior (evoking an earlier era—the Reconquest—in Spain's glorious past). It is the culminating moment in her seduction of the teacher, and shortly thereafter, he finally succumbs to his physical attraction for his pupil. Thus, a young girl tames the great warrior with whom Leticia has identified Don Daniel. The masculine exploits of the Spanish imperial past surrender to an intelligent, modern female who is unhampered by the conventional constraints on her gender.

Leticia writes her memoirs, a confession by Chacel's definition, to reaffirm her existence, to fill the chasm that opened in her life when her brief sexual encounter with Don Daniel became public and he committed suicide. From her "exile" in Switzerland, she writes to recapture a time when she felt that she was a live, physical presence in the world (as Chapter 6 shows, exile or emigration from Spain is a constant theme in women's novels with a feminist message). As Carol Maier points out, the narratee of the autodiegetic narration is Leticia herself (1992, 92 n. 17). Chacel may have believed that in *Leticia Valle* she was reversing Dostoyevsky's story of an older man who seduces a young girl. In fact, however, she has created a new kind of bildungsroman in which a person very much like herself, instead of coming of age in and being socialized into the values of the surrounding Spanish culture, struggles through a miasmically bipolarized social sexuality to listen to her own body and consciousness and find her own place essentially outside of social norms. In order to do so, she must kill the "father" (Don Daniel) and wound the "mother" (Luisa) whose polarized existences she struggles to reconcile. Leticia eliminates Don Daniel because he is the supreme patriarch, but Luisa's dependent model, despite the attractions that Luisa holds for Leticia, does not suit her either.[36]

Unamuno and Pérez de Ayala employed the feminized man (especially a feminine Don Juan) to raise red flags about nontraditional gender roles that were emerging in the 1920s in Spain. The messages embedded in their novels militate for male supremacy within conventional marriage. Burgos essayed sexual alternatives that challenged heterosexual marriage, and Chacel destroyed Luisa and Daniel's traditional marriage by introducing the bisexual or androgynous Leticia into their midst. The references to Spain as a nation via effeminate Don Juans, Calderonian themes, international settings, and imperial locations that weave through Pérez de Ayala's *Tigre Juan y El curandero de su honra;* Azorín's *Don Juan;* Burgos's *Ellas y ellos, ellos y ellas, El permisionario,* and *Quiero vivir mi vida;* and Chacel's *Memorias de Leticia Valle* remind us that the public debates on gender in the 1920s and 1930s coincided with the rising Republican movement, another major political upheaval for Spain. Chapter 6 examines a group of novels written by (mostly women) authors who sided with the Republican ideal and envisioned a new political order in which women and men shared equally in the public good.

CHAPTER 6
Vanguard Feminists Dream the Nation

Rosa Chacel charted brave new territory in her essays on gender and in her novel *Memorias de Leticia Valle,* but she did not spring from a vacuum. She may have encased feminist ideals in a more vanguard novelistic format, but Carmen de Burgos, Margarita Nelken, Federica Montseny, and Concha Espina, who, like Chacel, were pro-Republican feminists, paved the way for her messages on gender in Spain.[1] In the 1920s and 1930s, they enlisted fiction in a fairly realist mode to promote a more progressive nation where women would be men's equals and marriage would mean partnership rather than oppression. Like male vanguard art, women's vanguard fiction reflects the rapid changes of modern life, but it does not partake of the dehumanized aesthetic that José Ortega y Gasset defined in his famous 1925 essay and that is associated with such male novelists as Ramón Gómez de la Serna, Pedro Salinas, and Benjamín Jarnés.

It is hard to imagine a woman engaging in the kind of aggressive destruction that constituted much male vanguardism (for example, Marcel Duchamp's mischievous defacement of the Mona Lisa when he painted a moustache and beard on her timeless beauty). Jokes that centered on women similarly circulated among members of the Spanish vanguard. Attendees at a banquet in honor of Ramón del Valle-Inclán laughed at lines such as "La condesa de Noailles menstrúa como una vaca" (qtd. in Pariente 1999, 467). [Countess Noailles menstruates like a cow.] At a Residencia de Estudiantes avant-garde film showing, Luis Buñuel suggested to Pepín Bello that "[el] momento parecía indicado, ante aquel distinguido público, para anunciar la apertura de un concurso de menstruación y señalar el primer premio" (qtd. in Pariente 1999, 469) [it seemed like an apt moment before that distinguished public to announce the opening of a new menstruation contest and assign the first prize]. Obsession with female corporeality is central to canonized vanguardism and often provides the basis for its shock value. As Susan Suleiman points out, however, although the male vanguard imagination focused on the female body, it was not the body of a real woman; it "does not need to see the woman in order to imagine her, placing her at the center but only as an image, while the actual woman is now out of the picture altogether" (1990, 24). In surrealism, for example, women are the objects of male dreams, but they are not the dreamers.

In many ways the avant-garde is about women but without women. Two landmark male-authored Spanish vanguard fictions—Salinas's *Víspera del gozo* (1926) and Jarnés's *El convidado de papel* (1928)—focus on the erotic thoughts of a male protagonist. (Don Quixote's platonic imagination has now been eroticized.) In the several loosely associated narratives of *Víspera del gozo*, the real woman appears only at the end of the story, if at all. When the woman makes her brief appearance, it is to disclose that her physical reality does not match that of the imagined woman. The women who occupy the erotic imagination of Jarnés's protagonist are from magazine photographs, the "convidadas de papel" who substitute for the real women he has only fleetingly encountered outside the seminary.[2]

Women novelists writing in the 1920s and 1930s similarly narrated imagined women. Instead of being erotic fantasies, however, they are socially and politically committed new women, who do not yet exist in Spain but who are projected for the future. Like the male vanguard writers' protagonists, these women dream: They have a vision, but it is not of the female body; it is of a new body politic, of a different Spanish society in which women act alongside men. As Mary Nash observes, by the 1920s, slowly but surely the discourse on the "angel of the house" was replaced by discourse on the "new modern woman": "Although not as widely accepted as the traditional *Angel del Hogar*, this new cultural representation became incorporated into social values and collective imagery about gender norms'" (1999, 31). What Nash does not note is that women generated much of this discourse in their novels and essays. The imaginative qualities of the novelistic genre were a means of realizing the dream of a new sociopolitical order based on a personal freedom that included erotic freedom.

In many ways, the Second Republic (1931–39) was women's dream. Ernesto Giménez Caballero, who was well-known for promoting male vanguardism through his journal *La Gaceta Literaria,* wrote, "La República en España es el triunfo de la niña. Un éxito radicalmente femenino . . . [el] avance de la España ginecocrática" (qtd. in Hurtado 1998, 31). [The Republic in Spain is the girl's triumph. A radically feminine success . . . the advancement of gynecocratic Spain.] As I have noted, women's issues were central to the Republic's agenda—greater legal guarantees for women, women's suffrage, equal pay for equal work, and divorce. Not only were women a significant object of Republican policy; they were some of the most important political philosophers of the Republican movement. Their voices and writings, pervasively heard and read in the 1920s and 1930s, have faded from the cultural landscape, and the gynecocratic Spain to which Giménez Caballero referred is now viewed as a field of conflict for male liberals such as Miguel de Unamuno, Antonio Machado, José Ortega y Gasset, Pío Baroja, Azorín, Gregorio Marañón, Ramón Pérez de Ayala, whose anguish and wavering over the republic was chronicled by Victor Ouimette (1998) in *Los intelectuales españoles y el naufragio del liberalismo (1923–1936).* The erasure of the prominence of women and women's issues in 1920s and 1930s public discourse began while it was still in progress. Leaders of the highest ranks of the Republic revealed disdain for women politicians. For example, President Manuel Azaña, who served from 1931 to 1933, severely criticized the three women legislators. He labeled Nelken "vanidosa," and he ridiculed her speeches. He said that Victoria Kent was inept as director of prisons, although he thought her "simpática" and "correcta." He judged Clara Campoamor to be more intelligent than Kent but "antipática" (qtd. in Núñez Pérez 1993, 134–35). In a 1932 interview, the vanguard theorist and novelist José Díaz Fernández said that women should not have ministerial posts and should limit their activities to the apolitical sphere (Núñez Pérez 1993, 121).

If, as Ouimette claims, the older male intellectuals committed a *trahison des clercs,* waffling in their theorizing about and active support of the Republic, women writers and intellectuals (although the specifics of their imagined Republic differ) wavered much less in their enthusiasm for a Republican form of government.³ Carmen de Burgos's *La mujer moderna y sus derechos* (1927); Margarita Nelken's *La condición social de la mujer en España* (significantly subtitled *Su estado actual y su posible desarrollo,* emphasizing the future [n.d.]); María Martínez Sierra's *Cartas a las mujeres de España* (1916), *Feminismo, femininidad, españolismo,* and *Las nuevas cartas a las mujeres* (1917); Federica Montseny's articles in *La Revista Blanca* (1925, 1926, 1927a, and 1927b); Rosa Chacel's "Esquema de los problemas prácticos y actuales del amor" (1931); and María Zambrano's *Horizonte del liberalismo* (1930) envisioned a political system based on personal freedom centered on sexual liberation inside and outside of marriage. These women writers understood that without a new sexual order, there could be no new political order. The basis of the new women's sexual order was a theory of the self that included relationships with others—love, companionship, and community chief among them. Interestingly, as pointed out earlier, canonical male writers like Ramón Sender and Francisco Ayala, who actively supported the Republic and wrote politically committed fiction, did not engage with women's issues in their novels or essays. One exception is the semicanonical Díaz Fernández whose *La venus mecánica* (1980) I comment on briefly later.

The notion of "creative dreaming" that Zambrano posited in her novelized autobiography *Delirio y destino* (1989) aptly summarizes the women's vanguard project. "Creative dream" defines the manner in which one can conjure the new society that Zambrano later developed more extensively in her long essay *El sueño creador* (1955). For Zambrano, dreams are an imagined space in which one can shape the future. Creative dreaming is paired with "creative forgetfulness."⁴ Unlike *intrahistoria,* in which the present is sustained by past tradition, in creative forgetfulness, people and nations must abjure the past in order to transcend it with new personal and social forms. Thus, for Zambrano, dreams are not a reenactment of experiences already lived, as Sigmund Freud interpreted them, but an opportunity to fashion the future.⁵ For Zambrano, dreaming is conscious, rather than subconscious as it is in surrealism; it points the way to positive creation rather than self-crippling suppression. In dreaming of the nation, women of the vanguard era eschew the cool detachment of the male vanguardists and enlist passion and personalism to conjure their vision of a different Spain.

As with male vanguardism, conventional marriage was the subject of much female vanguard iconoclasm. If male vanguardists focused on woman as erotic fantasy rather than domestic partner, women writers aimed their iconoclasm at destroying both the image of traditional woman and woman as sexual fantasy. Women writers replaced these two male-generated versions of womanhood with images of publicly competent new women. Important to the project was the condemnation of the uneducated, superficial, materialistic Spanish woman who collaborates in perpetuating marriage as a sand trap (to borrow Nelken's term). The male protagonist's wife in Nelken's *La trampa del arenal* (1923) is a particularly egregious example, as is the mother/wife figure in Espina's *La virgen prudente* (1929). In *Memorias de Leticia Valle*, Chacel approached the traditional Spanish woman more subtly, giving her an artistic dimension and thus a more positive cast. She is, nonetheless, destroyed in order to make way for a new version of womanhood prophesied in Leticia.

Burgos was one of the earliest and most sustained dreamers of a modern Spanish society. As we have seen, she constructed a variety of new sociosexual arrangements to propose alternatives to traditional gender roles and instill an *olvido creador* regarding traditional sexual relationships. *La mujer moderna y sus derechos* is her longest theoretical essay about the history and future of womanhood. The book displays a vast knowledge of women's problems and accomplishments from classical Greek and Roman times through the 1920s, tracing developments in views of sexuality, women's education, work, family, marriage, religion, the military, fashion, politics, and suffrage (with special reference to the legal aspects of these topics). As noted in Chapter 5, her approach coincides in part with what today would be called "the social construction of gender," pointing at every turn to legal practices that privilege men and disadvantage women with no basis in fact.[6] She especially argued for allowing women to combine body and mind ("El cerebro (inteligencia) y el corazón (sensibilidad) marchan siempre de acuerdo" [91]), and she consistently favored uniform education for men and women. Some of her arguments can be traced to turn-of-the-century discourse in which women's education is intimately linked to the health of the nation: "Las naciones más cultas, donde el autor se enriquece con su trabajo, como Inglaterra y Norte América son países de mujeres cultas y aficionadas a la lectura" (92). [The most cultured nations, like England and North America, where authors can get rich with their work, are countries with cultured women who are fond of reading.] The state, she says, is a large national family and should imitate enlightened families that treat male and female children in an identical fashion. It is absolutely essential to national progress that there be in the home a "mujer consciente, no la *mujer reflejo*" (134, emphasis in original). (Burgos joined Martínez Sierra and Chacel in emphasizing consciousness in her theory of the new Spanish woman.) To support her case for women's enlightenment, she borrowed the Krausist notion of humanity's progressive movement toward perfection: "el deber primordial del ser humano a su perfeccionamiento" (92) [the primordial duty of human beings to perfect themselves]. and she infused her rationalism with a profound sense of right and justice.

Burgos's novels reveal a position akin to Jürgen Habermas's "communicative reason," which counters modernism's privileging of the individual subject with an alternative discourse. As noted in the Introduction to this book, Habermas's "communicatively mediated" knowledge includes intersubjective and moral dimensions that distinguish it from male modernist reason centered on aesthetics and expression. Burgos drew on and parodied all the major tenets of male modernism—emphasis on male subjectivity, linguistic virtuosity, the exalted role of the artist in society, and very traditional, even stereotypical, gender roles.[7] She did so, as discussed in Chapter 5, by employing gender in rather different ways from those deployed in the fiction of Spanish male modernists. Unlike novels by Ramón del Valle-Inclán, Miguel de Unamuno, Pío Baroja, Azorín, Ramón Pérez de Ayala, Gabriel Miró, Benjamín Jarnés, and Pedro Salinas that focus almost exclusively on a single (usually male) character, Burgos's short novels *El veneno del arte, El permisionario,* and *Ellas y ellos o ellos y ellas* feature collective as well as individual protagonists. Each novel alternates mixed-sex social scenes that focus on no particular character with intimate colloquies that reveal the subjectivity of individual male and female psyches. If art and subjectivity are the hallmarks of Spanish (and European) male modernism, sentiment and the authentically social self are the key features of Burgos's works.

Burgos's *El veneno del arte*, a novelette from 1910, is both iconoclastic and constructive. The first of the two parts of the novel critiques old Spanish society, whereas the second suggests a new paradigm or possibility. The first section casts an ironic eye on a typical artistic *tertulia*, including all the clichés of the age—a degenerate aristocracy that promotes false artistic values, bohemian hangers-on, rampant hypocrisy and social climbing, internecine squabbles between would-be avant-garde artists and intellectuals, and hostility toward the establishment. Some of the portraits refer directly to the early career experiences of Spanish modernist authors such as Valle-Inclán, Unamuno, Azorín, and Baroja in Madrid:

> Se habían reunido allí todos los jovencitos innominados, los provincianos, que llegaban con su caudal de ilusiones, dispuestos a *luchar* para hacer que se reconociera su genio, oculto por la falta de medios de exteriorizarlo; y hablaban con odio y desprecio de *los viejos* que les cerraban el paso. . . . Se animaban cuando se les presentaba ocasión de lucir sus opiniones de arte, *de su arte,* que tenía una sonrisa burlona para Galdós, Sorolla y Benlliure, y un desdén para Velázquez y Cervantes. Aprovechaban la ocasión de asomar cada uno el superhombre que creía llevar dentro y que procuraban revelar en las largas melenas y en el descuido de los trajes comprados en el Rastro. (1989b, 224).

> [All the young unknowns had gathered there, the provincials who arrived with their abundance of illusions to struggle to make known their genius hidden for lack of any way to publicize it; they spoke with hatred and contempt about the older generation that blocked their way. . . . They brightened when they had the opportunity to show off their opinions about art, *about their art,* which included a sneering smile for Galdós, Sorolla, and Benlliure, and scorn for Velázquez and Cervantes. Each seized upon the opportunity to display the superman that he believed he carried within and that he tried to reveal with long hair and shabby secondhand clothes.]

Here are summarized some of the characteristics associated with Spanish male modernists—complaints about the obstacles that the literary establishment placed in their path to renovating Spanish letters, the cult of Friedrich Nietzsche, the studied acquisition of a bohemian look, and the rejection of artistic realism.[8]

The effeminate Luis, an aristocrat and sometime poet (mostly of satirical pieces against his own class) who lives in his mother's mansion, provides the venue and refreshments for these motley soirées. The narrator sets Luis apart from the would-be artists and writers who frequent his *tertulias* at the same time that she includes him as part of the elaborately parodied decadent art scene. His face—with its "nariz enérgica," "boca carnosa, de gruesos labios, que el volumen de la lengua y el peso de la mandíbula inferior mantenían abiertos y colgantes" (222) [energetic nose, fleshy mouth with thick lips that the voluminous tongue and the weighty lower jaw kept hanging open]—bears traces of Oscar Wilde, as does his role as a mediator between the aristocracy and artistic bohemians. His mother also provides Luis with a monthly allowance, which he usually spends long before the end of each month. Thus, Luis's situation creates a double irony: He scornfully observes a superficial, vane, and artistically pretentious society, while, at the same time, he himself is placed in a dubious moral situation because of his homosexuality and his lack of substance. He is the quintessential degenerate aristocrat: "Su cutis era de un blancor lechoso; los ojos, de la clara transparencia de los albinos, miopes, ahuecados y saltones, parecían a flor del rostro. . . . Parecía que en aquel ser se daban batalla las influencias fisiológicas y psíquicas más encontradas" (222). [His skin was milky white; his eyes, of albino-like clear transparency, myopic, hollow, bulging, seemed even with his face. . . . It appeared as though the most contrary physiological and psychic influences engaged in battle in that being.]

Many of the attendees at Luis's *tertulias* are of ambiguous gender. Contributing to the "compañerismo femenil" are artists described as "jovencitos dulces, femeninos, soñadores, con los cabellos ensortijados, pintadas ojeras, perfumados y con el cutis lleno de *coldcream* virginal a la glicerina, que tenían siempre una sonrisa complaciente y una mirada humilde para las más absurdas teorías de los jóvenes genios" (226) [sweet, feminine, dreamy, perfumed young men with curled hair, rings painted under their eyes and skin covered with virginal glycerin cold cream who always had an indulgent smile and a humble look for the most absurd theories tendered by the young geniuses]. There is also a "mujer hombruna" who attracts a "grupo de efebos" (227). The pretensions to artistic talent fostered by the modernist mentality create an entirely false and hypocritical set of social motivations that are highlighted by the gender ambiguities. These kinds of alternative gender types (in fact any reference to alternative gender possibilities) are almost entirely absent from the Spanish male modernist novel.[9] Pérez de Ayala's *Troteras y danzaderas* (1913) contains similar parodies of the earlier generation of Spanish male modernists but without recourse to gender implications (he employs prostitute figures as the genuine purveyors of artistic understanding but portrays male artists as rather pathetic). As discussed in Chapter 5, Pérez de Ayala later joined Burgos in deploying gender role reversals to dissect the ills of Spanish society in his last published novels, *Tigre Juan y El curandero de su honra*. He did not, however, find it possible, as did Burgos, to allow an intelligent woman to reveal her subjectivity within his parody of gender categories.

In the second half of *El veneno del arte*, Burgos drops the ironic/parodic tone of the first part and allows the reader a glimpse inside two people—a man and a woman—who have chosen to live outside the bounds of traditional gender roles. The homosexual Luis visits the singer María, who declined to attend the *tertulia* in his home. Free of the society that surrounds them, the falseness and hypocrisy fall away and María and Luis engage in a frank and open revelation of their intimate selves, their respective past lives that have shaped their present sense of alienation, their longings, and their disappointments.[10] First, Luis tells María of his relationship with the daughter of a boardinghouse keeper. After the girl's mother caught her nude in his room, Luis promised to marry her, but his own mother intervened and interned him in a religious school. There, as he puts it, the teachers and other students did all in their power to alleviate his sentimental disappointment (in other words, encouraged homosexual activity). When it is María's turn to tell her story, she reveals that she lost the opportunity for personal fulfillment because she did not declare her love. "¡Maldita razón! ¡Maldito análisis!" (1989b, 259) arrested her moment of passion, and she could not recover it. Reason, the handmaiden of modernity, overwhelmed sentiment and ruined her chance for personal happiness.

This moment of shared communication is repeated nine years later when Luis and María meet again after a long hiatus. Luis has shed his bohemian pretensions and plans to adopt his mother's aristocratic lifestyle. Although he has not abandoned his homosexuality, he is considering marriage. He argues that he would be a better husband than most, presumably because he would not be vulnerable to heterosexual adultery. María remains a solitary woman artist, although she no longer performs. She seems to have a satisfactory life; at least she is independent and does as she wishes. She travels, and her lot is better than that of most Spanish women: "La vejez es sólo terrible para las pobres españolas que se encierran al lado del fuego a engordar rezando el rosario y tomando pectorales" (267). [Old age is awful only for the poor Spanish women who shut themselves up by the fire and grow fat saying the rosary and taking pectorals.] María tells Luis (who has been abroad for some time) that all their acquaintances—the would-be artists—have stagnated in mediocrity or have left the bohemian life altogether. Art, the shrine of modernism, has ceded to real life and its demands. This ending leaves us with the sense that gender and modernity continue in flux but that whatever becomes of modern society, gender considerations will be at the heart of its arrangements. This message is very different from the messages in novels by Valle-Inclán, Baroja, Unamuno, and Azorín, in which adulteresses die, male intellectuals accept bourgeois marriage (albeit with ambiguous results), and women who refuse to marry and preside over "normal" family life become social outcasts.

Many of Burgos's fictions, unlike those of her male contemporaries, center overtly on domestic situations. Personal domestic problems resonate with national concerns in well-crafted plots that include a foreign partner in a domestic relationship or a foreign venue. By focusing on the domestic, Burgos recreates a national indwelling through the basic institution of civil society, where tradition is firmly rooted in masculine and feminine roles within marriage. In these novels, Burgos might appear to be working from a philosophical position not unlike that of Unamuno, Azorín, and Baroja, who relied to an extent on biological determinism in defining national characteristics (Burgos pits Spain against other European countries—especially France—where greater equality between men and women is presumed).[11] In highlighting the institution of marriage, however, she suggests that sociopolitical rather than biological factors define the nation. The Spanish/foreign dichotomy that she posits is deployed through problems with solutions—moral behavior or civil and legal structures that can be changed or reformulated.[12]

One group of novels refers overtly to the legal parameters of matrimony in early twentieth-century Spain. Many laws that affected modern Spanish women derived from the Napoleonic code, which was particularly restrictive with regard to married women, who were "virtual legal appendages of their husbands" (Enders and Radcliff 1999, 21). For example, Article 57 of the Civil Code of 1889 stated that "the husband must protect his wife, and she must obey her husband" (Enders and Radcliff 1999, 21). Wives had to seek their husbands' approval to work, travel, or engage in financial dealings. Disobedience meant fines or imprisonment. As Victoria Lorée Enders and Pamela Beth Radcliff point out, there was little revision of the gender sections of the Civil Code until the Second Republic: "The regime transformation brought basic civil and political equality for women, including suffrage" (22). Burgos attempted to influence public opinion about marriage through popular fiction as well as social action. One of her first acts upon arriving in Madrid in the early century was to conduct the survey on divorce quoted earlier. In 1903, after reading about an organization called Club de Matrimonios Mal Avenidos—which catered to those who wanted to "exponer sus quejas y estudiar las bases de una ley de divorcio que solucione los problemas de estas parejas" (Castañeda 1994, 35) [expose their complaints and study the basis for a divorce that would solve the problems of these couples]—Burgos was inspired to bring the issue of divorce to the public's attention.

Burgos's *El abogado* (1915), for example, marshals the power of melodrama to reveal the snares and pitfalls in which the legal system entangles women who have children out of wedlock. Matilde, mother of a child by a self-centered man who refuses to marry her, seeks the aid of an even more unscrupulous lawyer. The lawyer's dealings with her represent the entire Spanish legal system, which allows men to prey on women without having to shoulder moral responsibility for their actions. Burgos's *La rampa* (1917), which Michael Ugarte judges to deal "more thoroughly with the condition of women in the city than any canonical Madrid novel in the early twentieth century" (1996, 95), also highlights the lack of legal protection for women who have children out of wedlock. The middle-class Isabel works and shares an apartment with another workingwoman. When she becomes pregnant by her boyfriend, Fernando, he abandons her, and she goes to a home for unwed mothers. Fernando agrees to live with her after the baby arrives, but he shows no interest in her or in the baby and finally, when the baby dies, he leaves her. She attempts to make a living by various means but finally ends up in a charitable institution.

The title *El artículo 438* (1921) refers to the Spanish law, which Burgos called "vergonzoso" [shameful] (1927, 81), that allowed husbands to punish (even murder) adulterous wives. Unamuno insinuates, although he does not explicitly mention, Article 438 in *Nada menos que todo un hombre* (1916), when Alejandro commits Julia to an insane asylum for claiming that she has had an affair. Burgos's similar story embodies a harsh critique of the Spanish legal system that Unamuno's novelette merely evokes to pose an existential problem. In *El artículo 438*, the daughter of wealthy parents who protect her from knowledge about the world falls in love with and marries a profligate man. After her parents' death, her husband (as entitled by law) takes control of his wife's fortune and spends it on licentious living. In order to live free of his abuse, the wife agrees to sell properties and turn over the proceeds to her hsuband so that he can live abroad, thus leaving her in peace. When she engages in a love affair with another man, the husband returns and kills her. Her lover is imprisoned, and—thanks to Article 458 and the fact that divorce does not exist in Spain—the cruel and wanton husband inherits the remainder of his wife's fortune.

Elizabeth Starcevic (1976, 87) points out that the protagonist of *El artículo 438* is singularly lacking consciousness (unlike other Burgos protagonists, most notably María of *El veneno del arte*). As Martínez Sierra was already arguing in the first decade, consciousness is paramount to women's avoidance of the traps of patriarchy. *El hombre negro* (1912; see Burgos 1980) presents a more self-conscious adulteress by rewriting the traditional novel of adultery—*Madame Bovary, Anna Karenina, La Regenta*—in which the adulterous woman is severely punished for her transgression. Drawing on the emotional impact of the gothic genre, Burgos's novel begins ominously with the observation, "Aquella mujer no podía soportar a aquel hombre" (29). [That woman abhorred that man.]¹³ In a society where there is no legal escape from an odious husband, the wife finds solace not only in committing adultery but also in financially ruining her spouse, who engages in shady business practices and has used his wife to achieve his goals.¹⁴ Importantly, in each of these novels in which the woman's bleak circumstances overwhelm or nearly overwhelm her, she always has a friend to confide in. This informal female solidarity represents a significant element in women's dream of a new Spain, and it was reflected in the growing organization of women's efforts to formally confront the Spanish legal system.

Another group of Burgos's novels on marriage implicates Spain as a nation in a different way. In *Los anticuarios* (1918), *Dos amores* (1919), *La flor de la playa* (1920), *La nostálgica* (1925), and *El extranjero* (1923), Burgos compares and contrasts Spanish domestic arrangements through characters whose married (or sexual) lives bridge national boundaries. These novels and novelettes center on Spaniards who live abroad or on foreigners who reside in Spain, thus occasioning situations in which Spain as a nation can be viewed from the position of an outsider. This strategy was not new to Spanish literature in the modernist/vanguardist period. We need only consider José Cadalso's *Cartas marruecas* (1774) or José Mariano de Larra's "Vuelva Ud. mañana" (1833). Burgos, who wrote a book on Larra, alludes to his articles in her novels. As detailed in Chapter 4, both Baroja and Azorin employed the foreign/Spanish dichotomy to highlight the situation for women in Spain.

In *Los anticuarios,* antiquarianism provides Burgos with the opportunity to explore a number of issues related to marriage and to the Spanish nation (a married couple buys and sells Spanish national treasures). The spirited Adelina marries the widower Fabián, who has pretensions to the aristocracy (in title but not in fortune).¹⁵ To make a living, Adelina and Fabián become antique dealers. She is the more business minded of the two and proves exceptionally astute at buying antique treasures at prices that allow her to resell them for a handsome profit. Even with their eight children, Adelina manages both the household and the business with great efficiency. She is the thoroughly modern woman who does it all, including taking frequent trips to Paris for the lucrative antique business. Even though her independence runs somewhat counter to Fabián's notion of Spanish honor or a bourgeois gentleman's concept of female virtue, he accepts her absences for economic expediency. Eventually, the entire family moves to Paris, where Adelina and Fabián work hard and their business flourishes; they begin to dream of retiring and returning to Spain. When they manage to falsify and sell a significant painting, they finally have the capital to end their business careers, but they do not carry out their plan to retire to Spain. Although the novel offers no explanation for their remaining in France, it implies that in their native country they would not be able to maintain their revised gender roles.

The underlying motif of the novel is *engaño:* Adelina and Fabián continually deceive the people they deal with in the antique trade. And, even though they do not deceive each other, the novel highlights the role-playing aspect of marriage. Adelina and Fabián have reversed the traditional roles of married couples; she is the chief breadwinner, and he, although he shares in the business partnership, is the stay-at-home father. Other elements in the novel represent modern sexual attitudes as well. Adelina is concerned that her daughters enjoy the same social freedom as her sons, and several characters display cross-gender characteristics. Medrano, a young Spanish painter who goes to Paris, where he believes that his new style will be more acceptable, Burgos describes as follows: "Era simpático, con una peligrosa hermosura de efebo. Parecía una muchachita vestida de hombre, con su rostro rosado, imberbe, de ojos verde claro, adornados de espesas pestañas rubias que le daban la expresión de cándida inocencia de una colegiala" (1989a, 137). [He was likable, with the dangerous beauty of a young boy. He seemed like a little girl dressed as a man, with his rosy, beardless face, clear green eyes adorned with thick blond lashes that gave him the expression of candid innocence of a schoolgirl.][16] There are also "hombres *enfaldados* . . . hombres [que] tenían que hacer alarde de que la mujer no los dominaba" (185) [men *with skirts* . . . men who had to make it look like women did not dominate them].

These reshapings of roles and falsifications of appearances within standard institutions mirror the national situation through Spain's priceless antique heritage. Many of the artifacts that denote the nation's glorious past are falsifications; for example, paintings in churches are copies, the originals having been sold to antique dealers or collectors. Similarly, the nation creates a false sense of stability in traditional social roles that

Spaniards can transgress only by living abroad. Spain hovers in the background of the novel as an unreal place, a fabrication, a country that time has passed by. Adelina and Fabián's antique store in Paris, "Antiquités Maison Espagnole," "excitaba la curiosidad hacia nuestro país de leyendas pintorescas" (82) [excited curiosity about our country of picturesque legends]. The genuine artifacts of Spain have been dismembered, wrenched from their national setting, and placed willy-nilly in the antique shops of Paris:

> España era un resumen de todo aquello. . . . Dentro del establecimiento los grandes muebles españoles, los sillones fraileros, los bargueños magníficos, las mesas sólidas; el espíritu de esa España severa de la Edad Media, tan grandioso y tan inimitable. Era Castilla misma la que representaban aquellas porcelanas de Talavera, con los colores amarillos y verdosos de los campos castellanos, y todo su ardor de sol y de resequedad, de falta de agua. (86)
>
> [Spain was a summary of all that. . . . Inside the establishment, the large Spanish furniture, the monk's chairs, the magnificent secretaries, the solid tables; the spirit of this severe medieval Spain, so grandiose and inimitable. Castile itself was represented in the Talavera porcelains with yellow and green colors of the Castilian countryside and all its sunny heat and dryness from lack of water.]

The antique business and thus the falsification of the national tradition are singularly Spanish. The narrator notes that other countries—England, Holland, Belgium, Germany, and even Greece—are not mined for antiques. Also making the connection with transgressive gender roles is the suggestion that the profession of antique dealing is carried out by *afeminados*. Thus, Spain's historical heritage—so avidly sought by the male members of the Generation of '98—is as slippery as defining gender roles within marriage or in society at large.

Dos amores, which also focuses on a Spaniard who resides outside Spain for a time, compares marriage and male-female relations at home and abroad in a different way. Mauricio, a young Spanish man, contemplates marriage to a Spanish girl and an Italian girl simultaneously. Before traveling to Florence for an extended visit, Mauricio becomes engaged to Margarita, whom he has known all his life and for whom he feels a strong attachment. While in Florence, he meets and falls in love with Blanca, to whom he also becomes engaged. He continues to correspond with Margarita in Spain while he sees Blanca daily in Florence. The two women become confused in his mind, and he cannot tell one from the other. When he is reading letters from Margarita, he is convinced that he still loves her; when he is with Blanca, he is completely absorbed by the Italian girl. After receiving desperate letters from Margarita about his long absence, he decides to provoke a break with Blanca and return to Spain. On the train home, he begins to regret the choice that he has made and comes to the conclusion that he will never be happy. Being with Margarita, surrounded by family, tradition, and the familiar, means having a predictable but dull future. It would seem that a Spaniard cannot find an appropriate marital situation inside or outside his country: "El recuerdo de la patria no era del agrado del joven, que nada contestó" (Burgos 1919, 2). [The reminder of his country did not please the young man, who did not reply.] Ultimately, Mauricio finds his niche at home and abandons his desire to transfer the freedom that he has found abroad to his homeland. The tension between the ideal foreign model and the need to preserve national tradition cannot be resolved. The native woman is too familiar, and the foreign one is too exotic.

La flor de la playa, which Shirley Mangini calls "herético" in *Las modernas de Madrid* (2001, 62), demonstrates how important it is for couples to find alternatives to bourgeois marriage or to experiment with marriage-like situations before they enter into a binding legal status (options available only outside Spanish borders). A young seamstress, who lives on her own earnings and shares a flat with another working-woman, is engaged in a long courtship with an office worker. They have not amassed enough money to marry, but he receives a pay raise that allows them to take a vacation together. The two decide to go to the Portuguese coast, where their unmarried status will attract less attention. When they arrive in the Portuguese resort village and take a room at the hotel "La flor de la playa," they pose as a typical married couple. The *novio* has bought a hat for his companion so that she will have the air of a respectable married woman. Anne Hardcastle notes that the trip itself is a "figurative honeymoon" (2001, 244).

The vacation is to last a month, but both the man and the woman find that they are soon tired of their domestic arrangements (they have set up their room at the hotel as they would their own domestic household). They manage to last out the month, but at the end of the vacation, they return to Madrid to go their separate ways, knowing that the relationship has ended. The decision to part is completely mutual, and the woman seems content to return to her previous life as a seamstress sharing a flat with a female friend. Burgos has set forth a rather utopian idea for early twentieth-century Spain—that a man and a woman who are contemplating marriage might have the opportunity to test the waters before they enter into a legal arrangement. Importantly, in order to find the right atmosphere in which to test the matrimonial state, they must temporarily leave Spain.

La nostálgica not only similarly reflects the desire of some Spaniards to find personal and marital liberation outside the confines of Spain but also addresses biological determinism in the construction of national identity (so common in Generation of '98 writing). Manuel, a doctor, marries Rosa, a beautiful but perennially unhappy woman. Manuel tries everything to cheer her up, including starting a family, but Rosa does not respond to any of his heroic efforts. Because she has vague feelings of a need for bright colors and a more cheerful ambience, Manuel takes her to Valencia; this elevates her mood for a few days, but the effect soon wears off. Manuel researches her family history and discovers that she had a great grandmother from Naples who always wanted to return there. Subsequently, they travel to Naples, where Rosa's melancholy finally disappears. The story resonates with not only the kind of Tainian geographical determinism that we associate particularly with Azorín and Baroja but also the suggestion of an essential transcendental national spirit theorized by Unamuno and Azorín at the turn of the century. It is important that the two male characters in the novel are, like some of Baroja's protagonists, doctors, men of science. In fact, Alfredo, a doctor friend of Manuel's makes pronouncements very reminiscent of those of some of Baroja's characters: "Es una cosa rara la influencia que ejerce la patria transmitiéndose de generación en generación" (Burgos 1925, 46). [The influence that the nation exercises transmitting itself from generation to generation is a strange thing.] As an example, Alfredo cites the Jews, whom, unlike Baroja's characters, he views favorably.

According to Alfredo, Manuel's wife suffers from *nostalgia*, which he defines in the following manner: "Verse lejos de la patria y de las personas queridas produce una verdadera enfermedad. Es el caso de tu mujer. Tiene un alma napolitana. Siente la soledad, la añoranza, y está enferma de nostalgia" (47). [To see oneself far from one's country and loved ones produces a true sickness. This is the case with your wife. She has a Neapolitan soul. She feels loneliness and longing, and she is ill from nostalgia.] The ending undermines the entire pseudoscientific view of Rosa's problem as one of geographical determinism by suggesting that Rosa is a reincarnation of her grandmother. Thus, Burgos negates the materialistic and deterministic principle on which much Generation of '98 thinking was founded. Although the male scientists decide that Rosa is biologically shaped by her genetic heritage, they also suggest, tongue-in-cheek, that there is another transcendent dimension to life that is not limited to biology:

> —Sé muy bien por lo que quieres que te engaña con una explicación científica que te tranquilice respecto a este misterio.
> —Te aseguro . . .
> —No te esfuerces. Tienes miedo de encontrarte casado con la bisabuela de tu mujer. (55)

> [—I know perfectly well that you want me to deceive you with a scientific explanation that will put you at ease about this mystery.
> —I assure you . . .
> —Don't get mad. You are afraid to find out that you have married your wife's great grandmother.]

In this novelette (in contrast to the message in *Dos amores*), Burgos posits that national borders can be crossed and new alliances forged without forgoing what is best in autochthonous Spain.

In *El extranjero*, Burgos ostensibly portrays the Calderonian honor code as a positive Spanish national tradition. Matilde, the oldest child of a family of four, is left to care for her sister and two brothers when their parents die. After trying heroically to care for them, she finally admits defeat and goes to live with an avaricious maiden aunt. Matilde, who has a romantic bent, becomes vulnerable to the courtship of Alfredo, a Sicilian playwright of Spanish heritage who is currently working and residing in Spain. Alfredo befriends the lonely Matilde, and they have an affair. She becomes pregnant, but Alfredo, who was showing signs of tiring of Matilde even before the pregnancy, now abandons her. She courageously seeks him out, and, when he will not let her into his apartment, she causes a scene. She is arrested, and her situation becomes a public scandal. Shunned by all, Matilde prepares for the arrival of her child alone. Her reflections at the end of the novelette are occupied less with her dishonorable position than with Alfredo's status as a foreigner. Matilde's notions are projected ironically through her romantic idealism. Her naiveté with regard to Alfredo is paralleled in the Spanish intellectuals' reception of him. The fact that Alfredo, a foreigner of dubious artistic talents, has been readily accepted into Madrid's artistic circles bespeaks a lack of critical judgment on the part of Spanish intellectuals, especially in adopting currents from abroad: "acogido por escritores y artistas con esa fácil bondad, quizá demasiado fácil, que los intelectuales españoles tienen para acoger a los extranjeros y darles carta de naturaleza entre ellos sin aquilatar méritos severamente ni hacer una verdadera selección" (1923, 9). Once more Burgos projects a view of the nation through a liaison between the sexes; the donjuanesque foreign artist deceives both Matilde and Madrid's intelligentsia.

Matilde considers racial characteristics as fundamental to the success of domestic arrangements. Her reflections on her situation focus especially on national differences. She believes that if she had become pregnant by a Spaniard, he would have "su parte de castigo en la deshonra de su propia raza, de la mujer semejante a su hermana y a su madre" (61) [his share of punishment in the dishonor of his own race, of a woman like his sister and his mother]. The foreigner, in contrast, "era otra cosa; se agravaba todo más. Era un abuso a la tierra que le acogía, a las personas que le tendían la mano. El extranjero se burlaba así de la nobleza, de la virginidad de toda la raza, que ella, en su noble orgullo castellano, consideraba superior. Le afligía la idea de tener el hijo de un ser inferior, de un macaco" (61) [was something else; it made everything worse. It was an abuse of the country that took him in, of the people that lent him a hand. The foreigner ridiculed the nobility, the virginity of the entire race, which she, with her noble Castilian pride, considered superior. The idea of having a child with an inferior being, with a monkey, gave her great pain]. Matilde's patent idealism can be understood as an allegory of the Generation of '98's faith in an essential Spain that (if it could only be determined) would be the salvation of the nation. She believes that her problem was having taken a foreign rather than a Spanish lover; a Spanish man would have wished to uphold the national honor.

The position of the implied author in *El extranjero*, as in most of Burgos's fictions, is rather ambiguous in her assessment of Spain as a nation. In each novel, Spain occupies an important place in the imagination of the central characters, which have an idealized notion of their native country. The idealizations are indirectly articulated through the characters' contacts with a foreigner or with a foreign milieu in the context of a marital or a potential matrimonial relationship. In practical daily life, the characters are unable to achieve personal fulfillment in their relationships within Spanish borders, a dilemma that leaves them in a state of perennial dissatisfaction. Even though there is a resolution in each novel—Adelina and Fabián remain in France, Mauricio chooses his Spanish fiancée, the seamstress and her fiancé decide not to marry, Manuel and Rosa move to Naples, and Matilde will have a child out of wedlock—none of the solutions is ideal. Spain has failed the characters in one way or another, and the foreign setting or foreign person cannot completely compensate for the vacuum created by Spanish deficiencies. Burgos does, however leave room for a future in which couples like Adelina and Fabián in *Los anticuarios* may retain their modified gender roles and live on Spanish soil or in which Mauricio in *Dos amores* would not feel that marriage in Spain was too confining.

Burgos's novelettes that incorporate foreign venues doubtless reflect her travels with Gómez de la Serna, her companion of twenty years. Gómez de la Serna, who was responsible for introducing many of the European vanguard currents into Spanish artistic circles through his journal *Prometeo* and his *tertulia* at Pombo, wrote fiction in a playful vanguard style in the 1920s (*El secreto del acueducto* [1922] and *El novelista* [1923], among others); by 1927, when he published *La mujer de ámbar*, however, he had doubtless fallen under the influence of his feminist partner.[17] Like many of Burgos's fictions, this novel, set in Naples, paints a dire portrait of women contemplating marriage. The Spaniard Lorenzo has gone to

Naples to enjoy the leisurely life there, but, feeling lonely, he begins to look for a female companion. From the outset, it is clear that his ideas about relations with women are exceptionally traditional; although he, like most male vanguard protagonists, dedicates a great deal of time to observing women, as he gazes at women in the park, he also thinks that "él prohibiría a su esposa que se pasease sola por el parque de los emboscados escultóricos" (1981, 9) [he would prohibit his wife from walking alone through the park with the sculpturesque draft dodgers]. He finally settles on Lucía, whose amber beauty inspires endless epithets. She is the soul of Naples (Gómez de la Serna could be mocking Unamuno and Azorín here); her eyes reveal "una mirada de iglesia entreabierta" (52); and she is the ideal woman for him (27, 106). Lorenzo and Lucía become engaged, but on their wedding day, Lucía, dressed in her wedding finery and with no explanation, jumps from the church balcony to her death. Lorenzo's artistic reformulations of womanhood—"muñeca cérea y de la cera virgen en que aún queda amarillez de polen, Lucía, en traje interior de encajes tenía hechura y compostura de muñeca mecánica" (154) [Lucía, waxen doll, of virgin wax in which there still remains the yellowness of pollen, in lace undergarments, had the makeup and bearing of a mechanical doll]—holds the clue to her desperation. The bond of intimate, authentic communication and women's dreams of a better future that Burgos suggests in so much of her fiction is buried under a tumult of artistic language in *La mujer de ámbar*. In 1929, two years after he published the novel, Gómez de la Serna entered into an affair with Burgos's daughter. Burgos and Gómez de la Serna's intimate relationship ended, and Burgos died in 1932, embittered by the betrayal of her longtime companion, whom she had inspired and whose career she had aided. Poignantly, Burgos died while delivering a lecture at the Ateneo in Madrid; her last words were allegedly "¡Viva la República!" Her Spanish nationalism was of a particular kind. When José Rico de Estasén asked her in a 1930 interview where she would like to live if she were not Spanish, she replied "En la República Española" (1930, 60).

Díaz Fernández represents an interesting contrast to both Burgos and Gómez de la Serna in terms of his approach to women, marriage, and feminism in the Spanish 1920s. A very active militant for the Spanish Republic and a great friend of Marañón's, Díaz Fernández (like Marañón) supported some of the feminist causes—especially, women's right to education and gainful employment. However, as noted earlier, he stopped short of approving of women's participation in politics. He is perhaps best known for his essay *El nuevo romanticismo,* which begins with a section on feminism in which Díaz Fernández clearly articulated his belief that womens and domestic issues should be subordinated to a revision of larger political and economic structures. Alluding to Marañón, he wrote that biologists should study women's hatred of men from an endocrinological perspective. Feminism, he avers, has done nothing to rectify women's social situation; in fact, it has confounded human collaboration: "Si los derechos políticos le han servido al hombre para tan poco, no sé por qué habían de servirle para más a la mujer, sobre todo si tener voto no significa tener pan" (1930, 15). The remainder of the two hundred–page book is devoted to political revolution in general and to the literary forms that can best accommodate it. Buried in the chapter titled "Objetivos de una generación" are two or three rather ambiguously worded pages on women's suffrage.

Díaz Fernández's novel *La venus mecánica,* first published in 1929, toward the end of Miguel Primo de Rivera's dictatorship and at the height of Spain's male vanguard movement, is a valiant attempt to counter the canonical male vanguardists' tendency to objectify women and reduce them to the geometrical and/or sensual forms of their bodies. The novel begins in typical male vanguard fashion with a male intellectual (the leftist journalist Víctor) engaged in a series of flirtations with superficial 1920s flappers, whose easy virtue can constitute not only a way of life but also a living. The narrative, however, reverses the vanguard tendency to deny female subjectivity. Víctor meets Obdulia in a dance hall, where she works as a dance partner for lack of any better way to make a living (her bourgeois education has not prepared her for the consequences of her parents' bankruptcy). She is endowed with a psychological depth and moral substance absent in the other women with whom Víctor has associated, and he is attracted to these qualities as much as or more than to her physical beauty.

The narrative focalizes through Obdulia for a long section in which she and Víctor are separated. When her hopes for a film career do not materialize, Obdulia's moral mindset prevents her from seeking financial assistance from Víctor. Then, believing that Víctor is involved with another woman, she breaks off with him and takes a job as a traveling fashion model (a "venus mecánica"). When she can no longer abide the bourgeois women to whom she sells clothes, she accepts the offer of financial support from a wealthy married man, an Asturian mining magnate. Her affair with the mine owner provides her with the opportunity to witness his abominable treatment of the miners and thus raises her social consciousness. By the time she realizes that she is pregnant by him, she abhors her patron and seeks out Víctor for assistance. After Obdulia obtains an abortion in France, she and Víctor take up residence together and have a child. Víctor is arrested and jailed, apparently for his antigovernment writings, and that very night the child dies of a fever. In the last scene, after a period in which Víctor is held incommunicado, Obdulia finally visits him in prison. The gap between the two very different agendas of these characters is apparent in the prison interview. Obdulia speaks to Víctor of revenge against the military dictatorship. Clearly, she is thinking of revenge for the death of her child, which she blames on the Spanish government. She believes that her anxiety over the house search and Víctor's arrest occasioned her inability to properly care for her ill child. Víctor, in contrast, appears to be thinking in less personal terms; he is more concerned about revenge against the oppressive and backward regime for more general political reasons.

The novel's dual focalization—Víctor and Obdulia—is reminiscent of some of Burgos's novels *(El veneno del arte, El permisionario, Ellas y ellos o ellos y ellas)*. However, this technique in Díaz Fernández's novel creates a tension between women's issues—work and relationships with men—and issues related to the Spanish political milieu, a tension that we do not see in most novels by women written during the pre-Republican and Republican era. Although women's issues—lack of appropriate education for meaningful work, prostitution, single motherhood, marriage—are important in this novel, the critique of Primo de Rivera's dictatorship emerges as the main issue. The dictator himself is represented in the character General Villagomil, who financially supports Elvira (one of Víctor's more frivolous female friends) as his lover. The oppressive nature of the regime—lack of freedom of expression, household searches, summary arrests that cause personal hardship, and the wanton spending of public funds—brings the novel to a close and overshadows the matters that have arisen through Obdulia's story. Importantly, Díaz Fernández began the novel while he was imprisoned under Primo de Rivera's dictatorial regime.

Both Nelken and Montseny, like Díaz Fernández, militated for the Republic from radical leftist positions, but many of their narratives manage to maintain their focus on women's special problems in a changing Spain. Nelken was first a socialist and later a communist, and Montseny was always identified with anarchism.[18] Nelken and Montseny not only supported the Republic and held office in its government; they took up the pen to narrate the possibilities for a new Spanish domesticity under a more liberal political form. Both women activists placed community and communicative reason at the center of their social theories and novelistic exercises.

Nelken was an exceptionally versatile woman. Born in Madrid in 1896 of German Jewish parents, she studied art in Paris and worked as an art historian and critic for many years. She lectured on both artistic and feminist subjects in a variety of venues and was elected as a representative to the Cortes from Badajoz in 1931 (reelected in 1933 and 1936).[19] Nelken spent a year in the Soviet Union (1934–35) where she was convinced that she witnessed the realization of her dream of women's emancipation. In her novel *La trampa del arenal* (1923), she considered work for remuneration the cornerstone of women's liberation, and in the Soviet Union she saw women actively participating in the workforce, liberated from the role of being mere appendages to their husbands.

Nelken accepted biological differences between the sexes, emphasizing women's maternal obligations, and she argued for special legislation for women on that basis. She promoted legislation against sexual harassment and in-home piecework and in favor of equal pay for equal work, female factory inspectors, a shorter work day, maternity assistance, and childcare facilities. She also fought for divorce and paternity investigations. She was, however, against women's suffrage because she believed that women were not yet sufficiently educated for the responsibility of voting: "Las mujeres españolas espiritualmente emancipadas son hoy todavía insuficientemente menos que las que irán a pedirle la orden al confesor o se dejarán dócilmente guiar por los que explotan su natural conservadurismo familiar femenino" (qtd. in Capel Martínez 1991, 165). [Spiritually emancipated Spanish women are still insufficiently fewer than those who will go to ask their confessors for the slate or who will docilely allow themselves to be guided by those who exploit their natural feminine conservativism on family matters.] In *La condición social de la mujer en España* (n.d.), Nelken called for the eradication of conventional social barriers between the sexes and classes to create "new communities and forge new alliances between groups that have been traditionally antagonistic or otherwise estranged" (Bretz 1998, 105). Nelken theorized a democratic community in which the two sexes would collaborate. During the Civil War, Nelken remained in Spain ideologically allied to the Communist Party, and she (along with Martínez Sierra) formed part of the Comité Nacional de Mujeres Antifascistas headed by Ibarruri.

Continuing the tradition of Burgos, Nelken introduced a complex set of class and gender distinctions in the novel *La trampa del arenal*. Subtle class and lifestyle differences motivate the story, especially in the figure of Libertad, a new type of "free woman." Thus, the general social concerns of the Spanish 1920s and 1930s that Díaz Fernández, Sender, and Ayala privileged over women's issues come to the fore in Nelken's novel. Luis, the protagonist, is the somewhat wayward son of a "modesto burgués, comerciante o pequeño rentista, de existencia metódica y normalmente vulgar" (1923, 12) [modest bourgeois, merchant or small-time rent collector, whose existence is methodical and common in a normal way], but the townspeople call him *muy señor* for his gallantry. Thus, the family represents the epitome of traditional bourgeois values of respectability. The novel opens with a detailed description of the family home, firmly establishing the comfortable middle-class milieu. Carefully orchestrated details reveal an uncomfortable relationship to modernity: "Pues [el padre] era aficionado al progreso, aunque, por falta de práctica en las cosas unas veces, y por exceso de confianza en las gentes otras, sus experimentos dábanle raramente buen resultado" (17). [Well the father was a fan of progress, although because he was sometimes unpracticed in things and other times did not have enough confidence in people, his experiments rarely turned out well for him.] This world of respectability confronts that of Salud, whom Luis is forced to marry when she becomes pregnant by him. Salud and her mother are the classic *cursis*, impoverished women of pretensions, "una de esas muchachas madrileñas, ni francamente artesanas ni burguesas, que dan, a quien las ve por la calle, la ilusión de una posible y fácil elevación en la escala social" (25) [one these Madrid girls, neither clearly of the artisan nor of the bourgeois class, who give the impression to those who see them in the street of a possible and easy elevation in social level]. Salud works, but she prefers to clerk in a stationery store, where she earns less money than she would in a factory, because in the store she is in contact with well-mannered people who speak to her courteously and call her *señorita*.

After the marriage takes place, Salud becomes the quintessential bourgeois wife; secure in her legal position, she insists on all the material trappings of her station. Legitimacy and keeping up appearances become the motivating forces of her life: "este paseo del matrimonio burgués ostentando su legitimidad" (63) [this walk of the bourgeois married couple showing off their legitimacy]. Bourgeois respectability is her creed. Salud fires a seamstress who confides to her that she was seduced and abandoned, although she hypocritically accepts the friendship of a "kept woman" because her male sponsor is wealthy and provides a carriage for excursions on which Salud is invited. The portrait of the vain, empty bourgeois wife in *La trampa del arenal* is unflattering: "Con la fácil facultad de olvido de las mujeres, que les permite recordar del pasado tan sólo lo que les conviene, y les hace trastrocar los hilos borrosos de su vida en trama luminosa, Salud, que sentía su belleza triunfante, llegó insensiblemente a creer que esa belleza había sido, por si sola, la conductora de su destino" (112) [With women's easy ability to forget, which allows them to remember only the aspects of the past that they wish to remember and makes them transform the fuzzy threads of their lives into a luminous plot, Salud, who felt her beauty triumphant, arrived without reflection at the idea that this beauty had been the sole conductor of her destiny.] Salud is the kind of Spanish woman that Nelken considered unprepared to vote.

Luis soon realizes that he has become imprisoned by boring office work and moral emptiness from which there is no escape. Just when he has resigned himself to this fate, Libertad, the "new woman," moves in next door: "una muchacha con tipo intermedio entre obrera y estudianta rusa, vestida muy modestamente, no fea, pero tampoco guapa; fresca, eso sí, con una carnación apetitosa de fruta madura, y una cabellera corta y dorada que le daba cierto aire de andrógino" (108) [a girl with a look somewhere between a woman worker and a Russian student, very modestly dressed, not ugly, but not good-looking either; but definitely fresh, with the appetizing flesh of a mature fruit, and short, golden hair that gave her a certain androgynous air]. She lives alone (after the departure of a male companion), works as a translator to support herself, and leads an independent life.

The contrast could not be greater between Salud's values and those of Libertad, who is free of all class pretensions. Libertad maintains a dignity not recognized by middle-class requirements of female dependency. After his father's death, Luis arranges for Salud and their child to spend a few months with his mother and sisters in the country, allowing him to pursue a platonic friendship with Libertad in the city. But when Salud returns and Luis is unable to maintain the same intensity in his relationship with Libertad, Libertad decides to accept a job in Paris, leaving Luis mired in a loveless marriage, with another child on the way and a new bureaucratic job that requires long hours of work. At the end of the novel, Luis recalls a picture in his father's office in which a man is sinking into quicksand. It is reminiscent of the final image of Luis Buñuel and Salvador Dalí's 1927 film *Un chien andalou*, in which a man and a woman, apparently either married or engaged, are buried in sand up to their necks. The film, however, does not offer the alternative of a lifestyle without marriage depicted in Nelken's Libertad.[20]

Federica Montseny approached women's situation in Spain from an anarchist perspective. Her father and mother, Juan Montseny and Teresa Mañé (whose pseudonyms were Federico Urales and Soledad Gustavo), were assiduous activists and enterprising editors of anarchist books and journals. In 1922, at only seventeen years of age, Federica began to publish her writings in such anarchist publications as *La Novela Roja, Nueva Senda, Tierra, Redención,* and *Acción Social Obrera*. In 1923, Federica not only encouraged her father to issue a second epoch of *La Revista Blanca* (biweekly) but also initiated the *La Novela Ideal* (a weekly novel series), *La Novela Libre, El Mundo al Día,* and *El Luchador* (all monthlies). Federica, like her parents, believed in the power of the word to transform society. Her articles in *La Revista Blanca* posit a political theory that, like those of many of her female contemporaries, centers on community (a "more community-focused organizational base" [Ackelsberg 1991, 23]). It was, however, through the some one hundred novelettes that she published in *La Novela Ideal* and *La Novela Libre* series that she most completely developed her sociopolitical ideas.

Montseny preferred to think of herself as a defender of liberty for all humankind rather than as a feminist (she was, in fact, an outspoken antifeminist, as she considered feminism a bourgeois movement). Many of her ideas are nonetheless compatible with feminist ideology. As Martha Ackelsberg points out, "A reorganization of sexual and family life and a reconstitution of women's roles were essential to [Montseny's] revolutionary vision" (26). Montseny wrote a number of novels that center on women's quest for equality with men and the obstacles that they face in finding male companions who will accept them as equals. She coincides with many of her modernist predecessors (Blanca de los Ríos, Sofía Casanova, Carmen de Burgos) in her concern with Spanish donjuanismo, which forced women into a kind of slavery. In "El ocaso del donjuanismo" published in *La Revista Blanca* in 1925, she wrote:

> Las mujeres han sido durante mucho tiempo, gatas sumisas y traidoras. Obligadas a estar sujetas al hombre, mantenidas con premeditada intención en un plano educativo física y moralmente muy inferior al del otro sexo, debieron sacar de la forzosa debilidad las fuerzas precisas para defenderse en las luchas por la vida. Ahora yergen la cabeza y dan la cara. No se vengan de su esclavitud con el veneno de falsas caricias, sino que se entregan con toda su alma y arman su brazo cuando se sienten burladas. (Qtd. in García-Maroto 1996, 45).

> [Women have been submissive traitor cats for a long time. Obliged to be subordinate to men, kept by premeditated design at an educational level that is physically and morally inferior to that of the other sex, they should draw from forced weakness the necessary power to defend themselves in the fight for life. Now they raise their heads and show their faces. They should not take revenge for their enslavement with the poison of false caresses; rather, they should give themselves with all their soul and take up arms when they feel that they are being ridiculed.]

Montseny's autobiographical novel *La indomable* (1928; see Montseny 1991) explores the problem of the politically active woman who negotiates class distinctions and freedom from the constraints of society but who also craves intimacy with a man. With the subversive clandestine politics of the Primo de Rivera dictatorship as a backdrop, this novel, like *La trampa del arenal,* has a deceptively simple plot. Vida, born to a politically active couple, grows up into a strong, socially engaged young woman. Instead of focusing on her political activity, however, the novel centers on Vida's attempts to find an appropriate male companion. Even though she has many feminine qualities—she cooks, sews, cleans house, and has a penchant for nurturing—she is too strong for all the men she meets, even the ones who, like her, are politically militant. Having been brought up "al margen de toda fórmula social" (Montseny 1991, 48) as a "pequeño Hércules femenino" (52), there is no place for her in the Spanish social system of the 1920s. She has strong, individualistic principles; for example, she turns down a scholarship to study abroad, an experience that she yearns for, because she would have to prove she has been baptized: "Por una beca no reniego yo de las ideas de mis padres, ni enajeno mi libertad" (70). [For a scholarship, I neither reject my parents' ideals nor give up my liberty.]

Through its structure and language, *La indomable* fields a complex philosophical notion of freedom. Vida is an idealist, capable of envisioning a Spain where men and women work together as equals, but her idealism is clearly distinguished from that of many male idealists:

> No pasó tampoco por ese período doloroso de todo idealista: la desilusión. Muchos hombres y muchas mujeres abrazan un ideal por el reflejo y la influencia de sus militantes. No profesan estas o aquellas ideas, porque las piensen o las sientan, porque las identifiquen con ellos mismos, sino porque son las ideas de este o de aquel, porque este o aquel a ellas les llevó. Entre ese género ambiguo de idealistas se reclutan los futuros réprobos, los que mañana, al primer desengaño o al primer embite, abandonarán la idealidad. (89)

> [She did not suffer disillusionment in this difficult period for any idealist. Many men and women embrace an ideal as a reflex reaction to and because of the influence of its militants. They do not profess these or those ideals

because they think or feel them, because they identify with them themselves, but because they are the ideals of one or another person, because that person carried them along. Among that ambiguous class of idealists are recruited the future reprobates, those who tomorrow, at the first disappointment or the first setback, will abandon their idealism.]

The notion of absolute freedom is a mark of this extreme idealism: "Hubiera podido abrirse la puerta de un gran diario, *La Avalancha*, y ella la desdeñó. Amaba, ante todo, la libertad; necesitaba escribir, trabajar, vivir, fuera de toda preocupación de salario, de todo límite patronal" (92). [She could have had an entrée into a great newspaper, *La Avalancha*, but she spurned it. Above all, she loved liberty; she needed to write, work, live, outside all concerns about salary, outside all limits of patronage.]

Vida has developed a theory of the person as an individual that is summarized by a fellow political worker, a young man in whom she has a romantic interest. He tells her that she is an individual by temperament, that ideas will find an intuitive renovation in her, "enriquecimiento de teorías basadas en [su] propia naturaleza" (106) [enrichment of theories based on her own nature]. Her theory of the personality and the will expressed in her writings emanate from her own character "un mundo individual en el acervo común de los mundos humanos" (106) [an individual world in undivided estate with all human worlds]. She herself recognizes that her ideas are born of a desire to carry them out; her idealism is an activist idealism: "La idea por la idea es como el arte por el arte: juego inútil de colores, de sonidos o de palabras" (109). [The idea for the idea is like art for art's sake: a useless game of colors, sounds, or words.] How different is this approach to thinking philosophically about the self from that of the reflective characters invented by Unamuno, Azorín, Baroja, Pérez de Ayala, Miró, and Jarnés and all the other male vanguard writers of the 1920s. The male characters are paralyzed, rather than motivated to action, by their ideas.

La indomable embodies a theory of the self and its relationship to society that is concrete and dialectical. Flying in the face of notions of the eternal unity of a subterranean history of Spain, society in this novel is a multiplicity, a variety of "razas, clases, profesiones, afinidades, ideales" (123). In each of these categories, there are further divisions, "hasta el infinito" (123). Society is a union of individuals "que se relacionan entre sí, atraídos por simpatías personales o por una identificación relativa del pensamiento" (123) [that relate among themselves, attracted by personal sympathy or by an identification relating to thought]. Vida's strength and idealism, however, ultimately cause the young man who is capable of understanding and interpreting her philosophy to turn away from her and propose marriage to one of her friends. The friend, who is more passive than Vida, reacts with surprise that she and not Vida receives the proposal of marriage: "¡El ideal! Pues el ideal es Vida.—Tú lo has dicho. Es el ideal, pero el ideal no lo podemos alcanzar" (120). [The ideal! Well, the ideal is Vida.—You have said it. She is the ideal, but we cannot reach the ideal.] [21] The only man capable of actually committing himself to a relationship with Vida is a neighbor she assisted while his wife was dying of tuberculosis. He is vaguely aware of her political activism but, more than any of the other eligible men who know her, he has seen her as a caregiver, to his ailing wife and to his frail, motherless daughter.

Like Martínez Sierra, Montseny opposed what she called the "masculinization" of womankind. Masculinization was not dignified or liberating; it was simply imitating the other sex, not a very lofty enterprise: "No debemos contentarnos con todos los derechos que *tiene el hombre*. Debemos aspirar con voluntad indomable a todos los derechos que *habría de tener*. . . . La mujer del porvenir no será un entecillo andrógino con la cabeza ajena de ideas y de pelo, el cabello aplastado sobre las sienes a fuerza de cosmético, shmoking [*sic*] impecable, cigarillo en boca y bastoncillo en ristre, una mujer mujer, no mujer-hombre ni mujer hembra" (qtd. in García-Maroto 1996, 54). [We should not be content with all the rights that *men have*. We should aspire with indomitable will to all the rights that *one ought to have*. . . . The woman of the future will not be a little androgynous being with a head empty of ideas and hair plastered down at the temples by cosmetics, with an impeccable evening jacket, a cigarette in her mouth, and a cane at rest, a woman woman, not a woman-man or a woman female.] She believed that women had special characteristics that should be socially affirmed.

La indomable ends without an ending, indicating that Vida's life can have no conclusion in the present age, but she is determined not to "ahogarse dentro de los límites de su época" (Montseny 1991, 158) [drown in the limitations of her epoch]. The "ahogarse" allusion is significant, and it reminds us of the sand trap metaphor of Nelken's *La trampa del arenal*. Women writers of the modernist/vanguardist period refused to accept the eternal sea of *intrahistoria*, the eternal national myth that would swallow them up and deny them a future of change and possibility. The nation with which they identify perhaps has no past or has forgotten its past in the "olvido creador" theorized by Zambrano. Their narratives of a new Spanish society suggest that the *tradición eterna* on which the myth of the Spanish nation was built needs to be dismantled, and a new more specific contemporary theory must be put in its place. As Ackelsberg notes, the emphasis is on creation: "The way to create a new society is to *create* new reality" (1991, 32). The novel was an ideal venue for this project.

Among the many novels and novelettes that Montseny wrote for *La Revista Blanca*'s two series, *La victoria* (Montseny n.d.) is especially interesting as it combines her usual concerns with humanity's and women's freedom with a metanovelistic, self-reflexive quality that we often associate with vanguard art. It is self-consciously subtitled *Novela en la que se narran los problemas de orden moral que se le presenten a una mujer de ideas modernas*. The novel foregrounds the power of creative fiction to perpetuate stereotypes or to take a new direction and offer an alternative, more progressive image of women in society. The protagonist, Clara, engages in several relationships with men who are finally unable to accept her desire for sexual equality. She pleads with her companion Roberto to think of her not as a woman "sino un . . . ¡cómo diré yo!, camarada quizá es pedir demasiado, pero le aseguro que si lograra que ustedes viesen en mí eso, me complacería más que todas las palabras amables que acostumbran . . . prodigar los hombres a las mujeres" (42) [but rather a . . . how can I say it, comrade perhaps is asking too much, but I assure you that if I could make you see me that way, it would please me more than all the pleasantries that men usually lavish on women]. Roberto seems sympathetic to Clara's goals, but ultimately he decides that she is just not womanly enough for him; she is "excesivamente fuerte y despojada de feminidad" (72) [excessively strong and lacking femininity]. To merit the qualification of "womanly," Clara must eschew ideology and enter into a dependent relationship with a man; she must be "más femenina, más dulce, menos abstraída por los conceptos ideológicos y más llena de palabras de amor. Ser más piadosa consigo misma y admitir el apoyo y la fortaleza de un hombre junto a su debilidad" (73) [more feminine, sweeter, less abstracted by ideological concepts and more full of loving words. Be more compassionate with herself and allow the support and strength of a man to accompany her weakness].

Once the extradiegetic narrator has fully characterized Clara as committed to a political agenda of freedom for women in all areas of life, several intradiegetic narrators, who are male writers, subject her to metacharacterizations. A male journalist pens mordant articles about her, calling her a "doctor con faldas, sin feminidad, sensibilidad, gracias ni encantos" and "un ser sin sexo," of a "género neutro," an "especie exótica e híbrida de mujer moderna, inepta para el amor y seca de todo sentimiento" (121) [a doctor in skirts, without femininity, sensitivity, graces, or charms and a sexless being of a neuter gender, an exotic hybrid species of modern woman, inept in love and immune to all sentiment]. Then Clara meets Fernando Oswald, author of popular "feminist" novels. Although she enjoys reading the novels, she disagrees with his romantic idealization of women: "Siempre pensó que el divinizar o sublimizar a la mujer traía aparejados serios peligros para ella, y Fernando Oswald convertía al sexo femenino en divinidad, que los hombres debían adorar devotamente, inmaterializándola y sublimizándola" (123). [She always believed that making a woman divine or sublime brought with it serious dangers for her, and Fernando Oswald converted the female sex into a divinity that men should adore devoutly, making her immaterial and sublime.] Here, Montseny points up the conflation of the terms "feminist" and "feminine" in many male authors' usage (recall, for example, Miró's article titled "Literatura feminista," in which he clearly meant "Literatura femenina").

Fernando and Clara engage in several heated discussions about their diverging views on women. Clara argues that women should be considered an equal part of humanity, whereas Fernando insists on placing women in a separate category—"una reina, una musa y un tesoro" for whom he would be "el defensor y el más rendido súbdito de su amor" (200) [a queen, a muse, and a treasure for whom he would be the defender and the most submissive subject of her love]. Finally, Fernando suggests that Clara's life would be a good topic for his next novel, but she strenuously objects to his authoring her story. She protests because, as a man, Fernando could not portray her accurately. According to Clara, men neither understand nor wish to understand women. Here Montseny goes beyond the usual message of her novels that argue for human liberty in general as well as for dignity and autonomy for women in particular. *La victoria* proposes writing as essential to these goals and theorizes that in advancing women's causes, women's authorship is essential. Montseny thus self-consciously vindicates her own activity as a prolific novelist of the 1920s. In her defense of *La victoria*, which was severely criticized for its revolutionary approach to single motherhood, she emphasized that it was essential to provide models for how women could achieve liberation (Ackelsberg 1991, 30).

Although she bears a child, Montseny's Clara refuses a permanent relationship with a man (*El hijo de Clara* [1929], sequel to *La victoria*, further develops the subject of single motherhood). Montseny believed that the traditional family must be eradicated to allow both men and women to achieve their own individuality: "Desde luego, partamos de la base de que el hogar irá desapareciendo poco a poco. La vida se irá individualizando, a medida que las condiciones sociales liberten a los hombres y a las mujeres de la necesidad de unirse para el mutuo apoyo. La familia subsistirá y con ella la forzosa sujeción de la mujer, mientras el porvenir de los hijos dependa de los padres" (Montseny 1927b, n.p.) [So, let's depart from the basic idea that the home will disappear little by little. Life will become more individualized as social conditions free men and women from the necessity of joining for mutual support. The family will subsist and with it the forced subjection of women, while the future of the children depends on the father.] Montseny considered marriage "la tumba del amor" (qtd. in García-Maroto 1996, 185).

Espina also addressed single motherhood in *La virgen prudente* (1929), possibly in answer to Montseny's novels on the subject, which caused quite a furor when they were published.[22] Even though Espina has always been considered one of the more Catholic and conservative women writers of her era, she was a self-styled communist: "Conducida, por mi sentimiento cristiano, hace tiempo que llegué al comunismo en la pura emoción filosófica" (qtd. in Lucientes 1981, 105). [Guided by my

Christian sentiments, I came to communism some time ago through pure philosophical emotion.] Espina was also an ardent supporter of the Republic: "La forma actual del gobierno tiene mis mayores esperanzas . . . porque mi ilusión política de toda la vida fue la República. En unos meses España ha recorrido muchos años. ¡Cómo no ser optimista!" (qtd. in Lucientes 1981, 105). [The present form of government has my greatest hopes . . . because the Republic was my political illusion during my entire life. In a few months Spain has covered many years. How can one not be optimistic!] She favored women's right to vote, because women are just as politically capable as men: "La incorporación de la mujer a la vida política equivale al descubrimiento de un tercer mundo" (qtd. in Lucientes 1981, 105). [The incorporation of women into political life is the equivalent of discovering the third world.] Even more surprisingly, she publicly supported divorce legislation ("El divorcio en España era, sencillamente, una necesidad social" [qtd. in Lucientes 1981, 105]), even though she realized that this stance might adversely affect the sales of her books (see Ortega 1928).

La virgen prudente, which Janet Pérez considers "Espina's most nearly feminist novel" (1988, 29), imagines how a woman might negotiate a path in the uncharted territory of public life. On the eve of the novel's publication, Espina herself believed that it would cause a furor "por lo avanzado de sus teorías y el atrevimiento con que están planteados" (qtd. in Don Galaor 1929, 45) [because of the advanced nature of its theories and the daring with which they are presented]. The protagonist, significantly named Aurora de España, represents the dawn of a new Spain in which women are able to develop as intellectuals.[23] Aurora attends the university and becomes a lawyer with a radical and controversial thesis on women's rights, although she positions herself as a Christian feminist. Her public thesis defense causes a minor scandal, which is fueled in the press, probably by her own mother, a very traditional woman whose second daughter by another marriage has been slighted by a suitor who favors Aurora. As noted earlier, the contrast of "la mujer nueva" and "la mujer vieja" reappears constantly throughout the woman-authored novel of the vanguard, pre-Republican, and Republican eras.[24] Aurora's stepfather articulates the contrast between the woman of the past and the woman of the future in a harsh rebuke to Aurora's mother: "[Aurora] es la mujer nueva, la íntegra mujer presentida. Y tú sólo has podido formar, a tu imagen y semejanza, una parodia de modernidad, un ser menor, un remedo enojoso y arbitrario de las virtudes que os sirven para la caza del hombre, porque de eso se trata únicamente" (Espina 1929, 53). [Aurora is the new woman, the complete woman as foreseen. And you have been able to forge, in your image and likeness, only a parody of modernity, a minor being, an irritating and arbitrary copy of qualities that help you trap men, because that's what it's all about.]

Unlike the traditional Spanish woman, Aurora has ideals and imagination. Her doctoral thesis argues for universal peace founded on love. Although some label her thesis feminist, she prefers to characterize it as an "asunto humano" (77), perhaps echoing Federica Montseny's Clara. Aurora's thesis declares that women must be given the same political rights as men without any limitations on their mutual association: "Ellas, como ellos, capacitados por la edad y la cultura con idénticas enseñanzas, deberían hacer un Tratado de Igualdad, unánime en privilegios, para actual unidos en todas las cuestiones postestativas, incluso las internacionales. Porque de cierto la mujer emplearía sus votos en exigir la paz del mundo, la protección a los niños y a todas las invalideces miserables, el imperio de la Justicia humana, en fin" (78). [Women, like men, enabled by age and culture through identical educations, should forge a Treaty of Equality with unanimous privileges, in order to act united in all facultative matters, including international ones. Because women would certainly employ their votes to demand world peace, protection for children and all the weak and the unfortunate, in a word, the empire of human justice.] Like many other female modernist/vanguardist novelists, Espina weaves a social theory into her narrative fabric. Aurora's arguments, however, are more universalizing than some; her idealism embraces a notion of male-female equality that could effect international peace.

Aurora recognizes that her ideal for women is perhaps too advanced for her epoch. Her vision of the modern woman's trials comes in a surrealistic and nightmarish dream scene, "una especie de sueño premonitorio" (138), about midway through the novel. In the dream, she sees a few women "debatirse fuera del redil, empeñadas en saltar lejos de su sombra, hasta donde el Sol *sale* para *todos*" (138) [fighting outside the fold, dedicated to landing far from its shadow, where the Sun *shines* for *everyone*]. Some generous and cultured men are helping them, but a larger group (mostly women) persecutes them. In her trance-like state, Aurora comprehends that her choices are to stand against this majority tide or to join the "muchedumbre ramplona, signo de los tiempos actuales, irreverentes mayorías congestionadas de pequeños individualismos, cada uno con presunciones de especialidad" (138–39) [vulgar crowd, sign of the present times, irreverent multitudes congested with petty individualism, each one with presumptions of specialness].

After the unpleasant experience of her thesis defense and the subsequent scandal, which sends her to bed for a while, Aurora agrees to marry a longtime doctor friend, who seems to appreciate her intelligence and professional ambitions. When she becomes pregnant by him, however, she realizes that he is just as patriarchal and possessive as other men. Bravely, she decides to break off her engagement and remain a single mother. Espina's solution for the liberated woman and unwed mother may have caused less of a scandal than Federica Montseny's novels on unwed motherhood, because Espina built into her protagonist's life the possibility that she will eventually marry. Courted by two suitors, she chose the wrong one. The rejected suitor, however, has conveniently waited in the wings and is willing to partner with her even though she will bear another man's child. The novel does not include the legal union of Aurora and this suitor, but when he befriends her toward the end, the possibility that their relationship will develop beyond platonic friendship is left open. In addition, the novel includes other positive male figures—Aurora's grandfather (Juan de España) and her stepfather.

As in most of the other fictions by Spanish women of the vanguard era, communicative reason is a motivating principle of *La virgen prudente*. Toward the end of the novel, Espina's narrator melds vanguard imagery (futurist emphasis on machinery and speed) with the protagonist's desire to forge a better world through women's united efforts. Aurora wishes that she could communicate her own mental state to the millions of women that she envisions as mired in a somnolent, domestic state. Her mind races as she experiences a loving spirit that wishes only for the good of others:

La unión, la fuerza sensitiva de tantas almas, ¿no daría por resultado un formidable poder? En los trenes actuales cada rueda compite con las alas del viento, como una rosa de frenesí que gira sobre el polvo y en el espacio, burlándose de las distancias. Y en la emoción de Aurora estas imágenes de la prisa moderna adquieren proporciones de vaticinio. Se figura que muchos entendimientos lumininosos de mujeres irán con ella a toda velocidad, como van unidos el calor y la sed, pidiendo las cosas justas, que parecen imposibles porque no se desean bastante. (300–301)

[Wouldn't the union, the sensitive force of so many souls produce a formidable power? In today's trains, each wheel competes with the wings of the wind, like a frenzied rose that whirls in space above the dust, laughing at the distances. And in Aurora's emotion, these images of modern rush acquire prophetic proportions. She imagines that many women's bright understandings will accompany her at high velocity, as heat and thirst go together, asking for just things that seem impossible because they are not desired enough.]

The speed of modern life informs Espina's portrayal of Aurora's mental processes as well as the protagonist's vision of a feminist social order. The dual purpose of Espina's vanguardist imagery—the fusion of futurist references with a sociopolitical message—is emblematic of women's narrative of the vanguard era.

Imagery and metaphor are also central to Zambrano's aesthetics (both in theory and practice), which are summarized in her central philosophical notion "poetic reason."[25] Through poetic reason, she transformed the Spanish soul of *intrahistoria,* which in Unamuno was introspective and contemplative, into a sociopolitical tool. Zambrano's arrival at this view of literature is circuitous. Her first book, *Horizonte del liberalismo,* published in 1930 in the heat of debates about Republicanism in Spain, called for a new liberalism, in which she posited a politics that needs society. Zambrano criticized a liberalism that places excessive emphasis on the individual at the expense of social considerations and argued instead for a "libertad . . . que no rompa los cables que al hombre le unen con el mundo, con la naturaleza, con lo sobrenatural. Libertad fundada, más que en la razón, en la fe en el amor" (1930, 139) [liberty . . . that does not break the chains that tie people to the world, to nature, to the supernatural. Liberty founded, rather than on reason, on faith in love]. Freedom is a social rather than an individual phenomenon.

Zambrano would doubtless have agreed with Simone de Beauvoir that to "will oneself moral is to will oneself free" (1994, 24) and that to "will oneself free is to will others free" (73), for "every man has to do with other men" (74). Also like Beauvoir, Zambrano believed that impersonal universal humanity is not a source of values but a plurality in which particular people project themselves toward their ends on the "basis of situations whose particularity is as radical and irreducible as subjectivity itself" (Beauvoir 1994, 17). In literature, Zambrano found the particularity necessary to formulate social values, because literary works (especially fiction and drama) embody the kinds of situations that enabled her to articulate concrete social, political, and ethical concerns.

Four years after she wrote her essay on liberalism, in an essay entitled "Hacia un saber sobre el alma" published in *Revista de Occidente* (see Zambrano 1987), Zambrano effected what might appear to be a 180-degree turn from external political concerns to the mostly intimate and internal sphere. Laying the foundations for much of her later work, she relates the innermost aspect of human life—what she calls the soul—and sociopolitical matters by using literature as an intermediary. "Hacia un saber sobre el alma" is essentially an argument for including the passions (alongside reason) in theorizing (philosophizing) about human life.[26] In that essay, Zambrano attempted to go beyond Benedict de Spinoza (the subject of her doctoral dissertation), because Spinoza posited "una Ética donde la psicología es metafísica aún; Metafísica, porque el estudio y clasificación naturalista de las pasiones iban dirigidas hacia un saber superior sobre el hombre y su vida; era un mirar las pasiones para encontrar con ellas, como instrumento, una vida feliz, una vida en la eternidad" (1987, 22) [an Ethics in which psychology is still metaphysics; Metaphysics, because the study and naturalistic classification of the passions are directed toward a superior knowledge over people and their lives; it considered the passions in order to use them as an instrument to find a happy life, a life in eternity].[27] According to Zambrano, the study of the soul was left to psychology, which approached it with a scientific eye. Under those circumstances, the soul turned to literature: "El alma buscaba a sí misma en la poesía, en la expresión poética" (23).

[The soul sought itself in poetry, in poetic expression.] The soul is key to the process of bringing external political and ethical matters into the realm of the individual subject, because it situates itself in that central and facilitating space between "el *yo* y el fuera de la naturaleza" (29) [the *I* and the exterior of nature].

The Civil War precipitated Zambrano's philosophical trajectory in the direction initiated in "Hacia un saber sobre el alma." Her avid Republican sympathies, based on a desire to free the human spirit through a more liberal political future, coalesced with her interest in the emotions as a philosophical subject. She found that these myriad and disperse projects could best be joined through literature, and here she coincides with Montseny's message (in *La victoria*) about the power of literature to influence real life. Of the twelve or so articles that Zanbrano wrote for *Hora de España,* a journal that she founded along with other Republican writers in 1937 to further the cause of the Republic during the Civil War, eight or nine are on literary topics. The journal's guiding principle was that art and the state are inseparable and that a way must be found for art to "coordinarse con el Estado sin perder su integridad y libertad" (1986b, 49) [coordinate with the State without losing its integrity and liberty]. For *Hora de España*'s founders, art is freedom and has a seminal role in maintaining a free political system. Zambrano believed that the history of Spain is essentially poetic, "no porque la hayan hecho los poetas, sino porque su hondo suceso es continua trasmutación poética" (60) [not because poets have made it, but because its deep course is a continuous poetic transmutation]. In an article on Machado, she asserted that in poetry political ideas achieve clarity: "¿Qué sería de nosotros, de todo hombre, si no supiésemos hoy y no nos lo supiesen recordar el saber último que con sencillez de agua nos susurran al oído las palabras poéticas de Machado?" (Zambrano 1986b, 61). [What would happen to us, to all humanity, if we did not know today and if we were not reminded of the ultimate knowledge that Machado's poetic words whisper in our ears with the simplicity of water?]

Poetry is the way in which ideas become social entities: "Al ser expresadas, al ser recibidas por cada uno en su perfecto lenguaje, ya no nos parecen nuestras, cosa individual, sino que nos parecen venir del fondo mismo de nuestra historia, adquieren categoría de palabras supremas"

(Zambrano 1986b, 62). [Upon being expressed, upon being received by each one in its perfect language, they no longer seem ours, an individual thing, but rather they seem to come from the depths of our history, they acquire the status of supreme words.][28] Poetry names that which allows a people to recognize itself and accept its destiny: "Es la mejor unidad de la poesía con la acción o como se dice con la política, la mejor y tal vez única forma de que la poesía puede colaborar en la lucha gigantesca de un pueblo: dando nombre a su destino, reafirmando a sus hijos todos los días su saber claro y misterioso del sino que le cumple, transformando la fatalidad ciega en expresión liberadora" (62–63). [It is the best union of poetry with action, or as one says with regard to politics, the best and perhaps the only form in which poetry can collaborate in the people's gigantic fight: naming its destiny, reaffirming to its children every day its clear and mysterious knowledge of the fate that it fulfills, transforming blind fatality into liberating expression.]

As noted earlier, Zambrano, like Chacel, wrote on confession as a literary genre. Her interest in confession may be related to her view of the literary author as a private/public voice. Zambrano defined confession as a genre that centers on hope—"por eso la Confesión supone una esperanza: la de algo más allá de la vida individual" (22) [for this reason, Confession means hope: hope of something beyond individual life]—and that has community as its ultimate goal: "Y es la mayor tragedia, porque si en la confesión se parte de la soledad, se termina siempre como San Agustín en comunidad" (35). [And it is the greatest tragedy, because if confession begins in solitude, it ends like Saint Augustine in community.] Terence Doody, without benefit of Zambrano's reflections, similarly observes that "confession is the deliberate, self-conscious attempt of an individual to explain his nature to the audience who represents the kind of community he needs to exist in and confirm him." For Doody, confession is "*always an act of community*, and the speaker's intention to realize himself in community is the formal purpose that distinguishes confession from other modes of autobiography or self-expression" (1980, 3, emphasis in original).

Doody, like Zambrano, links literature to the ethical through the notion of community: "Community is a moral relationship that implies mutual, personal responsibility" (6).[29] According to Zambrano, the poet serves as the mediator between the individual and the collectivity, the *pueblo*, because the poet is the people's voice (as Homer, for example, was the voice of Greece). Thus, *intrahistoria*, formed of the common daily practices of the folk, assumes a contemporary political agency. Such a move is possible because philosophical thought and poetry are inextricably united in a moral position, "el sentimiento de la responsabilidad" (Zambrano 1986b, 64). Machado, Zambrano observes, looked to the human being as the site where the philosophical and the poetic unite: "De esta *entereza* humana arranca la unidad moral, poética y filosófica de la poesía de Machado" (67). [From this human *integrity* derives the moral, poetic, and philosophical unity of Machado's poetry.] Zambrano then relates this *entereza* with that of the Republican soldiers who are fighting for the freedom of the Spanish people. For her, the Republic was the future, a possibility, a form of government that had limitless potential to make life better for many Spaniards, and Machado conveyed that prospect. Zambrano assimilated the model—a literature of possibility—learned not only from Machado but also from Cervantes and Galdós,[30] and went on, after her exile, first in Latin America and later in Rome, to write several works of a decidedly literary nature that conveyed this notion.

As discussed in the Introduction to this book, Zambrano transformed the Antigone story into one of hope rather than unmitigated tragedy. In her novelized autobiography, *Delirio y destino,* Zambrano refers to her sister as Antigone, a designation that places Zambrano in the position of Ismene, the sister who did not participate directly in the moral act. Zambrano's position as author is as an objective witness of the present and a visionary for the future. At the time that she composed *Delirio y destino,* Zambrano was living in Cuba, far removed from the horrors of World War II that her sister Araceli was experiencing daily.[31] Thus, she bore empathetic witness to her sister's tragedy and was affected by its emotional impact. Her role is akin to that of the judicious spectator posited by Adam Smith and revisited by Nussbaum in *Poetic Justice: The Literary Imagination and Public Life.* The position of judicious spectator allows literature a privileged place in ethical concerns because "literary readership . . . offers an artificial construction of the position of such a spectator. It thus supplies a filtering device for emotion of just the sort that Smith thought necessary for emotions to play the valuable role they ought to play in public life" (Nussbaum 1995, 72).

Zambrano's sister Araceli had experienced several devastating circumstances not narrated in *Delirio y destino*. Her second husband, a soldier in the Republican army during the Spanish Civil War, was extradited from France and executed by Francisco Franco's government. The Gestapo harassed Araceli herself. Her first husband, a militant Spanish communist during the Civil War, fought with the Russians in the Second World War, after which he was interned in Siberia. He escaped from his Siberian prison and made his way to Venezuela, where he committed suicide in despair over the Stalinist purges in Russia.[32] The sad event related in *Delirio y destino* is the death of the Zambrano sisters' mother, which left Araceli entirely alone in a foreign country and without any means of support: "La había llamado Antígona, durante todo este tiempo en que el destino las había separado apartándola a ella del lugar de la tragedia, mientras su hermana—Antígona—la arrostraba. Comenzó a llamarla así en su angustia, Antígona porque, inocente, soportaba la Historia; porque habiendo nacido para el amor la estaba devorando la piedad" (1989, 249). [She had called her Antigone throughout the entire time destiny had separated them, removing her from the site of tragedy, whereas her sister—Antigone—was having to face it. She began to call her sister that in her anguish, Antigone, because she was innocent but she was having to endure history; because her sister had been born for love but compassion was devouring her] (1998, 177).

Delirio y destino defies generic classification.[33] It was apparently dictated orally to Zambrano's friend Reyna Rivas in Cuba as a quick mode of composition to meet the deadline for a Swiss competition for the best novel or autobiography, which Zambrano wanted to win in order to help her sister with medical expenses. The book has two parts, the first of which interweaves history, autobiography, and philosophy in a seamless lyrical web to evoke the energy that young Republican sympathizers felt in 1929 and 1930 while they actively militated for the Second Republic. The Republic itself and its dissolution in the bloody Civil War receive mention only in passing, toward the end of the book. The bulk of the narrative focuses on Republicans' dreams (the delirium) for the future rather than on their laments for its death at the Francoist victory in 1939.

The second part of *Delirio y destino* comprises a series of *delirios*, which are part short story, part lyrical rhapsody.[34] Many of the *delirios* embody the kind of "aesthetics of possibility" evident in Zambrano's remake of the Antigone story. Fiction facilitates the dream of a future space in which individuals experience transcendence and community with others. The *delirios* incorporate vanguard techniques such as the evocation of subjective states through ellipsis, striking imagery, and metaphors. Two of the stories focus on women who have found means to escape the limitations of their historical circumstances (their destiny) through delirium (or fantasy); another two on communal experiences draw on the notion of self that Zambrano developed in *Horizonte del liberalismo:* that the individual is always a social, communal entity. Walter Benjamin stated the position in dialectical terms, asserting that there is "absolutely no use for such rigid isolated things at work, novel, book. [One] has to insert them into the living social context" (1978, 221).

In "La loca," a deranged girl who is always thirsty lives imprisoned in her parents' home. Before the strange malady of endless thirst overcame her, she had a fiancé and was apparently destined for a traditional female life. At one point, she regularly escapes from the house to go to the river, but after nearly drowning one day, she remains confined forever. Her life is reduced to her thirst and to her garbled, unintelligible shouts: "Empezó a gritar a media noche llamando a los vecinos y después contestando o llamando al gallo en la madrugada y quiso saltarse la ventana para ir a la copa de un árbol con un nido de ruiseñores que ella vio o se le figuró que había" (1989, 260) [The shrieking would start at midnight, when she would call to the neighbors, and then she would answer or call to the cock early in the morning, and she had tried to jump from the window so she could climb to the top of a tree where she had seen a nest of nightingales or thought she had] (1998, 186). She becomes obsessed with grapes, and she is brought large bunches of them, which she throws out the window. She sits and stares for hours at the cover of a raisin box that depicts a woman dancing "envuelta en unos velos de rojo fuego como llamas y tenía los cabellos entrelazdos con racimos de uvas negras y unos pámpanos que le caían por el cuello, una cabeza de mármol la miraba danzar sonriéndose con mucha burla" (1989, 261) [wrapped in some fiery red, flame-like veils with clusters of black grapes entwined in her hair and a few vine shoots falling around her neck, and sitting beside her there was a marble head that smiled mockingly as it watched her dance] (1998, 186). Finally, a great peace envelops her when she takes up religious practices just before her death. She has willed that her entire inheritance be used to help the poor, occasioning the opinion that if she had been sane, she would have been conferred a sainthood.

The good woman, the woman who has suffered and who has not found traditional fulfillment in life but who is capable of extraordinary imagination—the obsession with the beauty of water and the fascination with grapes—envisions a better life for those whom her worldly possessions might assist. The ending in which the townspeople and the church can only imagine a "sane" saint is highly ironic. The "rational spectator"—the implied and real reader—understands that this woman, whose "reason" has failed her, has in fact wrought more good than those who claim to have all their wits about them. There is a wry smile in the narrator's ending: "La gente la sintió mucho [the girl's death]. Una paloma andaba revolteando por encima de la caja por el camino y en el cementerio mientras la enterraban. Y se decía por el pueblo que había muerto inocente y santa, que de haber estado cuerda hubiera sido una Santa, que sólo le había faltado eso, estar cuerda para ser Santa" (1989, 261). [People felt very sad. A dove kept circling above the coffin on the way to the cemetery and while she was being buried. And in the village they said that she had died innocent and like a saint, that if she had been sane she would have been a saint, that sanity was all she lacked, sanity would have made her a saint] (1998, 187).

"La del dulce nombre" describes a young girl of extraordinary beauty who "empezó a espigarse y a embellecer de modo tan alarmante" (1989, 264) [began to grow tall and show such striking beauty, but alarming beauty] (1998, 189). She becomes so prodigiously beautiful that she finally encloses herself in the tower of her house and refuses to come out. In her tower, she has visions and takes on a miraculous air: "Parece que veía lo que pasaba lejos, sin asomarse siquiera a la ventana aunque hubiera sido igual, pues desde ella nada se veía sino tierra y más tierra, hasta que se junta con el cielo, y nada más" (1989, 265). [She seemed to see things that were happening far away, without even peering out the window, although it would not have made any difference since all she saw from her window was land and more land until it meets the sky and nothing else] (1998, 191). She sings songs that no one in the village has ever heard, and one day she appears with pearls of unknown provenance. At times, one hears musical instruments playing in the tower, and some strange birds—golden, blue, emerald green—alight on the tower window.

Her behavior and the circumstances of her life occasion considerable consternation with the townspeople, but she is finally left alone and forgotten, except when some stranger comes to town. Then the story is told, but the outsider does not seem to completely understand or value it: "¡Y es la desgracia que tenemos en estos pueblos tan pobres y tan apartados! ¡Señor, cómo se llama su Merced, señor alcabalero, que pasan cosas así, y luego no tenemos, no tendremos nunca quién las cuente!" (1989, 267). [And it's our misfortune, my Lord—what is your worship's name, sir Collector?—in these villages where we're so poor and isolated, that things like this happen, and afterwards we have no one, we'll never have anyone who can tell about them!] (1998, 192). The imagination and the telling of stories about the collectivity are essential to the community's sense of itself in the context of the rest of the world. The stories elevate one beyond the prosaic reality of everyday life—"el pueblo . . . polvoriento de rebaños, oliendo a vino y resonando juramentos de arrieros" (1989, 263) [thanks to so many flocks of sheep, the town was dusty; it reeked of wine and echoed with the cursing of muleteers] (1998, 189). The village, which had once been populated by stately homes, is now in full decline: "Todo se fue desmoronando y ni rastro había quedado, y el pueblo, para parecer más insignificante, era nuevo, pues no había ni ruinas como en otros" (1989, 263). [Evidently everything had gradually collapsed and not even a trace remained; and the village was new, which made it seem even more insignificant. There were not even any ruins the way there are in some villages] (1998, 189). The story of the beautiful girl in her tower accompanied by music and legendary birds keeps alive the possibility of recovering the splendor the town had enjoyed in better economic times. Both of Zambrano's *delirios* about imprisoned women echo Beauvoir's dictum that liberation occurs through resistance to material reality, "[ethics] is the triumph of freedom over facticity" (1994, 44).

If these two *delirios* focus on the individual as she is imagined by her society, the last two *delirios* of *Delirio y destino* relate the individual to her society in a more physical way. In "Corpus en Florencia," the female narrator, caught up in the emotion of the Florentine Corpus Christi celebration, experiences the collective sense of the religious festival: "Se sentía perfectamente encajada en aquella muchedumbre hasta por su traje azul muy celeste nada elegante, como si hubiera vestido de acuerdo, más que con la moda, con el esplendor del día" (1989, 288). [She felt that she fit in perfectly with the multitude, even her sky blue, rather plain dress, as if she had not chosen it to look stylish that day but to blend with the day's splendor] (1998, 207). She experiences the Corpus Christi celebration as a communal phenomenon. The emotion of the moment places her both at one with and separate from the rest of humanity.

The sights and sounds of Corpus Christi envelop the narrator as one in a large crowd of people witnessing the procession:

> [Las cruces] recubiertas por un dosel de terciopelo o damasco, cada una de color diferente, colores brillantes, todos recamados de oro. Y quedaron allí en hilera enfilando la Vía de San Joan, reverberando al rayo del sol poniente que las hería de costado. Y algunas daban contra el cielo y eran aves fabulosas, que se hubieran dejado apresar o que vinieran por su gusto al conjuro de una palabra mágica. . . . La multitud comenzó a desagregarse extrañamente silenciosa, como vuelta hacia si. (1989, 289–90)

> [The crosses were covered by brightly colored canopies made of velvet or damask—each canopy a different color, and each embroidered with gold. They stood in a row, lined up in the Vía de San Joan, shining in the ray of setting sun that wounded them obliquely. Some collided with the sky, and they were fabulous birds that had probably let themselves be caught or had come happily, pulled by a magic word. . . . The crowd began to break up, strangely silent, as if it were turning inward.] (1998, 208–9)

The imagery of the humanized crosses (wounded by the sun's ray, colliding with the sky, engaging in voluntary or involuntary action) reflects the collective experience of those who are viewing the procession and leads naturally into the crowd psychology expressed when the crowd "turns inward." The end of the piece summarizes a female vanguard aesthetic in which artistic form and human qualities come together to create a sense of community:

> Por todas partes, naturaleza y vida humana, la diferencia triunfaba; la cualidad y la cantidad marcaban sus abismos. ¡Oh el mundo de las categorías! El Mundo simplemente sustancia, pero en seguida cantidad y cualidad. Y allí, Señor, en tu Cruz no hay nada, en esa simple desnudez inapresable; nada de eso en la pura forma sustancia incorruptible donde toda cualidad ha sido resumida. ¿Señor, será así? Acabaremos de nacer del todo en Tu Paraíso? (1989, 291)

> [Everywhere nature and human life—difference—were triumphing; quality and quantity each was defining its abyss. Oh, the world of categories! Simply the world: substance, but then immediately quantity and quality. And there, on your cross, Lord, there is nothing in that simple ungraspable starkness—nothing of all this in pure form, incorruptible substance, where each and every quality has been totally reduced. Is this how it will be Lord? Will we finish being born once we are in your Paradise?] (1998, 109–10)

Religious (transcendent) sentiment similarly infuses Espina's protagonist's theory of self and community in *La virgen prudente*.

The *delirios* section of *Delirio y destino* ends with the very short "El cáliz," in which a female voice employs the image of passing the chalice to consider our nature as individual human beings. It begins with a run-on dialogue, a dispute between an unidentified voice and the voice of a woman about how a chalice is to be passed from one to another. The voice ponders two possible views of our relationship to things and to others. We can view ourselves as autonomous with rights of personal ownership, or we can view ourselves as part of a whole that supersedes individual rights. If we view the chalice as a possession, it becomes a source of social conflict. The vignette concludes by provocatively questioning whether it is legitimate to think in terms of private property: "¿Pero tengo yo algún cáliz, mío para mí, de mí? ¿No será uno, uno para todos del que me cae una sola gota, una gota sólo que no pasa, una gota de eternidad?" (1989, 294). [But do I even have a cup, one that is mine, mine alone? What if there is just one cup, one for all of us with one lone drop that falls to me, just one drop that cannot be passed on, one drop of eternity?] (1998, 211). Through powerful imagery, Zambrano's creative dreaming constructs a sense of the communal. In each of these lyrical narratives, the individual situation dissolves into a communal one; we are asked to consider the way in which we as individuals relate to society at large through the efforts of imagination. We imagine another's life and thought, an exercise that becomes, as Nussbaum says of Dickens's *Hard Times,* one in which "the vision of individual life quality afforded by novels proves compatible with, and actually motivates, serious institutional and political criticism" (1995, 71).

By positioning herself as Ismene, the observant rather than activist sister, vis-à-vis the stories that she narrates, Zambrano achieves the state that she calls *razón poética*. *Razón poética* is very like Nussbaum's "poetic justice" and Theodor Adorno's "subjective reason"—a reason that is guided and shaped by emotional content: "Both empathetic participation and external assessment are crucial in determining the degree of compassion it is rational to have for the person" (Nussbaum 1995, 73). This kind of reason, as Beauvoir notes in *The Ethics of Ambiguity,* always has a social dimension: "Passion is converted to genuine freedom only if one destines his existence to other existences through the being . . . at which he aims, without hoping to entrap it in the destiny of the in-itself" (1994, 62). Ismene/María Zambrano is an individual with a social conscience who finds in literature the means to channel the emotions toward social ends that encompass the possibility of a better future.

Nussbaum argues for a literature with the potential to make a contribution to "law in particular, public reasoning generally" (1995, xv). Burgos, Martínez Sierra, Nelken, Montseny, Chacel, and Zambrano similarly promoted the literary imagination as a public imagination, especially one that can envision new social configurations. Again Nussbaum's words are pertinent: "Literature focuses on the possible" (5). Via melodrama or vanguard imagery, women vanguard novelists placed the emotions at the heart of their literary ethics, because the emotions have the power to disturb and raise consciousness (all the reasons for which Plato banned the poets from the Republic). They understood that the emotions are most effective in influencing public policy if they are tempered by distance (or reason), which gives literature its unique role as mediator between raw passion and abstract aloofness.

Conclusion
A Legacy and a Prophecy

When the niña bonita, the Spanish Republic, succumbed to its own internal divisions and the superior Nationalist forces, women's dream of a new sociopolitical order metamorphosed into the thirty-five-year nightmare of Francisco Franco's dictatorial regime. The social revolution that included so many shifts in women's roles was dramatically reversed. The Franco government, which ruled from 1939 until 1975, rescinded most of the legal gains that women had made between 1920 and 1936. Women were now indoctrinated with the lessons of the Sección Femenina—sewing, cooking, and endless cheerfulness in a revived traditional patriarchy. The national political system (Franco, the dictator, as the symbolic father of the nation) was mirrored in the domestic sphere. Husbands had absolute legal rights over their wives. Legal barriers were imposed against a married woman's right to work outside the home and against a woman's right to property and even to her children (if she separated from her husband). The church regained the hegemony over personal life that it had lost during the Republican era, and divorce was once again prohibited.

Both literary and social modernism came to an abrupt end. The Lyceum Club, that emblematic location where women (mostly married and otherwise confined to the home) found intellectual nourishment, closed in 1939, when Franco's troops took Madrid. The Phalange Party confiscated the Lyceum's building at San Marcos 40, and the Sección Femenina converted it into the Medina Club. Unfortunately, the new occupants destroyed the Lyceum's archives. The writings of most of the women discussed in this book, which envisioned a Spain that provided greater equality for women, disappeared from the public record. The *novela rosa* and narratives about women who find felicity within conventional marriage, home, and child rearing became the most readily available fiction to a broad spectrum of women readers, replacing the novella series in which Carmen de Burgos, Margarita Nelken, and Federica Montseny had published their feminist novels.

The Republican era became a nostalgic memory for intellectuals and writers like María Zambrano, whose *Delirio y destino* so poignantly chronicles the exuberance that she and her contemporaries felt in 1929 as the Miguel Primo de Rivera dictatorship and the monarchy of Alfonso XIII were crumbling. Zambrano, like so many other Republican combatants and sympathizers (including María Martínez Sierra, Margarita Nelken, Federica Montseny, and Rosa Chacel), went into exile. Interestingly, Zambrano left the last vestiges of patriarchalism behind her when she departed Spain. As Franco's troops entered Barcelona in March 1939, Zambrano stood at the door of her apartment in the Catalan capital poised to leave her native land for exile in France and Latin America. There before her, packed in neat boxes, were all her notes from her classes with José Ortega y Gasset (who had been her principal teacher at the University of Madrid and who had directed her doctoral dissertation on Benedict de Spinoza). Although the boxes would have been easy to transport and although she did not fully understand her reasons at the time, she decided to leave them behind. She had disagreed with Ortega y Gasset over his lukewarm support of a republic in the late 1920s, and he had belittled her desire to find an alternative to Western rationalism.

Although some women attended the university and enjoyed a measure of intellectual freedom in the 1920s and 1930s, there were many subtle obstacles to overcome. Exile provided some women intellectuals with economic opportunities in addition to personal liberty that enabled them to continue to grow and develop. While she was in exile, Chacel wrote her best novels, *Memorias de Leticia Valle* and *La sinrazón* (1960), as well as *Saturnal* (1972), her seminal essay on gender (written under the auspices of a Guggenheim Fellowship in New York). Zambrano wrote *Delirio y destino* in Cuba and her other major books in Rome and Switzerland. From Argentina, María Martínez Sierra finally wrote and published several works under her own name (Gregorio died in 1947, thus invalidating her pen name). Shirley Mangini's *Memories of Resistance* (1995) chronicles the many memoirs written by women in prison or in exile during the postwar years. Even though exiled women writers continued to publish abroad, their writings were mostly unknown in Spain.

Despite the fact that the writings of women from the earlier part of the twentieth century and the writings of women in exile were largely ignored by the Spanish public in the Franco years, there arose a new wave of women writers who were not entirely unaware of their predecessors. Traces of the legacy of the prewar women writers are evident in the postwar era. For example, in Carmen Martín Gaite's novel *El cuarto de atrás*, the autobiographical protagonist (known as C.) notes that, when she was in high school, her mother gave her a book to read: María Martínez Sierra's *El amor catedrático*, "la historia de una chica que se atreve a estudiar carrera" (Martín Gaite 1978, 92). The mother, probably born in the late nineteenth century, would have loved to have attended the university, but in her day "no era costumbre, ni siquiera se le pasó por la cabeza" (92). Clearly, the mother wished to provide her daughter with models that were different from her own. C., however, was a little disappointed in the decision of the protagonist (Teresa) to marry her professor, who was much older than she and rather maniacal in the bargain: "tanto ilusionarse con los estudios y desafiar a la sociedad que le impedía a una mujer realizarlos, para luego salir por ahí, en plan *happy end*, que a saber si sería o no tan *happy*" (92).

C. projects beyond the novel's ending, beyond the nuptials, wondering why novels end with marriage, as though life stopped there. She is certain that sooner or later Teresa will become disillusioned with her marriage arrangement (C. does not take into consideration the important role that Teófilo plays in mitigating the "happy end" effect). C.'s enlightened mother, who has long harbored repressed desires for intellectual development, urges her daughter to follow Teresa's footsteps (at least in her studies). Instead of teaching C. the female arts of cooking and sewing, she has always encouraged her in her schoolwork.

Martínez Sierra had another indirect influence on postwar writers. She mentored Elena Fortún (the pen name of Encarnación Aragoneses Urquijo), the author of an important series of books for young readers. Fortún's books, which appeared from about 1929 until the end of the Civil War, were stories about a precocious and intelligent girl named

Celia. Martínez Sierra and Aragoneses Urquijo became acquainted at the Lyceum Club, where Aragoneses Urquijo regaled her fellow members with amusingly told stories. Martínez Sierra convinced her friend that instead of fortifying her domestic budget by selling vacuum cleaners, as she had planned, she should take advantage of a genre that was gaining popularity by putting her stories into writing for young people. As an adolescent in prewar Spain, Martín Gaite had been an avid reader of the Fortún stories, and doubtless many other girls her age had been similarly captivated by the narratives in which a young girl with a strong mind and voice questions all received wisdom, especially that of her mother. Martín Gaite points out that Fortún not only created a precocious female child; she also conjured sympathetic portraits of working-class people, which Martín Gaite believes may well have influenced male social realists of the 1950s. The collections titled *Celia, lo que dice, Celia en el colegio, Celia novelista, Celia en el mundo,* and *Celia y sus amigos* were reprinted in the 1990s and will perhaps continue to nourish youthful imaginations.

Despite the otherwise dismal outlook for intellectually and artistically inclined women in the early Franco years, Martín Gaite and many other young women attended the university in the 1940s. In 1944, Carmen Laforet's *Nada,* about an eighteen-year-old girl named Andrea who moves to Barcelona in the early postwar years to attend the university, won the first Nadal Prize for the novel. Women's education, which had been such a hotly contested issue some eighty years earlier, had finally become a perfectly acceptable plot motivator rather than a central theme. Even though Andrea's family (particularly her self-appointed guardian, Aunt Angustias) is very conservative about all matters concerning gender, no one questions Andrea's university education. At the university, Ena, another surprisingly independent young woman, befriends the protagonist and facilitates Andrea's break with her unenlightened family.

Although the momentum for a future of social and legal liberation that women modernists and vanguardists envisioned was stalled for nearly forty years, it only lay dormant (kept smoldering by an underground feminist movement) and was revived in 1975 when Franco finally died. Watching Franco's funeral on television, for example, inspired Martín Gaite to begin to write *El cuarto de atrás,* chronicling a future woman novelist's formation in the pre- and early postwar years. Chacel and Zambrano returned from exile about this time to the attention and accolades so long denied them in their homeland. Zambrano's approach to the self inspired many younger women writers (especially poets such as Amparo Amorós and María Victoria Atencia). Often in the public eye, Chacel gave a lecture in which she once again sought a model in *Don Quixote* to challenge what she perceived as some of the dangers of the renewed feminist cause. Returning to the theme of *Saturnal*, the couple as the fundamental unit of human life, she warned against the pitfalls of women's Marcela-like attempt to isolate themselves absolutely.

Male artists also reacted to the new post-Franco feminism. Although these manifestations were somewhat lighter in tone than the backlash of the 1920s and 1930s, they were pointed nonetheless. Take, for example, Fernando Trueba's comedic film *Belle Epoque,* set in 1931 on the eve of the Second Spanish Republic. Fernando, unworldly and innocent, an army deserter on the lamb, takes refuge with a Republican-sympathizing man and his four unmarried daughters, who are spending the summer holidays in their village away from their jobs in Madrid. The male protagonist's naiveté in sexual and other matters contrasts with the women's worldliness. One daughter, a lesbian, takes delight in seducing Fernando when she is dressed in his soldier's uniform and he in a maid's outfit for a costume party (the scene is reminiscent of Burgos's use of cross-dressing to evoke a national theme). A second daughter accepts Fernando into her bed even though she is engaged to another man, whose Carlist mother prefers a Republican to an Alphonsist daughter-in-law. The fiancée wants to postpone the wedding until the Republic is proclaimed, so that she will have the opportunity to divorce if she wishes. The widowed oldest sister also finds consolation in Fernando's youthful good looks. It is the youngest sister, Luz (played by Penelope Cruz), more demure and less sexually assertive than her siblings, who finally marries Fernando, whom she has secretly loved all the while.

It would seem that in the 1990s Trueba returned to messages about domestic felicity and female comportment that Miguel de Unamuno, Pío Baroja, Azorín, and Ramón Pérez de Ayala were fielding in their novels published during the rise of first-wave feminism in Spain. With women in most levels of the Spanish government and economic system today, it seems unlikely that this breezy backlash (if indeed it is backlash) could have the same restraining effects that it had in the prewar era, but it is certainly a phenomenon worthy of consideration. Current Spanish women's fiction—including novels by Rosa Montero, Carme Riera, Marina Mayoral, Soledad Puértolas, Cristina Fernández Cubas, Adelaida García Morales, Paloma Díaz-Mas, among many others—continue the work of social modernists Martínez Sierra, Burgos, Nelken, Montseny, and Chacel in staking a claim for women as equal partners in creating a modern Spanish nation.

Notes

Introduction

1. Such works as Gustavo Pérez Firmat's *Idle Fictions* (1982), Robert Spires's *Transparent Simulacra* (1988), and my own *Crossfire* (1993a), for example, treat male fiction almost exclusively. Notable exceptions are Maryellen Bieder's "Woman and the Twentieth Century Literary Canon" (1992), Michael Ugarte's *Madrid 1900* (1996), and Shirley Mangini's *Las modernas de Madrid* (2001). Bieder's pioneering article, which launched a Burgos "industry" in U.S. Hispanism, sets Burgos's intellectual and artistic endeavors within the context of canonical male modernist writing and is a model for this book. Ugarte's book includes a chapter on Burgos that analyzes a number of male authors who wrote about Madrid, and Mangini's study covers a number of women writers of the modernist era.

2. Eric J. Hobsbawm (1990) locates nationalism's origins in the nineteenth century and its culmination in the First World War. Citing the specific example of Spain, he points out that not until the 1884 edition did the *Diccionario de la Real Academia* begin to display the terminology of state, nation, and language as we understand them today. In this book, I extend Hobsbawm's end date for the European nationalist period beyond World War I to 1939, thus including the intense political debates on the Spanish nation in the Second Spanish Republic and the Civil War. This revised chronology not only better suits the situation in Spain but also allows consideration of the growing women's movement and such women writers as Burgos, who increasingly contributed to the conversation about Spain as the century moved beyond its infancy. This reconfiguration brings the study of Spanish modernity and nationalism into line with studies of these phenomena in other countries where a link has been made between the growth of national identity and a consciousness of women in new and more public spaces. Álvarez Junco traces the Spanish nationalist movement from the 1808 patriotic reaction to Napoléon Bonapart's invasion of Spain, but he finds that a true sense of nation did not gel in Spain until the 1898

war, remarking that with the Generation of '98 "un nacionalismo más activo y eficaz" was born (2001, 588). Politicians were alarmed at the lack of patriotism on the part of the masses when the Spanish navy was defeated and embarked on a concerted effort to raise public national consciousness (589).

3. This kind of imagery had earlier manifestations: "In the spring of 1869, when [General] Prim ordered a new round of conscription to sustain the colonial war in Cuba, militant republicans organized strikes in Málaga and Seville. Francisco Pi y Margall, the century's preeminent federalist ideologue, denounced Prim for destroying the 'sweet illusions' of Spanish mothers. Once again employing feminine imagery to counter the agenda of the *Gloriosa*'s martial leaders, federal republicans invoked the distraught mother, weeping for sons lost, to castigate the conservative revolution" (White 1999, 245). That references to the nation as mother had older origins is attested to by Álvarez Junco, who notes that during the French invasion of 1808, Spanish patriots were exhorted to "derramar por [la madre que nos acoge y protege] hasta la última gota de nuestra sangre" (2001, 33).

4. In a commentary on the initiative undertaken by Castro, C. Bernaldo Quirós offers a more typical slant on the aim of women's education: "Con el tiempo, estas pequeñas instruidas en los conocimientos que exige el vivir, iniciadas en la precisión mediante la Caja Escolar de Ahorros que existe en la Asociación, irán saliendo de ella transformadas en jóvenes animosas, dispuestas para comprender el sentido serio y elevado de la vida y compartirle con el hombre en la pareja sexual, donde cada parte tiene su papel dictado por la naturaleza. *'El hombre es la lucha; la mujer es el amor',* debe decirse siempre, con Thulié; la bella y novel frase que esgrimió contra las aberraciones del feminismo. El feminismo bueno ¿qué puede desear sino hacer a la mujer cada vez más femenina?" (1904, 8).

5. A partial list of other books on women that circulated in Spain in the late nineteenth and early twentieth centuries includes R. Abellán y Anta, *La mujer. Canto épico original* (1886); Serafín y Joaquín Álvarez Quintero, *La mujer española* (1917); Concepción Arenal, *La mujer del porvenir* (1869) and *La mujer de su casa* (1884); E. de Belmar, *El sacerdocio de la mujer* (1886); Valentín Brandau, *Caracteres de la mujer según la sociología contemporánea* (1908); J. P. Criado y Domínguez, *Literatas españolas del siglo XIX* (1889); Félix-Antoine-Philibert Dupanloup, *La educación de las Hijas de Familia y estudios que convienen a las mujeres en el mundo* (1880); E. Filogyno, *Las mujeres en las Academias* (1891); Concepción Gimeno de Flaquer, *La mujer española. Estudios acerca de sus facultades intelectuales* (1877), *Evangelio de la mujer* (1900), *La mujer intelectual* (1901), *El problema feminista* (1903), and *Mujeres de raza latina* (1904); E. Gómez Carrillo, *El libro de las mujeres* (1909); A. Gómez Torres, *¿Cuál es la educación física y moral de la*

mujer más conforme a los grandes destinos que le ha confiado la Providencia? (1866); Edmundo González Blanco, *El feminismo en las sociedades modernas* (1904); A. Jerez Perchet *El libro de la mujer. Educación social y familiar. Higiene y economía doméstica* (1899); E. Jiménez, *La mujer y el derecho. Indicaciones históricas sobre la condición de la mujer* (1892); Luisa Luna, *La misión de la mujer en la sociedad y la familia* (1881); A. Navarro, *Azul y Rojo. Pensamientos, máximas y anécdotas acerca de la mujer de los mejores autores antiguos y modernos* (1899); J. Nín y Tudó, *Para la mujer . . . Colección de pensamientos . . . sobre la mujer y el amor* (1881); M. de Palacio, *El amor, las mujeres y el matrimonio. Cuentos, pensamientos y reflexiones* (1864); F. Paláu and T. de J. Gil Lobo y Calvente, *El libro de las señoritas* (1876); J. Panadés y Poblet, *La educación de la mujer según los más ilustres moralistas e higienistas*, 3 vols. (1878); F. Rubio y Galí, *La mujer gaditana* (1902); Faustina Saez de Melgar, *Deberes de mujer* (1886); B. Santamaría, *La mujer* (1879); M. P. Sinués de Marco, *La mujer de nuestros días. Obra dedicada a las madres y a las hijas de familia* (1878), *Verdades dulces y amargas. Páginas para la mujer* (1882), and *La misión de la mujer* (1886); F. Vila, *Malo y bueno que se ha dicho de las mujeres* (1881). See the bibliographies in Jagoe, Blanco, and Enríquez Salamanca (1998) for additional book-length works that address women published in Spain during this period.

6. A number of Generation of '98 journals took note of the "woman question" and the progress of feminism. *Revista Nueva* carried a few articles, notably Manuel Bueno's 1899 "La Eva futura," which had a decidedly antifeminist tone. José María Llanas Aguilaniedo also thought of feminists in terms of "future Eves" in an article for *Juventud* but modulated his criticism of the current incarnation: he opined that the contemporary role of "administradora honrada, socia buena, humilde casera; una especie de animal doméstico sin inteligencia ni corazón a no ser para los hijos" (1901, n.p.) was the appropriate one for the modern woman. However, he did not believe that the future model had been found. Very masculine women—the worker or the intellectual—were insufferable.

Helios included the section "Fémina," directed by Margarita María de Monterrey, in nearly every issue. The column avoided the usual women's issues such as fashion, kitchen, and home, preferring human or social issues of concern to women such as "El dinero en el matrimonio" "De la influencia social del celibato sobre el feminismo. Capacidad política de la mujer," "La misión artista por Eleanora Duse," and "La poetisa polaca María Konopnitchka." These articles indicate a more progressive attitude toward women's capacity for intellectual reading (perhaps because of María Martínez Sierra's association with the journal), although they hardly represent a militant feminism. *Helios* also included some misogynist writing (notably a 1903 article by Rubén de Cendoya, an early pseudonym of José

Ortega y Gasset, and in an anonymous 1903 article titled "Glosario").

In 1904, *Alma Española* published some articles by Baroja that could be considered to have a feminist orientation ("Adulterio y divorcio," and "La secularización de las mujeres"). He condemned the discrepancy in the judgment of women's and men's adultery and favored the notion of "la unión libre" (qtd. in Celma Valero 1991, 100). He also railed against the lack of education for women and declared that progress was impossible without women's participation. In the same journal, 1904 articles by Bernaldo de Quirós ("Nueva asociación para la enseñanza de la mujer"), Joaquín Dicenta ("Atavismo"), and Fabián Vidal ("Las mujeres y el arte") also argue for the need to educate women in order to liberate and dignify them.

7. Timothy Brennan ascribes a central role to the novel in the national myth-making project: "Literary myth too has been complicit in the creation of nations.... And the rise of European nationalism coincides especially with one form of literature—the novel" (1990, 49). He further points out that the novel "historically accompanied the rise of nations by objectifying the 'one, yet many' of national life, and by mimicking the structure of the nation" (49).

8. See the collection *Referencias vivenciales femeninas en la literatura española (1830–1936)* (Porro 1997) for a number of titles of both male- and female-authored novels that focus on gender that are not included in this book.

9. A comment by Ramiro de Maeztu from his 1923 article "Diretes. Masculinidad" is emblematic: " 'Pide a Dios el señor Unamuno que proteja a la Inteligencia de España. Y escribe Inteligencia con mayúscula. ¡Dios la proteja! ¡Dios la perdone! Porque su pecado, '¡lengua sin manos!', consiste precisamente en no haber comprendido que los guardianes de la República de Platón han de ser 'tan guerreros como filósofos'. No ha visto en suma que la masculinidad no es meramente un don, sino una virtud del espíritu, que se cultivará cuando se santifica su nombre, que se descuidará cuando se menosprecia" (qtd. in Ouimette, 1998, 1:158).

Chapter 1

1. José Antonio Maravall paraphrases Miguel de Unamuno's *España y los españoles:* "El remedio [era] conquistar la españolidad, 'hacerse histórico, hacer su historia', por el camino que él nos señala (1986, 194).

2. After quoting a nineteenth-century article that appeared in *Anales Malagueños* in which the *pueblo* was invoked as the only means of cleansing the nation stained by an impure monarch, Sarah L. White (1999, 252) summarizes the concept in the following way: "The *pueblo*—the people—served

as an abstraction for the nation, the citizenry. In the more radical and romantic imagery of revolution, the *pueblo*—signifying the peasantry and the working classes—constituted the industrious backbone and virtuous heart of the body politic. The term, however, was essentially inclusive: the *pueblo*, when invoked in contrast to the monarch, referred to the common people, indicating both middle-class men of democratic sympathies and the laboring classes that constituted the bulk of the nation's population.

3. These kinds of associations can be found in the numerous books on women that were published in the early part of the twentieth century. For example, although it tried to appear modern, E. Gómez Carrillo's *El libro de las mujeres* is an exercise in classifying women geographically. Some of the chapter titles are "Mujeres de Biarritz," "¡Vienesa, rubia vienesa!," "El prestigio voluptuoso de las sevillanas," and "Estrasburgo y sus mujeres." Gómez Carrillo also classifies by stereotypes—the courtesan, the actress, the Salomé, dancers from a number of places. Spanish women form a special category: "—¡Una española!—exclamó mi amigo Alboni.—¡Véala usted y dígame si una mujer así puede confundirse con las de otros países! . . . Aunque no hubiese aquí sino esta española, España se llevaría la palma. Es una de esas bellezas que hacen la reputación de un país, de una raza, de una época." (1909, 37).

4. Jurkevich (1991, 5–6) provides a helpful analysis of this aspect of Unamuno's life within her Jungian study of Unamuno's fiction.

5. Without employing the term "essentialism" so prevalent now for such characterizations of women, a number of other critics also note that Unamuno relied on stock or traditional traits in the portrayal of women in his fiction. R. L. Predmore (1955) notes Unamuno's emphasis on the female body, especially the maternal breast and lap, which are closely related to woman's maternal and nurturing qualities. Lynette Hubbard Seator avers that "for Unamuno, natural woman is woman. Social woman does not exist" (1980, 51). Friedrich Schürr (1965, 71) also considers Unamuno's equation of woman and motherhood as essential, and Kathie Carruthers (1972) points out that Unamuno viewed matrimony as a natural state.

6. Unamuno's views of marriage found echoes in writings throughout the early twentieth century. José Castán Tobeñas's 1913 *La crisis del matrimonio*, for example, reflects the concern that an increasingly public and active female population aroused in conservative men. In terms that could easily have been Unamuno's, Castán Tobeñas defined marriage as a "remanso para el alma masculina." Men should find in marriage a rest for their nerves, repose for their intelligence, peace and contentment for their heart, something akin to the eternal life of heaven that the female "ángel del hogar" can facilitate: "Las ternuras del hogar, (. . .) son las que pueden proporcionarnos la felicidad, porque representando el orden, el equilibrio y la armonía de

lo humano, matizan la vida de apacibles alegrías, y parecen dilatar nuestro espíritu aproximándolo a los horizontes de la eternidad" (qtd. in Bussy Genevois 1997, 128).

7. For other discussions of Martínez Sierra's name and her collaboration with her husband, see M. Martínez Sierra 1953; O'Connor 1987; Blanco 1989; and Rodrigo 1994.

8. Like Burgos, Martínez Sierra was an active feminist who wrote a number of essays that supported the feminist cause in Spain, most of them signed by Gregorio (he also delivered the feminist lectures that she wrote). She founded the Asociación Femenina de Educación Cívica as a meeting center for middle-class workingwomen. Its purpose grew to include courses and lectures in order for the group to advance socially and culturally. Minister of Public Instruction Fernando de los Ríos attended the inauguration of the 1932–33 course. Martínez Sierra's feminist essays include *Cartas a las mujeres de España* (1916), *Feminismo, feminidad, españolismo* (1917), *La mujer moderna* (1920), *Eva curiosa* (1930), and *Nuevas cartas a las mujeres* (1932). In some ways, the message in these essays does not differ significantly from that of the late nineteenth-century male "feminists" who espoused women's education for nationalist purposes—women as mothers bear the responsibility of schooling sons who will uphold the national honor. Many of these essays were written during the First World War and should be interpreted in the context of the urgent need for the strongest possible fighting force (mostly male). As Blanco notes, "La voz femenina de *Gregorio Martínez Sierra* no solamente surgió dentro de este hostil contexto [especially the feminist polemics on suffrage] sino que fue, en gran parte, la que moldeó y estableció los fundamentos teóricos del debate en sus cinco libros de ensayos sobre el feminismo publicados entre 1916 y 1932" (1989, 25). For a more in-depth analysis of Martínez Sierra's feminist essays, see Blanco 1998.

9. Alda Blanco considers consciousness a central theme of *Cartas a la mujeres de España; Feminismo, feminidad, españolismo;* and *La mujer moderna:* "María Martínez Sierra's objective is to explain women's need to live in equality and to be a conscious being, that is a person who feels, thinks, desires, and functions with an awareness of what she is doing" (1998, 90). Burgos echoed Martínez Sierra in *La mujer moderna y sus derechos:* "Hay que buscar en el hogar la mujer consciente, no la *mujer reflejo,* que concebía Confucio al decir que 'el hombre es a la mujer lo que el sol a la luna, y ella necesita ser el reflejo para que reine la armonía'" (1927, 134, emphasis in original).

10. O'Connor's version of this incident follows Martínez Sierra's own account in *Gregorio y yo.* According to these versions, María accidentally fell into the sea while walking on a Barcelona beach, and only when the man who

rescued her pronounced the word "suicide" did she realize that she could have lost her life (1977, 28). Because María very carefully reconstructed every detail of her relationship with Gregorio in the autobiographical *Gregorio y yo* (leaving out all mention of Bárcena, for example), it would be risky to accept her interpretation.

11. Blanco (1998, 76) theorizes quite convincingly that Martínez Sierra employed a male pseudonym as well as a masculine voice in her feminist essays in order to gain the public hearing and credulity for a feminist message that would not have been accorded a female author.

12. In *Women in the Theater of Gregorio Martínez Sierra*, O'Connor studies the portrait of weak men in the theater of Martínez Sierra (1966, 106–25).

13. Women characters associated with nature that were created by male Generation of '98 novelists include Miguel de Unamuno's Josefa Ignacio and other minor characters in *Paz en la guerra* and Pío Baroja's Dolores in *Camino de perfección* (1902), who lives in the agriculturally rich Valencian region and is often depicted tending her plants.

14. In *Gregorio y yo*, Martínez Sierra reflected on her dramatic "role" as a woman author, her ability to evoke emotion in (especially male) spectators: "A mí, mujer al cabo, complacíame sobre todo haber hecho llorar a los hombres. Las mujeres tenemos fama de ultrasentimentales, por lo tanto no me sorprendía, aunque me halagase, el que las damas, olvidando el desastre del maquillaje, dejasen correr lágrimas abundantes; pero el que los caballeros, después de luchar bizarramente contra la emoción por aquello de 'un hombre no llora' que les han repetido desde niños, se rindieran a ella, me complacía extraordinariamente" (1953, 277). She also commented on the "masculine" role that she assumed in her friendships with men. For example, misogynist Santiago Rusiñol said of her, "'María no es una mujer: es un amigo'" (qtd. in M. Martínez Sierra, 1953, 54). Thus, María observed, began their loyal friendship: "Mas, para otorgármela, tuve que suprimir y olvidar de una vez para siempre, mi condición de mujer" (54). Frederica Montseny similarly found novelistic inventiveness and role-playing important during her exile in wartime France: "I lied with complete self-assurance, with the greatest cheekiness, utilizing my novelistic practices. I had to keep playing various roles at the same time. Here I was the wife of a Jew; there I was the possible widow of a hero, killed in the line of duty; for others . . . I was a featherbrained woman who dyed her hair in the absence of her husband to look younger and satisfy some 'heretic.' What did I care! What I wanted to do was confuse people and bring something for my children to eat" (qtd. in Mangini, 1995, 164).

15. Blanco analyzes Martínez Sierra's use of the letter format for her feminist essays. She points out that the "Letters to the Women of Spain" are penned

in a male voice, which "plays with notions of masculine authority." She notes that, while it creates the "illusion of impartiality which respect the feminist project," it also may seem paternalistic (1998, 85).

16. See Johnson 1996a for a full listing of the Golden Age works contained in Azorín's personal library.

17. See Rico Verdú 1971 for a more detailed discussion of Azorín's relationship with his father.

18. A partial list from Fox's *Azorín. Guía a la obra completa* (1992) includes the following: "Una mujer," *El País* (December 5, 1896); "Una mujer," *Madrid Cómico* (January 22, 1898); "Feminismo," *El Progreso* (February 10, 1898); "El divorcio," *España* (January 20, 1904); "Lolita. Historia de una niña que se hará grande," *Blanco y Negro* (September 8, 1904); "A mis amigas. Un almanaque de la ética en España. Silvela en el Ateneo," *España* (January 16, 1905); "La malloquina," *ABC* (September 21, 1905); "Unas sombrereras," *Blanco y Negro* (March 10, 1906); "Mujeres," *ABC* (March 25, 1906); "La moda," *ABC* (March 30, 1906); "Los amigos literarios. Una criada," *Blanco y Negro* (April 21, 1906); "Carolina Albert," *ABC* (May 3, 1906); "La vuelta con Josefina," *Blanco y Negro* (October 26, 1907); "La infanta Paz," *ABC* (June 8, 1909); "La familia," *Diario de Barcelona* (January 25, 1910); "El feminismo," *ABC* (May 4, 1912); "Andanzas y lecturas. Una mujer," *La Vanguardia* (June 24, 1913); "Rosalía de Castro," *Blanco y Negro* (January 11, 1914); "España. Exhortación a las majas," *ABC* (June 1, 1917); "Indicaciones. Una princesita y una reina," *La Vanguardia* (June 19, 1917); "Indicaciones. Doña Pendendo en Pombo," *La Vanguardia* (July 10, 1917); "Actualidad. El feminismo," *La Vanguardia* (August 28, 1917); "La vida española. Santa Teresa de Jesús," *La Prensa* (February 24, 1922); "La vida española. Feminismo," *La Prensa* (May 28, 1922); "Una doctrina feminista," *ABC* (June 3, 1922); "Autores del siglo XIX. Fernán Caballero," *ABC* (December 4, 1922); "Por unas monjas," *ABC* (May 2, 1925); "La mujer moderna," *La Prensa* (October 29, 1925); "El año femenino," *Blanco y Negro* (December 30, 1928); "Mujeres españolas. Pepa," *ABC* (March 1, 1929); "Concepción Arenal. Ideario," *ABC* (October 15, 1929); "Jorge Sand en Mallorca," *La Prensa* (October 27, 1929); "Mujeres," *La Prensa* (June 5, 1932); "Las mujeres de España," *La Prensa* (September 30, 1934); "A Concha Espina," *Arriba* (July 29, 1941); "La mujer española," *ABC* (September 6, 1942); "La Pardo Bazán," *Destino* (July 31, 1943); "La situación de Penélope," *Destino* (January 27, 1945); "Un retrato de mujer," *ABC* (April 13, 1946); "Fernán Caballero," *ABC* (July 24, 1946); "Santa Teresa todos los días," *ABC* (October 15, 1946); "La mujer del labrador," *ABC* (August 17, 1947); "Monjas de Burgos," *ABC* (December 14, 1948); "Dos españolas," *ABC* (February 26, 1949); "Las damas de antaño," *ABC* (October 6, 1949); "La fundadora," *ABC* (February 18, 1956).

19. His answer to Burgos's survey on divorce is highly ambiguous. He begins by saying that he has been divorced at least four times and by referring to the difficulty of establishing a lasting relationship with a woman. In the remainder of his response, he imagines what his life would be like with a wife, the vision suspiciously similar to the fate of Antonio Azorín in *La voluntad,* whose intellectual career is ruined by marriage.
20. Fernando Ibarra discusses Azorín's shift in attitude toward marriage in relation to Clarín's. He concludes, "En ellos sin duda trabajó con fuerza irresistible la gravitación hispana hacia lo tradicional. Los ardientes iconoclastas de los años mozos han vuelto al redil de las formas tradicionales y estáticas" (1972, 53)
21. Burgos similarly theorized fashion as a temporal marker in her 1922 *El arte de ser mujer:* "La mujer a la moda nos regala el presente, y como éste es tan efímero, ha de encarnarlo en algo efímero. . . . Tal vez la moda nos hace más humanas porque tiene la crueldad de señalarnos el paso del tiempo" (qtd. in Saitz 1990, 173). She also joins Azorín in finding in "los pequeños detalles de la historia y de la vida doméstica" the true history of people. In *La mujer moderna y sus derechos,* Burgos links fashion and the spirit of the Spanish people: "En ella [la moda] hay siempre algo muy importante, muy recóndito, capaz de revelar por sí sólo el alma de una época y el espíritu de un pueblo" (1927, 249). Burgos diverges from Azorín, however, in her interpretation of cross-dressing or the loss of clear gender definition in fashion. Instead of being alarmed by the "mujer peinada a *lo garçon,* con blusa camisero, levita o smoking de corte inglés, sombrero masculino y falda estrecha, de un hombre barbilampiño, con gran cuello de sport y pantalón ancho," she finds that "la moda tiende a igualarlo todo" (262). Fashion erases both class and gender distinctions.
22. Elaine Showalter (1990) analyzes the intersection of sexual issues and a sense of decline at the end of the nineteenth and twentieth centuries.
23. Convents also became targets of criticism for perceived sexual perversions (Balfour 1997, 128).
24. Azorín's interest in houses—domiciles, those spaces in which domestic activity is carried out—is quite remarkable. Think, for example, of the amount of prose devoted in *Doña Inés* (another classical *refundición*) to describing the title character's Segovian home and the daily activities of cleaning and cooking that take place there. In an article on Fernán Caballero, Azorín identified the nineteenth-century novelist as the very first to introduce the house into Spanish literature: "Por primera vez en nuestro arte un escritor siente la casa, se da cuenta de la importancia de la casa, pone su conato en descubrir la casa" (1922c, n.p.). Azorín thought it important that Fernán Caballero lived for a time in a government property under the shadow of

the *alcázar* in Seville, a kind of grace-and-favor abode from Isabel II. He notes that when Isabel was dethroned, Fernán Caballero had to move to a "pobre casita."

Chapter 2

1. Without elaborating on her tantalizing insight, Elena Catena points out that Generation of '98 members' knowledge of the *Quixote* "daría claves esclarecedoras sobre el hecho del renacimiento novelístico en el último tercio del siglo XIX" (1973, 1).
2. For a more detailed account of the differing versions of marriage that Baroja and Azorín present in these novels, see *Crossfire* (Johnson 1993a, 52–53).
3. Elaine Showalter indicates that a popular image in fin-de-siècle Britain was a "Donna Quixote," who, like Don Quixote, lived according to ideas acquired from books; however, "while Don Quixote is bedazzled by chivalric romance, the New Woman has been picking at radical literature" (1995, 12).
4. In a note in her edition of *Una mujer por caminos de España,* Alda Blanco points out the importance of the Quixote figure for Martínez Sierra: "La figura de Don Quijote es clave para María Martínez Sierra. En *Motivos, Gregorio Martínez Sierra* escribe un largo capítulo dedicado a este personaje cuya importancia resume de la siguiente manera: 'Y con la lectura [del *Quijote*] se va despertando una nueva vida en el espíritu del lector" (Blanco 1989, 82 n. 19).
5. Maeztu also published an essay on the *Quixote (Don Quijote o el amor),* later collected in *Don Quijote, Don Juan y la Celestina* (1925).
6. See Harriet S. Stevens, "Las novelitas intercaladas en *Niebla*" (1961) and Gayana Jurkevich, "Unamuno's Anecdotal Digressions" (1992) for detailed analyses of the interpolated stories in *Niebla.*
7. In "The Discourse of Class in *Niebla,*" Thomas Franz labels Uncle Fermín a feminist who asserts that "work is a means to a woman's emancipation" (1995, 526). Franz's article, although primarily about class, makes other points of interest to gender analysis, particularly those related to women, work, and economic matters. His analysis of the laundress Rosario's role is particularly illuminating (531–34). In another one of Franz's articles, "The Philosophical Bases of Fulgencio Entrambomares in Unamuno's 'Amor y Peadgogía'" (1977, 443), he reminds us that in 1902 Unamuno was already registering awareness of feminism in creating the antifeminist Fulgencio Entrambosmares.
8. Franz points out that Unamuno's personal psychology required a traditional family structure: "For Unamuno this moving point of reference was his

family—both wife and children, and the creatures of his pen—who daily reflected the objectified, socially juxtaposed Unamuno back onto the writer in his limited subjective state. To take a single human will, a single noble idea or hope, to lend it objectivity—make it 'other'—and then interact with it so as to multiply and vitalize it into endless variations—'casarse con una grande y pura idea para criar familia de ella'—this was spiritual fatherhood for Unamuno" (1980, 655). Gonzalo Navajas observes, "La familia se percibe como el territorio del amor y el orden que el sujeto no puede alcanzar legítimamente fuera de ella. Esos atributos parecen producirse en la familia desde siempre y su existencia y validez se presentan como incuestionables. La familia es la fortaleza segura que se opone a la destrucción apocalíptica. . . . La tendencia de Unamuno hacia la disrupción no se aplica a la famila. . . . La firmeza familiar se cimienta en una noción convencional del matrimonio. . . . La familia se constituye como un hogar tradicional. La seguridad de ese hogar se origina en la identificación de sus múltiples significados simbólicos" (1988, 116, 117, 123). In *Unamuno contemplativo* (1975), Carlos Blanco Aguinaga includes an entire chapter on "El refugio en la familia," and Juan Rof Carballo calls this aspect of Unamuno's thinking *epidemiología familiar* (1964, 84).

9. Rogelio is, in fact, a poet, who makes his living by his imagination, his writing; Félix is an engineering student, but his imagination and language associate him more with the artistic temperament.

10. Macdonald (1984) reveals that Miró began *Las cerezas del cementerio* in the first person, but for some reason changed the narrative voice to the third person while he kept intact large passages that filter the narrative through Félix's consciousness.

11. James Hoddie (1984) and Francisco Marquéz Villanueva (1972) give more detail on some of the literary intertexts that Miró employs in *Las cerezas del cementerio,* but they do not relate them to a general Mironian tendency to project an image of women through a masculine consciousness and canon.

12. See *Crossfire* (Johnson 1993a, 162–71) for a discussion of Miró's version of *intrahistoria* on the collective Spanish unconscious.

13. Beatriz is related to the moon on numerous other occasions in the novel (see Miró 1991, especially pages 95, 96, 100, 101, 103, 135, 137, 140, 141, 147, and 227). In many of these passages, the sea or other bodies of water are also present. Thus, Beatriz could be associated with the intrahistorical eternal feminine of Unamuno's and Azorín's early writings. She is, however, a less specifically Spanish feminine soul, as she is constructed of more universalizing references.

14. Félix is transformed into a Christ-like martyr through a number of strategies: His father's name is Lázaro, his story roughly follows the Christian

calendar, and the women with whom he associates are Virgen Mary archetypes or Mary Magdalenes.

15. As Elizabeth Rojas Auda points out, "Concha Espina relaciona la vida primitiva de la región maragata con la explotación de la mujer" (1998, 53). Rojas Auda goes so far as to give *La esfinge maragata* a feminist interpretation; she says that it shows women "doblegada hacia el yugo de la costumbre" and denounces "la situación de la mujer en la sociedad que la forma y la condiciona." In this sense, the "mujer maragata" is "emblemática de la mujer española" (57).

16. Rojas Auda also aligns Mariflor with modernity: "Mariflor en su actuar, con su independencia y sus modales pertenece completamente a la época moderna" (1998, 59). Thus, she stands apart from all the other women in the novel. I disagree with Rojas Auda's conclusion, however. She believes that the novel's ending represents a defeat and sacrifice on Mariflor's part (64), whereas I interpret Mariflor's action as a free and potentially liberating choice. Her marriage to the pragmatic cousin not only liberates her economically; it frees her of quixotic male visions in her marriage to the pragmatic cousin.

17. Martínez Sierra's view of marriage changed over time, doubtless reflecting her disillusionment with her own marriage. As Alda Blanco points out, in Martínez Sierra's 1917 essay "Maternidad," the author "caracterizaba el matrimonio como una institución esclavista" (1989, 18–19).

18. The connection between Martínez Sierra's relationship with Gregorio and the main characters in this novel is evidenced in her comment in *Gregorio y yo* that as a young girl she imagined herself as a professor's wife and helpmate to her husband in his work (1953, 22).

19. There was, for example, the sad case of Emilia Pardo Bazán who was named to a professorship at the University of Madrid, but no students attended her classes. The Menéndez Pidals were the epitome of this kind of collaboration and could well have been the model, in addition to the Martínez Sierras, for the couple in *El amor catedrático*. If Ramón Menéndez Pidal's wife, María Goyri (1873–1955), had written novels, she would be included in this study. She was the beneficiary of Krausist instigated education for women and was one of the first women to study Philosophy and Letters at Madrid's Central University (1892–93), where she was prohibited from speaking to other students in order to avoid "disorder." She entered a doctoral program in 1895 and married Ramón Menéndez Pidal in 1900. Ramón went on to become one of Spain's best-known medieval philologists. María and Ramón collaborated on their philological research, and María published some books under her own name. Even so, like María Martínez Sierra, she never emerged from her famous husband's shadow, and she is rarely mentioned as a medievalist of note.

20. Juan Ramón Jiménez is a likely model for Teófilo, as he was for the poet in *Tú eres la paz.* This identical situation—a woman's preference for an older, more traditional man over a younger one with progressive ideas about women—is repeated in Ramón Pérez de Ayala's *Tigre Juan y El curandero de su honra,* which I discuss in Chapter 5.
21. Many years later, Ortega y Gasset's last book, *Man and People,* critiques the generic term "humanity" or "human being." He tells of meeting an American woman who took umbrage at his treating her like a lady. He quips, "Evidently Lincoln had not struggled to win the War of Secession in order that I, a young Spaniard, could permit myself to treat her like a woman. In the United States of that time women were so modest that they thought there was something better than 'being a woman.'" The woman insisted that he talk to her as if she were a human being; his response was that he was not acquainted with this person she called a "human being"; he knew only "men" and "women." He attributes her "mistake" to having gone to "some college where she had suffered the rationalistic education of the time, and rationalism is a form of intellectual bigotry which, in thinking about reality, tries to take it into account as little as possible. In this case, it had produced the hypothesis of the abstraction 'human being'" (1957, 129).
22. This description of a woman via geometrical forms is clearly related to cubist technique in painting and literature. There are similar descriptions in novels by Jarnés—*El profesor inútil, El convidado de papel* (1928), and *Paula y Paulita*—as well as in Salinas's *Víspera del gozo* (1926). Azorín's playful geometrical portrait has a dimension not present in other vanguard novels, however, since the woman he is describing has a specific, identifiable social function as secretary of a club for intellectually inclined women.
23. See John Cruickshank (1974) for a more complete description of the development of Constant's thought and his relationships with his female interlocutors. For example, Cruickshank quotes a letter to Récamier in which the French thinker declared that he wanted Récamier to take complete control of his faculties in order to benefit France and enhance his fame.

Chapter 3

1. Arturo Ramoneda Salas provides a list of parodies of the classic versions of the Don Juan theme that appeared in the latter half of the nineteenth century and the early years of the twentieth century (unfortunately, without their dates of publication). Included in his list is *Doña Juana Tenorio* by R. María Liern and *Tenorio feminista* by Paso y Servet (1989, 503).
2. Maeztu published his essay on Don Juan in 1925 but his position on

Spanish nationalism and the Spanish literary tradition did not change from those that he expressed at the turn of the century. According to E. Inman Fox, even though Maeztu's politics shifted radically over the course of those twenty-five years (from socialism to conservatism), his ideas on classic literary figures remained constant (1977, 41–42).

3. Genara Pulido Tirado (1998) relates Maeztu's ideas on Don Juan as brute, instinctive energy to Friedrich Nietzsche's notion of the superman. Pulido Tirado also draws useful parallels between Maetzu and José Ortega y Gasset on the meaning of Don Juan as a national symbol.

4. Leda Schiavo (1989, 9) notes that fragments of the *Sonatas* appeared in newspapers and magazines from 1892 on.

5. Corpus Barga evinced a similar notion in a 1925 essay: "Lo esencial de Don Juan, no es lo que tiene de parecido a los hombres felices con las mujeres; es, claro está, lo que le distingue de ellos. Don Juan es el espíritu de desafío (la apuesta de Don Juan), capaz de atreverse a lo más terrible, que, en la moral mamífera, es mancillar a la mujer, a la familia. Don Juan es el desafío a la sociedad católica y a Dios" (1925a, 380).

6. The dates of publication of the *Sonatas* do not conform to the chronology of the life of the protagonist. *Sonata de primavera,* which records the earliest phase, was published third; *Sonata de estío,* chronicling the next period, was published second. *Sonata de otoño,* which narrates the Marqués's middle age, was published first; *Sonata de invierno,* which records the end of the Marqués's career as a Don Juan, was published last.

7. Those who have branded him as evil incarnate include Gerard C. Flynn, citing his "ethic of the bagatelle" as "diabolical" (1961, 120). Flynn fails to recognize that every time Bradomín is labeled *diablo* or *satanás* in the narratives, it is in a statement made about him by another character, usually by a woman in an extreme situation—such as one involving hysteria or death. Flynn (1962) compares Giacomo Casanova and Bradomín to highlight Bradomín's evil nature against Casanova's less morally objectionable one. Completely ignoring Flynn's article, which she does not cite, Barbara Terry (1967) finds numerous parallels between the details of the life that Casanova narrates in his memoirs and Bradomín's. In so doing, she counters the portrayal of Bradomín as a heartless Don Juan. She believes that Bradomín, like Casanova, is capable of love and is much less callous toward women than is Don Juan. In a more recent study, Ignacio-Javier López argues that despite Bradomín's cynicism and satanic qualities (manifested most prominently in *Sonata de primavera*), he possesses genuine religious sentiments. Thus, for López, "a pesar de lo que el Bradomín que escribe quiere hacer creer al lector, el que protagoniza la acción de la novela tiene un sustrato religioso, todo lo confuso que se quiera, y su satanismo y donjuanismo son mera

infatuación" (1986, 146). What makes Bradomín so compelling is that he has all and none of these characteristics. Valle-Inclán has created a modern character by grafting the turn-of-the-century amoral dandy onto a more traditional satanic Don Juan. As Verity Smith has observed, "Valle makes of his 'viejo dandy' a living symbol of the passing of an age and an expression of the author's personal nostalgia and grief at the decay of a society as he himself has visualized it'" (1964, 350).

8. For studies on aspects of the Marqués's self-construction, see Spires 1988 (35–47); Valis 1989; Epps 1993; and Loureiro 1993.

9. The complex narrative strategies in *Sonata de otoño* have given rise to a great deal of critical commentary. See especially Alberich 1965, Gulstad 1970–71, M. Predmore 1988, and Spires 1988.

10. See López 1986 (77–116) for detailed discussions of Don Juan figures in *La Regenta* and *Fortunata y Jacinta*.

11. See Capel Martínez 1986 and Perinat and Marrades 1980 for discussions of the social constraints placed on women in late nineteenth- and early twentieth-century Spain. Geraldine Scanlon argues that women's chastity was so important that a girl who had only one sexual encounter had no recourse (usually forced by male members of her household) but to become a prostitute (1976, 107). Margarita Nelken observes that "las prostitutas de las clases más bajas provienen en su mayor parte de ambientes campesinos y han acudido a la ciudad para ser muchachas de servicio. Muchas de ellas son víctimas del 'donjuanismo chulesco' que 'hace considerar como acto de bravura 'hacerle una barriga' a una muchacha" (n.d., 142).

12. See Vásquez Recio 1998 (382) for a complete bibliography of de los Ríos's essays on Don Juan.

13. Reyes Lázaro goes much farther; she relates *Las hijas de Don Juan* to Spanish national romanticism at the turn of the century and thus to Castilianocentric ideas of the Generation of '98. She points especially to the romantic views and characterization of the protagonist, Juan Fontilures, as having lost the legendary qualities of the classic Don Juans. His name "fuente o manantial de lo ibérico . . . lo unge como lo intrahistoricamente castizo" (1966, 472) She notes that he is superior to modern, decadent Don Juans (one presumes the Marqués de Bradomín) in being immoral rather than amoral.

14. Corpus Barga commented that a Don Juan with a wife would be better suited to a Pedro Muñoz Seca play: "Don Juan era del sexo masculino; de estado, soltero; de cuerpo sano y de espíritu extraordinario; lo que le llevó a morir de muerte sobrenatural" (1926, n.p.). In another male modernist version of the Don Juan figure, Serafín and Joaquín Álvarez Quintero put quite a different twist on the bourgeois Don Juan. Their play *Don Juan,*

buena persona casts Don Juan as a lawyer who gives money and other help to women with whom he has been involved. He eventually falls in love and marries in quintessentially bourgeois fashion. The play, like Unamuno's novels that incorporate the Don Juan theme, militates in favor of traditional male-female roles and marriage. The Álvarez Quintero brothers directly connect marriage and child rearing with the health of the nation: "¡Hay que dar ciudadanos a la patria!" (1918, 106), says a character at the end of *Don Juan, buena persona*. The message directly conveys that espoused by such politicians as Francisco Pi y Margall in the 1869 conference on women's education, whose lecture stated that the mission of women in society was not to be *literatas* but to be mothers (see Capel Martínez 1986, 119).

15. Nieves Vásquez Recio argues convincingly that *Las hijas de don Juan* bears an antimodernist message ("testimonio antimodernista" [1998, 388]). In this aspect of the novelette, de los Ríos could be alluding to Valle-Inclán, whose lifestyle and early prose were quintessentially *modernista*.

16. Nancy Chodorow (1978) theorizes female psychological development in terms of women's continuing identification with the mother, which contrasts with a male psychology that is marked by separation from the mother. She postulates that women's ongoing maternal attachment prompts women to approach life as a series of relationships, whereas men's lives are defined by independence and detachment.

17. Sander Gilman (1985) discusses the common view in fin de siècle Vienna that prostitution was inherent in some women, who were led into the profession by their lascivious natures. It is not unlikely that such views were held in other European countries as well. There was a widespread tendency to overlook economic necessity and the role that highly restrictive sexual practices and lack of birth control measures for "honest women" (married and unmarried) played in creating a demand for paid sex.

18. For discussions of artistic representations of women in fin de siècle Europe, see Pierrot 1981; Dijkstra 1986; Apter 1991; Charnon-Deutsch 1990a, 1990b; and Showalter 1990. Note, however, that these studies (except for Lou Charnon-Deutsch's) do not address the particular Spanish context, and note the extent to which the tendencies that they discuss are secondhand and diluted when they appear in Spain.

19. Ethnic or racial determinism is a philosophical position that unites male and female Spanish writers of the early twentieth century. Both were deeply influenced by Charles Darwin's and Hippolyte-Adolphe Taine's theories. Vásquez Recio (1998, 395) points out that genetic determination is an important theme of de los Rios's *Las hijas de don Juan*, and later chapters demonstrate that some of Burgos's novelettes similarly ally her with Unamuno, Baroja, and Azorín on inherited national characteristics.

20. The Marqués de Bradomín's narration is singularly reluctant to give voice to women. The four *Sonatas* have many passages in which the Marqués interrupts women's attempts to tell their stories or in which women's conversation is relegated to background murmuring (noise). See Ciplijauskaité 1987 for a discussion of this phenomenon, although not specifically in reference to the *Sonatas*.
21. Espina, however, was much less criticized for her independent lifestyle. Shirley Mangini (2001, 55–66) summarizes Rafael Cansinos-Asséns's unfavorable (to Burgos) comparison of the two. He even went so far as to point out that Espina's daughter was more respectable than Burgos's.
22. Gabriel Miró's Félix in *Las cerezas del cementerio* is another example in which a male character is endowed with both Quixote-like and Don Juan–like qualities. These hybrids become further refined in the Don Juans created by Unamuno and Azorín in the 1920s. These figures are stripped of their donjuanesque carnality and are endowed instead with quixotic spiritual qualities.
23. See Alberich (1965) on Bradomín's language as a parody of earlier literary styles.
24. For more details of Burgos's unconventional life, see Concepción Núñez Rey (1989). See also Starcevic (1976); Bieder (1992); Wood (1999–2000); and Mangini (2001).
25. Maryellen Bieder (1996) points out that the Pérez Blanco figure has certain characteristics in common with the novelist Pío Baroja: the headgear designed to cover baldness, the plaid robe and slippers. In addition, note that the name Pérez Blanco bears Baroja's initials and that *La entrometida* could be a response to Baroja's *El mundo es ansí* (published twelve years earlier) in which a male narrator edits the intimate letters and diary of the female protagonist, Sacha, and in which feminists are subjected to a bashing. I am indebted to Maryellen Bieder for supplying me with a copy of *La entrometida*, which has not been republished since its 1924 appearance in *La Novela Corta*.
26. Judith Kirkpatrick skillfully analyzes the authorial-patriarchal relationships between Pérez Blanco and Clarisa. She concludes, however, that Clarisa "remains trapped within the male fiction" (1992, 69), whereas I believe that Clarisa has achieved a measure of autonomy.
27. María Martínez Sierra also refers to feminism in her play *Don Juan de España* (see G. Martínez Sierra 1921), which includes a concise history of the Don Juan figure in the literary tradition and foretells some of the modernist versions. For example, a beggar calls Don Juan "Hermano Juan" (one year before Azorín used the same epithet and eight years before Unamuno did so, but Martínez Sierra's monkly nickname is much more ironic). He

is also called "El santo" with equal irony (185). Although the play ends, as does Zorrilla's, with the seduced woman praying for Don Juan's salvation, the feminist element is evident in speeches such as the following:

> Don Juan–*Sonriendo.* ¿Os pesa ser mujer?
> Casilda—¡Sí, puesto que hay hombres en el mundo! (111)

Like Valle-Inclán's Marqués de Bradomín, Martínez Sierra's Don Juan is older at forty than his classic prototypes. Her domestication of him goes beyond the serious condemnation of his amorality that we observed in de los Ríos, Casanova, and Espina.

28. In an early review of the novel, P. Romero Mendoza complained that Azorín had abandoned the essence of Don Juan, the legendary conqueror. Romero Mendoza prefers the Don Juan "gallardo, atrevido, escéptico, mujeriego, fanfarrón, insolente," whom he considers "pintado [por] la musa del pueblo" (qtd. in Martínez Cachero 1960, 123).

29. Ana Sofía Pérez-Bustamante Mourier places Azorín's *Don Juan* within the context of Maeztu's and Ortega's ideas on Don Juan as an emblematic national figure whose literary reworkings reflect the periods in which they are written. She argues that Azorín's novel parallels the author's own evolving view of his country's problems and their solution—here, a contemplative, beneficent national symbol. She points out that the most positive female figure is the maternal Virgin Mary (1998, 452) and the most negative a modern, seductive Parisian (458).

Chapter 4

1. Carlos Longhurst notes that Sacha's Russian background might have been inspired by the wedding of one of Baroja's friends to a Russian woman: "For it is well known that in 1909 Baroja was best man at his friend Paul Schmitz's wedding to a Russian woman in the Orthodox chapel in Biarritz, and the description of the wedding appears in the first chapter of the prologue" (1977, 70).

2. Carmen published one novelesque work, *Martinito, el de la Casa Grande* (1942). Another example of a Spanish Judith Shakespeare is Azorín's youngest sister, Amparo, who left the manuscript of her novel about a lonely woman named Soledad. Amparo did not publish the novel, she said, because she feared her brothers' derision. (The manuscript can be consulted in the Casa-Museo Azorín in Monóvar in Alicante Province.)

3. *El mundo es ansí* has received extensive critical commentary, much of which

focuses on its philosophical message (see, for example, Rodgers 1972) or its complex narrative devices (see, for example, Longhurst 1977).

4. Longhurst (1977, 72) considers this narrator to be Baroja's professional mask, but the editor is but one more voice in the overall heteroglossia of the novel. For example, the "implied author" provides an ironic view of this narrator/editor whose prurient interest in the story and particular slant on it are all too evident. Later, Longhurst asserts that "there is . . . a profound connection between author and fictional protagonist" (97). Anne Robinson Taylor's (1981) theory that male authors choose female protagonists as a mask for their own vulnerable position as authors and weaker members of a masculine society does not seem to apply in the case of any of the three male writers discussed in this chapter.

5. This narrative situation leads Longhurst to conclude that "Sacha is at bottom an aesthete, making up for her emotional shallowness by cultivating a sensitivity for nature and for words" (1977, 45).

6. Pío's nephew Julio Caro Baroja, a generation younger than his uncle, revealed an attitude toward Don Juan more akin to that of the women writers who treat the Don Juan figure: "No hay más que una solución. Don Juan es un arquetipo literario, basado en una sociedad: la del antiguo régimen. Su figura se deshace si dejan de existir las convicciones y convenciones sociales y religiosas que se dieron cuando se creó (1978, n.p.).

7. Unamuno similarly associated handwork with an insipid character in women; he especially disliked embroidery, which he characterized as "esos hórridos bordados en realce que tan reveledores son del característico mal gusto de nuestras mujeres" (1958, 7:651). For him, true art could not include this kind of work: "Estarán mejor o peor hechos, con ese primor de ejecución que no es sino destreza chinesca, pero carecen de sentido estético" (7:651–52).

8. Emilia Doyaga mentions the feminine context in her introduction and gives a number of quotations on the feminist movement from Unamuno's works but does not fully integrate these insights into interpretations of individual novels. María-Elena Bravo affirms that Unamuno's *La tía Tula* is much better understood in the context of feminist debates (1989, 138).

9. See Ribbans 1986 for an account the composition of *La tía Tula* and the novel's early origins. Geoffrey Ribbans reproduces "La tía," a 1902 manuscript version, in its entirety.

10. Ricardo Gullón, interprets *Dos madres* in a rather different way. He sees Berta's arrangement as the diabolical one, a selling of her soul, as it were: "Su hijo será el precio que está dispuesta a pagar por el alma de la otra. Negocio diabólico, en el objeto y en la causa; el diablo compra un alma,

pero no en forma clásica, directa, sino invirtiendo los papeles y presentándose como vendedor" (1961b, 46).

11. One exception might be Ossorio's relationship with his sexually perverse Aunt Laura, which is the immediate (if not ultimate) cause of his nervous exhaustion.

12. Ribbans argues forcefully for a philosophical interpretation of the novel that would see it as no different from Unamuno's novels with male protagonists: "*Como en las demás novelas agónicas, las raíces de su actuación son ontológicas y cae relacionarlas con dos afirmaciones teóricas de primera importancia: la necesidad de hacerse insustituibles que Unamuno articula en* Del sentimiento trágico *y la función primordial de la voluntad proferida en el* Prólogo *a las* Tres novelas ejemplares" (1987, 404, emphasis in original). Dennis Hannan, similarly argues for a philosophical interpretation: "El encasillar a Unamuno entre los precursores del existencialismo francés ha llegado a ser casi una tradición aunque se han notado también discrepancias importantes. Quisiera señalar yo que en este caso la lucha consigo misma de Gertrudis, a pesar de su fe ortodoxa, se acerca a la lucha consabida de los existencialistas por ser 'auténticos'—es decir, por encararse con su situación existencial" (1971, 299). Gullón considers Tula's ontological "sin" her "tentación de igualarse al Creador" (1964, 217).

13. Lynette Hubbard Seator asserts (I believe erroneously) that *no* woman in Unamuno's novels would be capable of posing the kinds of existential questions that Juan asks in *Dos Madres:* "Raquel reduces Juan to the condition of a child; yet as a rational child he must ask the crucial question. What did his life mean? (No woman in Unamuno's novels would be capable of posing such a question.)" (1980, 47). Seator's observation may hold true for most of Unamuno's novels, in which the female characters are not protagonists, but Tula certainly does engage in an existential quest. In the case of *Dos madres,* to which Seator primarily refers, however, neither Raquel nor Berta achieves such depth of personal inquiry.

14. Interestingly, in the unpublished 1902 version "La tía," the main character has none of the negative qualities that she manifests in the 1920 version. She has not manipulated her sister and Ramiro, and she cares for her sister's children as a charitable act, without the domineering and sinister overtones of the final published novel.

15. Feal concludes that Tula's feminist stance makes Unamuno himself a feminist: "Reconocemos aquí un acento que, energicamente, suena en textos feministas contemporáneos. Y me complace señalarlo como prueba (una prueba que añadir a otras posibles) de la actualidad del gran hombre, cuya memoria, a los cincuenta años de su muerte, honramos en esta ocasión" (1988, 77). Thomas Franz similarly finds a feminist message in the novel

through its many parallels to Henrik Ibsen's *Hedda Gabler*. He does, however, believe that "Unamuno eventually weakens his feminist perspective by taking from his protagonist some of the vigorous sexuality, the economically mandated compromises, and the guiltless will-to-power that Ibsen had given to Hedda" (2000, 6). Laura Hynes (1981) equates many of Tula's stands as conforming to those of contemporary radical feminists such as Shulamith Firestone, Jeffner Allan, Ann Oakley, and Andrea Dworkin, who advocate the elimination of biological motherhood. Faciencia Ortañón de Lope, however, opines that "el significado de *La tía Tula* se antoja poco claro en una primera lectura. Por la defensa que se hace de la mujer frente a la tiranía masculina, podría parecer una obra feminista. Gertrudis se rebela ante la condición de la hembra como ser social" (1986, 385). Matías Montes Huidobro, wavers. He states early on, "Interpretado el asunto de este modo [Tula's interpretation of marriage as for procreation only], lo que Tula hace es dar un paso atrás con respecto a los derechos de la mujer" (1984, 236). However, by the end of the article, he gives her a more feminist cast: "El feminismo de Tula se pone de manifiesto en su irritabilidad ante la caracterización que el hombre ha hecho de la luna, ofensiva a la condición de la mujer" (246).

16. Francisco Javier Díez de Revenga argues that the novel removes Inés from historical time to focus on the passage of time: "Su alma femenina se ve mediatizada más que por el ambiente, tan sabiamente captado, tan documentalmente creado, más que por los personajes que hay en su derredor, más que por la sociedad en la que vive, por su tiempo y por su inexorable paso" (1998, 478). I propose here that Azorín is dissecting contemporary (early twentieth-century) social mores alongside his philosophical concern with time as an abstract notion.

17. See Pieropán 1989 for such a reading.

18. Numerous other passages are deployed in the same way. They begin by mentioning Doña Inés's presence but immediately assume an objective descriptive viewpoint; see, especially, Chapters 8, 9, 17, 24, 27, and 37.

19. I disagree with Antonio Risco, who writes that Azorín "se opone decididamente a semejante imagen complementaria para ofrecernos a la mujer en su mismidad e independencia, dueña de sí, rica en recursos e ideas, propias e inteligentes" (1982, 173).

20. Kathleen Glenn (1990) argues convincingly that women are mostly art objects in Azorín's works.

21. Risco also calls the novel feminist. He points out that Azorín avoids women characters as mothers: "Así se afirma otra vez con valentía el feminismo de *Azorín*, al proponernos modelos de mujeres libres de tales servidumbres orgánicas" (1982, 174).

Chapter 5

1. Nash provides details of the means employed by the medical profession in its bid for influence on gender roles: "In the 1920s prestigious medical forums such as the *Sociedad Ginecológica Española,* the *Academia Nacional de Medicina,* and medical publications such as *El Siglo Médico,* systematically presented a medical discourse that attempted to influence gender patterns and cultural values. As in Europe, the politics of motherhood was a key construct in the modernization of social welfare and health services in Spain" (1999, 33). Nash stresses how powerful these arguments were in shaping social practices: "Challenging the modern redefinition of gender roles meant contesting the scientific basis for modernity while also engaging with traditional religious canons . . . a steep challenge indeed for Spanish women" (35).
2. See Paraíso (1998) for an overview of Marañón's many writings on Don Juan during his long career. Paraíso does not, however, mention the similarity of his ideas to those of Pérez de Ayala.
3. See Macklin 1980b (25–27) for a more complete exposition of Pérez de Ayala's ideas on Don Juan's sexuality and their debt to German thinkers. Macklin does not mention the Marañón connection.
4. Marañón quoted Pérez de Ayala in "Notas para la biología de Don Juan," remarking that the novelist distinguished between men who have many women for pleasure or peccadillo and the true Don Juan, who embodies a diabolical element. Women surrender body and soul to the true Don Juan with full knowledge of his diabolical nature or even because of it: "Entonces sí: se trata del Don Juan prístino, imperecedero y diabólico" (qtd. in Marañón 1924a, 37).
5. J. J. Macklin (1980b) mentions Marañón in relation to this novel only to point out that, through Marañón, Pérez de Ayala would have had contact with contemporary psychological theory, especially Carl Jung. Miguel Ángel Lozano Marco (1990, 36–37) discusses the interrelation between Pérez de Ayala's extranovelistic writings on Don Juan and Marañón's essays on the legendary figure without a detailed analysis of Marañón's presence in *Tigre Juan.*
6. Macklin (1980b, 25–30) interprets *Tigre Juan y El curandero de su honra* as developing Pérez de Ayala's own ideas on Don Juan set forth in the essays in *Las máscaras* (1963d), whereas I see the always ironic and complex Pérez de Ayala as parodying Marañón's extreme biological interpretation of those ideas. For example, in "Sobre feminismo: La metáfora antropomórfica en sociología," Pérez de Ayala argues against applying "determinismo biológico" to society in general (1929c, 212).
7. Both J. J. Macklin (1980b) and Magdalena Cueto Pérez (1980) mention

the dualities in Tigre Juan's character, but neither notes the important male/female polarity that he embodies.

8. Here Colás's role is identical to that of Teófilo in María Martínez Sierra's *El amor catedrático*. The woman spurns the less misogynist younger man, who espouses feminist ideas, in favor of an older *machista*. Because María signed the name Gregorio Martínez Sierra to the novel, Pérez de Ayala may have felt more comfortable taking it as a model than he would have if she had signed her own name.

9. Cueto Pérez (1980, 101) draws a parallel between the "feminoid" Vespasiano and Doña Iluminaca's dead husband.

10. Carlos Feal (1984, 78) observes that the Don Juan figure Vespasiano, instead of promoting Herminia to womanhood, maintains her in childlike status. As I show later, Tigre Juan's patriarchalism does little to advance her independence either.

11. Prostitution is a metaphor that Pérez de Ayala calls upon in other novels to make significant social points. Consider especially the role of Rosina in *Tinieblas en las cumbres* (1907) or that of Verónica in *Troteras y danzaderas* (1913). Ideas in Spain are decaying, prostituted: "—Usté es joven; el mundo en [sic] ancho. En este país las ideas están viejas, caducas, deterioradas, prostituidas todas ellas. Hasta las ideas de más respetable traza son alcahuetas de algún propósito incecente. Vaya usté con su compañera a un país lejano, de ideas vírgenes, donde el sol de verdad no sea satélite del negro orbe de la mentira, sino centro de gravitación de las almas" (1990, 269).

12. To his credit, Pérez de Ayala was genuinely concerned about the atrociously backward sex education in Spain. His novel *Trabajos de Urbano y Simona* (1923) details the disastrous results of a marriage between sexually ignorant youths. The sex education that he advocates in that novel takes place within the confines of traditional marriage and conventional roles for men and women.

13. Interestingly, toward the end of Miguel Primo de Rivera's dictatorship, Pérez de Ayala equated feminism and dictatorial government (1929a, 209). He also argued that women may make men (in biological terms), but "la historia la hacen los hombres" (1929c, 213).

14. I include Unamuno's play in this book on fiction, because it is an important response to Marañón's ideas and because it can be argued that Unamuno's theater is more to be read than performed.

15. Cascardi singles out Don Juan's meeting with the stone guest (the statue of the dead *comendador*, as demonstrating "the consciousness that Hegel would ascribe to the noble-spirited soul, to the master, that is to the one who seeks above all the certification of his honor in the recognition of another" (1988, 156).

16. Ortega y Gasset also elicited Don Juan as a philosophical example in his

meditations on vital reason. For Ortega y Gasset, Don Juan represents a revolt against traditional reason, and he enlists him as proof that life must be reincorporated into abstract reason. Don Juan's attraction for the modernist mind-set, which is constantly refining and polishing the legend's image "hasta dotarla de un sentido preciso," is that he turns against morality "porque la moral se había antes sublevado contra la vida." Ortega y Gasset believed that only if a substantial ethics existed "con la plenitud vital," would Don Juan be able to submit himself to it, but that would mean a new culture, a biological culture (1966b, 178).

Corpus Barga evinced a similar sentiment with specifically nationalistic purposes: "Lo esencial de Don Juan, no es lo que tiene de parecido a los hombres felices con las mujeres; es, claro está, lo que le distingue de ellos. Don Juan es el espíritu de desafío (la apuesta de Don Juan) capaz de atreverse a lo más terrible, que, en la moral mamífera, a la mancillar a la mujer a la familia. Don Juan es el desafío a la sociedad católica y a Dios" (1925a, 380).

17. Spain gained important economic benefits from the war, especially a spurt of industrialization. As mentioned in the Introduction, many women entered the workforce in Spain between 1914 and 1918.

18. Susan Cavallo (1993, 177 n. 6) notes the respect that Marañón's role in the feminist movement garnered him from feminists like Burgos. Cavallo interprets *Quiero vivir mi vida* as embracing Marañón's ideas less ambivalently than I do.

19. Maryellen Bieder aptly calls what Burgos does with Marañón's ideas "put[ing them] into play" (2001, 258). Burgos is also very likely alluding to Unamuno's Tía Tula, who embodies male and female characteristics. Like Tula, Isabel (the protagonist of *Quiero vivir mi vida*) rejects biological motherhood and eventually sex and has a sister named Rosa who is much more traditionally feminine than she.

20. According to Nash (1999, 41) Lucía Sánchez Saornil, cofounder of the anarchist Mujeres Libres, was the only feminist willing to openly challenge Marañón's ideas on gender, which she did in a series of articles in *Solidaridad Obrera* published in the early 1930s. Nash points out that Sánchez Saornil especially argued against Marañón's use of biological reproduction to define women.

21. Mario Parajón (1972) compares *Memorias de Leticia Valle* to Sartre's *Les Chemins de la liberté*.

22. She differed with Beauvoir on a number of points, however. For example, she counters Beauvoir's derision of women's "thinking with the glands" (1994) by responding that one can think quite well with the glands.

23. Chacel rejected the feminist label (Mangini 2001, 152), but she had strong,

independent female role models in her family, and the positions that she deploys in her novels and essays can certainly be interpreted as feminist.
24. See Johnson 1993a (91–92) for a discussion of the polemic between Unamuno and Ortega y Gasset over personalism in art.
25. Reyes Lázaro links Chacel's view of the will to that of members of the Generation of '98, especially Unamuno, and demonstrates that her notion of the will contradicts that of Ortega y Gasset: "Chacel rechaza doblemente lo que percibe como inconsecuente falta de voluntad confesional de su mentor" (1993, 66). Carol Maier situates *Las memorias de Leticia Valle* as "the result of an attempt to create 'un fantasma' for Ortega" (1992, 82).
26. Chacel, whose Republican sympathies were demonstrable in other ways (she served as a nurse in the Republican war effort and wrote for Republican journals), preferred to refer to political issues only very obliquely in her novels. She visited Spain a few times during the Franco years but did not return permanently until 1974, a year before Franco died.
27. Chacel's book on confession may have been inspired by Zambrano's *La confesión. Género literario y método*, first published in México in 1943. Since Zambrano and Chacel occasionally exchanged letters in the 1940s and 1950s, it does not seem unreasonable to conjecture that Chacel knew the book before writing her *La confesión* sometime between 1965 and 1968. The copyright date is 1970, but in the "Preámbulo" to the 1980 edition, she says it was written fifteen years earlier; the date 1968 appears at the end of the text. Chacel follows Zambrano's format, which analyzes the classic confessions of Saint Augustine and Jean-Jacques Rousseau, adding Søren Kierkegaard to the list. Despite Chacel's disclaimers, however, her book is oriented more toward literary criticism, as the largest portion is devoted to a commentary on Miguel de Cervantes, Benito Pérez Galdós, and Miguel de Unamuno, whereas Zambrano's book has a more philosophical quality. Chacel's (and Zambrano's) interest in confession appears to contradict Felski's observation that "the strong Protestant element in the feminist preoccupation with subjectivity as truth in turn explains why the feminist confession appears to be a relatively rare phenomenon within the Catholic and rhetorically conscious French tradition, whereas both the United States and West Germany have seen the development of a vast body of confessional literature in the last fifteen years" (1989, 114).
28. See Susan Suleiman's chapter "A Double Margin: Women Writers and the Avant-Garde in France" (1990, 11–32).
29. See Spires 1988 (35–47) for a discussion of Valle-Inclán's subversion of the confessional genre in *Sonata de otoño*. Chacel joins earlier women writers in resisting the aesthetics and meaning of Valle-Inclán's *Sonatas*.
30. According to Paul Julian Smith, "We have seen none the less, that there is

in Chacel a tension between the assertion of a pre-existing self (outside language and sociality) and the production of a new and singular self (within the constraints of gender, class and 'race')" (1992, 31).
31. Michel Foucault interprets confession as "the transformation of sex into discourse"(1980, 61).
32. I borrow the evocative term "pneumatic aesthetics" from Gustavo Pérez Firmat (1982, 40–65)
33. María Soledad Fernández Utrera analyzes Chacel's integration of nature and reason in *Estación. Ida y vuelta* through the creation of a "subjectividad hermafrodita" (1997, 509).
34. In her 1975 lecture "La mujer en galeras" at the Madrid Ateneo (which is published in *Los títulos* [1981c, 187–218]), Chacel reconfirmed her notion that a woman's knowledge begins in her body (199).
35. Elizabeth Scarlett (1994, 90–92) analyzes *Memorias de Leticia Valle* as an answer to Freud's *Fragment of an Analysis of a Case of Hysteria* (or *Dora*), in which he theorizes homoeroticism as a stage in adolescent development. Scarlett demonstrates convincingly that Leticia's attachments to women, especially to Luisa and her cousin Adriana, may represent this phase. She departs from the Dora model, however, in "her implementation of bodily means to reverse the existing power relationships" (90).
36. Scarlett interprets Leticia's conquest of Don Daniel as Chacel's putting to rest "once and for all the Father's law as represented by Ortega" (1994, 92).

Chapter 6

1. In a groundbreaking article, Janet Pérez (1988–89) lists Rosa María Arquimbau, Carmen de Burgos, Carmen Conde, Rosa Chacel, Ernestina Champourcín, María Teresa León, Carme Montorial i Puig, Elizabeth Mulder, Ana Mùria i Romani, and Mercè Rodoreda as women writers of note in the 1920s and 1930s. She observes that "while few if any of their works are masterpieces ... many are quite well-written, and almost all are of considerable sociological and documentary interest" (1988–89, 41). Fulgencio Castañar (1992, 281–86) adds Rosa Arciniega and Luisa Carnés to the list of women authors whose novels supported elements of the Republican agenda.
2. Robert Spires observes that "in spite of its label 'new art,' the Spanish vanguard movement perpetuated old practices at least as far as gender roles are concerned. Women were limited to being the object of men's gaze and quest" (2000, 220).
3. Robustiana Mújika Tene believed that women were more patriotic than

men: "De la forma que ésta [politics] es consecuencia del pensamiento, el patriotismo es consecuencia de una corazonada, es un amor; y debido a esto casi casi me atrevería a decir que nos corresponde más el patriotismo a las mujeres que a los hombres; porque si el bien de ellos es la inteligencia clara, el amor es el nuestro, es de las mujeres (qtd. in Aguado et al. 1994, 423). As M.U.S. points out in the introduction to the Tene quotation, in Catholic European countries, women employed indirect strategies to escape the domestic sphere, distancing themselves from U.S. and British feminism and adopting the discourse of the dominant gender to achieve their goals.

4. "Hubiera bastado quizá a aquella Europa aún envuelta en su propia falsificación una larga hora de paz, de esa paz que es lo más cerca de que no haya historia: un olvido creador" (Zambrano 1989, 173).

5. Martínez Sierra also drew on the dream analogy when she wrote about her generation's vision of a new political order: "Todos andábamos soñando la vida entre los dieciocho y los veinticinco. El porvenir no parecía ni fácil ni claro. España era una monarquía decadente con rey niño y regente hembra. Dos partidos—liberal y conservador—turnaban pacífica e ineficazmente en el poder procurando no tanto hacer patria e incorporarla al movimiento de material progreso que en el resto de Europa ya se hacía sentir vivamente como frenar el 'carro del Estado' para que no volcase y arrastrase en el vuelco a la dinastía reinante" (1953, 15).

6. Anne Hardcastle makes this point, comparing Burgos's position to that of Judith Butler (2001, 240–41). Maryellen Bieder's analysis of Burgos's thought, however, reminds us that we must acknowledge the remnants of biologism in Burgos's writings (2001, 265). Gabriela Pozzi even avers that Burgos "or at least her textual persona" is "a site where competing and irreconcilable discourses vie for hegemony" (2000, 109).

7. Catherine Davies calls Burgos's novellas "straightforward realist narrative, didactic and unsentimental, [which] reached a wide reading public of mature lower-middle-class or working-class women." She characterizes their purpose as to "provoke reform, to arouse public awareness, and to encourage female solidarity" (1991, 194).

8. See Johnson 1993a for discussions of the Spanish male modernists' quarrels with the older generation of writers, including Juan Valera, Benito Pérez Galdós, and Leopoldo Alas (Clarín).

9. Davies (1998, 135) calls *El veneno del arte* homophobic, but I believe that Burgos's portrayal of alternative gender types in this and other novels is rather more complex than the few examples found in male modernist novels (for example, Baroja's positing the bisexual Laura in *Camino de perfección* as Fernando Ossorio's torment). It is true that there is an element of caricature in *El veneno del arte*'s false world of would-be artists, but Luis's self-

reflection and genuine friendship with María mitigate the caricature. As María Pilar Rodríguez notes, Luis can also be interpreted as opposing bourgeois ideals of rational masculinity (1997, 177). In Luis, Burgos approaches the multifaceted portrayal of homosexuality and/or lesbianism that we find in other European modernists such as Oscar Wilde, Marcel Proust, Thomas Mann, and Virginia Woolf.

10. Rodríguez makes a similar point in her study of the use of space in *El veneno del arte*. She contrasts Luis's mother's palace, in which Luis and his bohemian group are relegated to the inferior parts of the edifice, to the "espacio íntimo y acogedor" (1997, 178) of María's apartment.

11. Nelly Clemessy calls Burgos's position "netamente naturalista" (1983, 44) because she conceives her characters as "productos del medio ambiente y condiciones por él" (44). This may appear to be the case, but the *medio ambiente*, which is social and legal, can be changed.

12. Carmen de Urioste (1983) provides an overview of Burgos's fiction, pointing out that it embodies female protagonists and themes of interest to women. She loosely classifies her novels according to the following subjects: women's lack of education and resulting incapacity to find work; marriage as women's only means of personal, social, or economic development; single women's virginity; maternity; and legal problems (murdering a husband, divorcing, denouncing a criminal husband).

13. Ugarte (1996, 89–94) studies in detail the deleterious effects of the city on the female protagonist, which convert this novel into a modern gothic narrative.

14. Burgos's efforts to secure divorce legislation in Spain finally yielded results in 1932, the year that she died. Although, on the whole, the law brought surprisingly few divorce proceedings, it inspired more petitions for divorce from women than from men. Many obstacles other than the purely legal barriers—including fear of the courts, fear of major life changes, and fear of religious interdictions that claimed that divorced persons would be denied the sacraments—slowed the demand for divorces (for details, see Núñez Pérez 1993, 37–40).

15. Here I concentrate on gender and marriage, but class is also important in Burgos's novels, another element that distinguishes her from her male contemporaries.

16. José María Marco's introduction to *Los anticuarios* is the only article-length piece on this novel. Curiously, he devotes most of the essay to critiquing Burgos's style and novelistic technique, which he reduces to "[el] afán por hallar, bajo la apariencia individual, el *tipo* característico" (Burgos 1989a, 23). In establishing what he considers the heart of her technique—"parejas de términos opuestos y complementarios" (21)—he lists "la relación de Adelina con su marido Fabián; la del matrimonio con sus hijos . . . la

relación entre España, de donde proceden Adelina y Fabián, y Francia, en cuya capital están instalados . . . la relación de lo verdadero con lo falso" (21); however, he does not perceive the intricate relationship that Burgos weaves between these elements.

17. Herlinda Charpentier Saitz dedicates a paragraph (1990, 175–76) to Burgos's literary influence on Gómez de la Serna, demonstrating that as early as 1913, he was borrowing her themes. One of his most blatant imitations is his 1937 "Ella + Ella—Él + Él." Saitz does not note that this is surely a play on Burgos's *Ellas y ellos o ellos y ellas*.

18. Mangini (1995, 30–31) quotes several passages in which Montseny explains what she calls Nelken's tragedy (her failure to achieve the lasting fame that she deserved). Montseny believed that Nelken had switched parties because she did not receive appropriate recognition as a socialist. Her bad luck was to join the Communist Party just when the charismatic Dolores Ibarruri—La Pasionaria—became its undisputed spokeswoman.

19. See Mangini 2001 (204–13) for a more complete biography of Nelken. Her concern with social issues is evident in her 1919 establishment of La Casa de los Niños de España to house illegitimate children and children of working mothers. After fund-raising complications forced Nelken to close the center, the bitter experience moved her in the direction of the Socialist Party, "único capaz de acabar con la miseria que empozoña la vida nacional y dar a España el nuevo rumbo que precisa" (qtd. in Capel Martínez 1991, 164).

20. Bieder does not view Libertad as a positive alternative: "[Nelken's] one unconventional character is also her only rewriting of female gender, but, to regender an earlier assertion, Libertad is also 'a woman's fantasy of a man's desire' for a new woman" (1992, 320). Since Libertad is not always focalized through Luis, and she escapes from Spain and the bourgeois strictures within which Luis lives, I see her as a more independent character. Davies (1991, 198–99) precedes me in this view, reminding us that Libertad refers to herself as a "señorita" for her unmarried state but also as a "señora" who demands respect. Davies, however, believes that class distinctions overshadow any of the novel's messages about gender.

21. Montseny's theory of love is extremely idealistic: "El amor ha de ser siempre superior a nosotros, porque de la superioridad y superación del amor depende la superioridad y superación de la vida futura y de todas las futuras vidas. Y toda mujer y todo hombre habría de rechazar, ha de rechazar, todo amor que no represente en sí mismo y en sus frutos superación" (Montseny 1927a, n.p.).

22. Montseny published a series of articles in *La Revista Blanca* ("En defensa de Clara" [Montseny 1925]) defending Clara's decision to have a child out of wedlock. She argues that love must be absolutely free, "porque poner sobre

el amor una cadena aunque sea de oro es matarlo" (qtd. in García-Maroto 1996, 65).
23. Brigette Magnien notes that in 1932 the novel was reissued with the title *Aurora de España*, a title that she considers "no menos emblemático" than *La virgen prudente* (1997, 21).
24. Elizabeth Rojas Auda studies the contrast between various types of women in *Aurora de España*—especially the old and the new—pointing out that the novel proposes "varios modelos de mujeres" (1998, 68). She calls the old-style woman "arcaica" after Julia Kristeva (61). The new woman, Aurora, is "la mujer autoconsciente" (69), a condition that puts her in the company of Ana María of Martínez Sierra's *Tú eres la paz* and many other female protagonists of the prefeminist and feminist eras.
25. See Johnson 1996b for a more complete discussion of "razón poética."
26. Zambrano's position is doubtless a response to Ortega y Gasset's interest in and emphasis on the place of reason in life *(razón vital)*. For a discussion of the conflicted relationship between Zambrano and her professor and mentor, Ortega y Gasset, see Johnson 1993a (209 n. 18).
27. Martha Nussbaum points out that Spinoza joined Plato, Epicurus, and the Stoics in considering judgments based on emotion to be false (1995, 56).
28. There are echoes of the Generation of '98 concept of *tradición eterna* or *intrahistoria* here that doubtless come from Zambrano's father, Blas Zambrano. Blas Zambrano was steeped in Krausist ideas, which as noted earlier, are compatible with the notion of a "spirit of the people" found in Unamuno and Azorín. (María Zambrano was attracted to many of Unamuno's ideas and attempted to reconcile his irrational approach to philosophical matters with Ortega y Gasset's rationalism.) Her use of an intrahistorical view of the human past must, however, be placed in the context of the Civil War, during which she was writing. It served her political purposes to project a unified view of the Spanish people, especially the "folk" (the working classes) that made up the largest share of the republican armies.
29. Zambrano similarly interprets the "guía" as a literary genre that bridges the gap between the individual and society. The "guía," which she considers a quintessentially Spanish genre, guides "un individuo o a un grupo de hombres determinados a salir de cierta situación, a atravesar ciertos escollos, que acaso reaparecen una y otra vez" (1971, 370).
30. In "La reforma del entendimiento español," Zambrano points out that only is a novel like *Don Quixote* equipped to deal with failure, a subject that traditional philosophy cannot approach (1986b, 93–101). She also wrote a series of articles on Galdós, concentrating particularly on *Misericordia*. See Johnson 1996b for a study of Zambrano's philosophical use of Galdós.
31. For example, in a letter to a friend, Araceli tells of events that she witnessed

under the Vichy regime in France: "Aquí he visto a tantos sufrir y a otros partir para siempre a esos campos de horror (entre ellos un niño de 14 años que vivió con nosotros y una amiga mía después de haber torturado y matado a su marido) que la vida, los hombres y todo me da horror, ha sido terrible y además de nuestro sufrimiento era raro el día que no teníamos que escuchar las desgracias la desgracia del uno o del otro y que después de lo de España nos daba la impresión de que la vida había sido y seguía siendo éso [sic] nada más. He tenido a veces verdadero miedo a la locura" (handwritten letter dated October 8, 1945, currently part of the Zambrano archive housed in the Fundación María Zambrano in Vélez-Málaga, Spain).

32. Araceli Zambrano's cousin Rafael Tomero-Alarcón related to me the information about her marital history and her life during the Second World War in France in a telephone interview on April 1, 1996.
33. Zambrano's novelized autobiography contains a number of theoretical threads, especially about the individual's relation to society and the role of history in shaping human destiny that are useful for analyzing women's fiction of the nationalist period. The autobiography maneuvers between personal and collective history in a narrative way achieved by the female novelists discussed here Zambrano, however, details the historical moment—the years leading up to the Republic—more explicitly.
34. These *delirios* were composed in the mid-1940s, when Zambrano returned to Europe for several years after her mother's death in Paris.

References

Ackelsberg, Martha A. 1991. *Free Women of Spain*. Bloomington: Indiana University Press.
Aguado, A. María, Rosa María Capel, T. González Calbet, Cándida Martínez López, Mary Nash, G. Nielfa, Margarita Ortega, Reyna Pastor, María Dolores Ramos, María X. Rodríguez Galdo, S. Tavera, and M. Ugalde, eds. 1994. *Textos para la historia de las mujeres en España*. Madrid: Cátedra.
Alayeto, Ofelia. 1992. *Sofía Casanova (1861–1958): Spanish Poet, Journalist and Author*. Potomac, Md.: Scripta Humanistica.
Alberich, José. 1965. "Ambigüedad y humorismo en las *Sonatas* de Valle Inclán." *Hispanic Review* 33:360–82.
Alborg, Concha. 1996. "*Una mujer por caminos de España*: La seudoautobiografía de María Martínez Sierra (1874–1974)." *Revista de Estudios Hispánicos* 30:485–95.
Alcalde, Carmen. 1983. *Federica Montseny. Palabra en rojo y negro*. Barcelona: Vergara.
Aldaraca, Bridget A. 1991. *El Ángel del Hogar: Galdós and the Ideology of Domesticity in Spain*. Chapel Hill: University of North Carolina Press.
Álvarez Junco, José. 2001. *Mater dolorosa. La idea de España en el siglo XIX*. Madrid: Taurus.
Álvarez Quintero, Serafín, and Joaquín Álvarez Quintero. 1918. *Don Juan, buena persona*. Madrid: Clásica Española.
Amorós, Amparo. 1992. "Pensamiento poético y filosofía: María Zambrano, el espacio de la reconciliación." In *Estudios sobre escritoras hispánicas en honor de Georgina Sabat-Rivers*. Edited by Lou Charnon-Deutsch, 17–30. Madrid: Castalia.
Andreu, Alicia G. 1982. *Galdós y la literatura popular*. Madrid: Sociedad General Española de Librería.
———. 1992 . "Ramón Pérez de Ayala y el mito de don Juan." *Anales de la Literatura Española Contemporánea* 17:381–94.
Apter, Emily. 1991. *Feminizing the Fetish: Psychoanalysis and Narrative Obsession in Turn-of-the-Century France*. Ithaca, N.Y.: Cornell University Press.

Aranguren, José Luis L. 1963. "La mujer, de 1923 a 1963." *Revista de Occidente* 1–2d epoch:231–43.

Arbeloa, Víctor M., and Miguel de Santiago, eds. 1981. *Intelectuales ante la Segunda República española*. Salamanca, Spain: Ediciones Almar.

Arenal, Concepción. 1869. *La mujer del provenir*. Madrid: Hospicio.

Auerbach, Eric. 1974. *Mimesis: The Representation of Reality in Western Literature*. Translated by Willard R. Trask. Princeton, N.J.: Princeton University Press.

Azorín [José Martínez Ruiz]. 1897. "Crónica." *El País*. January 23.

———. 1905. "Oviedo, las bellas amigas." *ABC*. August 25.

———. 1906a. "Los amigos literarios. Una criada." *Blanco y Negro*. April 21.

———. 1906b. "Unas sombrereras." *Blanco y Negro*. March 10.

———. 1922a. *Don Juan*. Madrid: Caro Raggio.

———. 1922b. "La vida española. Nueva patria." *La Prensa*. April 30.

———. 1922c. "Fernán Caballero." *ABC*. December 4.

———. 1925. "La mujer moderna." *La Prensa*. October 29.

———. 1929. "Concepción Arenal. Ideario." *ABC*. October 15.

———. 1947–54. *Obras completas*. Edited by Ángel Cruz Rueda. Madrid: Aguilar.

———. 1961. *La Generación del 98*. Salamanca-Madrid: Ediciones Anaya.

———. 1962. *Varios hombres y alguna mujer*. Barcelona: Aedos.

———. 1965. *El caballero inactual (Etopeya)*. 2d ed. Madrid: Espasa-Calpe.

———. 1973. *Doña Inés*. Edited by Elena Catena. Madrid: Castalia.

———. 1990a. *Las confesiones de un pequeño filósofo*. Edited by José María Martínez Cachero. Madrid: Espasa-Calpe.

———. 1990b. *Los pueblos*. Edited by Miguel Ángel Lozano. Alicante, Spain: Caja de Ahorros del Mediterráneo.

———. 1991. *Castilla*. Edited by Inman Fox. Madrid: Espasa-Calpe.

———. 1992. *La ruta de don Quijote*. Edited by José María Martínez Cachero. Madrid: Cátedra.

———. 1995. *El alma castellana*. Edited by María Dolores Dobón Antón. Alicante, Spain: Instituto de Cultura Juan Gil-Albert.

Balfour, Sebastian. 1995. "The Loss of Empire, Regenerationism, and the Forging of a Myth of National Identity." In *Spanish Cultural Studies*. Edited by Helen Graham and Jo Labanyi,. 25–31. Oxford, England: Oxford University Press.

———. 1996. "The Lion and the Pig." In *Nationalism and the Nation in the Iberian Peninsula: Competing and Conflicting Identities*. Edited by Clare Mar-Molinero and Angel Smith, 107–17. Oxford, England: Berg.

———. 1997. *The End of the Spanish Empire, 1898–1923*. Oxford, England: Clarendon.

Baroja, Carmen. 1948. *Martinito, el de la Casa Grande*. Barcelona: Editorial Juventud.
———. 1998. *Recuerdos de una mujer de la Generación del 98*. Edited by Amparo Hurtado. Barcelona: Tusquets.
Baroja, Pío. 1902. *Camino de perfección*. Madrid: Hernando.
———. 1906. *Paradox, rey*. Madrid: Hernando.
———. 1908. *La dama errante*. Madrid: Hernando.
———. 1909. *La ciudad de la niebla*. Madrid: Hernando.
———. 1911. *El árbol de la ciencia*. Madrid: Renacimiento.
———. 1934. "Don Juan." *Luz*. March 3.
———. 1990. *El mundo es así*. Edited by José Antonio Pérez Bowie. Madrid: Espasa-Calpe.
Beauvoir, Simone de. 1994. *The Ethics of Ambiguity*. Translated by Bernard Frechtman. N.Y.: Citadel Press.
Behler, Ernst. 1990. *Irony and the Discourse of Modernity*. Seattle: University of Washington Press.
Benjamin, Walter. 1978. *Reflections*. Edited by Peter Demetz. Translated by Edmund Jephcott. New York: Schocken.
Benstock, Shari. 1986. *Women of the Left Bank: Paris, 1900–1940*. Austin: University of Texas Press.
Bernaldo Quirós, C. 1904. "Nueva asociación para la enseñanza de la mujer." *Alma Española*. No. 11. January 17.
Bhabha, Homi K. 1990a. "DissemiNation: Time, Narrative, and the Margins of the Modern Nation." In *Nation and Narration*. Edited by Homi K. Bhabha, 290–322. London: Routledge.
———. 1990b. "Introduction: Narrating the Nation." In *Nation and Narration*. Edited by Homi K. Bhabha, 1–7. London: Routldege.
Bieder, Maryellen. 1992. "Woman and the Twentieth-Century Spanish Literary Canon: The Lady Vanishes." *Anales de la literatura española contemporánea* 17:301–24.
———. 1996. "Self-Reflexive Fiction and the Discourses of Gender in Carmen de Burgos." In *Self-Conscious Art: A Tribute to John Kronik*. Edited by Susan L. Fischer, 73–89. Lewisburg, Pa.: Bucknell University Press.
———. 2001. "Carmen de Burgos: Modern Spanish Women." In *Recovering Spain's Feminist Tradition*. Edited by Lisa Vollendorf, 241–59. New York. Modern Language Association of America.
Blackburn, Simon. 1994. *The Oxford Dictionary of Philosophy*. Oxford, England: Oxford University Press.
Blanco Aguinaga, Carlos. 1956. "La madre, su regazo y el 'sueño de dormir' en la obra de Unamuno." *Cuadernos de la Cátedra de Miguel de Unamuno* 7: 69–84.
———. 1975. *El Unamuno contemplativo*. Barcelona: Laia.

Blanco, Alda. 1989. "Introducción." *Una mujer por caminos de España*, by María Martínez Sierra, 7–46. Madrid: Castalia.

———. 1993. "The Moral Imperative for Women Writers." *Indiana Journal of Hispanic Literatures* 2:91–110.

———. 1998. "A las mujeres de España: The Feminist Essays of María Martínez Sierra." In *Spanish Women and the Essay: Gender, Politics, and the Self*. Edited by Kathleen M. Glenn and Mercedes Mazquiarán de Rodríguez, 75–99. Columbia: University of Missouri Press.

———. 2001. *Escritoras virtuosas: Narradoras de las domesticidad en la España isabelina*. Granada: U of Granada.

Blanco-Belmonte, M. H. 1924. *Homenaje tributado a la excelentísima señora Doña Blanca de los Ríos Lampérez el día 12 de marzo de 1924*. Madrid: Tip. de la "Rev. de Arch., Bibl. y Museos."

Boyd, Carolyn. 1997. *Historia Patria: Politics, History, and National Identity in Spain, 1875–1975*. Princeton, N.J.: Princeton University Press.

Bravo, María Elena. 1989. "Algunos aspectos del problema de la genericidad en *La tía Tula* de Miguel de Unamuno." In *Actas del congreso internacional cincuentenario de Unamuno*. Edited by Dolores Gómez Molleda, 409–16. Salamanca, Spain: Ediciones Universidad de Salamanca.

———. 1994. "Literatura y concienciación de la mujer en España." *Sistema* 123:125–38.

Brennan, Timothy. 1990. "The Longing for National Form." In *Nation and Narration*, ed. Homi K. Bhabha, 44–70. London: Routledge.

Bretz, Mary Lee. 1998. "Margarita Nelken's *La condición social de la mujer en España*: Between the Pedagogic and the Performative." In *Spanish Women Writers and the Essay: Gender, Politics, and the Self*. Edited by Kathleen M. Glenn and Mercedes Mazquiarán de Rodríguez, 100–126. Columbia: University of Missouri Press.

Burgos, Carmen de. 1915. *El abogado*. Los Contemporáneos. No. 340. July 2.

———. 1917a. *Ellas y ellos o ellos y ellas*. Madrid: Imprenta de "Alrededor del Mundo."

———. 1917b. *La rampa*. Madrid: Renacimiento.

———. 1919. *Dos amores*. Novela Corta 180 (June).

———. 1921. *El artículo 438*. Novela Semanal 1, no. 15.

———. 1923. *El extranjero*. Madrid: Publicaciones de la Prensa Gráfica..

———. 1924. *La entrometida*. Novela Corta 292.

———. 1925. *La nostálgica*. Novela Semanal 5, October 10.

———. 1927. *La mujer moderna y sus derechos*. Valencia, Spain: Editorial Sempere.

———. 1931. *Quiero vivir mi vida*. Madrid: Biblioteca Nueva.

———. 1980. *El hombre negro*. Madrid: Emiliano Escolar.

———. 1989a. *Los anticuarios.* Edited by José María Marco. Madrid: Biblioteca Nueva.

———. 1989b. *La flor de la playa y otras novelas cortas.* Edited by Concepción Núñez Rey. Madrid: Castalia.

———. 1990. *Los inadaptados.* Granada, Spain: Biblioteca General del Sur.

Bush, Peter. 1984. "*Montes de Oca:* Galdós's Critique of 1893 *quijotismo.*" *Bulletin of Hispanic Studies* 61:472–82.

Bussy Genevois, Danièle. 1997. "Carmen de Burgos c cómo sacar fuerzas de flaqueza." In *Referencias vivenciales femeninas en la literatura española (1830–1936).* Edited by María José Porro, 123–39. Córdoba, Spain: Universidad de Córdoba.

Butt, John. 1998. "Rage and Idea: Renewal and the Generation of '98." *Times Literary Supplement.* August 7, 4–5.

Camprubí, Zenobia. 1991. *Diario, I. Cuba (1937–1939).* Translated and edited by Graciela Palau de Nemes. Madrid: Alianza Editorial

Carballo, Juan Roí. 1964. "El erotismo en Unamuno." *Revista de Occidente* 7: 71–96.

Capel Martínez, Rosa María. 1991. *El sufragio femenino en la Segunda República española.* Madrid: horas y Horas.

Capel Martínez, Rosa María, et al. 1986. *Mujer y sociedad en España (1700–1975).* 2d ed. Madrid: Ministerio de Cultura, Instituto de la Mujer.

Caro Baroja, Julio. 1978 "Don Juan número treinta." *El País.* February 2.

Carruthers, Kathie. 1972. "Apunte para un estudio de la mujer y el problema de la personalidad en Unamuno." *Reflexión* 2 1.1:105–15.

Casalduero, Joaquín. 1954. "Elementos funcionales de las *Sonatas* de Valle-Inclán." *Clavileño* 5:20–27.

Casanova, Sofía. 1908. *Más que amor.* Madrid: R. Velasco.

———. 1989. *Princesa del amor hermoso.* In *Novelas breves de escritoras españolas, 1900–1936.* Edited by Ángela Ena Bordonoda, 151–94. Madrid: Castalia.

Cascardi, Anthony. 1988. "Don Juan and the Discourse of Modernism." In *Tirso's Don Juan: The Metamorphosis of a Theme.* Edited by Josep M. Solá-Solé and George E. Gingras, 151–63. Washington, D.C.: Catholic University Press.

Castán Tobeñas, José. 1913. *La crisis del matrimonio.* Zaragoza, Spain: Tipografía de P. Carras.

Castañar, Fulgencio. 1992. *El compromiso en la novela de la II República.* Madrid: Siglo Veintiuno.

Castañeda, Paloma. 1994. *Carmen de Burgos "Colombine."* Madrid: Horas y Horas.

Catena, Elena. 1973. "Azorín, cervantista y cervantino. Apuntes para una antología." *Anales Cervantinos* 12:73–113.

———. 1973. "Introducción." *Doña Inés.* Madrid: Castalia.

Cavallo, Susan. 1993. "El femenismo y la novela social española en los años treinta." *Letras Peninsulares* 6:169–78.
Celma Valero, María Pilar. 1991. *Literatura y periodismo en las Revistas del Fin de Siglo. Estudio e índices (1888–1907)*. Madrid: Ediciones Júcar.
Chacel, Rosa. 1930. *Estación. Ida y vuelta*. Madrid: Ulíses.
———. 1931. "Esquema de los problemas prácticos y actuales del amor." *Revista de Occidente* 92:129–80.
———. 1956. "Respuesta a Ortega. La novela no escrita." *Sur* 241:97–119.
———. 1960. *La sinrazón*. Buenos Aires: Lozada.
———. 1970. *La confesión*. Barcelona: EDHASA.
———. 1972. *Saturnal*. Barcelona: Editorial Seix Barral.
———. 1980a. *Alcancía. Ida*. Barcelona: Seix Barral.
———. 1980b. *Alcancía. Vuelta*. Barcelona: Seix Barral.
———. 1981a. *Desde el Amanecer*. Barcelona: Bruguera.
———. 1981b. *Memorias de Leticia Valle*. Barcelona: Bruguera.
———. 1981c. *Los títulos*. Barcelona: EDHASA.
Chambers, Ross. 1991. *Room for Maneuver: Reading Oppositional Narrative*. Chicago: University of Chicago Press.
Charnon-Deutsch, Lou. 1990a. *Gender and Representation*. Philadelphia: John Benjamins Publishing.
———. 1990b. "On Desire and Domesticity in Spanish Nineteenth-Century Women's Novels." *Revista Canadiense de Estudios Hispánicos* 14.3:395–414.
———. 1994. *Narratives of Desire: Nineteenth-Century Spanish Fiction by Women*. University Park: Pennsylvania State University Press.
Chodorow, Nancy. 1978. *The Reproduction of Mothering: Psychoanalysis and the Sociology of Gender*. Berkeley and Los Angeles: University of California Press.
Ciplijauskaité, Biruté. 1987. "La función del lenguaje en la configuración del personaje femenino valleinclanesco." In *Genio y virtuosismo de Valle-Inclán*. Edited by John P. Gabriele, 163–72. Madrid: Orígenes.
Clemessy, Nelly. 1983. "Carmen de Burgos. Novela española y feminismo hacia 1920." *Iris* 4:39–51.
Close, Anthony J. 2000. *Cervantes and the Comic Mind of His Age*. Oxford, England: Oxford University Press.
Corpus Barga. 1924. "Doña Inés y Doña Juana." *El Sol*. August 21.
———. 1925a. "Don Juan y los placeres renanos." *Revista de Occidente* (September): 374–88.
———. 1925b. "Otra Juana de Arco." *El Sol*. June 21.
———. 1926. "Don Juan y los doctores." *El Sol*. December 18.
Criado Miguel, Isabel. 1986. *Las novelas de Miguel de Unamuno*. Salamanca, Spain: Universidad de Salamanca.

Cruickshank, John. 1974. *Benjamin Constant*. Boston: Twayne.
Cueto Pérez, Magdalena. 1980. "El personaje literario. *Tigre Juan y El curandero de su honra.*" In *Homenaje a Ramón Pérez de Ayala*, 91–111. Oviedo, Spain: Universidad de Oviedo.
Davies, Catherine. 1991. "Feminist Writers in Spain Since 1900: From Political Strategy to Personal Inquiry." In *Textual Liberation: European Feminist Writing in the Twentieth Century.* Edited by Helena Forsås-Scott, 192–226. London: Routledge.
———. 1998. "The 'Red Lady': Carmen de Burgos (1867–1932)." In *Spanish Women's Writing, 1849–1996*, 117–36. London: Athlone Press.
de los Ríos, Blanca. 1906. *Tirso de Molina*. Madrid: Bernardo Rodríguez.
———. 1907. *La niña de Sanabria*. Madrid: Idamor Moreno.
———. 1910. *Las mujeres de Tirso. Conferencia leída por su autora en el Ateneo de Madrid el día 16 de marzo de 1910*. Madrid: Bernardo Rodríquez.
———. 1911. *Afirmación de la raza. Porvenir hispanoamericano*. Madrid: Bernardo Rodríguez.
———. 1989. *Las hijas de don Juan. Novelas breves de escritoras españolas, 1900–1936*. Edited by Ángela Eno Bordonada, 67–125. Madrid: Castalia.
Díaz Fernández, José. 1930. *El nuevo romanticismo. Polémica de arte, política y literatura*. Madrid: Editorial Zeus.
———. 1980. *La venus mecánica*. Edited by José Manuel López de Abiada. Barcelona: Laia.
Díaz-Peterson, Resendo. 1984. "*Paz en la guerra* vista por Unamuno." *Revista de Literatura* 46:89–99.
Dicenta, Joaquín. 1904. "Atavismo." *Alma Española* 21:2–3.
Díez de Revenga, Francisco Javier. 1998. "Doña Inés sin don Juan. En torno a *Doña Inés* (1925) de Azorín." In *Don Juan Tenorio en la España de siglo veinte. Literatura y cine*, ed. Ana Sofía Pérez-Bustamante, 477–85. Madrid: Cátedra.
Di Febo, Giuliana. 1976. "Orígenes del debate feminista en España. La escuela krausista y la Institución Libre de Enseñanza (1870–1890)." *Sistema. Revista de Ciencias Sociales* 12:49–82.
Dijkstra, Bram. 1986. *Idols of Perversity*. Oxford, England: Oxford University Press.
Doody, Terrence. 1980. *Confession and Community in the Novel*. Baton Rouge: Louisiana State University Press.
Don Galaor. 1929. "Concha Espina." *Bohemia* (Havana) 21:25, June 23, 44–45.
Doyaga, Emilia. 1969. *Unamuno y la mujer*. Newark, N.J.: Washington Irving Publishing.
Eakin, John Paul. 1992. *Touching the World: Reference in Autobiography*. Princeton, N.J.: Princeton University Press.

Elizalde, Ignacio. 1983. *Miguel de Unamuno y su novelística*. Zarautz, Spain: Caja de Ahorros Provincial de Guipuzcoa.

Enders, Victoria Lorée, and Pamela Beth Radcliff. 1999. "General Introduction: Contesting Identities/Contesting Categories," *Constructing Spanish Womanhood: Female Identity in Modern Spain*. Edited by Victoria Lorée Enders and Pamela Beth Radcliff, 1–24. Albany: State University of New York Press.

Enguídanos, Miguel. 1959. "Azorín en busca del tiempo divinal." *Papeles de Son Armadans* 25:13–32.

Enloe, Cynthia. 1989. *Bananas, Beaches, and Bases: Making Feminist Sense of International Politics*. Berkeley and Los Angeles: University of California Press.

Epps, Brad. 1993. "Recalling the Self: Autobiography, Genealogy, and Death in *Sonata de otoño*." *Journal of Interdisciplinary Literary Studies* 5:147–79.

Espina, Concha. 1916. *Las mujeres del Quijote*. Madrid: Renacimiento.

———. 1929. *La virgen prudente*. Madrid: Renacimiento.

———. 1985. *La niña de Luzmela*. 6th ed. Madrid: Espasa-Calpe.

———. 1989. *La esfinge maragata*. Madrid: Castalia.

Eysteinsson, Astradur. 1990. *The Concept of Modernism*. Ithaca, N.Y.: Cornell University Press.

Feal, Carlos. 1984. *El nombre de don Juan (estructura de un mito literario)*. Amsterdam: John Benjamins.

———. 1988. "Nada menos que toda una mujer: *La tía Tula* de Unamuno." In *Estelas, laberintos, nuevas sendas. Unamuno, Valle-Inclán, García Lorca, La Guerra Civil*. Edited by Ángel Loureiro, 65–79. Barcelona: Anthropos.

Feeny, Thomas. 1985. "More on the Antifeminism of Pérez de Ayala." *Hispanic Journal* 7.1:115–21.

Felski, Rita. 1989. *Beyond Feminist Aesthetics*. Cambridge, Mass.: Harvard University Press.

Fernández Cifuentes, Luis. 1982. *Teoría y mercado de la novela en España del 98 a la República*. Madrid: Gredos.

Fernández Utrera, María Soledad. 1997. "Construcción de la 'nueva mujer' en el discurso femenino de la Vanguardia histórica española *Estación. Ida y vuelta*, de Rosa Chacel." *Revista Canadiense de Estudios Hispánicos* 21:501–21.

Flynn, Gerard C. 1961. "The Adversary Bradomín." *Hispanic Review* 29:120–33.

———. 1962. "Casanova and Bradomín." *Hispanic Review* 30:133–41.

Fortún, Elena [Encarnación Aragoneses Urquijo]. 1939a. *Celia en el colegio*. Madrid: Aguilar.

———. 1939b. *Celia en el mundo*. Madrid: Aguilar.

———. 1939c. *Celia y sus amigos*. Madrid: Aguilar.

———. 1942. *Celia, novelista*. Madrid: Aguilar.

———. 1992. *Celia, lo que dice*. Madrid: Alianza Editorial.

Foster, David W. 1966. "The 'Belle Dame Sans Merci' in the Fiction of Miguel de Unamuno." *Symposium* 20:321–28.
Foucault, Michel. 1980. *The History of Sexuality.* Vol. 1. New York: Vintage.
Fox, E. Inman. 1977. "Estudio preliminar." In *Artículos desconocidos, 1897–1904*, by Ramiro de Maeztu, 7–47. Madrid: Castalia.
———. 1987. *La invención de España.* Madrid: Cátedra.
———. 1991. "Introducción." In *Castilla,* by Azorín. Edited by Inman Fox, 11–77. Madrid: Espasa-Calpe.
———. 1992. *Azorín. Guía a la obra completa.* Madrid: Castalia.
Francos Rodríguez, José. 1920. *La mujer y la política española.* Madrid: Editorial Pueyo.
Franz, Thomas R. 1977. "The Philosophical Bases of Fulgencio Entrambosmares in Unamuno's 'Amor y pedagogía.'" *Hispania* 60:443–51.
———. 1980. "Parenthood, Authorship, and Immortality in Unamuno's Narratives." *Hispania* 63:647–57.
———. 1995. "The Discourse of Class in *Niebla.*" *Revista de Estudios Hispánicos* 29:521–539.
———. 2000. "Ibsen's *Hedda Gabler* and the Question of Feminist Content in Unamuno's *La tía Tula.*" *Anales de la literatura española contemporánea* 25:77–98.
Ganivet, Ángel. 1897. *Idearium español.* Granada, Spain: Viuda e Hijos de Paulino V. Sabatel.
García-Maroto, María Ángeles. 1996. *La mujer en la prensa anarquista. España, 1900–1936.* Madrid: Fundación de Estudios Libertarios.
García Mercadal, J. 1963. "Prólogo." In *Obras completas,* vol. 1, by Ramón Pérez de Ayala. Edited by J. García Mercadal, 11–22. Madrid: Aguilar.
Gies, David T. 1994. "La subversión de don Juan. Parodias decimonónicas del *Tenorio.*" *España Contemporánea* 7:93–201.
Gilbert, Sandra M., and Susan Gubar. 1988. *No Man's Land: The Place of the Woman Writer in the Twentieth Century.* Vol. 1. *The War of the Words.* New Haven, Conn.: Yale University Press.
Gilman, Sander. 1985. *Difference and Pathology: Stereotypes of Sexuality, Race, and Madness.* Ithaca, N.Y.: Cornell University Press.
Glenn, Kathleen M. 1990. "Azorín y el retrato femenino." In *Divergencias y unidad. Perspectivas sobre la Generación del 98 y Antonio Machado.* Edited by John P. Gabriele, 161–70. Madrid: Orígenes.
———. 1991. "Fiction and Autobiography in Rosa Chacel's *Memorias de Leticia Valle.*" *Letras Peninsulares* 4.2–3:285–94.
———. 1999. "Demythification and Denunciation in Blanca de los Ríos' *Las hijas de don Juan.*" *Nuevas perspectivas sobre el 98.* Edited by John P. Gabriele, 223–30. Madrid: Iberoamericana.
Gómez Carrillo, E. 1909. *El libro de las mujeres.* Paris: Garnier Hermanos.

Gómez de la Serna, Ramón. 1922. *El secreto del acueducto*. Madrid: Biblioteca Nueva.
———. 1923. *El novelista*. Valencia, Spain: Sampere.
———. 1981. *La mujer de ámbar*. 8th ed. Madrid: Austral.
Gómez-Ferrer Morant, Guadalupe. 1986. "La imagen de la mujer en la novela de la Restauración." In *Mujer y sociedad en España, 1700–1975*. Edited by Rosa María Capel Martínez, 151–73. Madrid: Ministerio de Cultura, Instituto de la Mujer.
Graham, Helen. 1992. "Community, Nation and State in Republican Spain, 1931–1938." In *Nationalism and Nation in the Iberian Peninsula: Competing and Conflicting Identities*. Edited by Clare Mar Molnero and Angel Smith, 133–47. Oxford and Washington, DC: Berg.
———. 1995. "Women and Social Change." In *Spanish Cultural Studies*. Edited by Helen Graham and Jo Labanyi, 99–116. Oxford, England: Oxford University Press.
Graham, Helen, and Jo Labanyi, eds. 1995. *Spanish Cultural Studies: An Introduction: The Struggle for Modernity*. Oxford, England: Oxford University Press.
Greene, Patricia V. 1997. "Federica Montseny: Chronicler of an Anarcho-feminist Genealogy." *Letras Peninsulares* 10.2:333–54.
Gullón, Ricardo. 1961a. *Relaciones amistosas y literarias entre Juan Ramón Jiménez y los Martínez Sierra*. San Juan, P.R.: Ediciones de la Torre.
———. 1961b. "La voluntad de dominio en 'la madre' unamuniana." *Asomante* 17:41–59.
———. 1964. *Autobiografías de Unamuno*. Madrid: Gredos.
Gulstad, Daniel E. 1970–71. "Parody in Valle Inclán's *Sonata de otoño*." *Hispanic Review* 36:21–31.
Guss, Donald L. 1994. "The Power of Selfhood: Shakespeare's Hamlet and Milton's Samson." *Modern Language Quarterly* 54:483–511.
Habermas, Jürgen. 1987. *The Philosophical Discourse of Modernity*. Translated by F. Lawrence. Cambridge: Massachusetts Institute of Technology Press.
Hannan, Dennis. 1971. "Unamuno: *La tía Tula* como expresión novelesca del ensayo 'Sobre la soberbia.'" *Romance Notes* 12:296–301.
Hardcastle, Anne. 2001. "What a Trip! Marriage and Divorce in Carmen de Burgos's 'La Flor de la Playa.'" *Revista de Estudios Hispánicos* 35:239–56.
Highfill, Juli. 1999. *Portraits of Excess: Reading Character in the Modern Spanish Novel*. Boulder, Colo.: Society for Spanish and Spanish American Studies.
Hobsbawm, E. J. 1983. "Introduction: Inventing Tradition." In *The Invention of Tradition*. Edited by E. J., Hobsbawm and Terence Ranger, 1–14. Cambridge, England: Cambridge University Press.

———. 1990. *Nations and Nationalism Since 1780: Programme, Myth, Reality*. Cambridge, England: Cambridge University Press.
Hoddie, James H. 1984. "Ensayo de aproximación a *Las cerezas del cementerio* de Gabriel Miró." *Revista de Estudios Hispánicos* 11:163–85.
Hurtado, Amparo. 1996. "Biografía de una generación. Las escritoras del noventa y ocho." In *Breve historia feminista de la literatura española (en lengua castellana)*. Vol. 5., ed. Iris M. Zavala, 139–54. Barcelona: Anthropos.
———. 1998. "Prólogo." In *Recuerdos de una mujer de la Generación del 98*, by Carmen Baroja. Edited by Amparo Hurtado, 9–38. Barcelona: Tusquets.
Hutcheon, Linda. 1985. *A Theory of Parody*. New York: Methuen.
Hynes, Laura. 1981 "*La tía Tula*: Forerunner of Radical Feminism." *Hispanófila* 117 (1996): 45–51.
Ibarra, Fernando. 1972. "Clarín y Azorín: El matrimonio y el papel de la mujer española." *Hispania* 55:45–54.
Jagoe, Catherine. 1994. *Ambiguous Angels: Gender in the Novels of Galdós*. Berkeley and Los Angeles: University of California Press.
———. 1998. "La enseñanza femenina en la España decimonónica." In *La mujer y los discursos de género*. Edited by Catherine Jagoe, Alda Blanco, and Cristina Enríquez Salamanca. Barcelona: Icaria.
Jarnés, Benjamin. 1926. *El profesor inútil*. Madrid: Revista de Occidente.
———. 1928. *El convidado de papel*. Madrid: Historia Nueva.
———. 1929. *Paula y Paulita*. Madrid: Revista de Occidente.
Jay, Martin. 1984. *Adorno*. Cambridge, Mass.: Harvard University Press.
J.B.R. 1931. "Periodistas de izquierda. 'Azorín.' " *La Calle*. April 24.
Johnson, Roberta. 1992. "*El abuelo del rey:* Gabriel Miró's Saga of the Spanish Nineteenth Century." *Romance Quarterly* 39:101–08.
———. 1993a. *Crossfire: Philosophy and the Novel in Spain, 1900–1934*. Lexington: University Press of Kentucky.
———.1993b. "Historia y narrativa en Azorín." *Ínsula* 556:19–20.
———. 1993c. "El tiempo retrospectivo en *Doña Inés*." *Anales Azorinianos* 4:369–84.
———. 1996a. *Las bibliotecas de Azorín*. Alicante, Spain: Caja de Ahorros del Mediterráneo.
———.1996b. "María Zambrano's Theory of Literature as Knowledge and Contingency." *Hispania* 79:213–19.
———. 2001. "El método arqueológico en Azorín." *Hispania* 84:767–73.
Jurkevich, Gayana. 1991. *The Elusive Self: Archetypal Approaches to the Fiction of Miguel de Unamuno*. Columbia: University of Missouri Press.
———. 1992. "Unamuno's Anecdotal Digressions: Practical Joking and Narrative Structure in *Niebla*." *Revista Hispánica Moderna* 45:3–13.

Kirkpatrick, Judith A. 1992. "Redefining the Male Tradition: Novels by Early Twentieth-Century Spanish Women Writers." Ph.D. diss., Indiana University.

———. 1995. "From Male Text to Female Community: Concha Espina's *La esfinge maragata*." *Hispania* 78:262–71.

———. 1995–96. "Skeletons in the Closet: Carmen de Burgos Confronts the Literary Patriarchy." *Letras Peninsulares* 8–9:389–400.

———. 1997. "'La lengua pantalónica': Unamuno and Women's Relationship to the Literary Text." *Siglo Veinte/Twentieth Century* 15.1–2:95–108.

Kirkpatrick, Susan. 1999. "Gender and Modernist Discourse: Emilia Pardo Bazán's *Dulce dueño*." In *Modernism and Its Margins: Reinscribing Cultural Modernity from Spain and Latin America*. Edited by Anthony L. Geist and José B. Monleón, 117–39. New York: Garland.

Kirkpatrick, Susan, and Teresa Bordons. 1992. "Chacel's *Teresa* and Ortega's Canon." *Anales de la Literatura Española Contemporánea* 17:283–99.

Kristeva, Julia. 1980. *Desire in Language: A Semiotic Aproach to Literature and Art*. Edited by Leon S. Roudiez. Translated by Thomas Gora, Alice Jardine, and Leon S. Roudiez. New York: Columbia University Press.

Labanyi, Jo. 1994. "Nation, Narration, Naturalization: A Barthesian Critique of the 1898 Generation." In *New Hispanisms: Literature, Culture, Theory*, 127–49. Ottawa, Canada: Dovehouse Editions.

———. 2000. *Gender and Modernization in the Spanish Realist Novel*. Oxford, England: Oxford University Press,

Laforet, Carmen. 1945. *Nada*. Barcelona: Editorial Destino.

Langa Laorga, María Alicia. 1991. "Introducción." In *La indomable*, by Federica Montseny, 7–42. Madrid: Castalia.

Langland, Elizabeth. 1992. "Nobody's Angels: Domestic Ideology and Middle Class Women in the Victorian Novel." *PMLA* 107:299–304.

La Rubia Prado, Francisco. 1996. *Alegorías de la voluntad. Pensamiento orgánico, retórica y deconstrucción en la obra de Miguel de Unamuno*. Madrid: Ediciones Libertarias/Prodhufi.

Lázaro, Reyes. 1966. "Tiempo contra historia en las novelas de José Martínez Ruiz." *Homenaje a Rodríguez Moñino*. Vol. 1. Madrid: Castalia.

———. 1993. "*Desde el amanecer*: Confesiones de una hija voluntariosa." *Journal of Interdisciplinary Literary Studies* 5.1:61–73.

———. 2000. "El 'Don Juan' de Blanca de los Ríos y el nacional romanticismo español de principios de siglo." *Letras Peninsulares* 13.1:467–83.

León, María Teresa. 1970. *Memoria de la melancolía*. Buenos Aires: Losada.

Livingstone, Leon. 1970. *Tema y forma en las novelas de Azorín*. Madrid: Gredos.

Llanas Aguilaniedo, José María. 1901. "Eva futura." *Juventud* 1.

Longhurst, C. A. 1977. *Pío Baroja. El mundo es ansí.* London: Grant and Cutler.
López, Ignacio-Javier. 1986. *Caballero de novela. Ensayo sobre el donjuanismo en la novela española moderna, 1880–1930.* Barcelona: PPU.
Loureiro, Ángel G. 1993. "La estética y la mirada de la muerte. 'Sonata de otoño.'" *Revista Hispánica Moderna* 46:34–50.
Lozano Marco, Miguel Ángel. 1990. "Introducción." In *Tigre Juan y El curandero de su honra,* by Ramón Pérez de Ayala, 9–44. Madrid: Espasa-Calpe.
Lucientes, Francisco. 1981. "España en pocos meses ha recorrido muchos años." In *Los intelectuales ante la Segunda República española.* Edited by Víctor M. Arbeloa and Miguel de Santiago, 103–7. Salamanca, Spain: Ediciones Almar.
Macdonald, Ian. 1975. *Gabriel Miró: His Private Library and His Literary Background.* London: Tamesis.
———. 1984. "First Person to Third: An Early Version of Gabriel Miró's *Las cerezas del cementerio.*" In *What's Past Is Prologue: A Collection of Essays in Honor of L. J. Woodward.* Edited by Salvador Bacarisse, Bernard Bently, Mercedes Claraso, and Gifford Douglas, 95–106. Edinburgh: Scottish Academic Press.
Macklin, J. J. 1980a. "Myth and Nemesis: The Artistic Integrity of Pérez de Ayala's *Tigre Juan* and *El curandero de su honra.*" *Hispanic Review* 48:15–36.
———. 1980b. *Ramón Pérez de Ayala "Tigre Juan" and "El curandero de su honra."* London: Grant and Cutler.
Maeztu, Ramiro de. 1923. "Diretes. Masculinidad." *El Sol.* October 6.
———. 1925. *Don Quijote, Don Juan, y la Celestina.* Madrid: Espasa-Calpe.
Magnien, Brigette. 1997. "La mujer y el trabajo en la novela de los años treinta." In *Referencias vivenciales femeninas en la literatura española (1830–1936),* ed. María José Porro, 17–36 Córdoba, Spain: Universidad de Córdoba.
Maier, Carol. 1992. "Siting Leticia Valle." *Monographic Review/Revista Monográfica* 8 :79–97.
Maier, Carol, and Roberta Salper, eds. 1994. *Ramón María del Valle-Inclán: Questions of Gender.* Lewisburg, Pa.: Bucknell University Press.
Mandrell, James. 1992. *Don Juan and the Point of Honor: Seduction, Patriarchal Society, and Literary Tradition.* University Park: Pennsylvania State University Press.
Mangini, Shirley. 1995. *Memories of Resistance: Women's Voices from the Spanish Civil War.* New Haven, Conn.: Yale University Press.
———. 2001. *Las modernas de Madrid. Las grandes intelectuales españolas de la vanguardia.* Barcelona: Península.
Marañón, Gregorio. 1920. *Biología y feminismo.* Madrid: Sucesor de Enrique Teodoro.

———. 1924a. "Notas para la biología de don Juan." *Revista de Occidente* 3: 15–53.
———. 1924b. "Sexo y trabajo." *Revista de Occidente* 2:305–42.
———. 1931. "Prólogo. Breve ensayo sobre el sentido de los celos." In *Quiero vivir mi vida*, by Carmen de Burgos, 7–13. Madrid: Biblioteca Nueva.
———. 1969. *Tres ensayos sobre la vida sexual.* 4th ed. Madrid: Espasa-Calpe.
Maravall, José Antonio. 1966. "La imagen de la sociedad arcaica en Valle-Inclán." *Revista de Occidente* 4:225–56.
———. 1968. "Azorín. Idea y sentido de la microhistoria." *Cuadernos Hispanoamericanos* 226–27:28–77.
———. 1986. "De la intrahistoria a la historia." In *Volumen homenaje cincuentenario de Miguel de Unamuno*, 175–230. Salamanca, Spain: Casa-Museo de Unamuno.
Marco, José María. 1989. "Prólogo." In *Los anticuarios*, by Carmen de Burgos, 9–24. Madrid: Biblioteca Nueva.
Marías, Julián. 1943. *Miguel de Unamuno.* Madrid: Espasa-Calpe.
Márquez Villanueva, Francisco. 1972. "Sobre fuentes y estructura de *Las cerezas del cementerio*." In *Homenaje a Joaquín Casalduero*. Edited by Gonzalo Sobejano, 371–77. Madrid: Gredos.
Mar-Molinero, Claire, and Angel Smith, eds. 1996. *Nationalism and the Nation in the Iberian Peninsula: Competing and Conflicting Identities.* Oxford, England: Berg.
Martínez, Graciano. 1921. *La mujer española. Hacia un feminismo cuasi dogmático.* Madrid: Asilo de Huérfanos.
Martínez Cachero, José María. 1960. *Las novelas de Azorín.* Madrid: Ínsula.
Martínez Ruiz, José [Azorín, pseud.]. 1902. *La voluntad.* Martínez Sierra, Gregorio [María Martínez Sierra]. 1905. *La tristeza del Quijote.* Madrid: Biblioteca Nacional y Extranjera.
———. 1907. *Aventura. El Cuento Semanal* 18.
———. 1916. *Cartas a la mujer de España.* Madrid: Clásica Española.
———. 1917. *Feminismo, feminidad, españolismo.* Madrid: Renacimiento.
———. 1921. *Don Juan de España.* Madrid: Saturnino Callejo.
———. 1932. *Nuevas cartas a las mujeres.* Madrid: Renacimiento.
———. 1955. *El amor catedrático.* Buenos Aires: Espasa-Calpe.
———. 1965. *Tu eres la paz.* 3d ed. Madrid: Espasa-Calpe.
Martínez Sierra, María 1931. *La mujer ante la República.* Madrid: Ediciones de la Esfringe.
———. 1953. *Gregorio y yo. Medio siglo de colaboración.* Mexico City: Biografías Gandesa.
———. 1965. "Prólogo," In *Tú eres la paz*, 7–12. 3d ed. Madrid: Espasa-Calpe.

———. 1989. *Una mujer por caminos de España*. Edited by Alda Blanco. Madrid: Castalia.
Martín Gaite, Carmen. 1978. *El cuarto de atrás*. Barcelona: Ediciones Destino.
———. 1992. "Prólogo." In *Celia, lo que dice*, by Elena Fortún, 7–37. Madrid: Alianza.
Meehan, Thomas. 1969. "El desdoblamiento interior en *Doña Inés*." *Cuadernos Hispanoamericanos* 237:644–68.
Miguel, Amando de. 1995. *La España de nuestros abuelos. Historia íntima de una época*. Madrid: Espasa-Calpe.
Miró, Gabriel. 1991. *Las cerezas del cementerio*. Edited by Miguel Ángel Lozano. Madrid: Taurus.
———. 1992a. *El abuelo del rey*. Alicante, Spain: Instituto de Cultura Juan Gil-Albert.
———. 1992b. "Literatura feminista: Yolanda." In *Los artículos de Gabriel Miró en la prensa barcelonesa, 1911–1920)*. Edited by Marta E. Altisent, 74–77. Madrid: Editorial Pliegos.
Montero, Rosa. 1995. *Historias de mujeres*. Madrid: Alfaguara.
Montes Huidobro, Matias. 1984. "*La tía Tula*. Matrimonio en el cosmos." In *Estudios en honor a Ricardo Gullón*, 229–48. Lincoln: Nebr: Society for Spanish and Spanish American Studies.
Montseny, Federica. 1925. "En defensa de Clara." *Revista Blanca*. 2d epoch. May 1.
———. 1925. "El ocaso del donjuanismo." *Revista Blanca*. 2d epoch. April 15.
———. 1926. "La mujer nueva." *Revista Blanca*. 2d epoch. May 15.
———. 1927a. "Intermedio polémico. Armand y La Vitoria." *Revista Blanca*. 2d epoch. July 1.
———. 1927b. "La mujer problema del hombre." *Revista Blanca*. 2d epoch. April 1.
———. 1929. *El hijo de Clara*. Barcelona: Biblioteca de la Revista Blanca.
———. 1991. *La indomable*. Edited by María Alicia Langa Laorga. Madrid: Castalia.
———. n.d. *La victoria. Novela en la que se narran los problemas de orden moral que se le presentan a una mujer de ideas modernas*. 3d ed. Barcelona: Costa.
Mora, Magdalena. 1987. "La mujer y las mujeres en la *Revista de Occidente*: 1923–1936." *Revista de Occidente* 74–75:191–209.
Morales, Sister Carmen F. I. 1971. "Unamuno's Concept of Woman." *Fu Jen Studies: Natural Sciences and Foreign Languages* 5:91–100.
Mosse, George L. 1985. *Nationalism and Sexuality: Respectability and Abnormal Sexuality in Modern Europe*. New York: Howard Fertig.

Nash, Mary. 1999. "Un/Contested Identities: Motherhood, Sex Reform and the Modernization of Gender Identity in Early Twentieth-Century Spain." In *Constructing Spanish Womanhood: Female Identity in Modern Spain*. Edited by Victoria Lorée Enders and Pamela Beth Radcliff, 25–49. Albany: State University of New York Press.

Navajas, Gonzalo. 1975. "The Self and the Symbolic in Unamuno's *La tía Tula*." *Revista de Estudios Hispánicos* 9:117–37.

———. 1988. *Miguel de Unamuno. Bipolaridad y síntesis ficcional. Una lectura posmoderna*. Barcelona: PPU.

Nelken, Margarita. 1923. *La trampa del arenal*. Madrid: Librería de los Sucesores de Hernando.

———. 1930. *Las escritoras españolas*. Barcelona: Labor.

———. n.d. *La condición social de la mujer en España. Su estado actual y su posible desarrollo*. Barcelona: Minerva.

Novoa Santos, Roberto. 1929. *La mujer, nuestro sexto sentido y otros ensayos*. Madrid: n.p.

Nozick, Martin. 1971. *Miguel de Unamuno*. New York: Twayne.

Núñez Pérez, María Gloria. 1993. *Madrid 1931. Mujeres entre la permanencia y el cambio*. Madrid: Horas y Horas.

Núñez Rey, Concepción. 1989. "Introducción." In *La flor de la playa y otras novelas cortas*, by Carmen de Burgos. Madrid: Castalia.

Nussbaum, Martha. 1995. *Poetic Justice: The Literary Imagination and Public Life*. Boston: Beacon Press.

O'Connor, Patricia W. 1966. *Women in the Theater of Gregorio Martínez Sierra*. New York: American Press.

———. 1977. *Gregorio and María Martínez Sierra*. Boston: Twayne.

———. 1987. *Gregorio y María Martínez Sierra. Crónica de una colaboración*. Madrid: La Avispa.

Oñate, María del Pilar. 1938. *El feminismo en la literatura española*. Madrid: Espasa-Calpe.

Ontañón de Lope, Paciencia. 1986. "En Torno a *La tía Tula*." In *Actas del Octavo Congreso de la AIH*. Edited by David Kossoff, José Amor y Vázquez, Ruth H. Kossoff, and Geoffrey W. Ribbans, 383–89. Madrid: Ediciones Istmo.

Ortega. 1928. "En zig-zag por la España nueva. Concha Espina, novelista." *Social* (Havana) 13.5 (May): 12, 70–71.

Ortega, Esperanza. 1982. "Leticia Valle o la mirada perspicaz." *Cuadernos Hispanoamericanos* 390:645–61.

Ortega y Gasset, José. 1914. *Meditaciones del Quixote*. Madrid: Residencia de Estudiantes.

———. 1923. "Oknos el soguero." *Revista de Occidente* (August): 231–41.

———. 1926. "Para una caracterología." *Revista de Occidente* 14 (November): 241–53.

———. 1957. *Man and People*. Translated by Willard R. Trask. New York: W. W. Norton.

———. 1966a. *La deshumanización del arte. Obras completas*. Vol. 3. Madrid: Revista de Occidente.

———. 1966b. *El tema de nuestro tiempo. Obras completas*. Vol. 3. Madrid: Revista de Occidente.

———. 1967. *On Love*. Cleveland, Ohio: World Publishing.

Ouimette, Victor. 1998. *Los intelectuales españoles y el naufragio del liberalismo (1923–1936)*. 2 vols. Valencia, Spain: Pre-Textos.

Paraíso, Isabel. 1998. "La mirada de un biólogo reformista. Marañón ante don Juan." In *Don Juan Tenorio en la España del siglo veinte. Literatura y cine*. Edited by Ana Sofía Pérez-Bustamante, 317–33. Madrid: Cátedra.

Parajón, Mario. 1972. "Personajes, situaciones y objetos imaginarios en 1945 (Characters, situations and imaginary objects in 1945)." *Cuadernos Hispanoamericanos* 270:531–32.

Pardo Bazán, Emilia. 1892. "La educación del hombre y la mujer. Sus relaciones y diferencias." *Nuevo Teatro Crítico* 2.22.

Pariente, Ángel. 1999. "La poesía surrealista en lengua española." In *Bibliografía y antología crítica de las vanguardias literarias*. Edited by Harald Wentzlaff-Eggebert, 463–76. Madrid: Iberoamericana.

Parker, Andrew, Mary Russo, Doris Summer, and Patricia Yaeger, eds. 1992. *Nationalisms and Sexualities*. New York: Routledge.

Pérez, Janet. 1988. *Contemporary Women Writers of Spain*. Boston: Twayne.

———. 1988–89. "Vanguardism, Modernism and Spanish Women Writers in the Years Between the Wars." *Siglo Veinte/Twentieth Century* 6:40–47.

Pérez-Bustamante Mourier, Ana Sofia, ed. 1998. *Don Juan Tenorio en la España del siglo veinte. Literatura y cine*. Madrid: Cátedra.

Pérez de Ayala, Ramón. 1927. "Hombredad y femineidad." *Caras y Caretas* (Buenos Aires) 30, December 10, p. 1523.

———. 1929a. "Feminismo." *La Esfera*, January 1. Reprint, *Artículos y ensayos en los semanarios* España, Nuevo Mundo *y* La Esfera, by Ramón Pérez-Ayala. Edited by Florencio Friera Suárez, 208–9. Oviedo, Spain: Universidad de Oviedo.

———. 1929b. "Sobre feminismo. La edad y el sexo de las épocas históricas." *La Esfera*. January 29.

———. 1929c. "Sobre feminismo. La metáfora antropomórfica en sociología." *La Esfera*. February 2.

———. 1962. *Los trabajos de Urbano y Simona*. 3d ed. Buenos Aires: Losada.

———. 1963a. *La caída de los Limones*. In *Obras completas*, vol. 2, by Ramón Pérez Ayala. Edited by José García Mercadal, 673–723. Madrid: Aguilar.

1963b. "El donjuanismo." In *Obras completas*, vol. 3, by Ramón Pérez Ayala. Edited by José García Mercadal, 380–90. Madrid: Aguilar.

———. 1963c. *Luz de domingo.* In *Obras completas,* vol. 2, by Ramón Pérez Ayala. Edited by José García Mercadal, 637–72. Madrid: Aguilar.

———. 1963d. *Las máscaras.* In *Obras completas,* vol. 3, by Ramón Pérez de Ayala. Edited by José García Mercadal, 343–90. Madrid: Aguilar.

———. 1963e. *Prometeo.* In *Obras Completas,* vol. 2, by Ramón Pérez de Ayala. Edited by José García Mercadal, 589–635. Madrid: Aguilar.

———. 1963f. "El satanismo." In *Obras Completas,* vol. 3, by Ramón Pérez de Ayala. Edited by José García Mercadal, 374–80. Madrid: Aguilar.

———. 1963g. *Tinieblas en las cumbres.* In *Obras Completas,* vol. 1, by Ramón Pérez de Ayala. Edited by José García Mercadal, 3–236. Madrid: Aguilar.

———. 1963h. *Troteras y danzaderas.* In *Obras completas,* vol. 1, by Ramón Pérez de Ayala. Edited by José García Mercadal, 473–816. Madrid: Aguilar.

———. 1969. "Ensayo preliminar." *Ensayos sobre la vida sexual,* by Gregorio Marañón, 4th ed., 14–22. Madrid: Espasa-Calpe.

———. 1982. *Belarmino y Apolonio.* Edited by Andrés Amorós. Madrid: Cátedra.

———. 1990. *Tigre Juan y El curandero de su honra.* Edited by Miguel Ángel Lozano Marco. Madrid: Espasa-Calpe.

———. n.d. *Artículos y ensayos en los semanarios* España, Nuevo Mundo *y* La Esfera. Edited by Florencio Friera Suárez. Oviedo, Spain: Universidad de Oviedo.

Pérez Firmat, Gustavo. 1982. *Idle Fictions.* Durham, N.C.: Duke University Press.

Perinat, Adolfo, and María Isabel Marrades. 1980. *Mujer, prensa y sociedad en España, 1800–1939.* Madrid: Centro de Investigaciones Sociológicas.

Pieropán, María Doménica. 1989. "Una re-visión feminista del eterno retorno en *Doña Inés.*" *Hispania* 72:233–40.

Pierrot, Jean. 1981. *The Decadent Imagination, 1800–1900.* Translated by Derek Coltman. Chicago: University of Chicago Press.

Porro, María José, ed. 1997. *Referencias vivenciales femeninas en la literatura española (1830–1936).* Córdoba, Spain: Universidad de Córdoba.

Posada, Adolfo. 1899. *Feminismo.* Madrid: Fernando Fe.

Posada, Adolfo, and Urbano González Serrano. 1893. *La amistad y el sexo: Cartas sobre la educación de la mujer.* Madrid: Fernando Fe.

Pozzi, Gabriela. 2000. "Carmen de Burgos and the War in Morocco." *Modern Language Notes* 115:188–204.

Predmore, Michael C. 1988. "Satire in the *Sonata de primavera.*" *Hispanic Review* 56:307–17.

Predmore, R. L. 1955. "Flesh and Spirit in the Works of Unamuno." *PMLA* 70: 587–605.

Pulido Tirado, Genara. 1998. "El don Juan de Ramiro de Maetzu. Una teoría nacionalista y nietzscheana del mito." In *Don Juan Tenorio en la España del siglo veinte. Literatura y cine.* Edited by Ana Sofía Pérez-Bustamante, 339–59. Madrid: Cátedra.

Quinones, Ricardo J. 1985. *Mapping Literary Modernism: Time and Development.* Princeton, N.J.: Princeton University Press.

Radcliff, Pamela. 1999. "Women's Politics: Consumer Riots in Twentieth-Century Spain." In *Constructing Spanish Womanhood.* Edited by Victoria Lorée Enders and Pamela Beth Radcliff, 301–23. Albany: State University of New York Press.

Radhakrishnan, R. 1992. "Nationalism, Gender, and the Narrative of Identity." In *Nationalisms and Sexualities.* Edited by Andrew Parker, Mary Russo, Doris Summer, and Patricia Yaeger, 77–95. New York: Routledge.

Ramoneda Salas, Arturo. 1989. "Una polémica y una obrita olvidadas sobre don Juan." In *Homenaje al profesor Antonio Vilanova*, vol. 2. Edited by Marta Cristina Carbonell, 487–506. Barcelona: Universidad de Barcelona.

Ribbans, Geoffrey. 1986. "El autógrafo de parte de *La tía Tula* y su significado para la evolución de la novela." In *Volumen-homenaje a Miguel de Unamuno.* Edited by D. Gómez Molleda, 475–93. Salamanca, Spain: n.p.

———. 1987. "A New Look at *La tía Tula.*" *Revista Canadiense de Estudios Hispánicos* 11:404–20.

Rico de Estasén, José. 1930. 'La voz de la mujer española. Hablando con Carmen de Burgos (Colombine)." *Carteles* (Havana) 16 July 6, p. 27.

Rico Verdú, José. 1971. *Un Azorín desconocido. Estudio psicológico de su obra.* Alicante, Spain: Instituto de Estudios Alicantinos..

Riopérez y Milá, Santiago. 1979. *Azorín íntegro.* Madrid: Editorial Biblioteca Nueva.

Risco, Antonio. 1982. "La mujer en la novela de Azorín." *Cuadernos Hispanoamericanos* 385:172–200.

Roberson, Susan L. 1994. "Matriarchy and the Rhetoric of Domesticity." In *The Stowe Debate. Rhetorical Strategies in Uncle Tom's Cabin.* Edited by Mason I. Lowrance, Jr., Ellen E. Westbrok, and R. C. De Prospo, 116–37. Amherst: University of Massachusetts Press.

Robinson, Lilian, and Lise Vogel. 1971. "Modernism and History." *New Literary History* 3:178.

Rodgers, Eamann. 1972. "Realidad y realismo en Baroja. El tema de la soledad en *El mundo es ansí.*" *Cuadernos Hispanoamericanos* 265–67:575–90.

Rodrigo, Antonina. 1979. *Mujeres de España (las silenciadas).* Barcelona: Plaza y Janés.

———. 1994. *María Lejárraga, una mujer en la sombra.* Madrid: Ediciones Vosa.

Rodríguez, María Pilar. 1997. "Desviación y perversión en 'El veneno del arte' de Carmen de Burgos." *Symposium* 51:172–85.

Rojas Auda, Elizabeth. 1998. *Visión y ceguera de Concha Espina. Su obra comprometida*. Madrid: Editorial Pliegos.

Romero, Lora. 1991. "Domesticity and Fiction." In *The Columbia History of the American Novel*. Edited by Emory Elliot, 110–29. New York: Columbia University Press.

Romero Salvadó, Francisco J. 1996. "The Failure of the Liberal Project of the Spanish Nation-State, 1909–1923." In *Nationalism and the Nation in the Iberian Peninsula: Competing and Conflicting Identities*. Edited by Clare Mar-Molinero and Angel Smith, 119–32. Oxford, England: Berg.

Ruiz, Roberto. 1982. "El sentido existencial de 'Las cerezas del cementerio.'" In *Harvard Conference in Honor of Gabriel Miró (1879–1930)*. Edited by Francisco Márquez-Villanueva, 35–46. Cambridge, Mass.: Department of Romance Languages and Literatures.

Saitz, Herlinda Charpentier. 1990. "Carmen de Burgos (Columbine). Escritora española digna de ser recordada." In *La escritora hispánica*, 169–79. Miami: Ediciones Universal.

Salinas, Pedro. 1926. *Víspera del gozo*. Madrid: Revista de Occidente.

———.1995. "Letter to Margarita Bonmati." *Cuadernos Cervantes*. No. 2 (May): 31.

Scanlon, Geraldine. 1976. *La polémica feminista en la España contemporánea, 1868–1974*. Translated by Rafael Mazarrasa. Madrid: Siglo Veintiuno.

Scarlett, Elizabeth A. 1994. *Under Construction: The Body in Spanish Novels*. Charlottesville: University Press of Virginia.

Schiavo, Leda. 1989. "Introducción." *Sonata de otoño. Sonata de primavera*, by Ramón del Valle-Inclán. Edited by Leda Schiavo. Madrid: Espasa-Calpe.

Schürr, Friedrich. 1965. "El amor, problema existencial en la obra de Unamuno." *Cuadernos del Idioma* 1:63–93.

Seator, Lynette Hubbard. 1980. "Women and Men in the Novels of Unamuno." *Kentucky Romance Quarterly* 27:39–55.

Showalter, Elaine. 1990. *Sexual Anarchy: Gender and Culture at the Fin de Siècle*. New York: Viking.

———. 1995. "Smoking Room." *Times Literary Supplement*. June 16, p. 12.

Sieburth, Stephanie. 1994. *Inventing High and Low: Literature, Mass Culture, and Uneven Modernity in Spain*. Durham, N.C.: Duke University Press.

Silver, Philip W. 1985. "Ortega and National Separatism: A New Reading of *España invertebrada*." In *Ortega y Gasset Centennial/Centenario Ortega y Gasset*, 81–92. Madrid: José Porrúa Turanzas.

Simmel, Georg. 1923. "Lo masculino y lo femenino." *Revista de Occidente* 516 (November–December): 218–36, 336–63.

Six, Abigail Lee. 1992. "Perceiving the Family: Rosa Chacel's *Desde el amanecer*." In *Feminist Readings on Spanish and Latin American Literature*. Edited by L. P. Condé and S. M. Hart, 79–90. Lewiston, N.Y.: Mellon.
Smith, Angel, and Clare Mar-Molinero. 1996. "The Myths and Realities of Nation-Building in the Iberian Peninsula." In *Nationalism and the Nation in the Iberian Peninsula: Competing and Conflicting Identities*. Edited by Angel Smith and Clare Mar-Molinero, 1–30. Oxford, England: Berg.
Smith, Gilbert. 1989. "Feminism and Decadence in Baroja's *El mundo es ansí*." *Romance Quarterly* 36:361–68.
Smith, Paul Julian. 1992. "Rosa Chacel: The Repudiation of Femininity." In *Laws of Desire: Questions of Homosexuality in Spanish Writing and Film, 1960–1990*, 20–31. Oxford, England: Clarendon Press.
Smith, Verity. 1964. "Dandy Elements in the Marqués de Bradomín." *Hispanic Review* 32:340–50.
Sobejano, Gonzalo, ed. 1972. *Homenaje a Joaquín Casalduero*. Madrid: Gredos.
Spires, Robert C. 1988. *Transparent Simulacra*. Columbia: University of Missouri Press.
———. 1998. "Modernidad y mujer. La ficción española del principio del siglo XX." *Iberoamericana* 22:190–205.
———. 2000. "New Art, New Woman, Old Constructs: Gómez de la Serna, Pedro Solinas, and Vanguard Fiction." *Modern Language Notes* 115:205–23.
Starcevic, Elizabeth. 1976. *Carmen de Burgos. Defensora de la mujer*. Almería, Spain: Librería-Editorial Cajal.
Stevens, Harriet S. 1961. "Las novelitas intercaladas en *Niebla*." *Ínsula* 16:1.
Súarez Solís, Sara. 1986. "El antifeminismo de Pérez de Ayala." *Los Cuadernos del Norte* (Oviedo) 1.2:48–52.
Suleiman, Susan. 1990. *Subversive Intent: Gender, Politics, and the Avant-Garde*. Cambridge, Mass.: Harvard University Press.
Sullivan, Constance A. 1990. "On Spanish Literary History and the Politics of Gender." *Journal of the Midwest Modern Language Association* 23:26–41.
Taylor, Anne Robinson. 1981. *Male Novelists and Their Female Voices: Literary Masquerades*. Troy, N.Y. Whitson.
Terry, Barbara. 1967. "The Influence of Casanova and Barbey D'Áurevilly on the *Sonatas* of Valle-Inclán." *Revista de Estudios Hispánicos* 1:61–88.
Tirrell, Lynne. 1990. "Storytelling and Moral Agency." *Journal of Aesthetics and Art Criticism* 48.2:115–26.
Torrecilla, Jesús. 1998. "Exotismo y nacionalismo en *Sonata de estío*." *Hispanic Review* 66:35–56.

Turner, Harriet S. 1989. "Distorciones teresianas de *La tía Tula*." In *Los hallazgos de la lectura. Estudio dedicado a Miguel Enguídanos*. Edited by John Crispin, Enrique Pupo-Walker, Luis Lorenzo-Rivero, 131–51. Madrid: Porrúa Turranzas.

Ugarte, Michael. 1994. "The Generational Fallacy and Spanish Women Writing in Madrid at the Turn of the Century." *Siglo Veinte/Twentieth Century* 12:261–76.

———. 1996. *Madrid, 1900: The Capital as Cradle of Literature and Culture*. University Park: Pennsylvania State University Press.

Unamuno, Miguel de. 1902. *Amor y pedagogía*. Barcelona: Henrich.

———. 1920. *Tres novelas ejemplares y un prólogo*. Madrid: Espasa-Calpe.

———. 1929. *La vida de don Quijote y Sancho según Miguel de Cervantes Saavedra explicada y comentada*. 4th ed. Madrid: Renacimiento.

———. 1933. *San Manuel Bueno, mártir*. Madrid: Espasa-Calpe.

———. 1958. *Obras completas*. 16 vols. Edited by Manuel García Blanco. Barcelona: Vergara.

———. 1959. *Teatro completo*. Edited by Manuel García Blanco. Madrid: Aguilar.

———. 1966–71. *Obras completas*. 9 vols. Edited by Manuel García Blanco. Madrid: Escelicer.

———. 1970. *Ensayos*. 2 vols. Edited by Bernardo G. de Candamo. Madrid: Aguilar.

———. 1971. *En torno al casticismo*. Edited by Francisco Fernández Turienzo, Madrid: Ediciones Alcalá.

———. 1982. *Niebla*. Edited by Mario J. Valdés. Madrid: Cátedra.

———. 1983. *Peace in War*. Translated by Allen Lacy, Martin Nozick, and Anthony Kerrigan. Princeton, N.J.: Princeton University Press.

———. 1990. *La tía Tula*. Edited by Carlos A. Longhurst. Madrid: Cátedra.

———. 1995. *Abel Sánchez: Una historia de pasión*. Edited by Carlos Longhurst. Madrid: Cátedra.

Urbieta, Arantza de. 1977. "Estructura narrativa de *Paz en la guerra*." *Letras de Deusto* 7:129–60.

Urioste Carmen de. 1983. "Canonicidad y feminismo: Los textos de Carmen de Burgos." *Romance Language Quarterly* 5:527–32.

Valis, Noël M. 1989. "The Novel as Feminine Entrapment: Valle-Inclán's *Sonata de otoño*." *Modern Language Notes* 104:351–69.

Valle-Inclán, Ramón del. 1916. *La lámpara maravillosa*. Madrid: Sociedad General Española de Librería.

———. 1963. *Sonata de primavera. Sonata de estío*. Madrid: Espasa-Calpe. 5th ed.

———. 1989. *Sonata de otoño. Sonata de invierno*. Edited by Leda Schiavo. Madrid: Espasa-Calpe.

———. 1992. "Tula Varona." In *Femeninas. Epitalamio.* Edited by Joaquín del Valle-Inclán, 83–99. Madrid: Cátedra.
Vásquez Recio, Nieves. 1998. "*Las hijas de don Juan (1907)* de Blanca de los Ríos. Fin de siglo y mirada femenina." In *Don Juan Tenorio en la España del siglo veinte. Literatura y cine,* 379–403. Madrid: Cátedra.
Vernon, John. 1984. *Money and Fiction: Literary Realism in the Nineteenth and Early Twentieth Centuries.* Ithaca, N.Y.: Cornell University Press.
Vidal, Fabián. 1904. "Las mujeres y el arte." *Alma Española* 23:7–8.
Vilanova, Antonio. 1981. "El tradicionalismo anticastizo, universal y cosmopólita, de las 'Sonatas' de Valle-Inclán," In *Homenaje a Antonio Sánchez Barbudo. Ensayos de literatura española moderna,* 353–94. Madison: University of Wisconsin Press.
Vilarós, Teresa. 1991. "La escritura autobiográfica y el espejo. Propiedad, memoria y deseo en Rosa Chacel." *Anthropos* 125:49–53.
Watson, Peggy W. 1993. *Intra-historia in Miguel de Unamuno's Novels: A Continual Presence.* Potomac, Md.: Scripta Humanistica.
Weber, Max. 1958. *The Protestant Ethic and the Spirit of Capitalism.* Translated by Talcott Parsons. New York: Scribner.
Webber, Ruth House. 1964. "The *Bagatela* of Ramón del Valle-Inclán.' *Hispanic Review* 32:135–41.
White, Sarah L. 1999. "Liberty, Honor, Order." In *Constructing Spanish Womanhood: Female Identity in Modern Spain,* ed. Victoria Lorée Enders and Pamela Beth Radcliff, 233–57. Albany: State University of New York.
Williams, Raymond. 1959. "Realism and the Contemporary Novel." *Partisan Review* 24:200–13.
Wolstenholme, Susan. *Gothic (Re)visions: Writing Women as Readers.* Albany: State University of New York Press.
Wood, Jennifer J. 1999–2000. "A Woman Writing War in 1909: Colombine in Melilla." *Letras Peninsulares* 12.3:373–85.
Zambrano, María. 1930. *Horizonte del liberalismo.* Madrid: Morata.
———. 1948. "Delirio de Antígona." *Orígenes* 5.18:14–21.
———. 1965. *El sueño creador.* Xalapa, Mexico: Universidad Veracruzana.
———. 1967. *La tumba de Antígona.* Mexico City: Siglo Veinte.
———. 1971. "Una forma de pensamiento. La 'guía.'" In *Obras reunidas,* 359–71. Madrid: Aguilar.
———. 1986a. *De la aurora.* Madrid: Ediciones Turner.
———. 1986b. *Senderos.* Barcelona: Ánthropos.
———. 1987. "Hacia un saber sobre el alma." In *Hacia un saber sobre el alma.* Madrid: Alianza.
———. 1988. *La confesión. Género literario y método.* Madrid: Mondadori.
———. 1989. *Delirio y destino.* Madrid: Mondadori.

———. 1998. *Delirium and Destiny.* Translated by Carol Maier. Albany: State University of New York Press.

Zavala, Iris M., ed. 1996. *Breve historia feminista de la literatura española (en lengua castellana).* Vol. 3. *La mujer en la literatura española (del s. dieciocho a la actualidad).* Barcelona: Anthropos.

Index

Abellán y Anta, R., 282n5
Academia Nacional de Medicina, 301n1
Acción Social Obrera, 250
Ackelsberg, Martha, 251, 255
Adorno, Theodor, 3, 272
Aguado, A. María, 306n3
Alas, Leopoldo ("Clarín"), 289n19, 307n8; *La Regenta*, 122, 235, 295n8
Albareda, José Luis, 17
Alberich, José, 295n9, 297n23
Alberti, Rafael, 28
Albornoz, Álvaro de, 24
Alcalá Zamora, Niceto, 24
Aldaraca, Bridget, 11
Alfonso XIII, 14, 125, 145, 276, 279, 307n5
Allan, Jefner, 300n15
alma castellana, el, 19
Alma Española, 119, 284n6
Álvarez Junco, José, 13, 15, 20, 21, 22, 109, 111, 121, 164, 281n2, 282n3
Álvarez Quintero, Joaquín and Serafín: *Don Juan, buena persona*, 295–96n14; *El genio alegre*, 49; *La mujer española*, 282n5
Amorós, Amparo, 279
Anales de la literatura española contemporánea, xi
Anales Malagüeños, 284n1
Andreu, Alicia, 189
androgyny, 201, 215, 223, 254
"angel of the house" (*"ángel del hogar"*), 67, 99, 122, 168,170, 225, 285n6

Anna Karenina, 235
Antigone, 168; Zambrano, María on, 7–9, 265–66
Apter, Emily, 296n18
Aranguren, José Luis, 26
Arbeloa, Víctor M., 119, 147
Arciniega, Rosa, 306n1
Arenal, Concepción, 16, 81; *La mujer del porvenir*, 18, 282n5; *La mujer en su casa*, 282n5
Arendt, Hannah, 3
Arquimbau, Rosa María, 306n1
Asociación Nacional de Mujeres Españolas (ANME), 25–26, 145
Asociación para la Enseñanza de la Mujer, 16
Atencia, María Victoria, 279
Ateneo Artístico y Literario de Señoras, 16
Auerbach, Eric, 72
Ayala, Francisco, xi, 29, 227, 248
Azaña, Manuel, 24, 28, 226
Azcárate, Gumersindo, 16
Azorín (José Martínez Ruiz), 2, 5, 16, 18, 24, 46, 51, 95, 97, 125, 229, 230, 233; *El alma castellana*, ix, 31, 33, 34, 53, 56, 57–66, 73, 131, 174, 184; *El caballero inactual*, x, 28, 80, 104–9; *Castilla*, ix, 31, 33, 40, 53, 54, 56, 66–68, 174, 184; and determinism, 296n19; on divorce, 289n19; *Don Juan*, 112, 141–43, 171, 190, 200, 219, 223, 297n22, 297n27, 298nn28–29; *Doña Inés*, 17, 78, 141,

338   Gender and Nation in the Spanish Modernist Novel

Azorín, *continued*
146, 155, 170–84, 289n24, 301n18 (as feminist novel, 301n21); and houses, 289n24; and *intrahistoria* or *tradición eterna,* 35, 36, 37, 41, 50, 125, 126, 216, 240, 291n13, 310n28; and liberalism, 25, 226; on marriage, 39, 289nn19- 20, 290n2; on motherhood, 301n21; *La ruta de Don Quijote,* 71, 73–74, 78, 83, 84; *Salvadora de Olbena,* 173; on Santa Teresa, 107; on time, 33–34, 54, 177–78, 301n16; and vanguardism, 293n22; *La voluntad,* 4, 12, 71, 163, 289n19; and women, 54–57, 58, 145, 146, 178–82, 279, 288n18, 301n20; *See also* Generation of '98

Balfour, Sebastian, 19, 20, 21, 23, 35, 62, 289n23
Bárcena, Catalina, 47, 49, 52, 287n10
Baroja, Carmen, 29; *Martinito, el de la Casa Grande,* 298n2; *Recuerdos de una mujer del noventa y ocho,* 148–51; on Baroja, Pío, 149–151, 154
Baroja, Pío, 29, 51, 72, 95, 97, 145, 146, 171, 229, 230, 233, 240, 279, 281n1; *El árbol de la ciencia,* 4, 12; and Burgos, Carmen de, 297n25; *Camino de perfección,* 4, 12, 71, 163, 287n13, 299n11, 307n9; *La ciudad de la niebla,* 19, 141, 147; *La dama errante,* 19, 141, 147; and determinism, 296n19; on divorce, 147; on marriage, 290n2; *Memorias,* 151; *Memorias de un hombre de acción,* 2; *El mundo es ansí,* 27, 146, 147, 298n4, 151–59, 163, 177, 184 (critical commentary on, 298nn3–5; as intertext of Carmen de Burgos's *La entrometida,* 297n25); *Silvestre Paradox,* 146; and women, 146, 147, 279, 284n6
Baroja, Ricardo, 119, 150
Barrena, Jaime, 126
Barthes, Roland, 35, 217
Baudelaire, Charles, 131
Beauvoir, Simone de, 212, 262, 272, 304n22

Bécquer, Gustavo Adolfo, 14, 119, 131
Bécquer, Valeriano, 14
Behler, Ernst, 122
Bello, Pepín, 224
Belmar, E. de, 282n5
Benavente, Jacinto, 28
Benstock, Shari, 218
Bhabha, Homi, 3
Bieder, Mary Ellen, 140, 281n1, 297nn24–25, 304n19, 307n6, 308n20
bisexuality, 208, 223, 307n9
Blanco, Alda, 11, 15, 283n5, 286nn7–9, 287n11, 287–88n15, 290n4, 292n17
Blanco Aguinaga, Carlos, 38, 291n8
Blanco-Belmonte, M. H., 125, 126
Blasco Ibáñez, Vicente, 205
Bonaparte, Napoleon, 281n2
Bonmati, Margarita, 28
Bordons, Teresa, 213
Boyd, Carolyn, 13
Brandau, Valentín, 282n5
Bravo, María Elena, 168, 299n8
Brennan, Timothy, 284n7
Bretz, Mary Lee, 248
Bucknell University Press, xi
Bueno, Manuel, 283n6
Buñuel, Luis, 224; *Un Chien andalou,* 250
Burgos, Carmen de, vii, 5, 7, 25, 27, 30, 72, 122, 149, 185–86, 210, 213, 224, 229, 248, 276, 280, 297n21, 297n24, 306n1; *El abogado,* 234; *Los anticuarios,* 101, 236–38, 243, 308n16; *El artículo,* 438, 235; and biologism, 307n6, 307n11; on divorce, 39, 147, 234, 308n12, 308n14 (*See also* Azorín); *Dos amores,* 236, 238–39, 241, 243; *Ellas y ellos y ellos y ellas,* x, 204–7, 223, 229, 246, 308n17; *La entrometida,* x, 123, 132, 139–41, 143, 145, 184, 190, 192, 297nn25–26; *El extranjero,* 236, 241–43, 297nn25–26; on fashion, 289n21; as a feminist, 286nn8–9, 308n12; *La flor de la playa,* 121, 236, 239–40; *La flor de la playa y otras novelas cortas,* 19, 63; and the Generation of '98,

296n19; and Gómez de la Serna, Ramón, 243, 244 308n17; *El hombre negro*, 235; on Larra, José Mariano de, 236; and Marañón, Gregorio, 207–8, 304n18; on marriage, 97, 121, 196; *La mujer moderna y sus derechos*, 63, 70, 207, 208–10, 227, 228–29, 239n21; and the Moroccan Wars, 23; *La nostálgica*, 236, 240–41; on women's education, 130; *El permisionario*, x, 63, 204, 205, 207, 210, 223, 229, 246; *Quiero vivir mi vida*, x, 207, 208–210, 223, 304nn18–19; *La rampa*, 234; and the Second Spanish Republic, 26, 244; as a social modernist, 1, 280; on the Spanish nation, 135; *El venero del arte*, 19, 207, 229, 230–33, 235, 245, 307n9, 10; *See also* communicative reason; Spain (compared to other countries)
Bush, Peter, 69
Bussy Genevois, Danièle, 286n6
Butler, Judith, 307n6

Caballero, Fernán, 289–90n24
Cadalso, José: *Cartas marruecas*, 236
Calderón de la Barca, Pedro, 21, 22, 126, 143, 195; theme of honor in, 205, 209, 223, 241; *El médico de su honra*, 190
Campoamor, Clara, 28, 201, 226
Campoamor, Ramón del, 16
Camprubí, Zenobia, 217
Camus, Albert, 212
Cansinos-Asséns, Rafael, 297n21
Capel Martínez, Rosa María, 243, 295n11, 296n14, 296n14, 309n19
Carballo, Juan Rof, 160, 166, 169, 291n8
Carlism, 2, 14, 21, 118, 279
Carlist Wars, 41, 42, 43, 115–16, 172
Carlos V, 102, 114
Carnés, Luisa, 306n1
Caro Baroja, Julio: on Don Juan, 299n6
Caro Raggio, Rafael, 148, 150
Carruthers, Kathie, 285n5
Casa de los Niños, La, 309n19
Casalduero, Joaquín, 116
Casanova, Giacomo, 294n7

Casanova, Sofía, vii, 5, 7, 25, 30, 72, 122, 131–32, 137, 147, 149; *Más que amor*, 132–33, 141; *Princesa del amor hermoso*, x, 123, 132, 133–35, 192, 298n27
Casares Quiroga, Santiago, 24
Cascardi, Anthony, 198, 199, 303n15
Castán Tobeña, José, 285–86n6
Castañar, Fulgencio, 306n1
Castañeda, Paloma, 147, 234
Castelar, Emilio, 15
casticismo, 133
Castile, ix, 20, 34–35, 71, 73, 174, 216, 295n13
Castro, Fernando de, 15, 282n4
Castro, Rosalía de, 131
Catena, Elena, 172, 290n1
Catholicism, 20, 22, 26, 43, 57, 102, 103, 111, 121, 179, 275, 302n1, 304n16, 305n27, 306n3
Cavallo, Susan, 304n18
Celestina, La, 126
Centro Iberoamericano de Cultura Popular Femenina, 19
Cervantes, Miguel de, 72, 77, 78, 109, 125, 230, 265; *Don Quixote*, 21, 67, 69, 70, 72, 80, 203, 217, 279 (Chacel, Rosa on, 305n27; as intertext of *El amor catedrático*, 97–103; as intertext of *Cerezas del cementerio*, 84–89; as intertext of *La esfinge maragata*, 84–86; as intertext in *Niebla*, 80–83); *La ilustre fregona*, 67; *Novelas ejemplares*, 21; *See also* Generation of '98
Chacel, Rosa, vii, 5, 7, 9, 26, 77, 186, 212, 229, 272, 276, 279, 280; *Alcancía. Ida*, 217; *Alcancía. Vuelta*, 217; *La confesión*, 6, 216–218, 219, 222, 305n27, 306n1; *Desde el amanecer*, 217, 218, 219; "Esquema de los problemas prácticos y actuales del amor," 211, 213–15, 227; and essentialism, 305n30; *Estación Ida y vuelta*, 219, 302n33; as a feminist, 304n23; Guggenheim Fellowship, 276; *Memorias de Leticia Valle*, x, 23, 186, 210, 211, 212, 213, 215–23, 224, 228, 276, 304n21,

Chacel, Rosa, *continued*
304n25, 306nn35–36; and Ortega y Gasset, José, 212–13, 214, 215, 216, 219, 304n25, 306n36; as a Republican, 305n26; *Saturnal*, 213, 276; *La sinrazón*, 276; *Teresa*, 213; *Los títulos*, 305–6n34; and Valle-Inclán, Ramón del, 305n29; and vanguardism, 224; and Zambrano, María, 220, 305n27
Chambers, Ross, 121
Champourcín, Ernestina, 306n1
Charnon-Deutsch, Lou, 11, 296n18
Chodorow, Nancy, 296n16
Cid, El, 42
Cierva, Juan de la, 25
Ciplijauskaité, Biruté, 297n20
Claremont Mckenna College, xi
Clemessy, Nelly, 307n11
Close, Anthony, 70
Comité Nacional de Mujeres Antifascistas, 248
Communist Party, 309n18
communicative reason: Burgos, Carmen de and, 229; in Espina, Concha, 260; in Montseny, Federica; in Nelken, Margarita, 247; *See also* Habermas, Jürgen
community, 6, 8, 36, 84, 227, 247, 264, 271
Conde, Carmen, 306n1
Congreso Nacional Pedagógico, 17
Constant, Benjamin, 104, 106, 293n23
consumer riots, 59, 64
Contemporáneos, Los, 24
Coronado, Carolina, 131
Corpus Barga, 22, 171; on Don Juan, 294n5, 295n14, 304n16
Cortés, Hernán, 113
Counter-Reformation, 35, 113
Criado Miguel, Isabel, 163, 164
Criado y Domínguez, J. P., 282n5
cross-dressing, 62–63, 205; Azorín and, 289n21; Burgos, Carmen de and, 289n21
Cruikshank, John, 293n23
Cruz, Penelope, 279

Cubas, Cristina Fernández, 280
Cueto Pérez, Magdalena, 302nn7–9

Dalí, Salvador: *Un Chien andalou*, 250
Dante Alighieri, 85, 89
Darío, Rubén, 1
Darwin, Charles, 296n19
Dato, Eduardo, 25
Davies, Catherine, 307nn7–9, 309,n20
determinism, 302n6
Díaz Fernández, José, xi; *El nuevo romanticismo*, 5, 244; *La venus mecánica*, 227, 245–47; on women, 226, 244–45, 248
Díaz-Mas, Paloma, 280
Díaz-Peterson, Rosendo, 45
Dicenta, Joaquín, 284n6
Dickens, Charles, 8, 149; *Hard Times*, 272
Díez de Revenga, Javier, 301n16
Dijkstra, Bram, 296n18
divorce legislation, 26, 29, 30, 226, 275; *See also* Azorín; Baroja, Pío; Burgos, Carmen de; Unamuno, Miguel de
D'Óliver, Nicolau, 24
domesticity, x, 21, 38, 39, 146, 147, 306n3; in Azorín's works, 67, 146, 179–84, 289n21 (*See also* Azorín [houses]); and Baroja, Carmen, 149–50; and Baroja, Pío, 146, 147, 149–50, 156–58; in Carmen de Burgos's novels, 233, 244, 242, 289n21; in Marañón, Gregorio, 186; in María Martínez Sierra's novels, 48; in modernist novel, 11–12; in nineteenth-century novel, 10–11; in Pérez de Ayala, Ramón, 193, 195, 197; in Unamuno, Miguel de, 38, 39, 46, 53, 146. 170
Domingo, Marcelino, 24
Don Galaor, 258
Don Juan (as an archetype), x, 110, 223; in Azorín, 55, 171–72; in Baroja, Pío, 147, 154, 156, 157, 158; in Burgos, Carmen de, 242, 251; in Casanova, Sofía, 251; in Chacel, Rosa, 212, 215, 218; as diabolical, 294n7, 302n4; in male and female modernist novel, 111–44;

Marañón, Gregorio on, 186–89, 192, 302nn2–6; in Montseny, Federica, 251; as a national symbol, 22, 112, 294n3, 294n5, 295n13, 298n29, 304n16; in Ríos, Blanca de los, 64, 251; in Unamuno, Miguel de, 39, 75, 161, 163, 198–204; in Valle Inclán, Ramón del, 87; *See also* Caro Baroja, Julio; Corpus Barga; effeminacy; Ortega y Gasset, José; Pérez de Ayala, Ramón
donjuanism, 27, 120, 124, 128, 131, 134, 135, 140, 163, 192, 197, 251, 295n11
Don Quixote (as a character type), ix, x, 22, 42, 43, 69–80, 111, 133, 135, 137, 188, 202, 204, 225, 290n3, 310n30
Doody, Terence, 264
Dostoyevsky, Fyodor, 212, 223
Doyaga, Emilia, 159, 160, 299n8
Duchamp, Marcel, 224
Dupanloup, Félix-Antoine-Philibert, 179, 181, 282n5
Dworkin, Andrea, 300n15

Eakin, John Paul, 117
effeminacy, 15, 61, 169, 185, 186, 187, 192–93, 197, 200, 203, 205, 214, 223; and Don Juan, 302n9; in Carmen de Burgos's *Los anticuarios*, 237; in Carmen de Burgos's *El veneno del arte*, 231
Enders, Susan, 59, 234
Enguídanos, Miguel, 33
Enloe, Cynthia, 12
Enríquez Salamanca, Cristina, 15, 283n5
Epps, Brad, 295n8
Escuela de Institutrices, 16
Escuela Normal Central de Maestras, 17
España Contemporánea, La, 18
Espina, Concha, vii, 7, 25, 27, 30, 109, 122, 135, 149, 224; *Aurora de España*, 309nn23–24; on divorce, 258. *La esfinge maragata*, ix, 4, 27, 80, 84, 87, 89–95, 104, 123, 135, 137–39, 298n27 (as feminist novel, 292n15); *Las mujeres del Quijote*, 73, 77–80, 84; *La niña de Luzmela*, x, 123, 135–37, 146; 297n21; on the Second Spanish Republic, 257–58; on suffrage, 258; *La virgen prudente*, x, 27, 80, 228, 257, 258–61, 271; 309n23; on women, 292n15; *See also* communicative reason
essentialism, 285n5
eternal feminine, the, 20; in Azorín, 216; in Espina, Concha, 79; in Miró, Gabriel, 87–88; 89; in Unamuno, Miguel de, 216
Europeanization, 117
Eysteinsson, Astradur, 4

Falla, Manuel de, 52
Feal Deibe, Carlos, 168, 169, 300n15, 303n10
Federación de Obreras Católicas, 26
Feeny, Thomas, 163
Felski, Rita, 216, 305n27
femininity, 157, 159, 188–89, 192, 211, 214, 255, 256, 304n19
Fernández Utrera, María Soledad, 305n33
Fernando VII, 172
Filogyno, E., 282n5
Firestone, Shulamith, 300n15
Flynn, Gerard, 294n7
Fortún, Elena (Encarnación Aragoneses Urquijo), 277; *Celia en el colegio*, 278; *Celia, lo que dice*, 278; *Celia en el mundo*, 278; *Celia novelista*, 278; *Celia y sus amigos*, 278; *See also* Martín Gaite, Carmen
Foster, David W., 163
Foucault, Michel, 305n31
Fox, E. Inman, 13, 288n18, 294n2
Franco, Francisco, 146, 266, 267, 275, 276, 277, 278, 279, 305n26
Franz, Thomas, 290nn7–8, 300n15
French Revolution, 173
Freud, Sigmund, 208, 227, 306n35

Ganivet, Ángel, 69. *Idearium español*, 34
García Lorca, Federico, 28
García-Maroto, María Ángeles, 254, 257
García Mercadal, J., 187

García Morales, Adelaida, 280
gender (defined), ix
Generation of '14, vii
Generation of '98, vii, 12, 19, 46, 125, 198, 238, 240, 241, 295n13, 304n25, 310n28; defined by Azorín, 5; and Baroja, Carmen, 148; on Don Juan, 112; and Don Quixote, 290; journals associated with, 283n6; and Martínez Sierra, María, 148; novel of, 50, 51, 287n13; and de los Ríos, Blanca, 126
Generation of '27, vii
Gies, David, 111
Gil Lobo y Calvente, T. de J., 283n5
Gil y Carrasco, Enrique: *El señor de Bembibre*, 90
Gilbert, Sandra: *The War of the Words*, 30
Gilman, Sander, 296n17
Giménez Caballero, Ernesto, 29, 226; *La Gaceta Literaria*, 226
Gimeno de Flaquer, Concepción, 282n5
Giner de los Ríos, Francisco, 16, 19
Gjeltema, Emily, xi
Glenn, Kathleen, 128, 217, 301n20
Gómez Carillo, E.: *El libro de las mujeres*, 282n5, 285n3
Gómez de Avellaneda, Gertrudis, 131
Gómez de la Serna, Ramón, x, 105, 216, 218, 224, 243; "Ella+Ella--Él+Él," 308n17; *La mujer de ámbar*, 243–44; *El novelista*, 243; *El secreto del acueducto*, 243
Gómez Torres, A., 282n5
González Blanco, Edmundo, 283n5
González Serrano, Urbano, 16, 19
gothic novel, 4–5, 6
Goyrí, María, 292n19
Graciano Martínez, Father, *El libro de la mujer española, Hacia un feminismo cuasi dogmatico*, 26
Greco, El, 74
Gubar, Susan, *The War of the Words*, 30
Guggenheim Foundation, xi; See also Chacel, Rosa
Gullón, Ricardo, 44, 167, 169, 299n10, 300n12

Gulstad, Daniel E., 295n9
Guss, Donald, 219

Hanan, Dennis, 300n12
Habermas, Jürgen, 229; on communicative reason, 6–7
Hardcastle, Anne, 307n6
Hartzenbusch, Juan Eugenio, 16
Hegel, Georg, 303n15; on Antigone, 9
Helios, 283n6
Highfill, Juli, 210
historical novel, 2
Hobsbawm, Eric J., 20, 21, 281n2
Hoddie, James, 291n11
homosexuality, 201, 207, 232–33, 307n9
Hora de España, 263; See also, Zambrano, María
Huidobro, Vicente, 24, 301n15
Hurtado, Amparo, 29
Hutcheon, Linda, 121
Hynes, Laura, 300n15

Ibarra, Fernando, 289n19
Ibarruri, Dolores, 248, 309n18
Ibsen, Henrik: *Hedda Gabler*, 300n15
Institución Libre de Enseñanza, 24
Instituto Escuela, 24
Instrucción para la Mujer, 17
intrahistoria, 13, 19, 20, 31–33, 34, 35, 38, 39, 41, 43, 44, 53, 54, 68, 79, 117, 126, 227, 255, 265, 310n28; See also Miró, Gabriel; Unamuno, Miguel de; Valle-Inclán, Ramón del
Irigaray, Luce, 211
Iris de Paz, 28
irony, 121–22, 128–29, 156, 232; See also Valle-Inclán, Ramón del
Isabel II, 2, 14, 15, 118, 172, 290n24

Jagoe, Catherine, 11, 15, 17, 18, 283n5
Jardine, Alice, 219
Jarnés, Benjamín, xi, 105, 143, 216, 224, 229, 255; *El convidado de papel*, 143, 218, 225, 293n22; *Paula y Paulita*, 293n22; *El profesor inútil*, 293n22
Jerez Perchet, A., 283n5

Jiménez, Juan Ramón, 24, 50, 52; and Martínez Sierra, María, 293n20
Johnson, Roberta, vii, 172, 281n1, 288n16, 290n2, 291n12, 304n24, 307n8, 310n25, 310n30
Joyce, James, 12, 39
Jung, Carl, 302n5; and *Paz en la guerra*, 211, 214, 285n4
Jurkevich, Gayana, 38, 285n4, 290n6
Juventud, 283n6
Juventud Católica Femenina, 26

Kent, Victoria, 24, 28, 210, 226; El problema de la ética, la enseñanza de la moral, 27; Historia de la cultura europea. La edad moderna; grandeza y servidumbre; intento de ligar la historia pretérita a las circunstancias del mundo presente para hallar una explicación a los conflictos de la hora actual, 27
Kierkegaard, Søren, 305n27
Kirkpatrick, Judith, 84, 297n26
Kirkpatrick, Susan, 10, 213
Krausism, 15–17, 18, 19, 24, 31, 36, 229, 292n19, 310n28
Kristeva, Julia, 121

Labanyi, Jo, 35
Laforet, Carmen: *Nada*, 278
Langland, Elizabeth, 11
Largo Caballero, Francisco, 24
Larra, José Mariano de "Vuelva Ud. Mañana," 236
Lawrence, D. H., 39, 164
Lazarillo de Tormes, 21, 67, 71
Lázaro, Reyes, 131, 295n13, 304n25
Lázaro Montero, S., 223
Lejeune, Philippe, 217
León, Fray Luis de, 179, 180
León, María Teresa, 217, 306n1
Lerroux, Alejandro, 24
lesbianism, 203, 205, 206, 207, 307n9
Letras Peninsulares, xi
liberalism, 200, 226, 227
Lien, R. María, 293n1

Liga de Educación Política, 186
Livingston, Leon, 33, 178
Llanas Aguilaniedo, José María, 283n6
Longhurst, Carlos, 152, 155, 258n1, 298nn3–4, 299n5
López, Ignacio-Javier, 294n7, 295n10
Loureiro, Ángel, 295n8
Lozano Marco, Miguel Ángel, 97, 302n5
Luchador, El, 250
Lucientes, Francisco, 257, 258
Luna, Luisa, 283n5
Lutoslawski, Wincenty, 131–32
Lyceum Club, 27–29, 105, 108, 109, 150, 189, 194, 275

Macdonald, Ian, 84, 291n10
Machado, Antonio, 226; María Zambrano on, 262, 265
Macklin, J. J., 189, 302n3, 320nn5–7
Madame Bovary, 235
Magnien, Brigette, 309n23
Marco, José María, 308n16
Marías, Julián, 42
Maeztu, María de, 24, 27, 109, 109, 112, 179
Maeztu, Ramiro de, 69, 284n9; on Don Juan, 112–14, 133, 144, 293, 294nn2–3, 298n29; on Don Quixote, 290n5
Maier, Carol, 225, 304n25
Mañé, Teresa (Soledad Gustavo), 250
Mangini, Shirley, 93, 239, 276, 281n1, 287n14, 297n21, 297n24, 304n23, 308n18, 309n19
Mann, Thomas, 307n9
Marañón, Gregorio, 24, 27, 140, 185, 197, 211, 244–45; on Don Juan, 186–89, 191–92, 198, 200, 201, 203, 204, 207–9, 211, 304n20; *Biología y feminismo*, 186; *El conde-duque de Olivares (La pasión de mandar)*, 186; *La edad crítica*, 187; *Ensayo biológico sobre Enrique IV de Castilla y su tiempo*, 186; and feminism, 304n18; "Notas para una biología de Don Juan," 187–188, 302n4; and Pérez de Ayala, Ramón, 302nn2–6; *Raíz y decoro de España*,

Marañón, Gregorio, *continued*
  186; "Sexo y trabajo," 186; and Unamuno, Miguel de, 303n14; *See also* Burgos, Carmen de
Maraval, José Antonio, 31, 34, 36, 117–18, 284n1
Márquez Villanueva, Francisco, 291n11
Marrades, María Isabel, 295n11
Martín Gaite, Carmen: *El cuarto de atrás*, 277, 278; on Fortún, Elena, 278; and Martínez Sierra, María, 277
Martínez Barrio, Diego, 24
Martínez Cachero, José María, 112, 298n28
Martínez Ruiz, Amparo, 298n2
Martínez Sierra, Gregorio, 49–50, 52, 124, 159, 276, 286nn7–8, 286n10, 290n4, 297n27
Martínez Sierra, María [Gregorio Martínez Sierra], vii, 5, 25, 26, 30, 34, 38, 109, 122, 130, 148, 213, 248, 255, 272, 276, 277, 280, 283n6; *El amor catedrático*, x, 77, 80, 95, 96–103, 108, 277; 292n19, 302n8; *Aventura*, 34; *Cartas a las mujeres de España*, 227, 286nn8–9, 287n15; on Don Juan, 297n27; *Don Juan de España*, 297n27; on Don Quixote, 290n5; *Eva curiosa*, 286n8; on feminism, 297n27; *Feminismo, feminidad, españolismo*, 103, 124, 227, 286nn8–9; *Gregorio y yo*, 46, 87, 102, 286n10, 292n18; on marriage , 292n17; "Maternidad," 292n17; men in the theater of, 287n12; *Motivos*, 290n4; *La mujer ante la República*, 201, 286n8; *La mujer moderna*, 286nn8–9; *Una mujer por caminos de España*, 34, 73, 103–4, 217, 290n4; 307n5; name, 46, 286n7, 287n11, 302n8; *Las nuevas cartas a las mujeres*, 227, 286n8; relationship with Martínez Sierra, Gregorio, 46–47, 49–50, 96–97, 210, 276, 286n7, 287n14, 292nn18–19; *La tristeza del Quijote*, 73, 76–77; *Tú eres la paz*, ix, 31, 40, 46, 47–53, 72, 77, 96, 123–24, 180, 213, 277, 293n20, 309n24; *See also* Martín Gaite, Carmen; masculinity
masculinity, 78, 111, 122, 159, 161, 187, 188, 192, 195, 201, 211, 221, 299n4; in Carmen de Burgos's *El veneno del arte*, 307n9; and Martínez Sierra, María, 287n14, 287–88n15
masculine women, 155, 157, 159, 169, 184, 185, 199–200, 214, 231, 289n21, 304n19; *See also* Montseny, Federica
Maura, Antonio, 25, 56
Maura Gamazo, Miguel, 24
Mayoral, Marina, 280
Medina Club, 275
Meehan, Thomas, 33, 178
melodrama, 5, 48, 131
Menéndez Pidal, Ramón, 24, 292n19
Merleau-Ponty, Maurice, 219
Mirlo Blanco, El, 150
Miró, Gabriel, 2, 72, 95, 97, 109, 229, 255; *El abuelo del rey*, 2; *Las cerezas del cementerio*, x, 80, 84–89, 91, 291nn11–2; 297n22; and Don Juan, 297n22; and Don Quixote, 83–84, 297n22; on feminism, 86–87; and *intrahistoria*, 291n12
modernism (defined), 1–2, 9–10, 11–12
Monné, Carmen, 150
Montero, Rosa, 280
Monterrey, Margarita María de, 283n6
Montés, Eugenio, 24
Montorial y Puig, Carme, 306n1
Montseny, Federica, vii, 5, 7, 26, 27, 30, 224, 247, 260, 272, 276, 280, 287n14; as a feminist, 251; *El hijo de Clara*, 257, 259; *La indomable*, x, 252–55; on masculine women, 254; on Nelken, Margarita, 308n18; and *La Revista Blanca*, 227, 251, 255, 309n22; theory of love, 309nn21–22; *La victoria*, x, 255–58; *See also* communicative reason; *La Novela Ideal*; *La Novela Libre*
Montseny, Juan (Federico Urales), 250
Mora, Magdalena, 210, 211

Morales, Carmen, 44–45
Morrocan wars, 14, 22, 216; See also Burgos, Carmen de
Morocco, 22
Mosse, George, 19
motherhood, 161, 163, 167–68, 170, 185, 186, 193, 195–96, 203, 204, 211, 296n14, 300n15, 301n1; in *Quiero vivir mi vida*, 304n19, 308n12; unwed, 257, 258, 309n19, 309n22
Mujeres Libres, 304n20
Mújika Tene, Robustiana, 306n3
Mulder, Elizabeth, 306n1
Mundo del Día, El, 250
Mundo Femenino, 25
Muñoz Seca, Pedro, 295n14
Mùria i Romani, Ana, 306n1

Nash, Mary, 10, 11, 185, 225, 301n1, 302n1, 304n20
nation (defined), ix, 281n2
nationalism, 12, 13, 19, 20, 281–82n2, 284n7; See also Spanish nationalism
Navajas, Gonzalo, 169, 291n8
Navarro, A., 283n5
Nelken, Margarita, vii, 5, 7, 9, 26, 27, 30, 201, 224, 226, 247–48, 272, 276, 280, 295n11, 308n8, 309nn19–20; *La condición social de la mujer en España*, 227; on gender, 227; on suffrage, 247; *La trampa del arenal*, x, 228, 247, 248–50, 255, 309n20; See also communicative reason
new woman, 225, 228, 248
Nietzsche, Friedrich, 52, 110, 230, 294n3
Nín y Tudó, J., 283n5
Noailles, Countess, 224
Nordau, Max, 62
Novela Corta, La, 24, 139, 297n25
Novela de Hoy, La, 24
Novela Ideal, La, 250; Federica Montseny in, 251
Novela Libre, La, 250; Federica Montseny in, 251
Novela Roja, La, 250

novela rosa, 275
Novela Semanal, La, 24
Novoa Santos, Roberto, 199
Nozick, Martin, 41
Nueva Senda, 250
Núñez de Arce, Gaspar, 16
Núñez Pérez, María Gloria, 46, 226, 308n14
Núñez Rey, Concepción, 297n24
Nussbaum, Martha, 8, 265–66, 272, 310n27

Oakley, Ann, 300n15
O'Connor, Patricia, 46, 286n7 286n10, 287n12
Oñate, María del Pilar, 185
Ontañón de Lope, Paciencia, 159, 300n15
Ortega, 258
Ortega y Gasset, José, 24, 27, 29, 185, 186, 210; *La deshumanización del arte*, 218, 224; on Don Juan, 294n3, 298n29, 303n16; and liberalism, 226; on love, 213–14; *Man and People*, 292n21; *Meditaciones del Quijote*, 70; "Oknos el sogero," 211; on women, 211, 213, 214, 283–84n6, 293n21; See also Chacel, Rosa; Zambrano, María
Ouimette, Victor, 56, 57, 226, 284n9

Palacio, M. de, 283n5
Paláu, F., 283n5
Palencia, Isabel, 28
Panadés y Poblet, J., 283n5
Paraíso, Isabel, 186–87, 302n2
Parajón, Mario, 304n21
Pardo Bazán, Emilia, 17–18, 107, 146, 292n19
Pariente, Ángel, 224
Parker, Andrew, 13
paternity, 203; legislation on, 247
Pensamiento Femenino, El, 25
Pérez, Janet, 102, 258, 306n1
Pérez-Bustamante Mourier, Ana Sofía, 298n29
Pérez de Ayala, Ramón, 2, 24, 27, 143,

Pérez de Ayala, Ramón, *continued*
185, 186, 204, 205, 208, 209, 210, 255, 279; *Belarmino y Apolonio*, 2; *La caída de los Limones*, 189; on Don Juan, 187–88, 189–92, 197, 302nn2–6, 303n10; on feminism, 302n6, 303n13; and liberalism, 226; *Luz de domingo*, 189; *Las máscaras*, 186, 302n6; *Novelas poemáticas de la vida española*, 2, 189; *Prometeo*, 189; "El satanismo" 187; *Tigre Juan y El curandero de su honra*, x, 143, 189–198, 203–4, 223, 232, 291n20, 302n5; *Tinieblas en las cumbres*, 303n11; *Trabajos de Urbano y Simona*, 303n12; *Troteras y danzaderas*, 303n11; on women, 303n13; *See also* Marañón, Gregorio
Pérez Firmat, Gustavo, 281n1, 305n32
Pérez Galdós, Benito, 217, 230, 265, 307n8; Chacel, Rosa on, 305n27; *Electra*, 56; *Episodios nacionales*, 128; *Fortunata y Jacinta*, 67, 122, 295n10; *Misericordia*, 310n30
Perinat, Adolfo, 295n11
personal realism, *See* Williams, Raymond
Phalange Party, 275
Pi y Margall, Francisco, 16, 282n3, 296n14
Pieropán, María Doménica, 178, 301n17
Pierrot, Jean, 296n18
Plato, 273, 284n9, 310n27
Porro, María José, 284n7
Posada, Adolfo, 18; *Feminismo*, 18–19
Pound, Ezra, 12
Pozzi, Gabriela, 307n6
Predmore, Michael, 114, 285n5, 295n8
Prieto, Indalecio, 24
Prim, General, 282n3
Primo de Rivera, Miguel, 14, 145, 245, 246, 276, 303n13
prostitution, 64, 75–76, 122, 131, 195, 203, 295n11, 296n17, 303n11
Proust, Marcel, 39, 307n9
pueblo, 36, 91, 133, 284–85n2
Puértolas, Soledad, 280
Pulido Tirado, Genara, 294n3

Quinones, Ricardo J., xi, 1–2, 38–39, 164
Quirós, Bernaldo C., 282n4, 284n6

Radcliff, Pamela, 59, 64, 234
Radhakrishnan, R., 2
Ramoneda Salas, Arturo, 293n1
Ranger, Terence, 21
Raza Española, 125
Récamier, Juliette, 293n23
Regis, Celsia, 25
Renan, Ernest, 20
Rendición, 250
Residencia de Estudiantes, 24
Residencia de Señoritas, 24, 27, 179, 180
Restoration, 15, 128, 189
Revista Blanca, La, 250; *See also* Montseny, Federica
Revista Canadiense de Estudios Hispánicos, xi
Revista de Occidente, 185; and Chacel, Rosa, 186, 211–12, 214; on women, 210–11; María Zambrano in, 262
Revista Nueva, 283n6
Revolution of, 1840, 172, 173
Revolution of September ("La Gloriosa"), 189, 282n3
Ribbans, Geoffrey, 166, 299nn8–9, 12
Ricks, Mabel, 189, 194
Rico Verdú, 288n17
Riera, Carme, 280
Ríos, Blanca de los, vii, 5, 7, 9, 25, 30, 64, 72, 122, 135, 137, 147; on Don Juan, 295n12; *Las hijas de don Juan*, x, 123, 127–31, 133, 134, 192, 295n13, 296n15, 296n19, 298n27; *Melita Palma*, 127; *Las mujeres de Tirso*, 126; *La niña de Sanabria*, 127; *La Rondeña*, 127; *El salvador*, 127; *Sangre española*, 127; on Tirso de Molina, 124–27
Ríos, Fernando de los, 24, 286n8
Risco, Antonio, 301n19, 301n21
Rivas, Reyna, 266
Roberson, Susan L., 10
Robinson, Lilian, 3
Rodgers, Eamann, 298n3
Rodoreda, Mercé, 306n1

Rodrigo, Antonina, 28, 52, 286n7
Rodríguez, María Pilar, 307nn9–10
Rojas, Fernando de: *La celestina*, 21, 66
Rojas Auda, Elizabeth, 292nn15–16, 309n24
Romero, Francisco J., 23
Romero, Lora, 12
Romero Mendoza, P., 298n28
Rousseau, Jean-Jacques, 120, 305n27
Rubens, Peter, 37
Rubio y Galí, F., 283n5
Rubio, Timoteo, 212
Ruisiñol, Santiago, 287n14
Ruiz de Quevedo, Martín, 16

Saez de Melgar, Faustina, 16, 283n5
Saint Augustine, 120, 264, 305n27
Saitz, Herlinda Charpentier, 289n21, 308n17
Salinas, Pedro, xi, 24, 28, 105, 224, 229; *Víspera del gozo*, 225, 293n22
Santa Teresa, 105, 106, 107, 108, 109, 129; *Camino de perfección*, 71
Santamaría, B., 283n5
Santiago, Miguel de, 119, 147
Sánchez Saornil, Lucía, 304n20
Sartre, Jean-Paul, 212, 217, 219; *Les Chemins de la liberté*, 304n21
Scanlon, Geraldine, 13, 18, 23, 26, 29, 295n11
Scarlett, Elizabeth, 306nn35–36
Schiavo, Leda, 294n4
Schopenhauer, Arthur, 71, 120, 137, 189, 208
Schürr, Friedrich, 285n5
Seator, Lynette Hubbard, 44, 285n5, 300n13
Sección Femenina, 275
Second Spanish Republic, x, 3, 14, 24, 26, 29, 46, 72, 79, 80, 145, 147, 159, 201, 204, 210, 213, 223, 227, 244, 246, 258, 262, 263, 265, 266–67, 275, 276, 279, 281n2, 306n1, 310n28; and feminism, 224, 226–27; *See also* Burgos, Carmen de

self-consciousness (as feminist strategy), 6, 50, 51, 52–53, 213, 222, 229, 286n9, 309n14
Sender, Ramón, xi, 29, 227, 248
sentimental novel, 5, 52
Sharistanian, Janet, xi
Showalter, Elaine, 289n22, 296n18
Siglo Médico, El, 301n1
Simancas Archive, 216
Simmel, Georg, 186, 211, 214
Sinués de Marco, M. P., 283n5
Six, Abigail Lee, 222
Sobejano, Gonzalo, 178
social modernism, vii, viii, 1, 30; *See also* Burgos, Carmen de
Socialist Party, 309n19
Sociedad Ginecológica Española, 301n1
Solidaridad Obrera, 304n20
Sophocles, 9
Sorolla, Joaquín, 230
Smith, Adam, 265–66
Smith, Gilbert, 152, 158
Smith, Paul Julian, 305n30
Smith, Verity, 295n7
Spain (compared to other countries), 102, 141, 147, 152–63, 155, 184, 197, 222, 229; in Burgos, Carmen de, 233–34, 236, 238, 239, 242–43
Spanish American War, 14–15, 22, 23, 27, 31, 69, 113, 282n2
Spanish Civil War, 14, 24, 149, 248, 262, 266, 277, 281n2, 310n28
Spanish Empire, 20, 21, 102, 108, 111, 112, 113, 115, 116, 125, 195, 216, 221, 222, 223
Spanish feminism, x, 18, 25, 119, 139, 143, 144, 145–46, 147, 152, 159, 161, 168, 185, 199, 210, 226, 279, 281n2, 282n4, 283n6, 286nn8–9, 290n8, 299n8, 310n24; Díaz Fernández, José on, 244–45; feminist novel, 27; 29–30, 152, 175, 212, 222, 256, 258, 280, 307n7; suffrage, 25–26, 30, 226, 286n8; *See also* Espina, Concha; Nelken, Margarita

Spanish nationalism, 13–14, 20, 21, 102, 103, 121, 125, 196, 244, 281n2, 294n2; See also Don Juan (as national legend)
Spinoza, Benedict de, 262, 310n27
Spires, Robert C., 281n1, 295n8, 305n29, 306n2
Staël, Madame de, 104, 106, 107, 154
Starcevic, Elizabeth, 235, 297n24
Stoics, 310n27
Suárez Solís, Sara, 193
Suleiman, Susan, 219, 222, 225, 305n28
Sur, 210
surrealism, 225

Taine, Hippolyte-Adolphe, 296n19
Taylor, Anne Robinson, 299n4
Tirrell, Lynne, 7
Tirso de Molina, 21, 111, 112, 114, 116, 124–27, 129, 171, 174
Tomero Alarcón, Rafael, 310n32
Tompkins, Jane, 30
tradición eterna, la, 19, 20, 21, 31, 33, 40, 41, 43, 54, 68, 109, 117, 125, 142, 240, 255, 310n28
transvestism, 205
Trigo, Felipe, viii
Tristán, Flora, 172–173
Trueba, Fernando: *Belle Epoque*, 279
Turner, Harriet (Harriet S. Stevens) 169, 290n6

Ugarte, Michael, 30, 93, 234, 281n1, 308n13
Unamuno, Miguel de, 32–33, 36–37, 38–40, 51,53, 69, 83, 84, 95, 97, 109, 112, 125, 126, 143, 145, 146, 171, 185, 186, 212, 213, 216, 217, 229, 230, 233, 244, 253, 284n9; *Abel Sánchez*, 42, 160, 166; *Amor y pedagogía*, 42, 44, 71, 76, 290n7; Chacel, Rosa on, 305n27; *Del sentimiento trágico de la vida*, 300n12; on determinism, 296n19; on divorce, 39; on Don Juan, 296n14; *Don Quijote y Sancho*, 70–71, 73, 74–76, 78; *Dos madres*, 27, 75, 161–64, 167, 184, 193, 198, 204, 299n10, 300n13; *En torno al casticismo*, 34, 39, 41; *España y los españoles*, 284n1; on the family, 290–91n8; on feminism, 159–60, 290n7, 299n8; *El hermano Juan*, 112, 141–42, 198–204, 219, 223, 297n27; on *intrahistoria*, 20, 31–33, 34, 86, 91, 117, 126, 291n13; on liberalism, 226; *El marqués de Lumbría*, 161, 164–65, 167; on marriage, 285–86n5, 286n6, 291n8; *Nada menos que todo un hombre*, 161, 165–66, 235; *Niebla*, viii, ix, 4, 19, 27, 29, 42,50, 71, 72, 76, 80–83, 159, 160, 161, 166, 167, 168, 204, 290n7; and Ortega y Gasset, José, 304n24, 25; *Paz en la guerra* ix, 2, 31, 33, 40–44, 45, 46, 47, 50, 75, 78, 83, 287n13 (See also, Jung, Carl); *Raquel encadenada*, 28; *San Manuel Bueno, mártir*, 42, 45; "La tía," 299n9, 300n14; *La tía Tula*, 12, 27, 45, 75, 82, 144, 146, 155, 160, 161, 166–70, 184, 299nn8–9, 300n12, 304n19 (as feminist novel, 300–301n15); *Tres novelas ejemplares y un prólogo*, 160, 161, 300n12; on women, 38–40, 146–47, 160–61, 279, 299nn7–8, 300n13; See also Chacel, Rosa, Marañón, Gregorio; Zambrano, María
University of Kansas, xi
Unruh, Vicky, xi
Urbieta, Arantza de, 45
Urrioste, Carmen de, 308n12

Valera, Celma, 284n6
Valera, Juan, 16; *Pepita Jiménez*, 67, 307n8
Valis, Noël, 295n8
Valle-Inclán, Ramón del, 51, 72, 95, 97, 112, 118–19, 126, 145, 224, 229, 230, 233; and *intrahistoria*, 117–18; and irony, 121–22; *La lámpara maravillosa*, 118; *El ruedo ibérico* x, 2; *Sonata de estío*, 115, 116, 120, 294n6; *Sonata de invierno*, 115–17, 120–21, 123, 294n6; *Sonata de otoño*, 47, 115, 116, 118, 119, 120, 305n29 (critics on, 295n9;

as intertext of Carmen de Burgos's *La entrometida*, 139–41; as intertext of Concha Espina's *La esfinge maragata*, 138–39 and *La niña de Luzmela*, 135–37; as intertext of María Martínez Sierra's *Tú eres la paz*, 123–24; as intertext of Blanca de los Ríos's *Las hijas de don Juan*, 134, 296n15 and *Más que amor*, 132 128); *Sonata de primavera*, 114–15, 116, 120, 294nn6–7; *Sonatas* x, 4, 47, 87, 114, 112, 114–18, 119, 120–22, 123, 131, 132, 134, 140, 163, 212, 297n20 (Marqués de Bradomín, 29–95nn6–8, 295n13, 296n20, 297n23, 298n27); *Tula varona*, 63–64; on women, 119–20
vanguardism, 243; in male writers, 224–25, 226, 228, 245, 306n2; in female writers, 224–25, 227–28, 255 260–61, 305n28; *See also* Azorín; Chacel, Rosa
Vázquez Recio, Nieves, 295n12, 296n15, 296n19
Vega, Lope de, 126
Velázquez, Diego de, 230
Vernon, John, 4
Vidal, Fabián, 284n6
Vila, F., 283n5
Vilanova, Antonio, 113, 117
Vilela, Concepción, 1
Vogel, Lise, 3
Volksgeist, 36
Voz de la mujer, La, 25

Watson, Peggy, 43
Webber, Ruth House, 122
Weber, Max: *The Protestant Ethic and the Spirit of Capitalism*, 21
Weininger, Otto, 187, 189, 208
Werther, 39, 77
White, Sarah L., 282n3, 284n2

Wilde, Oscar, 325, 307n9
Williams, Raymond on personal realism, 5–6, 8, 40, 91, 213, 224
Wolstenholme, Susan, 5
woman as evil, 80–83, 89, 161, 162, 164–65, 191, 194, 200, 299n10
women's education, 16–19, 185, 179–82, 216, 278, 282n4, 284n6, 295n14, 308n12; *See also* Burgos, Carmen de
Wood, Jennifer, 297n24
Woolf, Virginia, vii, 307n9
World War I, ix, 14, 19, 23, 24, 96, 145, 160, 168, 173, 187, 205, 207, 281n2, 286n8, 304n17
World War II, 265, 266

Zambrano, Araceli, 265–66, 310n31, 32
Zambrano, Blas, 310n28
Zambrano, María, vii, 5, 7, 26, 77, 79, 80, 213, 279; *La confesión . Género litrario y método*, 6, 264, 305n27; *Delirio y destino*, x, 3, 7, 217, 220, 227, 265, 266–72, 276, 306–7n4, 311n33; on "guía," 310n29; "Hacia un saber sobre el alma," 211, 262; in *Hora de España*, 263; *Horizonte del liberalismo*, 227, 262, 267; and liberalism, 261–62; and Ortega y Gasset, José, 276, 310n26, 310n23; on "olvido creador," 77, 228, 255; on Pérez Galdós, Benito, 310n30; on poetic reason, 261–65, 272; "La reforma del entendimiento español," 310n30; and republicanism, 263, 276; *El sueño creador*, 227; *La tumba de Antigone*, 7–9; and Unamuno, Miguel de, 310n28; *See also* Antigone; Chacel, Rosa; Machado, Antonio
Zorrilla, José, 119, 222; *Don Juan Tenorio*, 90, 111, 112, 113, 114, 129, 132, 171–72, 174, 297n27

www.ingramcontent.com/pod-product-compliance
Lightning Source LLC
Chambersburg PA
CBHW030105010526
44116CB00005B/103